Just TEACH ME, Mrs. K.

Just TEACH ME, Mrs. K.

Talking, Reading, and Writing with Resistant Adolescent Learners

Mary Mercer Krogness

HEINEMANN
Portsmouth, NH

Heinemann
A division of Reed Elsevier Inc.
361 Hanover Street
Portsmouth, New Hampshire 03801-3912
Offices and agents throughout the world

Editor: Philippa Stratton and Dawn Boyer
Production: Nancy Sheridan
Cover design: Jenny Jensen Greenleaf
Interior photographs: John M. Krogness
Front and back cover photographs: Sara Wasserman

A bio of Marcus (front cover): A complex boy, Marcus, a seventh grader, increasingly demonstrated shining moments of intelligence, rich imagination, and curiosity. His being a member of the classroom community—a safe and accepting place—supported Marcus in his desire to be successful in school and develop his considerable talent. As the school year wore on, Marcus took more control of his life and demonstrated a more highly developed sense of himself and his capability. By spring, he expressed pleasure in the person he was becoming.

A bio of Rolanda (back cover): Rolanda, a seventh grader, derived great pleasure from weekly art therapy sessions guided by Sara Wasserman, art therapist. Through art, Rolanda demonstrated her remarkable sense of color and design; art freed her to express feelings and thus become a contributing member of the language arts class. Like the delicate flowers she carefully designed and colored with pastels, Rolanda bloomed magnificently. For Rolanda, making art was crucial in bringing what was on the inside, out.

Credit lines and copyright information begin on page xv.

Library of Congress Cataloging-in-Publication Data

Krogness, Mary.
    Just teach me, Mrs. K. : talking, reading, and writing
with resistant adolescent learners / Mary Krogness.
       p.   cm.
    Includes bibliographical references and index.
    ISBN 0-435-08815-7
    1. Socially handicapped children—Education—Ohio—Shaker Heights—
Language arts. 2. Language arts (Secondary)—Ohio—Shaker Heights.
I. Title.
LC4085.K76 1994
371.96'7–dc20
                                   94-11488
                                      CIP

Printed in the United States of America on acid-free paper.
99 98 97 96 95   BB   1 2 3 4 5 6 7 8 9

For my husband, John,
and for my parents,
Edith and Tom Mercer

CONTENTS

FOREWORD

*As told to Mary Krogness by
one of her former students,
Quinten Johnson,
21 years old.*
12/28/93

First day of school: you came in all smiling and wearing long earrings and crazy socks and a jump suit. You started telling us what we was going to be doing all year, and how much fun we was going to have, and we all looked at each other and said, "Yeah, right." But it—the fun—turned out to be pretty much true.

At first the fun was getting to do what we wanted—like reading—what was that little skinny book called? It [*The Children's Story* by James Clavell] was the only book I ever really read. It kept my attention because I could read between the lines; I guess it was symbolic. We got to pick books we wanted to read, not just the recommended school books. Our class was fun because we could do independent projects, like the time I wrote "Boot Camp," a story about the way I saw school. And remember that time I wrote a story about a cat and you told me I had a poem? That was fun. Learning was so easy in our class, maybe because we didn't have to read those textbooks and because you wrote us long notes on our papers. I liked those notes because they answered questions for me like what was good about my writing and what wasn't so good. Grades and points sure couldn't explain anything.

I remember the time we made dictionaries of black slang. That project kinda just popped up out of nowhere after the class and you talked about words. Me and all the black kids taught *you* what all the slang (black expressions) like *dissin'* and *def* and *straight* meant. Teachers should be students; they should hear what students say instead of doing all the talking. We all talked a lot in our class—about everything, especially when we worked in groups. Maybe that's why we got along so well. But when kids (like me) got bad—like springs springing out of control—you let the "springs" be released; you didn't suppress us. We had a lot of freedom of expression. But I remember when you suddenly changed. I think you was regretful that you was so nice and patient with us; so you started acting like all the other teachers. I was disappointed; but you came around again, and acted kind and patient and never raised your voice. You didn't even kick me out of class—except maybe once.

Our class was a hands-on type of class. We did more of the "do" than listening to the teacher talk. I liked that because I was—still am—an active person who likes to do rather than sit. But I remember that I learned how much I like to write—express myself. Remember, I used to come in after school to talk and to work; I didn't have to come in, but I wanted to. We worked hard after school. You—remember I used to call you Special K.? You was sort of like my mom in school because you accepted me.

I remember that taped interview that I did for my final project in our class. I dubbed in raps and rock for the answers, and everyone laughed when I played it. I was the D.J. who was asking big questions and making sly comments about my classmates. Those were nice times. I *still* pull out my writing spirals—remember I filled two—and look at what I wrote in eighth grade. Kinda corny, but the writing I did is still important to me. Every time I move, I pack up the two writing spirals and take 'em with me.

ACKNOWLEDGMENTS

Whatever its subject, a book is a composite of the author's life and experience. But it is also a composite of many other people's effort and influence. With this notion in mind, I would like to thank particular people and groups of people—family, friends, colleagues, students, readers and responders, and my editor—all of whom helped me to bring this book to fruition.

In writing these acknowledgments, I am reminded that I began thinking of myself as a writer a long time ago, when I was an elementary school student. Not that I wrote in school very often; rather, at home on Saturdays, I would sit on a high chair at our ancient tiger maple secretary and try to imitate my favorite authors—Mary O'Hara, who wrote *My Friend Flicka* and other horse stories; or Louisa May Alcott, whose *Little Women, Little Men, Jo's Boys,* and *Eight Cousins* I tried to emulate in creating my characters. I was invariably disappointed that my fiction didn't turn out like theirs. At that age—maybe ten or eleven—I didn't know that real writers had to work hard. But I am grateful to my parents, Edith and Tom Mercer, who encouraged me to write whatever I wanted and praised me for my effort.

I also thank my parents for nurturing my imagination and for allowing me great freedom to explore life and language from an early age. In high school, I wrote for the school's weekly newspaper, the "Quaker"—first short feature articles and then a column; finally I became co-editor. I am grateful to the late Ruth Loop, the able advisor, who led me to write evocative editorials and pungent headlines and to edit other students' work, and gave me the opportunity to become a better writer myself.

When I began teaching, I had the great good fortune to have had a dynamic and visionary principal, the late Orville Jenkins, who not only encouraged me to try all manner of interesting approaches to classroom teaching but inspired me when he *insisted* that I begin writing articles for professional journals! It was Orville Jenkins who challenged me to write about my teaching, neatly dovetailing my interest in writing with my evolving classroom practice.

Bee Page, a published novelist, became my unofficial mentor when she and I and several others formed a writing group. I credit Bee with showing me the meaning of the writer's craft—especially in compressing and arranging words. She led me to appreciate the writer who distills language to its purest form, letting it speak for itself.

At Bread Loaf, Tony Burgess, our remarkable writing teacher, encouraged my classmates and me to be resolute in our dreams of reforming public schools, and do so by keeping ideas alive. Writing articles for professional publications and writing this book have been my way of keeping ideas alive and clarifying my philosophy and my approach to working with young people. Writing has been a long, hard process of growth and discovery. Writing has been a demanding teacher.

While working with resistant adolescent language learners during the last half-dozen years, I have been fortunate to have had colleagues and friends who have willingly read and responded to the manuscript for this book and have done so with clarity and honesty. I sought the advice and informed insights of Gail Rose, my department chair; Esther Mathews, library aide at the Shaker Heights Middle School, and her daughter, Angela Mathews; and Rudine Sims Bishop of the Ohio State University, who read parts of the manuscript and helped me to be sensitive to educational and social issues, particularly those that relate to people of color.

Supportive colleagues and friends Ruth Blair; Doris Blough; Theresa and Charles Bruckerhoff; Holly Burgess; Mark Freeman, our superintendent; Gladys Haddad; Jane Healy; Ray Levi; Mary Murphy; Mary Orear; Becky Thomas; Jeanette Throne; Betty Salomon; Liz Strickler; and Jill Schumacher read with an eye for authenticity and organization. As educators, they individually and collectively provided me with a marvelous sounding board, because they raised important questions that spurred me to hone my thinking and my prose. Many wrote copious notes and suggestions, which I took seriously. Thanks to Jeannine Rajewski and Judith Bratt, who worked side-by-side with me in 1988 and gave my students and me tremendous support. A thank you also to countless other colleagues and friends who encouraged me, and to Nancy Weingart who helped me recognize that a student's comment was a great book title.

Patrick Dias of McGill University, whose poetry response workshop I attended at an NCTE conference, graciously read my poetry chapter, which included a description of his hands-off method of bringing young people to poetry and engaging them collaboratively in responding to it *without* the teacher's direction or intervention, an approach that I have used successfully. A thank you to my long-time great friend and colleague, Marlene Birkman of Webster University, who has counseled and cheered me and introduced me to new possibilities. My dear friend, Sara Wasserman, art therapist at the Shaker Heights Youth Center and Shaker Middle School, with whom I worked hand-in-glove each week to bring around my most recalcitrant students, helped me to stand back and regain perspective when my classroom was most turbulent.

While you're a teacher in the trenches, you also need friends to come to your aid in locating poetry titles, authors, and publishers, and my good and loyal friend, Pat Poe, administrative secretary at the Teaching Media Center, Shaker Heights Schools, graciously performed that task. Mary and David Bartholic were also among those who performed other similar time-consuming tasks. The wonderful women at Shaker Secretarial Service, Inc.—Stefanie Hiles, Marion Matczynski, Arlene Swick, Ann Tanski, Diane Travnikar—bailed me out more than once when I was too overwhelmed to retype newly revised drafts.

Michael Ginsburg of Louisville, Kentucky, read the manuscript (the second of five drafts) from start to finish and raised important questions about the order and number of chapters (I subsequently rethought the order of the table of contents and dumped seven chapters). Although Michael was gentle and generous with his comments, he showed me the big picture through a detailed overview and wrote letters in which he conversed with me about each chapter. Michael's commentary forced me to focus, redevelop, delete, and let my voice be heard. I am grateful to Michael and also to Maureen Barbieri, a good friend and middle school teacher, who read the manuscript with her usual keen eye for concept, clarity, and craft. When Maureen praised my classroom stories extravagantly, she buoyed my spirits.

And then there was Jane Harrigan of the University of New Hampshire, who read draft four and had plenty to say about excessive prose! With the incisiveness of a brain surgeon, Jane used her scalpel to cut through the fat; she was brilliant at plucking pieces from one chapter or another and weaving them in somewhere else. I wish I could have been a student sitting next to Jane while she worked over what I eventually fashioned into the fifth draft. I'm in complete awe and admiration of her unimaginable ability to at once see the whole and help an author find ways to tighten, sharpen, and reshape a manuscript. I will always be indebted to her.

I credit Philippa Stratton, former Editor-in-Chief at Heinemann, for staying with me for half a decade, gracefully making suggestions while letting me have full control and responsibility for my work. As my editor, Philippa set the stage for me much as a deft classroom teacher does for her students. She allowed me (and I'm certain other authors) to take the time to find my classroom stories. I will always remember and appreciate her quiet counsel, immediate response to my questions, and abiding good humor.

Nancy Sheridan, production editor; Linda Howe, copy editor; Dawn Boyer; Ray Coutu; Michael Gibbons; Jenny Greenleaf; Melissa Inglis; Renee LeVerrier; and Elizabeth Valway of Heinemann worked collaboratively with me to bring this book to fruition. I thank them all.

My husband, John, was a veritable saint throughout the five years I worked on this book and cheerfully gave up going on summer vacations because I had to use the precious summer months to write. John was with me every page of the way—he was willing to teach me how to use the infernal computer back in 1989; he spent time in my classes taking photographs of my students and me in action; he ran the printer all hours of the night and day; he helped me package drafts to be mailed; and he gave me complete and patient support every day. When I told an eighth-grade class of disbelieving students how much my husband had helped me, they wondered aloud if I were paying him. I couldn't put a price on his love and support.

Finally, I want to thank my seventh and eighth graders at Shaker Heights Middle School who are the ballast of this book. It is they who needled and sparred with and inspired and taught me.

Author's note: The names of the students in this book are their true names, with the exception of several in Chapter 1 whose privacy I wanted to protect. Their writing is in its original form. Spelling, punctuation, and usage errors do exist; so does nonstandard dialect. My aim was to show authentic writing done by students who were, maybe for the first time, learning how to take charge of language learning and themselves.

CREDIT LINES

ONE

In the Trenches,
But Not Entrenched

On a blustery day in March, fifteen-year-old Tyvonny was sitting at a back table in my seventh-grade language arts/reading class, staring glumly at the action and participating as little as possible. When it came time to collect the students' spiral notebooks that day, Tyvonny pushed his open notebook to the edge of his table, intending for me to read the letter he'd written. Figure 1-1 shows Tyvonny's unedited draft.

Holding the notebook and trying not to shout with delight, I stood at Tyvonny's desk. "What a wonderful note!" I told the intense boy (softly so as not to bring him unwanted attention). "Of course I'll help you learn where to put periods and commas."

Tyvonny focused his fierce brown eyes on my face and said five words that echo still: "Just teach me, Mrs. K.!"

Throughout my twenty-nine years in education, that mission has sustained me. But "just teach me" is a whole lot harder than it sounds. If I hadn't realized that already, I certainly would have learned it during the six years I spent teaching language arts to resistant seventh and eighth graders at Shaker Heights Middle School in Ohio. My students there taught me as much as I taught them, and their strongest lesson was a frightening one: adolescents who have not been successful—have failed—in traditional classrooms are at risk. Unless we find ways to engage them, they will shut down. If we continue to focus only on identifying deficits and devising sterile remedies, these students will surely use their energy and talent for unproductive purposes—or not at all.

When I left elementary school, where I'd taught for more than twenty years, to move to the middle school, where I'd be teaching low- or underachieving seventh and eighth graders, I felt like a seasoned mountain climber tackling the Matterhorn. I had the technique and, I was sure, the stamina. I'd accepted the new job eagerly because I wanted still another kind of challenge when I returned to the classroom from a year of teaching at Cleveland State University. I'd already taught a broad spectrum of students—kindergarten through sixth grade, and college undergraduate and graduate students in teacher education. I'd taught writing and all of the language arts to elementary students in urban Cleveland, Ohio, and in the District of Columbia public schools. For many years I'd taught academically talented sixth graders in suburban Shaker Heights. During one year I was released from the classroom to write and produce a writing series, *Tyger, Tyger Burning Bright,* for PBS. During all the years I'd been a teacher, I wrote for publication.

Dear Mrs. Krogness

I really want to get ahead
in English, and language arts. I want to
learn were to put my . and any , in and I can't
learn by myself . I would really appreciate
if ya help me

Sincerly Tyvonny

FIG. 1-1   *Tyvonny's Letter*

But helping young people recognize their intellectual and creative gifts and then guiding them to develop their talents were what really made my adrenaline rush. I aimed to set these seventh and eighth graders on fire not only about language but about themselves as learners. Yet, even a veteran teacher with broad experience, I was in for a shock. I'd heard about the low test scores and negative teacher assessments of the kids I would teach, but I'm not sure anything could have fully prepared me for the students I was about to encounter—their recalcitrance, lack of focus and short attention span, outlandish behavior, or worse, stony passivity and apparent lack of interest in learning. An increasing number of my students were overage, underprepared, and weighted down by serious emotional baggage. But an occasional glimpse of their creativity and their fetching personalities captured my imagination, even though too many came to class ready to "pick with" each other.

Laden with boxes of paperbacks and bags of ideology, I arrived at Shaker Heights Middle School as a hybrid: simultaneously a twenty-three-year veteran and a first-year novice. In my missionary zeal, I thought I could change the world, or at least this corner of it. But first I had to learn the lay of the land.

Exploring new territory

Shaker Heights, where I'd taught for more than twenty years, is an old upper-middle-class suburb on the east side of Cleveland, Ohio, that is predominantly white. Thirty years ago, Shaker residents committed themselves to racial integration by supporting open housing and voluntary busing of students (African American and white) who lived within the boundaries of the Shaker Heights school district in order to achieve racial balance. Today, the suburb is home to a majority of older white residents, many of whose children are beyond school age. Most of the younger black citizenry have school-age children, so that about half of the school system's students are African American.

Shaker Heights Middle School (a middle school in name only) is a solid, traditional, academically rigorous junior high school of close to nine hundred seventh- and

Danny bursting into our classroom, #226. Late!

eighth-grade students who are taught by eighty or so faculty. Subjects are usually taught as discrete entities, and the school day is neatly divided into eight forty-two-minute periods. Students are grouped, or tracked, in advanced, regular, or skills English, math, and science classes according to how they fare on the Stanford Achievement Test and on the I.Q. test, and how this information fits into a matrix designed to be an impartial way of grouping students. Occasionally, a young person is moved, from a regular English class to an advanced class, for example, when his or her teacher observes exceptional ability.

Generally, SMS teachers, most of whom are seasoned educators with master's degrees and fifteen or more years of experience, approach teaching their subject matter in a solidly traditional way: teachers lecture while students take notes; students read and discuss the assignments (often from textbooks), do the questions at ends of chapters, work on teacher-prepared sheets, do homework (the amount and type vary), do library research, practice doing exercises (or labs) designed to enhance learning, and take tests (often mechanically graded ones) on the material covered. Projects, usually done at home, abound, and teachers put great emphasis on science fairs and preparing for and entering writing, math, and science competitions at the local, regional, and state levels, where participants often receive impressive commendations and awards. Teacher-led discussions are typical, although an increasing number of SMS teachers engage their students in small-group work and student-centered conversations. Modest inroads in trying to design an integrated curriculum that weaves together language arts, history, science, and math and to introduce team-teaching were recently made by interested teachers, who met regularly to plan. But so far, administrators have not made a definite commitment to a pilot program. The majority of Shaker students achieve at least adequately; a significant number excel.

For the first couple of years at SMS, I was assigned five language arts/reading classes (small in comparison to regular or advanced classes, whose size generally numbers somewhere between the low and upper twenties) in which I was free to use my elementary school experience and student-centered philosophy to nurture low or under-achieving students and engage them productively in using the language. During the last several years, however, my principal balanced my skewed schedule of teaching only skills students by assigning me a regular English class or two; one year I taught an advanced seventh-grade English class along with four language arts/reading classes. I was given free rein to approach language learning in whatever ways I chose, supported in my effort by my principal and interested colleagues.

My students were different from other Shaker Heights students in important ways. In contrast to the majority of mainstream Shaker Heights students (more than 90 percent of whom would eventually go to college), my kids generally scored in the 70s, 80s, or 90s on the I.Q. test. They also scored at or below the local third stanine in reading comprehension and vocabulary on the Standard Achievement Test, requiring them to take language arts/reading in addition to English. Nearly all of my students, young people outside the mainstream of a traditionally academic middle school, were assigned to at least one skills English, math, or science class, and some were placed in all three. A few of my students were placed in one, or perhaps two regular classes; rarely were they assigned to advanced classes. One of my language arts/reading students, Ameer, who was originally placed in an advanced math class, was later moved to a regular math class when he dropped behind. In most cases, my students traveled together from class to class and subject to subject because of tracking.

I made the best of this situation. I didn't spend much class time clinically assessing my students' reading and writing problems so that I could produce an appropriate diagnosis for each one. (Only a few had been identified as having learning disabilities, and they were already meeting with L.D. tutors several times a week.) The large majority of my language arts/reading students with gaping holes in their learning had already had a mighty dose of reading skill-builders during their school careers. I saw no point in becoming a plasterer who filled in persistent cracks, spending all of our precious class time diagnosing and then drilling on isolated skills in which a few, some, or all were deficient. My aim was to hook my students on talking, reading, and writing, to immerse them in language and give them plenty of practice in doing what they'd learned not to like or feel good about.

The test and I.Q. scores—those infernal numbers—didn't tell the whole story. I quickly realized that my students were bright. Not by any stretch of the imagination were they bright according to traditional school standards, such as skill in test-taking (standardized and teacher-prepared), doing homework and completing projects on time, using certain standard writing conventions, or demonstrating thought and organization in preparing work. Where they were smart was in their uncanny ability to size up people's feelings or interpret attitudes, actions, reactions, tone of voice, and body language. Sadly, this place called school still tends to define academic excellence and even literacy too narrowly, especially when these definitions are applied to poor and minority students.

The numbers didn't reflect the single biggest factor in students' academic achievement: the world in which they lived.

My students' lives

Graham burst into first-period class one Monday morning and announced breathlessly: "Mrs. Krogness, you should be happy to see me today! I almost got killed last night. I was walkin' down my street from my friend's house. Three guys jumped me and put a gun to my head. They asked what was my name and then said I was lucky. They was lookin' for somebody else!"

When we asked Graham how he managed to escape unharmed, he grinned: "I just kept walkin' and didn't say nothin'. I kept my mouth shut."

Graham's experience hints at what life is like for my students: full of dangers, but supported, in some cases, by loving families. My students at Shaker Middle School were mostly boys and mostly African American. They lived in what they proudly called "the hood," a neighborhood in Shaker Heights that abuts Cleveland proper and consists of modest rental homes—mostly duplexes—and apartments. With money tight and family composition constantly changing, transience was a fact of life in the hood. Several students moved two or three times during the school year. Kenetta's resumé which lists the ten schools she has already attended, illustrates such transience. Often, when I tried to call a student's family, I found that the number had been changed or suddenly become unlisted, or that the telephone had been disconnected.

In more than one of my classes, all of my students (or all but one) lived in single-parent households, and in nearly all these cases that parent was the mother. Some students lived with their mothers and new boyfriends or husbands, while others lived with grandmothers or large extended families. It wasn't unusual for students to shuttle between two households, depending on which family member was able and willing to have them. Two of my students were foster children. A growing number of students lived with guardians.

The adult family members worked as skilled or unskilled laborers, waitresses, nurses' or teachers' aides, practical nurses, lab technicians, and postal workers; many worked two jobs. Most had high school diplomas, some had started taking courses at our community college and a few had finished. A few parents were professionals. But an increasing number of my students' parents or other family members were exceedingly young and relied, at least in part, on public assistance.

Hurdles to clear

The experiences of many of these young people's lives rivaled those of people living in a war zone. Besides hearing an occasional gunshot outside their bedroom window and wondering what was going to happen next, they learned to expect that plans would be cancelled. Dawn wanted to enter an important playwriting contest open to students living in Greater Cleveland. Her mother, a single parent who worked long hours at the post office, promised Dawn that she'd type her daughter's play before the deadline. Dawn had spent two months writing and lovingly polishing the play in language arts/reading class. On the absolute last day for submission, she came to class, put her arms around me, and said: "Mrs. Krogness, I'm sorry but my mom didn't finish typing my play. First she ran out of paper. Then she got sick and couldn't type any more of it. I'm so sorry." Dawn seemed resigned.

Dawn's mother wasn't the only parent who couldn't come through for her child. Impediments such as layoffs from work and illness often precluded parents from following through on important home and school-related issues. When Mrs. B, Danny's mother, fell at work, tearing ligaments in her knee, she could no longer take public transportation. She had to cancel an appointment with the psychotherapist who had agreed to talk with her and evaluate her son's problems. Mrs. B also had trouble keeping her apartment clean while cooking and caring for her four-year-old daughter. Her own mother, an elderly woman, tried to help, but when both women expected Danny to mop the floors, straighten his own bedroom, and babysit his little sister, Danny rebelled. Rather than go home after school, he stayed out late, and more than once, the police brought him home. Later that spring, the boy talked wistfully about the possibility of working the next summer with his dad, who had moved out of their upstairs duplex the previous year.

Many of my kids made the best of fractured home lives that victimized them emotionally and intellectually. In an impassioned letter expressed in a single run-on sentence, Aretha explains why she has an "attitude" (see Figure 1-2). Having been "tossed here and there" and left by both parents is, as Aretha says, confusing.

Philipe, an only child, was raised by an aunt and uncle in another city. He returned to Cleveland to live with his mother, a single parent who physically abused and ridiculed her son even though she provided him with nice clothes and surroundings. Philipe frequently exploded in school and became embroiled in ugly confrontations with other students and teachers. Through counseling with our art therapist, his school counselor, the assistant principal, and various teachers, Philipe managed to hold together well enough to achieve Bs and Cs except for science; he even earned an occasional A in Dick Woods' American history class. Philipe found comfort in the older

> 2/14/90
>
> Dear Mrs. Kragness
>
> I think that my family is confused about a lot of things it seems like I don't fit in because I don't live with my mother nor my father my mother ~~left~~ left me when I was 8 years old and I see her every other 5 months or so my father has his own ~~woman~~ that he is like ignoring me when ever I go over their so I am glad I'm living with my grandma because what ever I'm going threw shes always there and before she came from New York I used to get beatings almost every day and I've been ~~tossed~~ hear + there and I ~~think~~ think thats the only reason why I get my attitude alot by the situation.
>
> Sincerely,
> Aretha

FIG. 1-2　*Aretha's Letter*

sister of a classmate, whom he alternately called his big sister *and* his mother. In class, Philipe wrote a love story based on that young woman, who attended our language arts/reading department's Family Night with Philipe and came to see him perform in the school play.

When home or school became too tough to deal with, some of these young people acted out inappropriately, even violently; others became so dull and passive that they seemed to have pulled down a mental window shade. When David repeatedly stared into space during class, apparently preoccupied, I asked: "Hey, David, do you have a blood pressure?" He looked quizzically at me. "In other words, are you dead or alive?" I laughed. He grinned back knowingly.

Much to my consternation, a few students often put their heads down on their desks; one fell sound asleep during my eighth-period class. I overheard kids say that Therone, a quiet and obedient boy, had a drinking problem (which I later investigated). An astonishing number of these thirteen- and fourteen-year-old boys and girls sucked their thumbs in class; during one school year, nine of my seventh and eighth graders were chronic thumb-suckers. One fourteen-year-old thumb sucker became pregnant and planned to keep her baby.

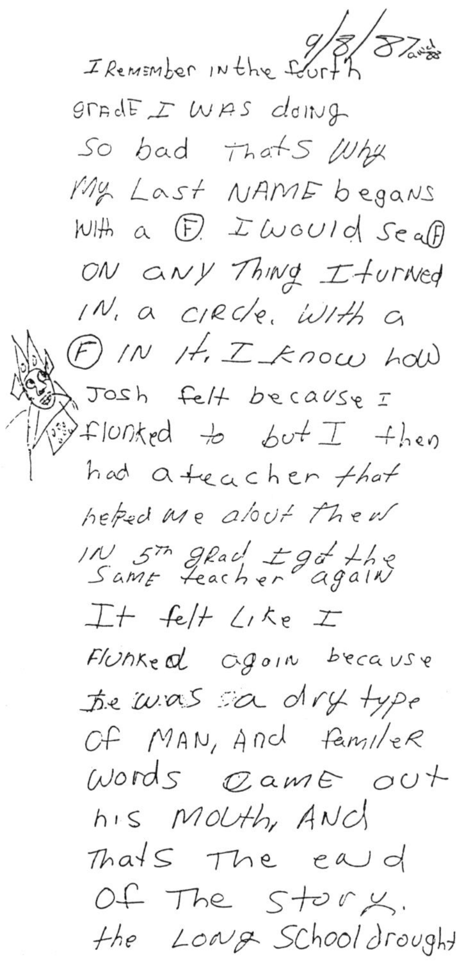

9/8/87

I Remember in the fourth grade I WAS doing So bad Thats Why My Last NAME begans With a (F) I would see (F) ON any Thing I turned IN, a circle. With a (F) IN it, I know how Josh felt because I flonked to but I then had a teacher that heped me about them IN 5th grad I got the Same teacher again It felt Like I Flonked agoin because he was sa dry type of MAN, And familer words came out his Mouth, AND Thats The end Of The story. the Long School drought

FIG. 1-3 *Micah's Response*

A history of failure

During the first week of seventh grade, we read *The Flunking of Joshua T. Bates,* a short, easy novel by Susan Shreve. I asked my students to respond to the dilemma of the main character, Josh, who is failing in school, and to write about a school experience that gave them similar feelings. Figure 1-3 shows the response of Micah, a self-effacing thirteen-year-old who had never recovered from his father's suicide seven years before.

This response could have been written by any number of my students. They knew they were different from the kids in the regular or advanced classes. Many didn't see themselves as learners or achievers, and years of poor report cards only reinforced their views. Often their grades were low, and their behavior frequently brought them negative attention.

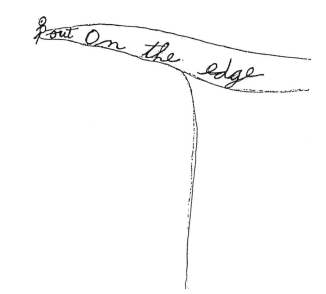

FIG. 1-4   *Micah's Cartoon*

Micah drew two cartoons that say it all: When kids are left out, they are out on the edge (see Figure 1-4). "What it all boils down to . . ." cleverly conveys a feeling of disappointment and rage at being a school failure (see Figure 1-5).

A significant number of the students in the language arts/reading program were considered serious behavior problems, and a growing portion of this group was known by local law enforcement officials and juvenile court. During school hours, teachers referred these misbehaving young people to the office, where they were usually dealt with firmly. Serious disrupters were assigned to in-school ATS (alternative to suspension), where they spent all or part of a day and as much as several days.

Students who fought, stole, or seriously disrupted class were suspended from school, usually for three or five days. Their parents were required to accompany their children to school when they returned. For exceedingly serious misdemeanors, such as brandishing a weapon, a student was summoned to a formal hearing by school author-ities and could count on being expelled for an entire semester.

The students who did not excel and did not misbehave fit another, more nebulous category. They didn't read, write, or think as effectively as their peers. Many didn't keep up with assignments. Consequently, they often said with their voices and actions (or inaction) that they didn't like to read or write. By the time they got to middle school, the academic gap between students who excelled and those who failed was wide. And the gap continued to widen.

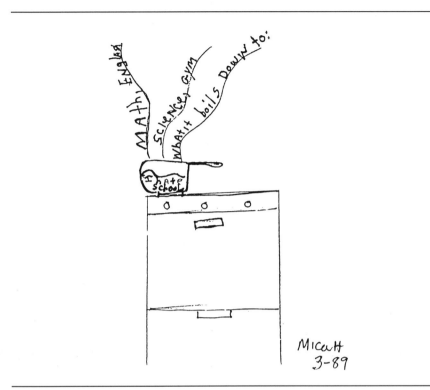

FIG. 1-5   *Micah's Cartoon*

Painful revelations

Society and school are powerful teachers and standard setters. Insidiously, they convey majority values about who is smart, who is best, and who will succeed. My students had already decided that those groups did not include them. The first week of school, I asked them to write letters to themselves about their intentions and expectations for the year. Figure 1-6 shows three representative letters.

As if low grades weren't enough. These students faced other challenges to their self-esteem. One day Graham observed that black kids never won Trivial Pursuit when his history class played. "I don't know the answers to all them history questions," he said. "My *mother* don't even know the answers. But them white kids—they know 'em!"

"Why might that be?" I asked Graham and his classmates.

"Maybe black people—they not as smart as white people." Graham, a class leader, looked around the room, grinning at his classmates. In customary fashion, he had provoked a response. Many class members sat on the edge of their seats.

"White people just *be* smarter than black people." Graham was pushing his class-mates to think as I had been unable to do. The class steamed, but they weren't brave enough to take on Graham, who leered impishly.

"Then why *do* them nerdy white kids know all the answers to Trivial Pursuit and make the best grades? Why do *they* clean up at the honors day assembly, except in track?" Graham, a track star, challenged his classmates and me.

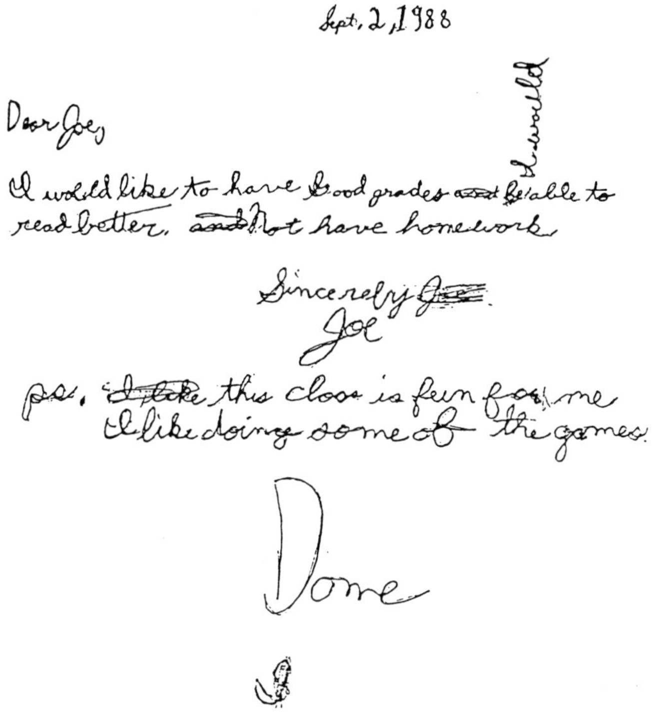

Sept. 2, 1988

Dear Joe,

I would like to have Good grades and be able to (should)
read better. and Not have homework.

Sincerely Joe

Joe

p.s. I take this class is fun for me
I like doing some of the games.

Done

FIG. 1-6A   *Joe's Letter*

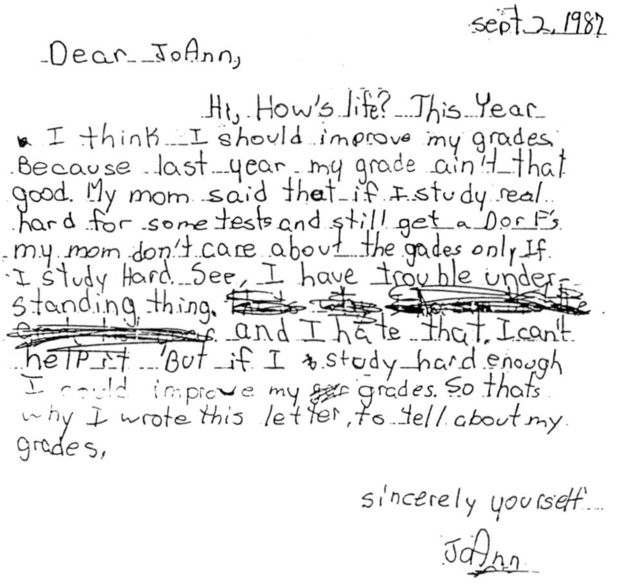

---

sept 2, 1987

Dear JoAnn,

Hi, How's life? This Year
I think I should improve my grades
Because last year my grade ain't that
good. My mom said that if I study real
hard for some tests and still get a D or F's
my mom don't care about the gades only If.
I study Hard. See, I have trouble understanding thing. and I hate that. I can't
help it. But if I study hard enough
I could improve my grades. So that's
why I wrote this letter, to tell about my
grades,

sincerely yourself.

JoAnn

FIG. 1-6B   *JoAnn's Letter*

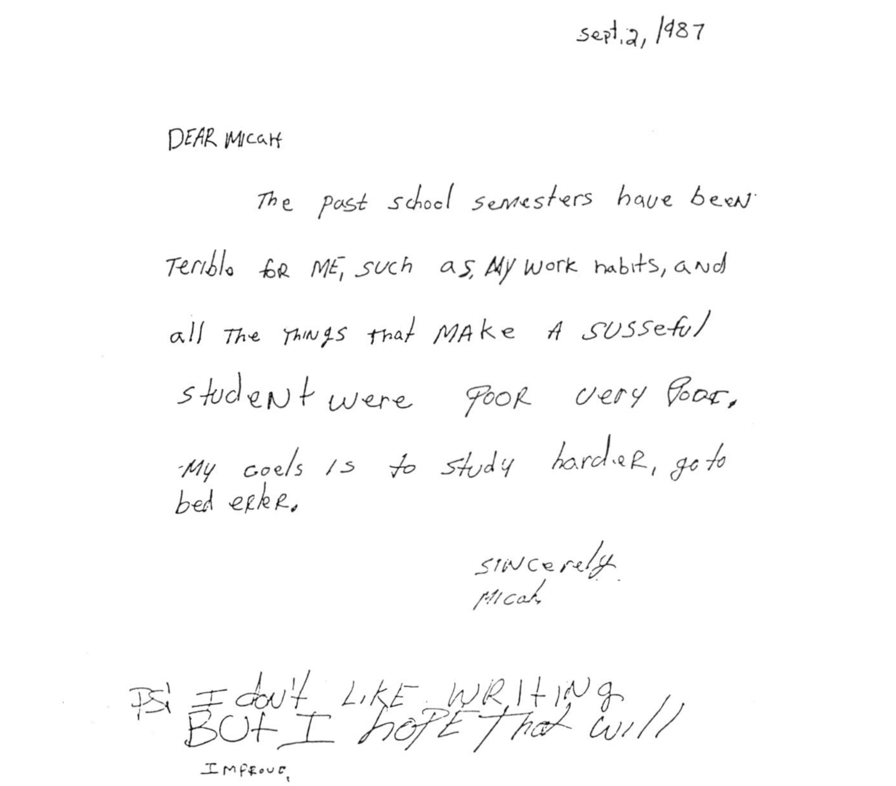

sept. 2, 1987

DEAR MICAH

The past school semesters have been Terible for ME, such as, MY work habits, and all The Things that MAKe A sussefol student were poor very poor.

My coels is to study hardier, go to bed erker.

SINCERELY
Micah

PS: I don't LIKE WRITING BUT I hope That will IMProve.

FIG. 1-6C   *Micah's Letter*

Jacqui shot back: "We have to do *better* than white kids. Every black person knows that!" But Graham ignored Jacqui's argument and pressed his peers to engage in the volatile verbal battle he'd started.

A bleak landscape

Though a gifted talker and leader, Graham was a good example of the deficits many of my students faced. Until I brought a pile of picture books to class, he knew little of fairy tales; he hadn't heard *Goodnight, Moon* or *Where the Wild Things Are*. Neither had many of his classmates. Because few had been read to by their parents, they had not developed a sense of story or sentence, a feel for language or a love for it.

A child's language landscape develops between birth and age five, when the mind is supple and the imagination alert to new sounds and stories. He begins to build the complex, colorful, and constantly changing backdrop that frees him to imagine and make sense of a world expanding in all directions. In *Joining the Literacy Club*, Frank Smith says that young children learn to be literate "not by programs or formal instruction. They learn—usually without anyone being aware they are learning—by practicing in literate activities with people who know how and why to do these things. They join the literacy club" (p. 9).

I knew that Graham had begun to join the literacy club when he piped up in class one day. "Books beautify the brain," he said in his best imitation of my voice. "Little kids need to be raised on books," he'd heard me say. Then Graham ceremoniously gathered his classmates around him—"just like my kindergarten teacher used to do"— and read aloud *Where the Wild Things Are*. " 'And now,' cried Max, 'let the wild rumpus start!' " A week or so later, Graham sashayed into class announcing that he'd won a thousand dollars on "Jeopardy" (or would have, if he'd been *on* TV instead of just watching it!) because he knew the answer to a question on children's literature. "Who's that dude that wrote about them wild things and the little boy name Max?" he asked.

For students like Graham, whose language landscapes differ from those of traditional mainstream students, ordinary school processes—listening and talking, reading and writing to learn—seem unnatural and exotic; they simply aren't part of the student's history. So when these young people come to school they're overwhelmed by the magnitude of formalized learning. In response, they shrink into themselves or act out in a variety of outlandish and inappropriate ways. The school, in turn, reacts by labeling and isolating these children, and the cycle continues. What the students don't know leads to errors, which lead to misunderstanding, which establishes more impediments to learning and to life.

A note of hope

The challenges are huge, frustrating, and infuriating, and traditional schools' ideas about how to meet the challenges are often more infuriating still. But there's reason for hope. Like all young people, underachieving students have dreams. Many of them honestly want to learn, or would if they could come to believe that success is possible. Even their errors of language can provide a springboard for discussion.

The day we returned from Christmas break, fifteen-year-old Jawan called out, "Hey, Mrs. K! Let's talk about our New Year's revolutions."

"Do you mean *resolutions*?" I asked.

"They're called RESolutions?" Jawan said in disbelief. "We always call them *revolutions*." Many of his seventh-grade classmates nodded in agreement.

I wrote *resolve* on the chalkboard. "To resolve means to promise," I told the group. "So a New Year's resolution would be a promise to improve in some way." Scribbling *revolt* on the board, I continued, "To revolt is to overthrow someone or something, like a government. A revolution, then is an overthrow."

"So, Jawan, are you trying to promise? Or are you trying to start a revolution in here?" Most of the kids now understood the joke.

My students were champion resolution-makers. No matter how the system beat them down, many of them sprang back, ready to try again. On report card day, they'd huddle together in the hallways to compare grades. With more zeal than realism, I'd overhear them promise, "Next report card I'm going to get all As." One seventh grader, Deone, said, "No offense, Mrs. Krogness, but I want to retreat out [get out] of your class and go to a high advanced class." Maybe Deone *did* want "to retreat," but I think he also wanted to gain the same respect that students in advanced and even regular classes enjoyed.

In the face of daunting daily discouragement, my students and their families mustered astounding courage and hope. Many of my students' families had made huge financial and personal sacrifices to move from Cleveland to Shaker Heights, and now they dreamed of the opportunities that would open to their children. "My daughter's father and I aren't living together anymore, but we both want Sarita to do well in school," one mother told me. "I went out and spent a hundred dollars on a study lamp and desk. But the problem is, I don't know how to help Sarita with her school work."

During another conference, Lashonda's mother said, "I work two shifts so I can keep my daughter in the Shaker schools. I want her to have the advantages I didn't have. I want her to go to college."

The students, too, dreamed big dreams. Big Malcolm wanted to be a basketball star, and even in eighth grade he was courted by coaches. Graham wore green surgical garb to class the day he gave a speech on aspirations. "I want to be a doctor so I can make lots of money and make my younger cousins know that someone in our family has made it," he said.

Perhaps the grandest dream was Julius's, shown in this epitaph he wrote for himself:

An epitaph

Julius H. was a strong Black leader because he opened the eyes of his people. Julius helped people less fortunate than he. Julius H. was a great speaker. His voice rolled like the sea. Julius' humor was gigantic. He was friendly with all. We shall miss Julius H., God rest his soul. May Julius have a great time in heaven. Amen.

Julius

The more I got to know these students, the more worried I became about doing justice to their dreams—but the more excited I got about trying. I knew—or, at least, most days I *hoped*—that there had to be a way to plug them into learning, to expand their vision, as Jawan aptly put it, "beyond our world." Faced with the warmth and generosity of spirit exhibited in this poem by Julie, what choice did I have but to try?

My World
by Julie

If this was my world
there would be no
sadness—
everyone would be
happier than
happy.
There would be no
drugs.
Everything would be so
clean and everyone
would have to be smart.

If only this world was
mine
there would be no
broken hearts.
Everyone would live
forever.
There would be no
sin—
Only if this world was
mine

TWO

Dreams with Design
Classroom Goals and Management

rs. Krogness, we want you to holler at us!" Lisa M. screamed angrily one day early in the school year. Like many of her eighth-grade classmates, she relied on adults to establish limits; she had not developed the internal controls that many children begin cultivating as preschoolers. Lisa was asking me to take control for her. She wanted me to put her into harness by "hollering," to scare her into shutting up and doing her work. But that wasn't the kind of classroom culture I planned to create.

From my first day at the middle school, I knew atmosphere and attitude would be crucial. Of course, issues of curriculum and discipline would occupy many of my waking (and even more of my should-have-been-sleeping) moments, but they weren't my immediate priorities. First I wanted to set goals; then I would figure out how to help my resistant students reach them.

Lofty goals

Each day I spent at the middle school, I moved a little closer to what Nancie Atwell calls the art and heart of teaching the young people from whom many had turned away. My goals for them were high, and by no means did we always attain them. But we kept them in sight.

Above all, I longed to immerse my resistant learners in language. I wanted to hook them on talking to learn. I wanted my classroom to be noisy with conversation, because talking is essential to intellectual commitment and camaraderie. I wanted my students to use the language in a myriad of ways, for a variety of purposes and for a variety of audiences. If I could help them harness their adolescent energy by enticing them with different modes of expression, together, I hoped, we would create an atmosphere in which everyone would feel free to talk, wonder, question, or disagree—without fear of silent mockery or verbal asides.

I wanted my students to develop intellectual stamina and to exercise their imaginations in the bargain. I wanted them to connect school with real life, to see that their "street smarts," their amazingly well-developed ability to size people up quickly, could be applied to analyzing literature or interpreting current events. Most ambitious of all, I wanted to help them move forward, to expand their vision of the possible. As strongly as I knew what I wanted, I also knew what I did *not* want: didactic worksheets and connect-the-dots skillbuilders, the traditional death sentence of the under- or low achiever.

The typical remedial program is a perfect example of what Micah, in a response to literature shown in Figure 1-3, called "the long school draught." Skill-building exercises reward predictability over vitality, perpetuating the notion that students learn by circling answers and filling in blanks. Too often, however, resistant students learn that creative, challenging academic work is for others, not for them—they're condemned to routinized exercises that render them intellectually and socially dependent. Numbed by years of academic pablum, they relinquish both their right and their desire to learn.

Of course, worksheets do occasionally have their place for teaching specific skills, and they've been known to corral the energy that an obstreperous young person might otherwise use to create classroom chaos. On bad days, I sometimes threatened to give worksheets, just to settle everyone down! But before the school year began, I had no intention of photocopying quantities of skill-builders or using other packaged materials.

Points of departure

Though I wanted to create a brave new classroom world, I started by behaving in a thoroughly traditional manner. I read our course of study to be sure of the middle school's expectations, requirements, and policies. Then I interpreted these general, philosophic goals, such as reading for meaning, in my own way. Instead of writing answers to questions, for example, we wrote responses to the literature we were reading. I took off, working within our school's broad guidelines to create a more flexible and imaginative program. I wanted to engage my resistant learners in nontraditional ways.

In designing the curriculum, I took leads from my kids. When I noticed how much importance they attached to their families, for example, especially their grandparents, I organized an oral history experience. We developed a set of questions and then taped interviews with family members and friends. Although my students rarely told me of their interests directly, everything they said and did gave me clues. I brought in ideas, projects, literature, speakers—anything or anyone that might whet their appetite for learning. Rather than hammer them with *have tos, oughts, musts,* and *shoulds,* or load them with assignments to be done at home where their classmates and I couldn't help them, I invited my students to get involved *during* class. I never sent the good stuff home.

The spiral writing notebooks, too, were sacred to the classroom and never to be taken home. Of all the experiments I tried with my new students, the spirals were perhaps the most satisfying. On the second day of school, I presented each student with a notebook of one-hundred pages that cost each person less than a dollar, thereby standardizing the size and quality of each writer's spiral. Into these notebooks would go all their writing—and all my responses to their writing. No one could take a writing spiral home, where it might be damaged or worse, lost. No one could tear out a page, no matter how messy. I instructed my students to draw single lines through material they wanted to delete rather than erase it; that way, the spirals would become their writing history, the record of their progress.

Keeping our writing notebooks—our archives—upright, orderly, and always at school.

Taking off

As the year went on, I watched with pleasure as my students ran into class and grabbed their writing spirals from the record racks where we kept them, eager to read my latest comments or just to thumb reverently through their work. We were creating our own archives, and our history together was changing all the time. We tried everything—reading poetry and performing it, writing our own poems, writing and performing our own plays, and improvising dramas based on the news of the day or the literature we were reading.

Together we cultivated an ability to see the commonplace through new eyes: a chair becomes a whole new entity when you look at it upside-down! We viewed dozens of slides of the Noguchi sculpture *Portal,* a black metal behemoth that looms in front of the Justice Center in downtown Cleveland. We noticed that it curved and pushed toward the sky, to a place far beyond its industrial home. From these discussions of perspective and point of view, we moved on to the points of view of characters in books, the way characters' understanding varies with age, experience, and the particular angle from which they view the action.

As my students wrote and talked more often, we began to do some serious fooling around: we played with words. They had heard of a school of fish and a herd of elephants. Now I introduced them to other animal groupings: a pride of lions, a gaggle of geese, a bevy of quail, a pod of whales, a leap of leopards. Then, during two class periods, we brainstormed our own groups of animals and the results delighted us. Michael J. proposed "a thundering of elephants." Daniell came up with a "skyscraper of giraffes." Tristin engaged all our ears with a "scissoring of crocodiles," and Louis created a sharp visual image with "a piano of zebras." These spare and striking word pictures came after I'd primed the pump with questions and recorded many kids' ideas on the board, after we'd had time—maybe a whole class period—to play with words. I felt as if I were living an experiment proving what I recall hearing E. Paul Torrance say: the more ideas a person—or a group—generates, the better those ideas become.

Ready to learn

At the annual meeting of NCTE (National Council of Teachers of English) in 1990, Elliot Eisner described curriculum as "a mind-altering device in which teachers' choices affect what students can do in the world." How true! But the best curriculum becomes useless if students aren't primed to learn. My initial task, then, was to establish the kind of classroom atmosphere that would encourage my students to do their best work.

Here is how I began. On the first day of school I set the tone by giving students a concrete message: "When you cross the threshold of this classroom, I expect you to develop a mindset for learning. I expect you to get yourself ready to pay attention to what *everyone* says about ideas, the literature we read, and the writing we do. I expect you to be prepared to think and ask questions, to be ready to talk, read, and write each day that you come into this room." I demonstrated coming into class and sitting down quietly.

I asked my seventh graders to get out of their chairs and practice the act of coming into class, preparing themselves emotionally and intellectually for working in their new school. We practiced crossing the threshold—that tangible line separating the class-room from the conflagration of the corridors—several times during that next week or two, thus establishing simple, observable standards of behavior and attitudes that I considered important for the act of learning. The eighth graders, old hands at being students in our school, would have scoffed at this little exercise.

After I talked to them about crossing the threshold in preparation for learning, I asked them to consider what interests they brought to our classroom and what they could do to ensure that we would work together for everyone's benefit. I asked several classroom recorders/reporters (perhaps potential problem students) to list their class-mates' ideas on a large sheet of paper that eventually hung in our classroom.

To establish order and continuity, I didn't shy away from ritual: the writing notebooks, for example, were always placed spiral down and cover facing forward in the record racks. I also passed out dashing homework folders, the vividly colored ones with two inside pockets that can be bought in bulk at any office supply store. Ceremoniously, I asked my new students to neatly write their name, the subject, my name, and the year on the front. I took time to explain that this folder should contain only papers that pertained to my class. I carefully instructed them to take this folder home each day and bring it back filled with the previous night's homework, which always consisted of short (not more than fifteen to twenty minutes' worth) of manageable activity. For example, I asked them to jot notes detailing a room in their home, to listen to the evening news and find a local, national, or international event, to do a practice skills sheet, or to read aloud to a younger child. When the folders bulged with ragged assignments, we took five minutes of class time to reorder them and get organized. Upon occasion, we spent after-school conference periods excavating book bags that

Language learning is social as well as intellectual.

resembled archaeological sites, all in an attempt to help students practice the art of orderliness.

Orderliness may not be next to godliness, but it's a good step toward the elusive goal of classroom management. Management is not something "done to" students. Rather, it's a teacher's way of thinking, behaving, orchestrating, and envisioning; in short, it is a way of treating people. As such, classroom management is not a neat paradigm a teacher can simply copy from a manual and superimpose on a class. Although management does include discipline and order, these are just one piece of the classroom management pie.

For me, classroom management is a balancing act between the practical and the intangible. The practical means organization: seeing that tables and chairs, supplies and equipment are in place, planning lessons, grading papers, lining up speakers and field trips. These considerations gave my students and me a sense of order, direction, and continuity.

The intangibles are human matters of the mind and heart: sizing up a class, figuring out what makes students tick and what would turn them on to learning, understanding who works well with whom, using time effectively, seizing the magic moments and bringing a motley group together for everyone's benefit.

Sharing responsibility

During the first few days of school, I conveyed through my words and my attitude that I wanted my students to come along with me. "Join me," I said. "Together we will learn how to talk to learn, read to learn, and write to learn. We will find out that learning can be pleasurable rather than boring or intimidating."

Throughout the school year I gave what I called "sermonettes" designed to help them refocus and regain belief in themselves. Here is an example: "Many of you don't like to read books or write; some of you don't like school at all. Many of you are having a hard time—and you're discouraged. Maybe you're having trouble *not* because you're not *smart* enough, but because you have not had the *experience* doing this kind of work that many of your classmates have had. You have not had the *practice*. You are behind because you lack experience and practice in listening, talking, reading, writing, and thinking. None of this is your fault. But now it is *your* responsibility to become active learners. *You,* not I, will talk about ideas; *you,* not I, will ask questions; *you,* not I, will say, 'Will you help me to learn?' Are you with me?"

When I'd give one of my sermonettes, my students would listen intently, for I had not blamed them for what they couldn't do or weren't ready to do. Rather, I'd put the responsibility in everyone's hands. If they'd do one thing—join me—school success could eventually become a reality!

Another way I showed my students my philosophy was by letting them make certain decisions—little ones at first. While many teachers assigned seats on the first day of school, I let students choose where they wanted to sit. I told my new students I would encourage them to exercise choice until their choices began to interfere with their own learning or that of others. By letting them choose their seats during the first few days of school, I also gained immediate insight into the group's dynamics: who was friendly with whom, who was an isolate, and so forth.

Sizing up every class

During the first days and weeks of school, I observed my students as individuals and as members of the group. Meanwhile, they were sizing me up, too. Early in the year, classroom leaders sent signals; they established their brand of leadership by entertaining their classmates or settling down to learn. I was alert to ways that I could most effectively tap the energy of those leaders, who had the potential to either derail our class or support me. I could give them responsibility immediately, engage them in language-learning opportunities quickly, or take time to build a foundation for working together.

Without labeling individuals or whole classes as incorrigible or passive, the two extremes that often characterize a seventh- or eighth-grade skills class, I considered the dynamics of each one of my five classes. I knew that disruptive behavior is due at least in part to students' low self-esteem and feelings of inadequacy, neither of which they know how to change. The students may subconsciously believe that behaving badly is all they can do well, or that their inadequacy won't be noticed if they create anarchy. Often, students who behave badly have never been in contact with peers who honestly aim to excel in school. The reason is the outmoded, educationally unsound practice of tracking students according to their apparent ability and skill.

The dynamics of a class depend on many variables: the teacher's competence, confidence, and style; the combination of student personalities; and the ratio of boys to girls. The degree of transiency within a class dramatically affects the dynamics, too. Each time a new student enrolls in or exits a class, the dynamics change.

Variables that rock the boat

In one constantly shifting, unsettled and unsettling eighth-grade class in which for many months boys outnumbered girls, a sudden change took place. Ladell, a solid student and effective leader who was friendly with everyone, moved away unexpect-edly. All signs pointed to trouble, but once again I learned that predictions are useless. While Ladell had been in the class, his best friend Mosay regularly gave me trouble by sashaying in late, then yelling out incendiary comments or making people laugh by his boisterous antics. I often sensed that Mosay was trying to gain Ladell's approval and compete with his friend for the key leadership position.

After Ladell left our school, Mosay moved into the "catbird seat." Shortly there-after, to my surprise, he calmed down, became more settled, and for the most part acted relatively respectable. Kaleem, another member of this class and a newcomer to our school, had been expelled from a Cleveland public school for carrying a gun to class; Shaker Heights authorities believed he was engaged in illegal activities. At the middle school, Kaleem, who carried a beeper and referred to his "partners," enjoyed moving at a snail's pace down the corridor and then making a late entrance into class, his voice sky-rocketing in pitch and intensity if I commented on his passive-aggressive ways. Curiously, he, too, simmered down after Ladell left, as did another of his fellow troublemakers.

Within a month—between the time of our winter holiday in December and the end of the first semester in late January—the class gained three girls, among them a very bright and refined Japanese girl; not only was she perplexed by the language and cultural barriers, but her eyes were out on stems at the animated vocabulary she heard and the body language she witnessed in this motley eighth-grade class!

Regaining and then maintaining classroom decorum in this case was not simply a task of moving ahead with our work, for the classroom dynamics had shifted dramati-cally; eight young people had entered and exited between mid-September and January. We quite literally had to regroup. My being calm and quiet (both difficult for me) was paramount to our working things out again. We were trying to shift from being a male-dominated classroom to being one with a majority of females who'd learned to be quiet when the macho boys were making themselves heard. To further complicate matters, the major project we'd been working on, a film we'd been creating and shooting with one of our librarians since October, had to be reorganized because we'd lost (or gained) writers and performers.

Forging a partnership with parents

This wasn't the first time I'd gotten parents involved. During the first few weeks of school, I called them all, introduced myself, and asked for their support. Most students' hopes are high during those early weeks; the new year means a fresh start, especially for those who haven't fared well in the past. The teacher who calls home early, *before* young people have gotten into serious difficulty, is usually received warmly. I found that by calling parents or other caretakers in the fall, I could count on their support for the rest of the year. They were willing to help me set limits and resolve their children's disruptive behavior.

After my initial call in September, I telephoned families when I wanted to report personal and academic progress or ask for help. I kept a log (see Figure 2-1) noting the date, the content and tone of each phone conversation. The log allowed me not only to look for patterns, but also to substantiate my contacts when necessary. Each year, I logged between two hundred and three hundred telephone calls home.

Telephone Log
1992-93

1. Darnell 9-8-92 Introduced myself to D.'s grandmother w/ whom he lives. She was at 1st anxious that I'd called so early in year. Was pleased to know—relieved—that grandson's attitude was positive. Have Mrs. B's support. She explained that D. had just moved in w/ her during summer. She plans to attend SMS OPEN House 9-28.

2. "Marshay" 9/9/92 Mom works night shift. Spoke w/ stepfather who seemed disinterested in his stepdaughter & my call. Abrupt. Gave me his wife's work #. She & I need to talk soon about "M's rage that has already been in evidence: glowers, yells out in class—at me & other students; defies requests & ignores assignments.

3. Devon 9/10/92 What a doll! Has already offered to share book he's rdg. Demonstrates vivid imagination & propensity for using lang. (orally & in writing) richly! Mom—so pleased to get a ++ report early!

FIG. 2-1 *Mary's Telephone Log*

When all else fails

I usually dealt with the most common misdemeanors—arriving late, disrupting class, not doing the work, talking back—at school. I tried always to keep my voice quiet but firm, and not to overreact to provocative comments designed to put the responsibility on my shoulders or distract me from the student's misdemeanor. Remaining calm and quiet, though often difficult, helped me subdue the riled adolescent.

Sometimes I used humor to defuse the kids' mood: "What can you expect from a 'doogleberry' like Jawan?" I'd ask the rest of the class.

"But what's a doogleberry?" another student might wonder, asking me to define my invented word.

"Jawan fits the description of a doogleberry perfectly," I'd answer.

Calling my rambunctious students silly-sounding, invented names that were not malicious—such as "doogleberries" and "doinkburgers"—caused us to laugh and often prevented our becoming engaged in unnecessary struggles. And through humor I was able to send some of them the message that they needed to take better charge of themselves.

I also tried to listen to students' points of view. If they were late to class, for instance, perhaps a teacher from the previous class had asked them to stay. But when I needed to be fully in charge of a situation, I said, "This is not a conversation. I am telling you to move. I want you to stop talking. We are not discussing why I am taking this action."

The student's common retort: "But I'm not doin' nothin'!"

"That's right. You're *not* doing nothin'. And that's why I'm distressed! Get in gear and engage in the work that we're doing, and I'll stop accusing you." (This sort of conversation brought me great pleasure.)

When a student pushed beyond acceptable limits, I borrowed a wonderful line from a bumper sticker: "Which part of NO don't you understand?" I tried (but did not always succeed) to refrain from talking too much and being dragged into the imbroglio. My aim, always, was to help the angry or manipulative student rechannel her or his energy to engage in learning.

Occasionally I would take a chronically unruly student to the office after class and tell the student to call his or her parents at work to explain the problem. Then I got on the telephone and explained to the student's parent or grandparent why I'd asked the student to call. This technique—used sparingly and judiciously—got action! It gave the misbehaving student responsibility, and explaining what had happened often helped that young person come to grips with the difficulties at hand.

When I was unsuccessful in talking through a problem with a student or enlisting a parent's help, I sent the student to the office, wrote a referral, and asked an assistant principal to talk with the student and use her or his judgment about assigning detention, sending the student to ATS (alternative to suspension), or calling the parents to make a conference appointment.

If a fight broke out in my class (and this happened only once), I quickly asked a student to call the office and summon help. I asked a few kids to help me separate and soothe the combatants. I also mailed a form letter, "We're Worried!" created by our new principal for unresponsive parents of chronically misbehaving students. I jotted down major difficulties and checked the appropriate misdemeanors on the list. I mailed the "We're Worried!" letters in plain envelopes (without the school letterhead) so that the young people would not intercept them. The duplicate copies served as records for me and whoever else would read the misbehaving student's file.

If I could not corral a student and help her or him redirect energy, or if one student prevented my being effective with the rest for too long, I asked that that student be removed from my class and placed in another section of language arts/reading. This strategy worked on several occasions. Even in a big school of nearly nine hundred seventh and eighth graders, rescheduling is possible when you make yourself heard and don't resort to this tactic too often.

Finding the tempo

While I was sizing up my students and endeavoring to set a tone during those early days and weeks of school, I tried to sense the tempo of each class. Finding various ways to start class quickly and effectively is important: different classes respond to different beginnings. Would this group go for a brief but interesting conversation? Should I try fast-paced calisthenics such as recognizing the difference between *their, there,* and *they're;* or, between *feel* and *fell* or *now* and *know*? Was reading poetry or a story aloud a good way to settle everyone down? Or should I try some word play, such as *Have you ever seen . . . a milk shake, a back rub, a brain wash, a salad dressing*?

In sizing up my five classes each fall, I tried to think of the best ways to group and regroup the students for discussions, poetry responses, and fast-paced drills. When a class has strong leaders who can follow directions and work independently, small groups can learn to work together for short periods early in the school year.

Learning to group, grouping to learn

Grouping young people for different activities and purposes is an integral part of classroom management, because it is directly related to classroom dynamics, but it also helps kids develop initiative, independence, and leadership. I often paired students (or let them choose partners) for brief, well-defined activities such as interviewing each other, generating lists, or responding to a single question. This five- to ten-minute exercise in working together, which I demonstrated before the pairs met, served as early preparation for more sustained small-group work. When certain students could not manage to work effectively for even a few minutes, I knew I would have to bring them to the conference table and take charge.

If too many students needed constant supervision, I devised other ways of working with them. For a while, I led the entire class in brief, well-defined activities so that everyone could practice a few simple procedures. I asked them to pair up with people sitting near them, and we repeated the procedures. I taught them quite explicitly. If students managed to accomplish one or two simple tasks, I asked them to work together again.

Some students simply could not control their behavior, while others couldn't accomplish the simplest tasks in a group situation, so I brought these students together and worked through the process with them. A few students could not manage even when I was their leader, and I either let them sit and watch what was going on or asked them to sit outside the classroom to complete a short, manageable task alone.

If they couldn't work quietly in the hall, I sent them to the office. Then I called their parents and arranged a parent/teacher/student conference to put together a plan of action for which the student would be held accountable. In certain cases, I wrote up simple contracts that the student would read and sign in the presence of one or both of his adult family members. Although I never insisted that a parent come to class and sit with his or her son or daughter for a day or more (a management technique that can work very well), I do believe that when teachers and parents work together, students benefit.

Thus, my students and I *practiced* working in pairs and then in small groups. We learned how to talk to each other more effectively and to accomplish more sophisticated tasks. But if a particularly disruptive student was having a bad day, I scotched my plans for small-group work and shifted into a more contained lesson. In the majority of my language arts/reading classes, students eventually learned how to work together because we took time to practice this skill throughout the school year.

The big picture

Recognizing the direct relationship between classroom management and long-term planning can make day-to-day operations smoother and more fulfilling for everyone. Looking at class time as a continuum rather than as short, discrete chunks allows the teacher to build continuity and support students' full engagement. Long-term projects are also an integral part of classroom management. I designed projects that extended from a few days to several months. These projects engaged the language learner in generating ideas, planning, conferring with others and responding to questions, reading, researching, writing, and rewriting or revising—all of the language arts woven together.

The flip side of being visionary is being resourceful. Many principals have discretionary funds for special projects or supplies. In a one-page proposal to the principal, you can include a brief, clear description of your plan and its objectives, as well as a list of necessary supplies.

Inventive teachers often apply to charitable foundations for mini-grants or even for substantial grants that enable them to buy supplies or pay for field trips or speakers. Mary Murphy, a new teacher and an indefatigable source of energy and imagination, was exceedingly resourceful even during the first year or two that she taught in one Cleveland public school. She was awarded grants of more than five thousand dollars from several of Cleveland's charitable foundations to implement special language and math programs in her sixth-grade class, among them a drama program in which African American actors worked with young people after school.

Mary Murphy's ingenuity led her to the greater community. For example, a meeting with African storytellers when she and her husband attended an international fair in downtown Cleveland led her to conceive an African day in her classroom. In preparation for the event, for which students and their parents prepared authentic African food, Mary engaged her sixth graders in researching African culture, music, art, and language. Using multiple paperbacks purchased with money from her principal's discretionary fund, Mary and her students read about the politics of South Africa and the practice of apartheid in Beverley Naidoo's powerful story, *Journey to Jo'Burg*. They read and listened to tapes of African folk tales before African storytellers, also paid for out of the discretionary fund, came to class and shared in the festivities.

Teachers who reach out to the community find a treasure trove of talent. By inviting parents and other community members to school to speak about a vocation, give demonstrations on quilting, sing gospel, tell stories, or engage young people in special projects, the teacher breaks down the walls that separate the school from the community's real life. By bringing talent from the outside into her classroom, Mary Murphy broadened her students' perception of the world and added to their language landscape. For her students, school became a hive of intellectual inquiry and activity as well as a safe and purposeful place to be.

Cultivating a vision and devising open-ended flexible plans are key to a language-rich, well-orchestrated classroom. As important as classroom management is, it cannot be separated from the everyday life of the group. And each group's story changes daily. By no means have I figured out all the answers. On my road to some imagined classroom nirvana, it seems I'm forever encountering a roadblock, a detour, or a rough stretch under construction. For every student who suddenly catches fire and soars in ways neither of us could have dreamed, there's another who just keeps sitting passively, or who takes one faltering step forward and falls two giant steps back. But every day I am learning—to listen, to be patient, to plant the seeds and not worry that it might be others who reap the results.

THREE
Inside Seventh Grade

n general, seventh graders are nice little critters whose eyes are wide with fear and expectation. By the time the school year starts, they've already heard about their big new school, certain teachers, and those mean eighth graders who are out to get them. During the first semester, the seventh graders' desire to please often keeps them in line. They are cowed by all that is new and daunting—finding their way to class on time, dressing for gym, adjusting to the peculiar styles of eight or more teachers, and taking lots of tests. In relative terms, seventh graders—especially alongside eighth graders—are manageable. However, some of the seventh graders I am about to introduce don't exactly fit this description. (But that is the danger of making generalizations.) Here is Chi, an immigrant from Vietnam, commenting on Mildred Taylor's *Roll of Thunder, Hear My Cry:* "I don't like Cassie because she write this story so hard." Chi expressed what many of my seventh graders felt but didn't usually say. Almost all of my kids were overwhelmed by print, either because they had failed so miserably in trying to understand it or because English, for a few students, was still very new to them.

Many of my seventh graders read at a third- or fourth-grade level, and a few at a second-grade level. They usually didn't fare well in other subjects either. Not surprisingly, they lacked competence and confidence in language learning. Chi expressed her frustration in a poem: "The mountain also hot and hard to claim [climb]."

The young people in my language arts/reading classes didn't view themselves as readers or writers. From the survey that I passed out during the first week of school, I learned how they felt about reading and writing and, therefore, about themselves. Here are some of their answers to the question "Why do you like or dislike reading?": "I hate to read because it's boring." "My eyes get tired." "My head gets to hurting." "My butt gets sore from sitting so long." "Most books are too long." Even the rare students who enjoyed reading often forgot what they'd just read or didn't really understand the story. The magnitude of their language-learning problems was overwhelming—certainly to them, and often to those of us who were trying to teach them. I didn't think of my students' academic problems as *reading* problems; rather, they reflected an all-encompassing difficulty in using language.

Except for Lisa S., all of the members of this particular seventh-grade class experienced difficulty in simply decoding words. They reversed letters and confused or missed consonant and vowel sounds, diphthongs, and blends. They started and stumbled, hesitated and halted. It was painful indeed to witness big boys and girls of twelve, thirteen, fourteen, and even fifteen working so hard to eke out an education word by word, sentence by sentence. It all took so long.

Steam and esteem

No wonder this group of students avoided reading. To them, print must have seemed an interminable number of terrible little black marks marching across more pages than they cared to consider. I often saw them leafing through the new paperback books I'd passed out, counting the pages that for them promised not adventure but drudgery.

Ironically, making meaning from a text often seemed more problematic for the few students who were fluent at the mechanics of reading than for those who had trouble decoding words. Lisa S., for example, could read aloud almost flawlessly, but she often couldn't remember what she'd read.

So my students experienced fear and even hatred of reading and writing (though they usually directed less anger toward writing, because they had been told they had serious *reading,* not writing problems). I, in turn, faced the complex task of figuring out what to do instead of filling their days with just the kind of reading skill-builders that hadn't solved their problems. I wanted to tap into other possibilities, ones that had probably gone unnoticed—for instance, nurturing the imagination or helping them translate their street-smartness to book smartness. Together my students and I had to find ways to talk and listen, to read and write our way through seventh grade, to give everyone practice and experience in doing what had become so unpalatable. I believed that we could accomplish these goals by meeting the language freshly and learning to enjoy it together.

An eclectic group

It was a motley crew that assembled in that classroom. Let me introduce some of the key players—many of whose names began with "J."

Jawan (Big J.) was big and explosive, charming and smart, but seriously underprepared. He had come from an urban school in Cleveland and would be fifteen in the spring. Jawan met regularly with his probation officer because he'd been caught by the police damaging school property, among other misdemeanors. When Big J. tilted back in his chair, yawned, sneezed, and thrust his hands into Jamar's face, he automatically started a cacophony of cross words and incendiary remarks.

Jermaine, Jawan's sidekick, a Spike Lee look-alike, was sneaky and manipulative, yet somehow appealing, especially when he let down his guard and allowed his vulnerabilities to show. He was quick to understand demanding questions about characters or situations; he took to improvised drama. But his life outside school pulled him in the wrong direction.

Jamar was a smiling fellow, delightfully whimsical and playful, but scattered. He wanted to excel and to please his teacher. His brand of humor is evident in his comic strip "D. J. Peterjohn," starring our principal, Dr. R. C. Peterjohn, who usually called male students "Big Guy" (see Figure 3-1). Sometimes, to please his father, Jamar tried to shed his natural gentleness in favor of a military-like machismo.

Joe, an eager-to-please but uncertain little blond fellow, picked at scabs on his plump, little-boy arms until they bled. Although he came to class with a considerable amount of knowledge, he often wasn't able to use it because he was distracted and fraught with angst. He lugged around a horrific amount of emotional

FIG. 3-1   *Jamar's Comic Strip*

baggage and also had a learning disability that all but stopped him from putting pencil to paper.

Jung, who'd recently come from Korea and an educated upper-middle-class home, was fragile and resisted not only reading and writing, but talking, too. Jung was trying to learn English and a new culture at the same time.

Tiawan, a tentative fellow, who trembled with anxiety and doubted himself, had also come from a Cleveland school. His oral reading revealed a probable learning disability, as did his writing, which was replete with syntactical difficulties, omissions, and idiosyncratic spelling. Tiawan nervously watched for approval until one day during the second semester, when quite suddenly he moved out of our school district.

Then there was the very bright and affable Chris M., who quietly put on the brakes the moment he approached success and often ran out of psychic energy before he'd finished a long-term project. Chris asked penetrating questions.

Deontay, who came to our class from a Cleveland public school at the end of first semester, smiled often, was pleasant and obedient, but distant. He followed orders but was unaccustomed to talking in class.

Rhonda, a hostile and frightened girl, had a talent for writing but frequently demonstrated what she herself described as "an attitude." She worked so long and hard at dividing the students in this class that late in the fall I asked that Rhonda be transferred to another section.

Chi, whom we have already met, was a fetching, hard-working girl. Her tiny stature belied her nearly fifteen years. She had come with her family from Vietnam and was happy learning the language and being a class member.

Lisa S., who loved to write and even to revise stories, was an anxious girl. She was capable of excellent work when she wasn't preoccupied. She desperately wanted to make friends and fit in.

And last, but certainly not least, was full-of-fire Marie, all-a-twinkle, all-a-twitch, and all smiles, who tried masking her sadness and anxiety by attempting to take hold of her life. Marie, alias Nefertiti, alias Sugar Rae, alias Marie, along with Chris, Jermaine, Jamar, and Jawan, had been transferred from another English class early in October. Marie was alternately petulant and positively exuberant. She, Chi, and Lisa wound up being the only girls in our class.

And also very much a part of our class was Jeannine Rajewski, a remarkable student teacher from Hiram College in Ohio, whom the English department chair shared with me for three months during the fall. Sara Wasserman, our talented art therapist from the Shaker Heights Youth Center, became a staple in our class, as did Judith Bratt, a teacher from England who volunteered once a week.

Orchestrating chaos

I was glad for all the adult help I could get, for this cadre of kids seemed to delight in what I called "zooing around." Joe often took to turning in his seat and quietly laying small verbal bombs, detonating a classmate's easily ignited fuse. Tiawan screeched his raucous laugh and mumbled little asides that inevitably triggered a response from at least one of his confreres. Lisa and Chi, friends for the most part, occasionally became embroiled in spats about one important thing or another.

Rhonda, meanwhile, rolled her eyes until I thought they would be lost forever in the inner regions of her head. Once I overheard Rhonda telling another student about me in a sharp, staccato voice: "She-gets-on-my-nerves!" As she spoke with hands on hips, her shoulders moved and her head swiveled to the beat.

Jermaine, whom I called Spicy Meatball, always found the jugular vein, especially when someone was feeling a little vulnerable. He inevitably knew when I wasn't feeling as strong as usual. (Do you see what I mean about being smart?) Chris and Jamar, both of whom were kind, polite boys, occasionally got into a verbal struggle with each other or with someone else.

Jung, who resisted doing much work in class, was certainly learning Western ways—mostly raw language and hand gestures. He delighted many of his teenage mentors when he uttered a four-letter word in his soft Korean accent or surreptitiously gave someone the finger.

There was no escape from Jawan, Jermaine, Chris, and Jamar when they started what they called "nappin' " (fussing or "picking with" each other). I recall wondering why I *ever* declared a desperate need for more class time.

Seventh graders, at twelve and thirteen years of age, are as a rule still young, innocent, and unsophisticated. They are fast-growing young people who try to fit in. Although they lack confidence and feel anxious about being in a new school, and occasionally admit to being scared, they behave in adolescent ways: they are silly and noisy. Generally, however, I found them to be more tractable and desirous of pleasing the teacher than eighth graders.

I was the community planner for all of them: the street-smart and the innocent, the provocative and the preoccupied, the volatile and the obedient, the native-born and the recent immigrant, the black male majority and the white female minority.

Do I hear a waltz?

Before I could bring some semblance of order to this chaotic community, I had to create a perfect setting—and, as far as I was concerned, the usual forty-two-minute class was far from perfect. So during a joint meeting of the English and language arts/reading departments the previous spring, I had begged for more time to work with the seventh graders. To my delight, our principal, the English and the language arts/reading departments, and Marty Wynne, our chief scheduler, agreed. So in September I was able to tell my seventh graders that this class would be special not only for its atmosphere and content but for its time—two uninterrupted back-to-back periods totaling eighty-four minutes. For a teacher, a short class can be a frantic cha-cha. I hoped the longer one would become a graceful waltz.

I learned to believe in the importance of time—uninterrupted blocks of time. When I was a high school sophomore, my mother used to drag me out of bed at six each morning to practice plane geometry. "You can do these problems," she'd say. "Anything is possible if you have enough time." Now, as an adult, I knew that forty-two minutes simply wasn't enough time—not for a teacher who had never been good at dividing a short class into even shorter segments, and not for students who had already encountered so much failure in school. Too many students, and a frightening number of teachers, believe that a student who is slow to catch on to concepts is inept or even hopeless. But all students learn at their own pace. If I wanted these seventh graders not just to learn but to learn in a new way—by talking, listening, responding, and thinking through possible answers rather than trying to outguess the teacher—I would have to give them time to change.

At first, of course, my students groused that the class was too long. After all, this was their first year of moving from class to class rather than staying with a single teacher, and now I was cramping their style. As a compromise, I used the four-minute bell time between the two periods as a short break. If the students returned and settled down quickly after this break, I permitted them a seventh-inning stretch in the hall later, or a trip to the lavatory and drinking fountain.

Once the students grew accustomed to the rhythm of the longer class, it began to work the magic I'd hoped. The double class period gave me a block of time. I could decide to develop a slow, easy-paced lesson on revision that might last a whole period or more; or this extended time would allow me the flexibility to weave together a literature lesson; an improvised drama; a short, fast-paced skills practice; and a read-aloud. One of the best things about a double period was having the luxury to talk expansively. We had time to meet up with poetry and prose, speakers and projects; we had time to write and talk, go off on tangents, and meet one another as learners and people. Time spent together brought us together. I fondly remember this class as one of the most diverse, energetic, and ultimately compatible groups I've taught. And I believe time was the key.

Chi

When I take a test
I see my watch go
so fast look like
Tic Tat Tic Tat

The ways we worked together

Every class develops its own tempo. Because talking, by design, became central to our curriculum, I usually started class by inquiring: "What have you observed or figured out since we last met?" This wide-open question elicited only shrugs.

Talking in class to learn didn't come naturally to my underachieving seventh graders, although they talked to one another incessantly. Although they knew perfectly well how to talk to each other during lunch, in the halls, and on the telephone at night, they had little experience in initiating classroom conversation. My students had been the receivers of information rather than the generators—if, indeed, they had retained much school information at all. Taking time to talk with one another each day eventually allowed us to come together emotionally and intellectually.

I kept urging my kids to ask questions, questions about all the things that concerned or interested them but whose importance they had probably dismissed. I invited them to share insights and opinions regarding a news event, a school issue (such as the famous Shaker Middle School book bag debate), the literature that we were reading together, or the writing that everyone was engaged in doing.

Judith Bratt, who arrived each Thursday brimming with excitement, often started our classroom conversation as she blew in the door. During those early weeks of school, our five- to fifteen-minute warm-up conversations usually began painfully slowly and ended uncommonly quickly. After much practice, certain beginning-of-the-period discussions eventually served as springboards to illuminating, animated conversations. Here again, time mattered. These young people needed plenty of it to warm up and become comfortable with the notion that they had something important to say. As their teacher and the designer of the language arts curriculum, I was sure that my seventh graders' natural propensity to be social and to talk would eventually translate into intellectual conversations during class. And my hunch was right.

In praise of tangents

One day after we'd finished looking through an assortment of brand new picture books from publishers, Chi picked up a book with an Asian child on the jacket and quite unexpectedly said: "That looks like me." Without hesitation, she quietly began to talk about Vietnam, her home. She talked about her village near Saigon, her family of many children, and the woman with whom she then lived and called Mother. As Chi talked, her classmates moved their chairs closer. Chi explained that her own mother (and father) had so many offspring to care for that they gave away some of their children to neighbors and friends. Chi told us about feeding the chickens: "Here chick, chick, chick." She and her classmates giggled.

Suddenly, Chi became self-conscious and stopped talking. But Marie coaxed her to tell more. The rest of Chi's classmates—unusually quiet and respectful—wanted to hear more, too. Next, she told us about school. Everyone groaned when Chi explained that it lasted for six hours a day, six days a week. Her classmates were shocked when they heard that the students—as many as sixty in a class—stood up and greeted their teacher when she entered the classroom. When she told us that her teacher used a ruler to reprimand talkative students, they rolled their eyes.

But these kids were in awe when Chi, who had opened up to us quite spontaneously, confided that she spoke four languages: Vietnamese, Chinese (her father was Chinese), a little French, and now she was learning English! Marie begged Chi to speak in all four languages. "And now Chi's doing a wonderful job learning our language!" Marie interjected enthusiastically.

Everyone applauded Chi's accomplishment and her story. Until that day in March, Chi had told us few personal facts about her life in southeast Asia. She had shown little confidence in taking the lead and asserting herself in class. The small adolescent girl with the winning smile showed us and proved to herself that she was doing a remarkable job in taking control of her new language, adjusting to a new culture, and trusting her fellow students and her teacher by making them privy to her early life in Vietnam. She did it because she felt free to talk.

Language alive!

One bleak January day, Jawan asked Judith a question that paid many dividends: "Hey, Ms. Bratt, where did you get that nice [British] accent?" Big J. raised this promising question just a few minutes after he'd stepped in the path of two angry boys who were preparing to get in a few licks. With a few calming words and a large hand on each boy's chest, he simmered them down. Now Jawan's thought-provoking question set us talking and asking, asking and talking for *much* more than one period.

Judith, a live wire and a gifted teacher, grinned broadly, then promptly demonstrated her linguistic prowess by imitating four different dialects from the United Kingdom. First came the West Midlands, where she had been raised. Next she demonstrated the ups and downs of a Welsh dialect, then the dialect typical of one who hails from Newcastle, which Judith described as the "Geordie" dialect. She was in rare form when she shifted into high gear and spoke Cockney, a speech pattern typical of London's East End. The seventh graders laughed appreciatively as Judith slid like an agile gymnast from one British dialect to another. These kids, spellbound by few intellectual conversations, were positively wide-eyed and slack-jawed at this revelation: that in every country of the world, people speak in a multitude of dialects and cadences.

A bombardment of questions

Then, miracle of miracles, it happened. Almost all of the students bombarded Judith with questions. First, Marie, a girl who could just as easily incite a group to chaos as infuse it with energy, asked: "How did you learn *all* those English accents, Ms. Bratt?"

"How do we learn different accents?" Tiawan asked timidly.

"Are there different dialects spoken in Cleveland?" Lisa, who often turned her attention to private thoughts, wondered.

Joe demonstrated his curiosity by asking, "How many different accents are there in England?"

"How many different accents are there in the USA?" Jamar asked.

Chi ventured forth by asking, "How many language are there in world?"

Bright and thoughtful Chris wondered if Judith could almost always determine where an English person was from just by the way that he or she spoke.

Jawan, who had been the prime mover of this impromptu conversation, remarked about his own changing speech pattern: "My cousins from Cleveland say, 'Jawan, now that you been living in Shaker, you talkin' different.' "

I asked Jawan in what ways his speech patterns had changed since he'd moved from urban Cleveland to suburban Shaker Heights.

"They say I talk proper. Fancy." Big J. laughed. Although he was unable to pinpoint specific changes, his cousins had discerned that his speech was in certain ways becoming more standardized. His comment about the changes in his own speech and Jamar's question about the number of different dialects in our country led us to discuss the concept of dialect and the characteristics of various standard and nonstandard dialects used by different groups and races of people: the speech patterns, cadences, pitch, volume, and expression dictated by occasion and audience. Thus, Jawan's question to Judith, "Hey, Ms. Bratt, where did you get that nice accent?" really started us rolling on the subject of language, the nature of language, and the nurturing of language.

On another day, Chris M. asked a stunning question: "Who actually makes the language?" I seized upon this magic moment.

"Who *does* make the language—either a long time ago or today?" I asked my class.

"People who write dictionaries make up words," Jermaine speculated.

"The language is pretty old. Maybe it's handed down from one family to another," Jamar thought.

"People bring it from other country," Chi offered shyly.

"Yeah, but expressions like *'home boy'* and *'home girl,' 'trippin,' 'doggin'* and *'dissin,' 'def,' 'bad,' 'scrillo,' 'rust bucket'* or *'old hooptie'* and other words come and go. Black people out on the street just make 'em up," Jawan observed.

"Actually, you're all correct. Yes, the language is passed down from generation to generation. Yes, people from other countries, immigrants like Chi and Jung, bring their languages with them and share them in the new country, enriching their new language with their own." I told an anecdote about a Soviet émigré who'd recently immigrated from Russia to Cleveland, a man who publicly thanked his sponsors and benefactors although he hadn't quite mastered the American idiom. He smiled broadly and said: "Thank you from the heart of my bottom!" The kids laughed appreciatively.

Building a dictionary

One day, we talked about people creating new words to meet new needs—computer experts, scientists, advertising people, and all of us. Jermaine brought up a word in black vernacular, *ganked*. According to Jermaine and other classmates, being *ganked* means being taken advantage of, as in "You've been ganked." A good *hookup* is a good

Jermaine is beginning to view himself as a reader, writer, and thinker.

combination of clothes put together by the wearer. (Formerly, a fashion-conscious person would have referred to a good *hookup* as good *threads*.)

At this point, I remembered hearing the ethnographer and linguist Shirley Brice Heath, who spoke at the English Coalition Conference the summer of 1987, suggest that we engage kids in making dictionaries. Since Jawan had made the point that many expressions are invented on the street and Jermaine had brought up words such as *ganked*, I suggested that they might like to create a dictionary of expressions African Americans use when they talk among themselves. Jawan, Jermaine, Jamar, Chris, Deontay, Jung, and a few other boys pulled their chairs into a circle and worked enthusiastically on a dictionary of current black expressions.

While this project was connected to our classroom conversations, it helped my students and me put black English dialect into a larger perspective, legitimizing it alongside all language. I explained that all languages—standard or nonstandard dialects—help us to think and convey meaning. I also explained that every dialect has its own set of rules or grammar. For example, the verb *be,* as in "I be going to school every day," connotes habit.

"My mother, she be comin' up to *this* school since we moved into Shaker!" Jawan laughed knowingly.

Collecting nonstandard words and expressions that originated in the black community and on the street led us to another realization about a person's language: the speaker must know her or his audience to decide whether standard or nonstandard English is appropriate. For instance, we all talk differently with our family and close friends than we do during class or in other public situations. My kids acknowledged that they usually used nonstandard speech at home but said they tried to use standard speech patterns at school.

I never referred to standard English dialect as correct or nonstandard dialect as incorrect. I taught my students what I learned in Howard Mims' dialect class at

Jermaine B.
Jawan M.
Black Expression — 1990

1. yeah boy = I Like that
2. Beano = Dollar
3. Let's kicket = Let's go somewere
4. I'm out = I'm about to go
5. dimhip = I no what you mean
6. ganked = somoone took it
7. gangster lean = having your seat all the way back while driving.
8. scrilla = money
9. your a sucka = you played me
10. dised = dogged
11. jam = is a party
12. High rollers = someone make a lot of $
13. mula = money
14. doe = money
15. hook me up = give me a little bit
16. you straight = means what do you need?

17. dopeman = someone who sells drugs
18. bone = a dollar
19. my boy means = he's hooked on to me
20. pad = house
21. jockin = someone who stairs at you or folows you

FIG. 3-2   *Dictionary of Black Expressions*

Cleveland State University: the accepted dialect spoken and taught in school happens to be the standard of speech that is determined by the group in power! Respect for *every*one's language was implicit in our class. After all, a person's language reflects the person. We also noticed that the language changes. Expressions and words change because the language users and makers—the people—cause it to change. And that keeps the language vibrant and healthy, I told my students. Figure 3-2 shows part of a brief dictionary of black vernacular and expressions that Jawan, Jermaine, and others collected and occasionally defined.

Another day, another start

Each day when I started class, I tried to capitalize on my seventh graders' needs—and not only their intellectual needs. Since I had to defuse their anxiety about school nearly each day, I needed to find ways to reassure them and redirect their energy. I took full advantage of their natural desire to be members of a group.

Starting class with a conversation, a question, or a story wasn't always our modus operandi. On certain days, I started right off by reading aloud, especially when my students came into class acting as though they'd been shot out of a cannon, or dragged in looking burdened by the weight of the world.

"Come on, Mrs. K., read *The Doll House Murder,*" Marie might plead. I'd honor her request by reading a favorite novel of theirs (and, for that matter, of many kids in Ohio) for ten minutes. Often, however, I'd save reading aloud until the last forty-two-minute period, after they had worked hard and were ready to relax and enjoy.

Occasionally I would begin class with an exercise on a language skill I'd recently introduced or an old one we'd been practicing. For instance, we worked on starting sentences with dependent clauses: "When Chi was walking down the street, she. . . ." Many kids had been instructed by their elementary school teachers never to begin a sentence with *because* or *when*. I knew the reason for this arbitrary-sounding ban: too often, kids wound up writing dependent clauses, not full sentences. But for the sake of expanding my students' repertoires, I introduced and, yes, briefly drilled them in using adverb clauses. We practiced so that we could *hear* the need to finish the dependent clauses.

" 'When Chi was walking down the street' is a leaner. It needs to lean on or be supported by a strong and independent part of this sentence," I would say. Then I'd demonstrate (without ever using the term *clauses*) by saying the fragment aloud, letting the cadence and my voice illustrate the need for something more.

"What does this part of a sentence need in order to support or prop it up?" I'd ask. By practicing aloud, most of my kids learned how to use adverb clauses in their talking and writing: "When Chi was walking down the street, she met her best friend. When Chi was walking down the street, she saw her teacher. When Chi was walking down the street, her boyfriend, Jamar, stopped to talk with her!" They loved inventing personal sentences that began with adverb clauses.

Sometimes I started class by practicing vocabulary building—certainly *not* by asking kids to look up isolated words in the dictionary, write down the meanings, and memorize them. Rather, I showed my kids how to figure out the meaning of unfamiliar words by looking at their roots and trying to think of familiar words that were first cousins.

Here is how we unlocked unfamiliar words such as *genetic*. I would say, "First, try to pronounce the new word out loud so that you can *hear* its sound. Then look at what probably is the main part of the word, its root. Think about words you already know that are related to the unfamiliar word. Let's try to think of as many words as we can that might be related to *genetic*." Here is our list, which I recorded on the chalkboard: *gene, genius, generic, genesis, genealogy, general, generate,* and *gender*. I added three more related words: *genocide, geneticist,* and *congenital*. I was surprised that no one connected *congenital* with *genital*, but that was one word relative I didn't bring to their attention!

The next step was to see which words someone might already know or be willing to speculate about. Then we generalized about the probable relationship of all of these words. We talked specifically about the meaning of *genius, gene,* and *genesis*.

"A genius is a real smart person," Joe offered.

"A gene is what we get from our parents," Jamar said.

"It's the microscopic carrier of characteristics such as height, body build, coloring, temperament, intelligence, and talent," I added. "What about genesis?" I asked.

"Genesis is in the Bible," Jermaine offered.

"Which book of the Bible is it?" I pushed them to see the relationship between Genesis, the first book of the Bible, and genetic inheritance from long-gone, distant relatives.

After Chris had nicely synthesized the general meaning of all of the words that we'd listed, I asked them to consider the other words and their meanings. Everyone knew about generic soap and other products that were general, not specifically identified. *Generic* and *general* strayed in meaning from the others that specifically were related to genetic inheritance.

Few knew what a genealogy was. So we looked at the ending, *ology*. "*Ology* always means 'the study of'—the study of animals as in zoology, the study of plants and animals as in biology. *Bi* means two (that is, plants and animals), and *ology* means the study of. So what would you imagine or speculate that *genealogy* means?"

"The study of genes." Jamar interpreted the word's meaning quite literally.

"You're very close, Jamar, but in actuality a genealogy is a family tree or chart in which someone, a genealogist, traces a family and the relationship of all of its members." We worked our way through the entire list of words the kids had *generated* so they could develop a strategy for unlocking unfamiliar words when they encountered them in their reading. Finally, I asked them to figure out the meaning of *genocide,* one of the word relatives that I'd added to our list. I prompted their thinking by asking them to look at the ending, *cide*. Someone thought about the word *suicide*.

"What, then, would *genocide* mean?" Marie quite literally defined *genocide* as the killing of genes. I referred to the Nazis' systematic killing of the Jews and other people. Because we'd just finished reading *Alan and Naomi* by Myron Levoy, they brought knowledge of the word *genocide* to this vocabulary experience. They weren't sure about the meaning of *geneticist,* so I used the word in context.

"Finish these sentences," I said. "A *geneticist* is someone who studies (*genes*). If one has a *congenital* heart problem, he developed it before he was (*born with it*)." After this sort of word-connecting and speculating was over, we'd sometimes refer to the dictionary for precise and multiple definitions. We practiced figuring out other unfamiliar words by listing probable relatives: *provocative* related to *provoke; initiative* to *initiate*; *ridicule* to *ridiculous*; *indomitable* to *dominate*; *scholarly* to *school* and *scholastic*; *elevator* to *elevate* and *elevation*; *escalate* to *escalator*; *evolution* to *evolve*; *revolutionary* to *revolt*; *strategic* to *strategy*; *minimal* to *mini*. These exercises took anywhere from ten to thirty minutes. Thirty minutes is most of a regular class period. But what are class periods for if not to explore? All of our skills 'n' drills were done *together, out loud* and *during class,* at the board or on the overhead projector. Rarely did we do paper and pencil skills exercises alone.

Homework also was a point of departure and a means of settling into English/language arts class, although I rarely let the homework assignment of the night before bog us down or hold us up for long. Each day we began class by moving from a brief conversation or a skill-builder or a word-play and into a long-term project. Finally, sinking our teeth into literature required our full attention.

Sinking our teeth into literature

I am reminded of Chi's words: "I don't like Cassie because she write this story so hard." *Roll of Thunder, Hear My Cry* by Mildred Taylor was a long and difficult story not only for us but for the characters, especially Cassie, the storyteller. This powerful YA novel unfolds against the backdrop of the 1930s and the deep South, Great Depression and Jim Crow.

We certainly did *not* begin reading Mildred Taylor's classic novel by merely taking out a stack of books and reading. No, sir. We spent five to ten days building a scaffolding for understanding: identifying important historic events and attitudes and then arranging them in chronological order.

I began this deliberate preparation by first telling the kids that this story had taken place in Mississippi, which we located on our map, during the 1930s when Jim Crow Laws (which I would explain later) were still in effect, the Ku Klux Klan was operating openly, the effects of the Great Depression were still being felt, and Hitler's genocide of six million Jews would soon be in Europe.

Only Joe knew about the Great Depression, when people were out of work and very shortly out of food. For the majority of the class, 1929 and the decades that followed seemed as far removed as the Civil War. They lacked time perspective and critical background information. So I drew a time line from 1900 to the present (see Figure 3-3). Together we filled in important dates: the two world wars, the Great Depression, the election of Franklin D. Roosevelt.

I asked which other big events should be included. Someone mentioned the Civil Rights movement of the 1960s. I explained that starting in the 1950s with *Brown v. Board of Education* of Topeka, Kansas, the Civil Rights movement under Dr. King's and Malcolm X's leadership gained great momentum. The voting rights acts engineered by President Lyndon Johnson came during the 1960s. Because Marie and several others had wanted to include the Civil War in this century, I drew two other time lines to give them a larger perspective, particularly the events in American history that certainly had an impact on this story.

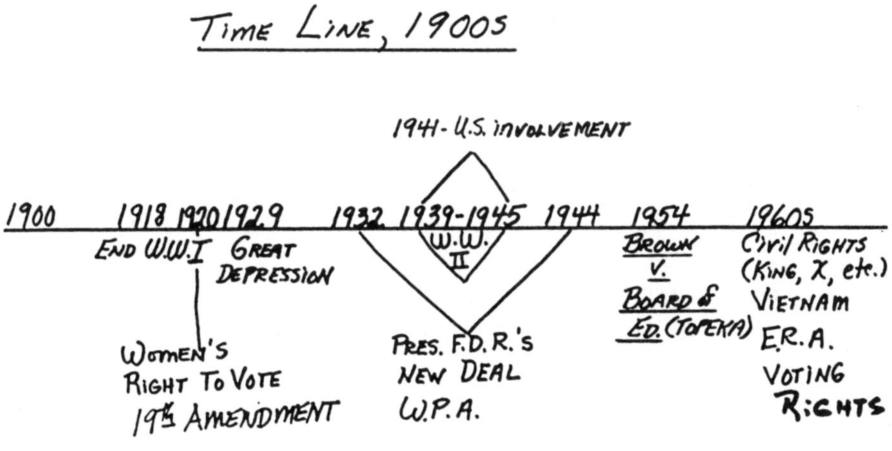

FIG. 3-3   *Time Line*

On the time line of the 1800s, I included the Civil War, Lincoln's Emancipation Proclamation, and two events none of them had heard of: Reconstruction and the *Plessy v. Ferguson* case of 1896, in which the U.S. Supreme Court upheld the right to "separate but equal schools" for blacks. (This phenomenon figures powerfully in Taylor's autobiographical novel.)

The time line for the 1700s contained only the dates of the American Revolution and our country's independence from Great Britain, because freedom and human rights figured heavily in *Roll of Thunder, Hear My Cry,* the novel we were preparing to read.

But we didn't merely identify important events. We talked about what they meant and how they related to the novel. During our regular weekly library period, several kids scouted out books on the Civil War, presidents Lincoln and Roosevelt, and the Great Depression.

After we had hashed over Jim Crow Laws, I read aloud another of Taylor's books, a very short and manageable one, to provide more background. *The Gold Cadillac* is about a black family traveling by car caravan down South from Ohio during the 1950s. They pack baskets of food for a series of picnics, since black people—then called Negroes—weren't permitted to eat in public restaurants or to sleep in hotels. This was a big reading project that embraced us fully. After I had read *The Gold Cadillac* aloud, we read *Song of the Trees* together; it was the first book in Taylor's trilogy and the precursor to *Roll of Thunder, Hear My Cry.*

We cheered again and again as Cassie, only nine years old, stands up for her own and her family's rights as human beings first and Americans second. When Mr. Andersen, a white man who tries to cheat the Logan family by forcing them to sell the giant old trees on their property, orders the Logan children to get on home and out of *their* forest, Cassie Logan speaks up: " 'We *are* home,' I said. 'You're the one who's on our land' " (p. 39).

Marie, Jawan, and Jamar jumped out of their seats and onto their feet to cheer after we read this passage: " 'One thing you can't seem to understand, Andersen,' Papa said, 'is that a black man's always gotta be ready to die. And it don't make me any difference if I die today or tomorrow. Just as long as I die right' " (p. 49). The rest of us got to our feet and cheered, too. In fifty-two pages, Mildred Taylor's words and characters had touched us deeply.

Before we even picked up *Roll of Thunder, Hear My Cry,* we talked about history.

"I didn't know that we was studying history," Jamar commented.

"Yeah, I thought this was a reading class," Chris chuckled.

"But a language arts class includes *everything*!" I answered emphatically. "Because reading includes all of language and all subjects, we will study every subject in here"—a revelation for my students.

"You see, learning isn't separated into neat little packages: an English package, a history package, a math package, a science package, and so forth. Learning is hooked together. Subjects are all woven together like a big tapestry, and language lets us make these connections." Armed with an understanding of the era and its attitudes, my kids and I were, at long last, ready to embark on *Roll of Thunder, Hear My Cry.*

Crawling inside the novel

Being together was key to the success of this literary experience. I never made the students slog through every page of a book. We took turns reading *Roll of Thunder*;

everyone who wanted to got a chance to read aloud to a captive audience. Because the book is long and very dense, I became the storyteller who narrated the parts of the story bridging the big events we relished reading aloud, such as the school bus incident; the issuance of worn, out-dated textbooks to black children in a "separate but equal school"; and the courage and resourcefulness of the Logan family in the face of racial hatred.

Raising important questions

While we read, we talked and raised questions informally, especially when we wondered or felt indignant. For instance, why does Miss Daisy Crocker, the Logan children's teacher, buy into whites' racist attitudes by defending separate but equal schools? And why does T. J. Avery, a young black boy, seek friendship with two white Southern rednecks, Melvin and R. W. Simms? What makes the Logans different from other black people who lived in Mississippi in the 1930s? Why was owning land so important to them? What are some of the most important suggestions or evidences of racism and prejudice in this story? What are primary examples of the Jim Crow laws? How are honor, self-respect, strength of character, strong family ties, and sacrifice conveyed to everyone who reads this story? How might this story have been different if someone else besides Cassie had told it?

To address these questions, a student and I co-led a discussion of the book. I knew that Joe, a smart and informed boy, would benefit from the structure that co-leading a book discussion offered. While co-leading allowed me to support an able student through an unfamiliar process, it also provided the other students with a model of a lively give-and-take. During the after-school conference period available to all students, Joe and I brainstormed questions: How do people learn to be prejudiced? How have you (classmates) been put down by someone of another color? How did you feel? What did you do? What can be done about racism in America? Do you think racism will always exist? Why? Why not?

Joe and I decided that since many of our class discussions had already centered on students' own brushes with racism, it might be time to broaden the scope. We boiled all of our questions down to three big ones: (1) How is life for black people in America today different from the days when the Logans lived in the deep South? (2) What rights and opportunities do African Americans have now that they didn't have in the 1930s, 1940s, and 1950s? (3) What rights *don't* African Americans have yet that they should have?

The first question allowed us to talk about the federal government's move to ban segregated schools and enforce busing. I told this class about the desegregation of the first public school in the nation in Little Rock, Arkansas, and about James Meredith, the first black student to enter the University of Mississippi. This question also prompted me to tell my students about Shaker Heights, a white community that during the Civil Rights movement of the 1960s became an integrated suburb.

"And now yellow people they live in Shaker Heights," Chi laughed. Chi and Jung were often puzzled by this and other classroom conversations, so we stopped often to explain to them in simple terms what was being said.

This question led us to discuss the banning of segregated public restrooms and water fountains, which triggered Chris's recalling *The Autobiography of Miss Jane Pittman*. Lisa recalled reading about Rosa Parks's courage, which led to the

Montgomery bus boycott. I pointed out that the Voting Rights Acts during Lyndon Johnson's presidency gave clout to people of color. I told my kids that in the midsixties, Cleveland elected Carl Stokes, the first black mayor in the country, which prompted many other cities and even small Southern towns to vote African Americans into public office.

The second question (What rights and opportunities do African Americans have now that they didn't have before?) also brought interesting responses. We recognized that although black people still suffer from prejudice, many more go on to college, hold responsible positions in business and politics, live in the neighborhood of their choice, and are financially secure.

Jawan talked about Jackie Robinson playing for the Brooklyn Dodgers, thus opening up professional sports for black people. Marie pointed out that black people, both men and women, used to straighten their hair in the old days, but later (in the 1960s, I reminded her) they let their hair go natural and wore Afros.

Joe's and my last question (What rights *don't* African Americans have yet?) was the most subtle of the three and the one that most personally and immediately affected my students, especially my black students. Jawan said that white kids at our school usually didn't get into as much or as serious trouble as black kids. Everyone, including my two white kids, agreed that this was true.

Jermaine told us about the times he'd been eyed suspiciously when he and his black friends went into the local deli or drugstore. All of the black students concurred that this happened frequently. Jermaine wondered if the white kids in the class had had the same problem. Lisa had not experienced this sort of scrutiny, but Joe said that he had. Marie talked about white kids at our school who sat together during lunch and banded together at school socials on Friday nights. Jawan reminded Marie that black kids also hung out exclusively together. Marie said somewhat wistfully: "We could sure teach some of them white kids a thing or two about dancin' and being live!"

Thoughtful Chris M. said he and a couple of his black friends were walking down the street when two white boys on bicycles approached them. The two white boys got off their bikes and walked cautiously past the black boys on foot, and Chris concluded that the white kids were afraid.

"I think white people *are* afraid of black people. And that's probably because they don't know us," he said softly. Typically, Chris was willing to empathize with the white boys' fear. "They have a right to be scared of us because you're always hearing about blacks stealing, using guns on people, and scaring them."

Because no one brought up academic expectations, I asked whether teachers seemed to ask as much of the black students as they did of the white students. The answers from both black and white students in our class were mixed. Many thought that expectations depended on the individual teacher; others thought that certain black students who had developed a bad reputation weren't always given a fair chance. But they concurred that certain kids deserved whatever they got. A couple of the kids, ones who were considered major troublemakers, blamed the system entirely.

My seventh graders, Jeannine Rajewski, and I were wrapping up our six-week study revolving around *Roll of Thunder, Hear My Cry*. As I was heading for the fall conference of the National Council of Teachers of English, I placed Jeannine in charge of bringing closure to this rich literature study. She decided to give a traditional test—and what a test! (see Figure 3-4). Those kids must have worn themselves out during the better part of two class periods doing their level best to measure up to Jeannine's high standards. What I call remarkable results are shown in Figures 3-5, 3-6, and 3-7.

TEST QUESTIONS, created by Mrs. J. Rajewski, student teacher

Roll of Thunder, Hear My Cry by Mildred Taylor

Directions: Answer the following questions in complete sentences on a separate sheet of paper. Be sure to write as much as you can and use examples from the book whenever possible.

1. Who is your favorite character in the book? Why do you like this character best?

2. Why did the Logan children get mad when they saw their 'new' textbooks? What did Mrs. Logan do about it?

3. Who were the night riders and what did they do to people? Why?

4. How did Stacey disobey Mama? Was he right or wrong? Why?

5. Why does Stacey get into a fight with T.J.? Would you have done the same thing? If not, what would you have done?

6. Why is Mr. Morrison living with the Logans? Give Mr. Logan's reason and the real reason.

7. Why did Mr. Tatum call the store keeper a liar? What happened to Mr. Tatum?

8. What does it mean to "tar and feather" someone?

9. Describe T.J. Do the Logan children like him? Do you like him?

10. What if the children's plan for revenge on the bus driver had backfired? Describe a situation that could have happened different from what did happen in the book.

11. Why is it important to be accepting of and kind to all people regardless of how they look or act, what they believe, how they speak or what color their skin is?

12. Draw a picture of the Logan family and write the name under each character. You can include their home and farm and Mr. Morrison if you want.

FIG. 3-4   *Jeannine's Test*

Mildred Taylor had become a household name in our class. We read Taylor's *The Friendship*, a story that, like *The Gold Cadillac* and *Song of the Trees*, would have been a fine precursor to the big novel. I decided against plunging into *Let the Circle Be Unbroken*, a powerful sequel to *Roll of Thunder* that is more suitable for eighth grade.

Later in the year we read Beverley Naidoo's *Journey to Jo'Burg*, a manageable novel about apartheid in South Africa. I bought multiple copies of a book of short stories—a commodity that I rarely find—entitled *Somehow Tenderness Survives: Stories of South Africa*, selected by Hazel Rochman, which will be on my reading list from

---

① I don't like CASSIE because she 1-88 write Chi this story so hard, and in this book the words are hard to understand.

② because they are black children is not have a new book they are have everything to old, only white children have new book, that why they are black children so mad.

FIG. 3-5   *Excerpts from Chi's Test*

---

6. Mr. Morrison is living with the Logans to help them with their chores so he'll have a job to do.

9. TJ is a very sneaky kind of boy, sometimes he lies. The Logan children does not like him alot. I don't like him (because...)

FIG. 3-6   *Excerpts from Lisa's Test*

now on. And, of course, we read and performed plenty of poetry by Lucille Clifton, Nikki Giovanni, Eloise Greenfield, Maya Angelou, Langston Hughes, Gwendolyn Brooks, and other African American poets.

Because we were becoming authorities on oppressors and the oppressed, we went on to read Myron Levoy's *Alan and Naomi,* a touching story about the Holocaust (another new vocabulary word). We compared this story in terms of the era and human problems to the Logans' battle with racism in America.

Sara Wasserman, our beloved art therapist who was Jewish, came to talk with us about prejudice. Sara explained her feelings about being a Jew and carrying the burden of persecution and denigration even though she'd not been a survivor of a concentration camp. She brought pictures of the Holocaust and the internment camps, and read from the collection of poems written by children at Teriezenstat, *I Never Saw Another Butterfly*. Sara helped us explore our own prejudice toward people whose lives and culture were different from ours.

"So black people aren't the only people who have been beaten down into the dirt?" Jamar asked. "I didn't know much about the Jews and the concentration camps before we all started talking about . . . what's that word that mean pressed down on?" Joe remarked, "It looks like the Ku Klux Klan and Hitler and the Nazis are a lot alike."

Jermaine B.
11-23-88

1. I like T.J. because he likes to cause trouble and intimadate people.

2. One of the Logon's got mad about those hand medown books. So they stood up for His right, Mrs Logan didn't say anything she stayed quite because she didn't won't to lose her job as teacher. (Mrs. L. did not speak up??)

3. The night rider's were some white men, if someone (black) would do something wrong they would hang them or burn there house, but now they put tar on people then dump feather's on him. (white people lynched & burned black people for no reason — any reason)

4. Stacey went down to the wallace store were they sell beer. In a way he was wrong he disobeyhis mother by going down their but she also had a good reason. When he went down their he got in a fight

5. Stacey and T.J. fought because he (T.J.) was cheating in class on a test. Stacey said: "put them away hen Stacey mom came T.J. gave the notes to stacey, Then Mrs. Logan cought him (T.J.) cheating and she wipped and failed him. Maybe I would maybe wouldn't I would beat him (T.J.) up then tell him to say sorry.

8. Tar & feather means when someone do something wrong someone throws tar own them then dumps feathers all over there hole body.

9. T.J. is a cruel and ubnocious person who always looking for trouble. none of the Logan's like him. Yes I like him long as he doesn't mess with me!

10. If it back fired they should try again. If they would of got caught putting that hole in the ground theywould of been hung, tar & feathers or got their house burned.

11. It is important to accept others or you will never have freinds or you will regret living

---

FIG. 3-7   *Excerpts from Jermaine's Test*

Right on the heels of this serious synthesis, Joe smiled as he said, "Mrs. K., come here and read this information about Adolf Hitler." Joe wanted me to read aloud a portion of a journal kept by Hitler's physician about his infamous patient's medical history. It seems that Adolf Hitler, who aimed to rule the world, suffered from an acute gastro-intestinal problem: gas! This bit of trivia brought the house down, a much needed bit of comic relief.

As the year went on, we read other novels: Katharine Paterson's *The Bridge to Terabithia,* Natalie Babbitt's *Tuck Everlasting,* Susan Shreve's *The Flunking of Joshua T. Bates,* Patricia MacLachlan's *Sarah, Plain and Tall,* Robert Newton Peck's *A Day No Pigs Would Die.* One day in the spring Chris, our sage, asked: "Mrs. Krogness, did you purposely pick out all of these books because you knew ahead of time that they'd all fit together?"

I answered, "Because you're becoming such expert readers, you're seeing the big connections between these stories. I really just chose books I thought you might enjoy. But, let's think about Chris's question some more. How do all of you think that the stories we've read are connected?"

As they talked animatedly about oppression and the survival of Cassie Logan and her family, they also talked about Naomi and her mother who escaped Hitler's death camps. They brought in Beverley Naidoo's characters, Naledi and Tiro, victims of South Africa's apartheid, who risked their lives to save their seriously ill baby sister.

I remember that warm May day when my kids and I reflected on all the literature we'd read and the characters we'd met. Maybe it was Marie who said, "For the first time in my life, I see why reading is fun." Then Big Jawan said, "These stories—especially *Roll of Thunder*—have taken us beyond our world."

FOUR
Inside Eighth Grade

A n eighth grader: animal, vegetable, or mineral? Eighth grade defies explanation. Hormones run rampant in bodies that are changing perceptibly. One day a boy comes to class with underdeveloped little-boy arms (no doubt left over from seventh grade) camouflaged by a baggy sweater. Within a few months, this same young man has donned a short-sleeved T-shirt and takes time out in class to stroke his budding biceps. Another eighth-grade boy interrupts class one day to ask, "Mrs. Krogness, can I go to the lav for just a few minutes to comb my mustache? P-l-l-l-e-e-a-a-s-e?"

I watched another physically developed student in my fifth-period class stretch the neckline of his sweater to sneak a peek at his brawny chest. Not more than a week later, he shed a bulky sweater as soon as he arrived in the classroom. Underneath he was wearing a tight black tank top (a definite no-no at our school) that had been slit wide open on the sides. Girls *and* boys were interested (I decided that the better part of valor was to ignore him).

A proclivity for provocation

The boys didn't have a corner on the hedonistic market. I will never forget Lisa M. sashaying into class sporting a snug-fitting T-shirt with two grotesque plastic hands jutting out, calling attention to the inscription emblazoned across her chest: "I Have a Hold of Myself."

Natalie, a girl preoccupied by adolescence (and untold other distractions), breathily whispered to me one afternoon that she'd gone all day without having made a trip to the lavatory. This was eighth period and she simply couldn't wait. I acquiesced. When Natalie hadn't returned to class after five or six minutes, I made a fast dash down the hall and found her in the girls' lavatory, gazing into the mirror while she penciled in the last stroke of lilac eye liner and puckered her lips to work in a heavy coat of purple lipstick. When I called Natalie's home that evening, her mother didn't seem the least surprised.

Body and soul, from eighth-grade boys and girls young adults are emerging. These mysterious young people vacillate between behaving like toddlers who are going through the terrible twos and acting like young adults who scrutinize their parents' and teachers' behavior and debate what's equitable and inequitable with these authority figures. At times, the girls who have already blossomed are impatient with the boys' infantile behavior. Certain girls play the role of mother to boys who haven't quite caught up. I recall Wandy's remark, which reflected more about the boys in our class

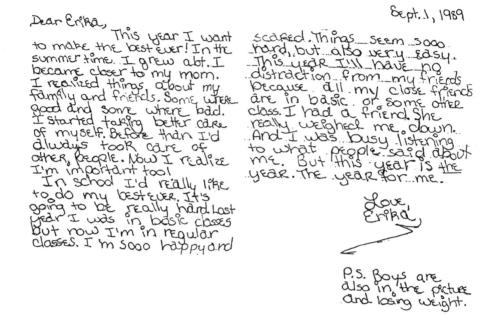

Dear Erika,
Sept. 1, 1989

This year I want to make the best ever! In the summer time. I grew abt. I became closer to my mom. I realized things about my family and friends. Some where good and some where bad. I started taking better care of myself. Before than I'd always took care of other people. Now I realize I'm important too!
In school I'd really like to do my best ever. It's going to be really hard. Last year I was in basic classes but now I'm in regular classes. I'm sooo happy and

scared. Things seem sooo hard, but also very easy. This year I'll have no distraction from my friends because all my close friends are in basic or some other class. I had a friend. She really weighed me down. And I was busy listening to what people said about me. But this year is the year. The year for me.

Love,
Erika

P.S. Boys are also in the picture and losing weight.

FIG. 4-1 *Erika's Letter of Intention*

than it did about Wandy. "Once a mother, always a mother," she sighed. "Sometimes I can't imagine some of these boys as adults!" another girl wryly observed, and a boy sitting near her visibly withered. How vulnerable eighth graders are! Personal hygiene, hair, bodies, and being popular are high priorities for most of them.

But alongside their preoccupation with changing physiques and self-study, their ever-changing moods and proclivity for provocation is the promise of the future. Eighth graders are on the cusp of adult life. They are novice philosophers who adamantly seek answers to questions about themselves and others. They are prone to ask the major existential questions: Who am I? Why am I here? Where do I fit into the scheme of things? Why can't adults understand me? What are my values? Is there a God?

Eighth graders also have dreams for themselves. Erika's letter of intention, for example, pushed far beyond our classroom and into her own life (see Figure 4-1). But eighth graders are ambivalent creatures. They struggle simultaneously to hang onto and let go of the last vestiges of their childhood; they both wish for and fear adulthood. For eighth graders and the adults who work with them, the process is often painful. Erika expresses this unease in her piece entitled *"Who I Am"* (see Figure 4-2).

Teaching eighth graders, then, can feel like a roller coaster ride. Knowing all of this ahead of time helps, but it doesn't ensure that a teacher will keep things in perspective. Eighth graders, although they may feel even more scared and fragile than seventh graders, exercise power by challenging adult authority and zeroing in on their parents' and their teachers' flaws. They are experts at causing an adult who is feeling vulnerable to come unglued. By testing their own mettle, eighth graders test ours.

Yet these young people can sense the moment and the feelings of others—even their teachers. To quote Quinten, "Mrs. K., we lift you up." And often they did lift me up. I've not forgotten that Quinn clandestinely organized his first-period cohorts to

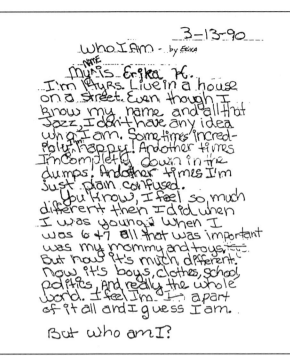

FIG. 4-2 *Erika's Piece*

make get-well cards for my mother when she became critically ill. Danny, a former student who had moved to another school system at the beginning of eighth grade, wrote a note to me during our winter holiday: "Thank you for the time and effort put into my writing. And I wish you great sucess in your book."

Crystal also wrote me a note on the front page of her final project, perhaps in part as a palliative for getting the project in late:

> First of all I would like to thank Mrs. Mary Krogness for pushing me through out the year and making me see and know that I can do anything I can as long as I put my mind to it. I just want you to know that I love you and that I am going to miss you.

Derrick wrote an acrostic poem after I'd served him and his classmates quiche for improving their attitudes (see Figure 4-3). Quinten—bright, ubiquitous Q.—sent me a postcard during the summer after eighth grade, a greeting to "Special K.," as a reminder, I imagine (see Figure 4-4). Who wants to be forgotten? No one who has ever taught eighth graders has emerged untouched!

An ancient riddle

How do adults help thirteen- and fourteen-year-olds harness their energy, sublimating all those new and arresting drives so that they can be still long enough to learn? Although no secret formulas exist, I tried to use the qualities—being provocative, challenging authority, finding their own individuality, seeking justice, and believing in their own immortality—that set eighth graders apart as a way to hook them on language

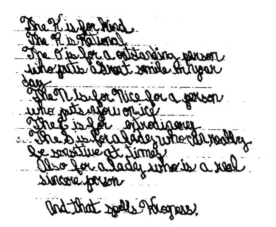

FIG. 4-3   *Derrick's Acrostic Poem*

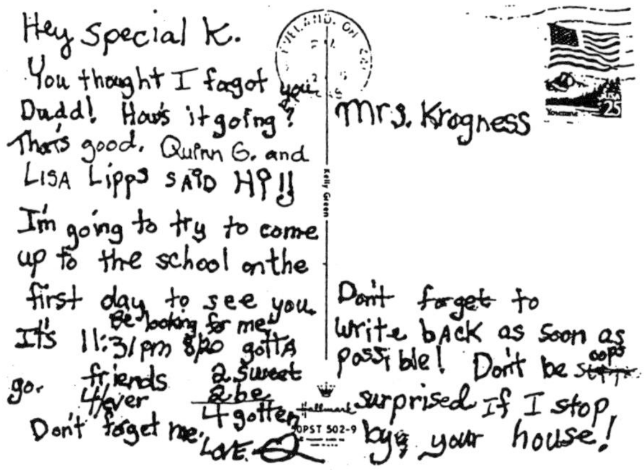

FIG. 4-4   *Quinten's Postcard*

learning. I chose to tap rather than to fight those peculiar tendencies. I tried to capitalize on eighth graders' desire to be in charge of their lives. By design I connected the special projects we did, the formal debates we had, and the literature we read with the temperament of rapidly changing adolescents.

The Children's Story

One little book—and I mean little—that meshes nicely with eighth graders' unique tendencies is James Clavell's *The Children's Story*. The students would inevitably start off scorning the book, which has large print, often on just one side of the page, as an insult to their intelligence. Before they knew it, however, they'd been captivated by this morally arresting and intellectually challenging story, which tells about New Teacher, a beautiful young infiltrator, dressed from head to toe in a suspicious shade of drab green, who brainwashes a class of third graders. Each time I use this novel with eighth graders, I end up feeling a momentary smugness at catching these full-blown adolescents unaware.

An allegory such as *The Children's Story* can be introduced and taught in a variety of ways. Although I approached it differently each time I taught it, new words such as *dictator* and *dictatorship, tyrant* and *tyranny, oppressor* and *oppression, predator* and *prey, anarchist* and *anarchy, skeptic* and *skepticism, totalitarian* and *propaganda*— vocabulary that appeals to eighth graders—inevitably filtered into our introductory conversations.

Important discussion of notorious tyrants preceded our reading *The Children's Story,* too. I made the kids into experts by drawing on their general knowledge of infamous oppressors, mainly Adolf Hitler. The eighth graders had read *The Diary of Anne Frank* in English class, so they knew about Hitler and the Holocaust. Many boys were intrigued by Hitler and his hideous insignia, the swastika.

While we discussed Hitler and the Nazis, Mussolini, Stalin, and the long line of white leaders who had ruled the black continent of Africa, I recorded our thoughts on the chalk board. We talked about owning and selling slaves in America's antebellum South and de facto segregation in the North, both practiced in a democracy. Some students brought up the Ku Klux Klan; others had seen movies about the beheading of King Louis XVI and Marie Antoinette. All of this material suited my eighth graders' sensibilities.

I mentioned the Ayatollah Khomeini of Iran, Saddam Hussein of Iraq, Idi Amin of Uganda, Hafez al-Assad of Syria, Muammar al-Qaddafi of Libya, Manuel Noriega of Panama, Ferdinand and Imelda Marcos, the husband-wife team of the Philippines, Eva and Juan Peron of Argentina, and Nicolae Ceauşescu and his wife, Elena, of Romania, explaining to students that throughout history, the world has been beleaguered by evil oppressors.

Before reading *The Children's Story,* the eighth graders and I considered several questions: What happens when people are oppressed—pressed down on—for too long? What does it finally take to galvanize a group of people to fight back? (I used vocabulary such as "to galvanize" because I respected their intelligence.) With them, I wanted to uncover why humans become corroded by evil.

I had laid the groundwork. Now, it was time for me to read aloud the first page of James Clavell's *The Children's Story*:"THE TEACHER WAS AFRAID. And the children were afraid. All except Johnny. He watched the classroom door with hate. He felt the hatred deep within his stomach. It gave him strength. It was two minutes to nine."

A jarring foreshadowing of terror in just thirty-seven words! I would usually stop dead at the end of that first spellbinding page and ask a wide-open question, such as: "What are your thoughts and feelings so far?" My most vociferous students would say: "It's stupid. We haven't read nothin' yet." Or "It's a baby book!" (God forbid that they would deign to read a baby book, they, the ultimate in sophistication!) But I would read on, never rushing to finish the book, which could probably be read aloud in twenty-five minutes, the time it takes New Teacher to take over the third-grade class. Rather, I would read the important parts of the story dramatically and emphatically. I played the role of the young, sweet-smelling infiltrator, anonymously referred to as New Teacher; the tired third-grade teacher, Miss Worden, who is dethroned; and little eight-year-old Johnny, the skeptic. Soon many students eagerly took turns reading aloud.

I would interrupt the reading frequently to talk about tyranny and to consider what motivates someone to become a tyrant or how a tyrant intimidates the vulnerable.

Finally, we would consider what inevitably happens in this predator-prey relationship. Speculating about questions like these can and should consume more than one class period. Eighth graders are emotionally capable of uncovering issues and making connections, and I wanted to involve them in this kind of thinking. These issues came up again and again as we read and discussed the story, as we connected it with our lives and the news of the day, taking time to return to our earlier list of notorious tyrants and oppressors throughout history.

Inciting thinking

One day I dared to ask—or rather, provoke—my eighth graders to think: "What is good about participating in a revolution?" A few kids who were paying close attention looked at me in disbelief. Then they began to speculate about the possibilities: a revolution ensures the passing of power from the oppressor to the oppressed. The oppressive regime is done away with, leaving a clean slate. Plotting a revolution unites like-minded people to fight for a common cause. I reminded them that the colonists revolted against the controlling British.

But I cautioned my students about the hidden liabilities of ridding a society of corrosive power. Ironically, oppressors who have been dethroned are often succeeded by leaders who are even more evil and greedy. In Orwell's *Animal Farm,* for example, the sodden Farmer Jones lets his barnyard go to rack and ruin, but his successors, Napoleon and Snowball, the two pigs, resort to the most evil and oppressive tactics perpetrated by humankind. These tangents let *The Children's Story* educate us in the ways of humans and in the pitfalls and promise of history. Our conversations captivated many of the students and helped even some of the most diffident readers become more invested in literature.

Usually, a good number of students would volunteer and even beg to read aloud to us about the persuasive New Teacher, letting the story unfold a little at a time. Although others were impatient to finish the book, I refused to rush through it quickly. I told my least patient kids that this stop-start operation could probably take several weeks or even a month to complete. They looked at me incredulously, slumped in their chairs, and groaned.

The Children's Story simply contains too much rich material to slide through quickly. We needed time to generalize and synthesize the big ideas embedded in its deceptively easy language. For example, New Teacher cradles frightened Sandra, isolates the skeptic Johnny, discredits the children's parents, their flag, and their God. She finally destroys their values because they are innocent and vulnerable and she is shrewd and well trained. As impatient as eighth graders are to get on with life, I insisted that we take time to understand each of the tactics New Teacher uses to take over her subjects.

Labeling takeover tactics

I started with the term *intimidate,* a key tactic in almost any coup and one the majority of my eighth graders knew and some even practiced. "How do eighth graders intimidate or frighten each other?" I asked.

Radha offered: "Everyone knows how to intimidate other kids. All you do is just look at them." Then Radha stood up and assumed a menacing posture and facial expression intended to convey intimidation.

"When certain vulnerable kids have been intimidated, how do they respond? What do they do?" I asked.

"They run!" Khalilah laughed.

"Or, they try to get tight with the person who intimidates them," Erika observed.

"Yes, that survival technique is called 'identifying with the aggressor'—in your words, the perpetrator," I said. "Getting close to the frightening, intimidating person and gaining favor is a tactic a vulnerable person might use." Then I returned to the novel: "What else has New Teacher done to infiltrate, or sneakily make her way into this innocent group of children to take them over?"

"She puts down Miss Worden, that pitiful old third-grade teacher," Endrico replied. Right then, I gave them two synonyms for *to put down: to discredit* and *to devalue,* a common takeover tactic.

I asked Endrico and the others to return to the text and locate the passages we'd read so far that clearly show New Teacher (we don't know her name) discrediting Miss Worden. Later, we discovered that New Teacher discredits other important adults (the third graders' parents) and raises serious questions about rote learning and such symbols as flag and family. New Teacher also questions the efficacy of praying to God.

By reading and stopping to talk, we discovered that New Teacher knows how and when to *intimidate, immobilize, flatter, soothe,* and *comfort*; *to build trust,* and *isolate* a dissident or skeptic such as Johnny. She senses the moment to *entice, bribe, discredit* or *devalue, brainwash* or *condition, infantilize* and *render helpless, seduce, divide and conquer,* and finally *take over* a group of vulnerable children. We located examples of all these strategies in the text.

"But this [a takeover] would never happen to a class of eighth graders!" Radha said assuredly.

"Yeah, I can see how this could happen to a bunch of little third graders—even seventh graders," Khalilah smirked knowingly.

"But not to us!" Radha added emphatically. Everyone agreed that eighth graders couldn't possibly be swayed, even by an enchantress as beguiling as New Teacher.

"What makes you so sure?" I asked.

"Eighth graders are almost grown," Kenny said. "We know better." This strong comment was one of Kenny's first ventures into class discussion, a major coup for a student who had declared at the beginning of the year that he could not read or write.

"Kenny, what do you mean that you'd know better?" I pressed. Kenny and the rest of the class continued to insist that mature people exercised judgment, that they were strong—even invincible—in the face of intimidation.

"But what about all of the Germans who were intimidated enough to go along with Adolf Hitler's plan to exterminate six million Jews?" I asked. "The German citizens were grown up. Many of them were strong adults." We were wrestling with important ethical and human questions.

I went on to pose other important questions that appealed to their sense of morality: "How can a group of people—a country rather than just a class of third graders—prevent a takeover or even genocide? How can we as a country be prepared so that an Adolf Hitler isn't able to come in and assume power? How can we prevent the kinds of conditions (poverty, illiteracy, racism, vulnerability of all sorts) that weaken a country, thus making it ripe for such an invasion?"

I was encouraging my students to see *The Children's Story* as an allegory. I asked them to consider what New Teacher might symbolize. I wanted them to figure out that Johnny, the skeptic, represents a very small group of strong, clear-thinking, ethical people in a society. I urged them to figure out that the majority of citizens in a society—likely all of us—would play the role of Sandra, the naive, or frightened follower. I was being quite directive at this point.

As we read aloud the last page of *The Children's Story*, "It was 9:23," we were struck with the short amount of time required for New Teacher to manage the takeover. We admired James Clavell's clever way of seducing *us*, his readers, with a title, plot, characters, and format that masked the many levels of meaning in his story.

"Do you still think that *The Children's Story* is a picture book for little children?" I asked.

"Even though first graders could read this book—pronounce all the words—they couldn't *really* understand it," Erika exclaimed with conviction. Although many seventh graders can understand this story, they don't relate to it in the same way eighth graders do. Somehow the additional year of maturity and experience enables the eighth graders to grasp the terror and feel passionately about it.

Responding to literature

The eighth graders and I not only raised questions, talked about, and created improvised dramas based on *The Children's Story*, we responded in writing to New Teacher's takeover tactics, her motives and methods for takeover, and the story's symbolic meaning (see Figures 4-5 and 4-6).

9/8/87

Response To Children's Story. Erik

Childrens Story is practical but sad. It's sad Because the New Teacher is really a kaniving witch manipulating the childrens minds by using kindness, and beauty. It's not right for her to do that and she knows it. She has all of the childrens trust except Johnny's. I feel that Johnny is right by not putting trust in her. Probably because people are not always what they might seem to be. Most people these days aren't. Most of the time when I put my trust in somebody, my feelings usually get hurt, or I get taken advantage of. That's why I feel Johnny is smart by not trusting her, because for some reason, I think that She has other plans for those children.

ERIK'S ASSESSMENT OF HIS RESPONSE:
I Think I have made Important points and the pieces hold together. I didn't develop too many Ideas.

FIG. 4-5   *Erik's Response*

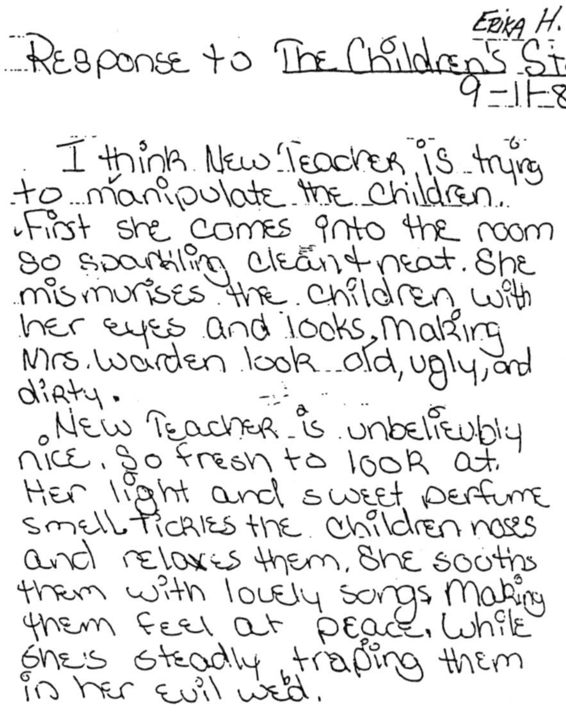

Erika H.

Response to The Children's Story
9-11-89

I think New Teacher is trying to manipulate the children. First she comes into the room so sparkling clean & neat. She mismurises the children with her eyes and looks, making Mrs. Warden look old, ugly, and dirty.

New Teacher is unbelievibly nice. So fresh to look at. Her light and sweet perfume smell Tickles the children noses and relaxes them. She sooths them with lovely songs making them feel at peace. While she's steadly traping them in her evil web.

FIG. 4-6   *Erika's Response*

Quinten was so powerfully influenced by this story that several months later he wrote his own allegory about school, a rather satiric piece about the intimidation tactics of the oppressive military establishment (certain administrators and teachers, including me) and the poor students, the recruits, lowest in rank and clearly the victims of oppression. The following is an excerpt from Quinten's "Boot Camp."

Boot Camp

"Ok! here's the plan — at 8:04 AM. you will report to homeroom military base until you have received all instructions for the day. at 8:12 AM the dismissal alarm will sound and you will "quickly" move to your next destination which is Fort History. Here you will aquire accurate knowledge of the world and you must get there in the limited time given or you must suffer the consequences. Such consequences could be 45 minutes of hard labor after the base is closed. And if this continues it could further your stay in the war!

I'm tired of walking and foot-running to drill so I decide to take it easy, and because of me taking it easy I'm late to my next field. The leader there in #226 hounded me because I was a few "seconds" late. . . . So she sends me to the torture chamber. Then I run into my head commander again and said, "Man that Mrs. Anonymous is really wierd! Ya see this is what happened. . . . ."

"Down here again huh, Quinten? I got cha now!"

"But all those other recruits were late too!

By the time I finished arguing I had already missed a English battle and it was chow time. I could tell it was chow time 'cause of the smell of frozen pizza and left over weinnies in the air!

Becoming investigative reporters

I borrowed dramatist-teacher Cecily O'Neill's drama technique to further engage the kids in responding to *The Children's Story*: becoming investigative reporters. We went to the library to tape an improvisation in which a student playing a reporter would ask classmates playing story characters important questions related to the story. We didn't use previously prepared questions or scripts. I started by telling the students that we were going to play various roles. Some of us would be reporters, while others would play the roles of New Teacher, Johnny, Sandra, and Miss Worden.

"If you want to play the role of an investigative reporter, think of some big *how* and *why* questions, maybe ones that we've already raised during class," I said. "If you don't want to be an investigative reporter, consider which character you'd like to play and then expect to be interviewed. Think how you would react if you played New Teacher, who is well trained in take-over tactics, or Johnny, who doubts and asks questions."

When everyone knew which role she or he wanted to play, at least for the moment (certain kids played different roles during the interview), we started the tape recorder and I signaled the first reporter to begin the questioning.

Rachel asked Marquita: "How did you feel when New Teacher walked into Miss Worden's classroom?"

"She just came walking into the class all dressed up in that green uniform. I got scared—especially when she (New Teacher) told Miss Worden to leave." Rachel paused. As the sideline coach, I prompted Rachel to repeat her question or ask another related one.

"What did you think might happen?" Rachel asked.

Ominicka worried that New Teacher would use her in the army in a master plot to conquer a defenseless country. At that point another investigative reporter took over and began to question Ominicka about her fear of going to war and not seeing her mother again.

Then Rachel posed her original question again, this time to Keith: "How did you feel when New Teacher walked into Miss Worden's class?"

Keith answered: "I was afraid she was going to hurt us. I didn't really know what to expect. The only thing I knew was what my father had told me."

I coached Rachel to pick up on what Keith was saying about his father: "What *did* your father tell you?" By asking related questions, Rachel was helping her classmates make good connections.

Keith, who was playing the role of a third grader in Miss Worden's class, couldn't think of the word for distorted information spread systematically. When I suggested *propaganda,* he nodded vigorously. Keith was worried that his father was being maligned by this savvy infiltrator. Chris N., an investigative reporter, asked Keith: "*Now* what do you think of New Teacher?" Although no one answered directly, it provided a lovely springboard for a whole series of questions. This high quality give-and-take hadn't come naturally; we had practiced talking and asking good questions in our classroom for several months. I played the role of sideline coach, who watched and listened and entered into the investigations when necessary while these kids were learning how it felt to be the experts in charge of generating ideas and interacting with each other in school.

Ghoulish treats

Besides being strong supporters of egalitarianism and human rights, eighth graders are social creatures. Because Halloween was just around the corner and one class was asking for a party, I considered their request and imagined making our menu poetry. Fourteen-year-olds don't feel neutral about much of anything. They *love* (their favorite verb) to talk among themselves, even if they resist responding in class. They *love* to throw parties and eat, even if they deride the cafeteria food.

Though they boo and hiss and say that they *hate* (another favorite verb) the poetry that I like to peddle, it was one of my eighth graders who suggested that we memorize the first stanza from the poem, "Witches' Spells" by L. Frank Baum (from *Queen Zixi of Ix*), entitled "Miss Trust's Incantation": "Erig-a-ma-role, erig-a-ma-ree / Jig-ger-nut, jog-er-nit, que-jig-ger-ee."

Though some kids wanted a party, they felt silly chanting Halloween poems, one of my prerequisites for having a bash. But after their self-consciousness melted away, they had fun using their voices in unison to chant Lilian Moore's "Witch Goes Shopping":

Witch rides off
Upon her broom
Finds a space
To park it.
Takes a shiny shopping cart
Into the supermarket.

X. J. Kennedy's "Wicked Witch's Kitchen" made them laugh:

You're in the mood for freaky food?
You feel your taste buds itchin'
For nice fresh poison ivy greens?
Try Wicked Witch's kitchen.

Of course, we memorized William Shakespeare's "The Making of a Charm" from *MacBeth,* Act IV, Scene 1:

Double, double toil and trouble;
Fire burn and cauldron bubble.

But their favorite Halloween poem was "Witches' Menu" by Sonja Nikolay:

Live lizard, dead lizard
Marinated, fried.
Poached lizard, pickled lizard
Salty lizard hide.

Hot lizard, cold lizard
Lizard over ice.
Baked lizard, boiled lizard
Lizard served with spice.

Sweet lizard, sour lizard
Smoked lizard heart,
Leg of lizard, loin of lizard
Lizard à la carte.

By using our voices and letting the incantations roll off our tongues, we were warming up and freeing ourselves to fool around with words—invented and ghoulish— and then maybe write our own Halloween poems.

Making poetry menus

Khalilah popped her hand up one day while we were chanting the Halloween poems and said, "Mrs. Krogness, why don't we make our own Halloween menus—something like 'Witches' Menu?' " So, after we'd chanted "Witches' Menu" five or six times, we did just that. First, we *talked* for twenty or so minutes about possible ghoulish menu items, such as sheeps' eyeballs and pigs' hearts, monkey blood, and toad brains, all of which I jotted on the chalkboard. We spun off a list of culinary terms—*marinate, parboil, sauté, poach, bake, broil*—that I added to the idea bank. We talked about ways of concocting a ghastly porridge: a pinch of this, a dash of that.

During this prewriting warm-up, we imagined cauldrons bubbling and boiling with our word recipes: a nasty gruel spiced with sage; a simmering stew laced with lavender. Excitement brewed as we all put pencil to paper. Even Kenny, who during the first week of school had adamantly declared, "Don't expect me to write; I can't," got busy on a poem. Laughter punctuated stretches of silence as we all composed our menus in verse.

"Let me read my start," Crystal laughed. "I'm thinking of a diner where they serve only weird breakfasts. How's this? Fried brains, scrambled, poached / Sunnyside up, $1.75."

We all applauded Crystal. Then others wanted to try out their beginning lines. "My restaurant is fancy—a French restaurant with a wine list and what do you call that man who seats the guests?" Erika asked. I gave her the French word, *maître d'*.

"Here's my start," Erika said. "Blood of Cherie / Blood of Maitre d' / Venom of snake / A vulture's quake.

Radha's poem featured Chucklebelly's Deli. The puns, too, began to burgeon: Endrico, in his rather extraordinary poem, featured "strawberry shortsnake" for dessert, while Crystal imagined "pansnakes—plump and juicy," and "oatheel—most nutritious." Here are some of their creations, spiked with imagination, wit, and humor.

Kenetta's Kitchen

by Kenetta

If you like freaky foods—
Come to Kenetta's Kitchen.
I'll serve you tender toes on rice—
Then walrus warts served with spice.
If that doesn't tempt your tummy,
I'll give you something really yummy—
Like cat tails with hardened nails.
That should make you go home and YELL—
HAPPY HALLOWEEN!

Red Bloodster Guts Restaurant

by Crystal

BREAKFAST   Fried brains—scrambled, poached,
Sunnyside up, $1.75.
Pansnakes—plump and juicy,
Cream of guts—most delicious,
Oatheel—most nutritious!

LUNCH   Spaghetti veins served with
baboon's blood,

Lamb burgers,
A goat's eye and a rat's tail,
Molded soup of floating snails.
COME EAT AT RED BLOODSTER GUTS RESTAURANT—
A nice treat for a total creep!

Chucklebelly's Deli
by Radha

Green snails fried with bloody scales,
And marinated bunny tails.
All for sale at Chucklebelly's Deli!
Stale snake skin,
Live cats, *very* thin.
Specialty of the day?
Buzzards' hearts baked in clay.

Filét Mignon Paté
by Tequila

Pigs and cows all served with spice,
Wolf tongue and cat tails—
Oh, wouldn't that be nice?
Dog ears, dog tails and pigs' feet on rye,
Chicken vein soup along with one big lizard's eye.
Fish scales and snail shells, already sautéed,
Eat sheep's hearts and turtles' heads at
Filet Mignon Paté!

(Tequila couldn't think of a food that rhymed nicely with *sauté,* so I suggested *paté.*)
I've saved the most tantalizing morsel for last, Endrico's poem, with its tight, rhythmic cadence and sound effects.

How 'Bout Some Strawberry Shortsnake?
by Endrico

Spiders' eggs and a bat's blood,
A gargoyle's glands mixed with mud.
Pink pigtails that are lightly poached,
Legs of an eagle and ribs of a roach.
Eyes of a beaver, and alligator à la mode.
Ears of a dog with a spine of a toad.
And for dessert, a strawberry shortsnake!

Making the poems stimulated the students' interest in poetry. Creating unsavory concoctions such as a "gargoyle's glands mixed with mud" stirred their interest in the language, too. We had fun fooling around with language together.

My eighth graders and I did as Lee Bennett Hopkins, who wrote *Pass the Poetry, Please,* said and passed the poetry to another class on Halloween because we needed an audience. In full costume, we served up a delicious feast of poetic goodies to our eighth-grade, eighth-period compatriots and their teacher, Gail Rose. As the seventh-period class cleared out, we rushed around to decorate our improvised banquet table, covering it with a festive pumpkin-orange and black-cat paper table cloth, taking care to place our poetry menus, neatly printed up on shirt cardboards, at each diner's plate. Endrico was in charge of putting on a tape of ghoulish background music and helping Kenny and the girls serve the cookies, chips, and cider.

Our poetry banquet began with hosts and guests joining in a choral reading of Shakespeare's "Double, double toil and trouble / fire burn and cauldron bubble." A couple of the students recited Halloween poems they'd memorized for the occasion. Then I asked everyone to think of answers to the Ghoulish Gags I'd collected: "What kind of fruit does a ghost like best?" (Boo-berries). "What kind of beans do monsters eat?" (Human-beans). "Which jewel does a witch like to wear?" (A tomb stone).

The most important part of the festivities was serving up our original poetry. Each chef stood behind his or her guest at the banquet table and read his or her poem aloud. When Kenny's turn came, I quietly signaled him, letting my least confident and competent and most resistant reader off the hook. "I can read it *myself,*" Kenny replied, impatient that I would even consider his letting someone else read his masterpiece. After the poetry reading, we all washed the ghoulish runes down with cookies and cider. How like a little kids' party this was. How happy my suave fourteen-year-olds were to play gracious hosts to our neighbors.

Taking off in new directions

Toward the end of the year, the students in one eighth-grade class were independent and motivated enough to take off on their own projects. Erika decided to write a collection of poems about the struggle of being a young-black-girl-soon-to-be-a-woman. Tequila, a lovely, gentle girl who at the beginning of the school year didn't consider herself a writer, labored over a story about a young black slave boy with imagination and dreams; the sequel, one hundred or so years later, is the story of the slave boy's great grandson. Both of these exceptional stories seemed to have been stored in Tequila's mind for many, many years. She and Erika often shared their writing in progress with the rest of us. Figure 4-7 shows an excerpt from Tequila's story.

Endrico worked quietly on a wonderfully imaginative coloring book about a boy named Roy who thought that everyone had forgotten his birthday.

No one remembers my birthday

Page 1   "Wow! It's my 8th birthday," said a little boy named Roy.
          "I hope I get lots & lots of presents."

Page 2   "Hi Mom, you know what today is don't you."
          "Of course, it's Tuesday," said Roy's mother

Page 3   But today's a special Tuesday. said Roy
          "Oh yeah? Today I have to pay the phone bill, thanks for reminding me."

Page 4   "My own mother didn't remember my birthday," cried Roy.
          Roy walked off unhappy into his room.
          He didn't want to be bothered.

FIG. 4-7   *Excerpt from Tequila's Story*

Page 5	"Hi, son," said Roy's father.
	"Do you know what today is Dad?"
	Roys father answered, "Yes, today is Friday the 13th. Why do you want to know?"
	"OH, I just asked," said Roy.
Page 6	Roy walked off.
	"My own father didn't remember my birthday." cried Roy.
Page 7	Roy went outside to play with his friends.
	But none of his friends were out.
Page 8	Roy walked for hours crying. This seemed to be the loneliest day of his life.
Page 9	Roy had nowhere else to go so he went home
Page 10	He opened the front door and . . .
Page 11	Surprise!

I wondered if this little story reflected Endrico's own sadness about not being noticed or valued.

Crystal created a news and advice tabloid, while Twilla created a stunning little book of suggested activities for babysitters or parents to use with children. Here are some excerpts from Twilla's book:

Activity book

If you have little kids & you don't know what to do with them, here are some suggestions just for you. As a parent you can do alot of things with your child or children to expand their minds, develop senses, teach them to get along with other children, to have fun with their friends, & to let them get educated & to see what the world is like.

Make Believe	You can get child some clothes and let your young child dress up as an imaginary person. For example if they wanted to dress up as a playmother you could get them some grownups clothes & heels to wear & maybe a hat & some make-up.
Play House	Let them get a cardboard box & let them cut it into different shapes & form it into a house then they can paint it & let it dry so they can play house.
Puppet Show	Have a puppet show with them. Get some old socks or paper bags & make puppet faces out of them. Then let them be behind a wall or something. For example you can act out the 3 little pigs or little red riding hood.
Parades	Letting them make parades with balloons, bicycles & wagons is a good idea. For example get your childs bicycle or big wheel & tie some ballons on it. Then start your parade.
Making Food	The kids also can try to make there own food such as a peanut butter & jelly sandwich or a bologny sandwich.
Kool-aid Cubes	Let them make kool-aid ice cubes. For example fill up a ice tray with kool-aid & let it freeze for about an half-hour.
Making A Mess	If they make a mess somewhere let them try to clean it up. For example wiping the table is an easy job. First you have to show them *how* to clean the table though.

Kenetta loved to write fiction. She worked on a story, "The Polka Dot Party," about a funny little boy, Tony, and his eccentric babysitter, Mrs. Noodlesoup. Radha kept changing her mind—first she wanted to write a novella, an episodic piece about her and her friends, but then she dropped it in favor of a promising short story, "The Abolishment of Slavery." But she dropped this idea in favor of a dictionary of current African American expressions. Then, much to my sadness and her discomfort, Radha took her project home and lost it.

Khalilah waxed and waned on her writing project, giving it a half-hearted amount of effort. Kenny, though he dawdled a bit, planned the talk show he wanted to produce and tape—live—in the school library. Much to our pleasure and pride, his "The Kenny C. Show," starring all of us, became a reality! We'd come a long way together and we savored our progress in talking to learn, reading to wonder, and writing to know.

The push-pull of eighth grade

Yes, my students raised heady questions and did promising original writing. But there was no escaping the many hard times when my eighth graders pushed and I pulled. I remember the day Rachel slumped in her chair and spread her legs apart, her face contorted.

"Sit up straight, Rachel," I said emphatically.

"I got cramps," she announced to everyone in the class.

Another time I chastised Quinten and his buddies for taking their sweet time coming down the hall to class until they saw me standing at the door. Then they ran and slid into their seats just as the bell was ringing. "But we *are* on time, Mrs. Krogness. Don't you see, we're in our seats and the bell's just now ringing." Splitting hairs was a favorite pastime of certain eighth graders. So were leaning back in their chairs, breaking pencils, tearing up paper, and telling others to shut up when they, too, were talking. Here are some all-too-familiar eighth-grade scenarios:

Student: "You *always* pick on me for talking out, but what about Cherise, Tyrone, and Jamal? You never get P.O.ed at them."

(**I think**: "But it's just that you talk without respite.")

Student: "You *never* call on me and I *always* have my hand up."

(**I think**: "You *finally* put your hand up just as I called on someone else.")

Student: "I already learned how to do this in first grade."

(**I think**: "If you had learned it in first grade, I wouldn't have to teach it to you now.")

Student: "But it's so *borrrrring*."

(**I think**: "Why is it that the people who complain about boredom are the ones who never do anything to make class interesting?")

Nothing makes me more angry and defensive than a student complaining of boredom. But on many days, boredom was the least of my worries. In eighth grade, I never knew when the temper of even the most cooperative student would flare.

Take Erika, the girl who raised many thoughtful questions and wrote a lovely collection of poetry and prose. In late March, she and the rest of this compatible, collaborative class had begun to let down and coast. One day I delivered a sermonette about settling down to serious work again. After class that day, Dalia Sak, a French teacher a couple of doors down the hall, witnessed Erika's angry diatribe about me to one of her friends.

"That woman talks about *our* attitude," Erika seethed. "What about hers? I hate her." (As I've said before, no one who teaches eighth graders emerges un-scathed.)

That evening I called Erika at home: "Erika," I said quietly, "this is Mrs. Krogness." A long pause. "Erika, I'm sorry that you were so angry with me. It's perfectly all right to express anger. But when you feel angry with me, tell me directly and as kindly as you can that you feel upset about my attitude or about something that I've said in class. We've been good friends for six months now. It's better when friends talk openly and get their grievances out, rather than store the fury and then back-stab the friend." I waited for Erika to speak.

"I'm sorry, Mrs. Krogness," she replied. "I don't know what got into me. But it seems that your attitude toward our class has changed. You seem disappointed with us. And that made me mad."

"I'm not disappointed with you; I just don't want you to shut down now that we're in the home stretch. All of you have made good progress; a few of you—

for instance, you, Erika—have made excellent progress. The reason that I called you at home is that you are someone who uses the language so well; you are so able to understand and express feelings. I want you to use the language to say what's in your mind and heart, even if it's not positive. Of course, always try to be kind and sensitive while you're speaking your mind! I hope that you and I are still friends."

"Everything's all right now," Erika said. "I'm relieved you called. Thank you, Mrs. Krogness." Now this is an example of the maturity eighth graders are capable of expressing.

Setting limits and letting go

Not all scenarios played out as positively as the one between Erika and me. I wrote more than one impassioned referral (a form filled out by teachers about misbehaving

---

Administration Action _____
Documentation _____

SHAKER MIDDLE SCHOOL

REFERRAL

STUDENT'S NAME ____ _____ - _____

REASON FOR REFERRAL: Date of Occurrence _4-1-88_
                              Date of Referral _4-1-88_
                              Parent Contacted _✓_

HE MUTTERS, MUMBLES AND GROUSES ABOUT ME AND THIS BORING CLASS—BUT DOES EVERYTHING TO DERAIL US AND PRECIOUS LITTLE TO ENLIVEN THE CONVERSATION. HE NEEDS TO TAKE A LITTLE RESPONSIBILITY.

Staff Originator _Mary M. Krogness_

Student's Comment: Agree _____   Disagree _____
         If "disagree" is checked, please write your comment on back of sheet.

ADMINISTRATION ACTION:

Administrator _____

FIG. 4-8   *Referral Form*

SHAKER MIDDLE SCHOOL

Administration Action _____
Documentation _____

REFERRAL

STUDENT'S NAME _____

REASON FOR REFERRAL:

Date of Occurrence **5-2-88**
Date of Referral **5-2-88**
Parent Contacted _____✓_____

Ho-Hum. This guy has yet to lift a pencil, discuss his thoughts, enter into class, open his writing spiral. The only thing he is quick to do is say: "WE DON'T DO ANYTHING IN HERE!" His inertia truly is infectious. WHERE DO WE GO FROM HERE?

Staff Originator *Mary Krogness* ✓

Student's Comment: Agree _____   Disagree ___✓___
   If "disagree" is checked, please write your comment on back of sheet.

ADMINISTRATION ACTION:

Administrator_____

FIG. 4-9   *Referral Form*

students and read by the assistant principals) before the year was over (see Figures 4-8 and 4-9).

Separating from people who have worked hard to make life a little more accessible and promising is very difficult for all young people, but it is particularly so for eighth graders. And because eighth graders are also trying hard—in some cases, desperately—to break free from the adults in their lives, they can resort to hardball tactics.

Certain kids like Dwight, whom I'll introduce later, said with their downcast eyes that they were separating; others would self-consciously turn their heads away when we'd pass each other in the corridors. They needed to pull away.

Julie, the gifted poet who had flourished during eighth grade and had chosen to make me the beneficiary of more than fifty of her poems, brazenly told me during the last week of school that she'd dumped her copy of *Kaleidoscope,* the all-school publication containing several of her poems, in the trash. "I had too much other stuff to carry," she announced blithely. How cold. How cavalier. How scared. How

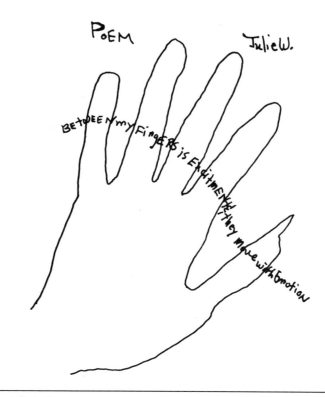

FIG. 4-10   *Julie's Poem*

protective. But as Julie's poem conveys (see Figure 4-10), eighth graders can and do express feelings openly and passionately.

Trippin' out

Each day with eighth graders is different. They blast you with their independence or deny your hope through their indifference. Then without warning, they unite and act civil—even sweet. By April, eighth graders—like the forsythia, daffodils, magnolias, lilacs, and hyacinths—had blossomed. They were beautiful young people whose faces finally fit their noses! They radiated a zest for living, contained a ready supply of energy, and upon occasion, exuded warmth that could bring tears to your eyes. The middle school students wanted to spread their wings and fly.

"Can't we go on a trip, Mrs. K.?" they started asking early in April.

"Yeah, all day. After all, you're always saying that language is made in and outside the classroom," another student reminded me.

"Where would you like to go? Keep in mind that I'll have to be able to justify the trip to Dr. Peterjohn and your parents." We started brainstorming: Geauga Lake, an amusement park, was first on the list; then going to a movie or a sports event downtown. Everyone wanted to see Tower City, the newly redesigned Terminal Tower building that sparkled with stylish shops and restaurants. After fantasizing about the almost infinite possibilities, they finally began getting serious about a trip that would qualify as being "educationally sound."

I suggested that going to Tower City was a possibility, along with touring Play House Square's historic, renovated theaters, The Palace, The State, and The Ohio. The most historically important building in Cleveland, the Arcade, was also a possibility. Or we might cross the Cuyahoga River, which separates the East and West sides of Cleveland, and visit the historic West Side Market. Could we pack so many tantalizing places into just one day? Quickly I scheduled a school bus and telephoned Play House Square to arrange a tour of the three theaters.

One Saturday, I took a trial run downtown with my husband, John, charting the route from Play House Square to Tower City, and from Tower City down the narrow and circuitous roads through The Flats and over the bridge to the West Side Market. The timing worked even if we stopped to eat and had to get back to school in time for our bus driver to make his usual run. I was relieved that several mothers agreed to accompany us on our trek downtown. After careful plans had been made and possible problems ironed out, we were set to enjoy a gorgeous Friday in May exploring our city.

Preparing to trip out

In preparation for our end-of-the-year outing, I brought booklets and playbills from all three of the old theaters; we raised questions about the buildings' unique features and the reasons for keeping old buildings. Going to the West Side Market was appealing because each vendor's stall was uniquely his and his family's, passed down from generation to generation.

I regaled the students with stories about the chicken man, who used to "candle" eggs before high technology sorted the eggs and caught imperfections. I told them about Rita Grau, the lively woman who made delicious peanut butter, pickles, and preserves that she enjoyed sharing with customers. I told them about the old man who used to climb an unimaginable number of steps to hand-wind the clock at the top of the Market's tower. One day, a step gave way and the clock-winder nearly fell to his death. Shortly thereafter, an electrical clock was installed. I told the kids to listen for Arabic, Russian, Spanish, Polish, Czech, Indian, Appalachian, and black dialects—a veritable smorgasbord of languages being spoken at the West Side Market.

One student said, "Planning this trip is probably even more fun than the real trip." The pleasure principle was in operation when we discussed Tower City's enticing shops and food hall—which of course led to *the* big question: "When we get to Tower City, can we please be on our own for just a little while?" I needed time to think about the huge responsibility. Herding more than sixty kids around the three-tiered building would certainly be unwieldy. It would spoil the fun, too. I talked with assistant principal Bill Jarvie about the benefits and the hazards, since he was an old hand at field trips. He encouraged me to lay careful plans with my students, set a few firm guidelines, and let them go free in Tower City for forty-five minutes!

I carefully worded a letter of permission to each parent, explaining in specific language each leg of our journey and the terms according to which their sons and daughters would be on their own within the confines of Tower City for forty-five minutes: to eat lunch with partners and shop if any time was left over, always with the knowledge that I would be stationed by the fountain in case of emergency.

Walk, never run!

The kids and I spent ten minutes of six or seven class periods talking about being responsible, using acceptable behavior, and exercising good manners and judgment. Together we established four rules: (1) *always* remain with your partner and stay *within* the confines of Tower City; (2) walk, never run; (3) check the time frequently (I advised them to eat first and then shop so that both might be accomplished within the allotted time period—between 11:30 A.M. and 12:15 P.M., thereby getting a head start on the regular lunch crowd that would invade the food hall by noon); (4) return to the appointed meeting place at the appointed time (both of which *I* established). We also discussed appropriate dress and a suitable amount of money to bring.

Safety precautions were also a topic of conversation: staying with your partner and keeping money out of reach of passersby. If a pair of students became disoriented, or even lost, they could ask a police officer or go to the information booth to find out the location of the fountain, where I would be permanently stationed. I emphasized that going on such an elaborate field trip such as this one was a pleasure and a privilege, and that one irresponsible act could spoil the trip for everyone.

A day downtown

The day finally came. The parents, kids, and I piled into the school bus and headed downtown. First stop: Play House Square, where we were greeted by a docent who took us to the State Theatre. We all stood in what is considered to be the longest lobby in the world, looking up at the stunning rococo ceiling and crystal chandeliers that hung from a great height. We admired the walls, which were covered by an exotic frieze. But the most fun was getting up on stage—all sixty of us—to tap dance, sing, M.C. a show, bow and twirl, and entertain a hypothetical audience of three thousand people.

The students asked astute questions about the history of the theaters and the actors who had played on these stages in the 1920s. They asked how the renovators had repaired the tall ceilings and brushed the gold leaf on; they wondered about the actors' dressing room, the Green Room, where, we were told, ghosts resided. The students were enchanted by the theaters' grandeur and appreciated the anecdotes. Their questions and observations were the best evidence of their personal and academic growth— certainly more significant than an end-of-year test.

Second stop: Tower City. I could feel the tension. But before I let them go free, I showed everyone the fountain, where we would meet and where they could always find me. I pointed in the direction of the information booth, where they could ask questions about the location of shops. I also pointed the way to the lavatories and reminded them of our rules. In pairs, they headed out.

A lone sentinel, I paced back and forth near the fountain. I spent the forty-five minutes casting my eyes expectantly over the crowd, hoping to catch a glimpse of my students on holiday. When I saw them, they'd flash a smile, wave, and then dash off, knowing that they had more time to spend.

A few minutes before the appointed return time, I held my breath hoping that they'd all show up. By 12:15 P.M., perhaps a third of them had arrived. I began to count bobbing heads. The kids talked about their discoveries and the wonderful extravagances they'd purchased or had just looked at longingly. Besides the compact disc shop, they had fallen in love with the Disney store, replete with its mouse memorabilia. After they'd all been accounted for, Derrick pleaded with me to be allowed to return to one

A day downtown; a day of freedom.

shop so he could buy a poster and a sweatshirt. How could I turn him down? After all, they'd all been so cooperative and appreciative. I snapped pictures of my crowd of happy kids and the four mothers while they jostled each other and laughed, ready to board the bus and move on to the third and last destination: The West Side Market.

By comparison to Tower City, the Market was small and contained. I let them loose again, first admonishing them to look at the ceiling of the market, open their ears to the language, let their olfactory systems appreciate the aromas, and visit Rita Grau's stand to get a pickle or a taste of peanut butter, free. I reminded them to stay with their partners and be careful not to endanger people by running down the aisles. My last order was to meet me at the tower in thirty minutes. Only one student and her mother came back to the bus late, but they were laden with delicious treats.

Beyond the classroom walls

Back at school and with little time left before the last bell rang, we shared the food we'd bought at the Market—to my delight, gummy bears and grapes—and basked in the fun of our day together. The kids savored their independence, expressing pleasure that this day away from school had surpassed their expectations. I finally relaxed, knowing that the day hadn't been flawed by rain or marred by accident or mishap. I also celebrated the responsibility and judgment they'd shown.

A field trip stimulates interest and imagination while signifying to both kids and adults that learning can take place outside of class. This field trip, which these young people had helped design, developed their confidence in generating ideas and making decisions. One student observed: *"We* got to go on an all-day field trip for a change." (My kids often felt that because they were in skills classes, they were automatically excluded from certain privileges they perceived other students enjoying.)

For Laurelia and her peers, learning can and does happen beyond school's four walls.

After the trip, we talked about what we had observed, learned, and enjoyed. We also talked about the consequences of exemplary behavior, thereby connecting students' decorum and personal responsibility with privilege and success. Although I can't quantifiably measure the positive effects of such an experience, I can assess its importance by the students' responses.

Erika wrote me a card of appreciation:

Dear Mrs. Krogness,

Thank you for taking us downtown. I liked Playhouse Square and the West Side Market. I *loved* Tower City.

Thank you for teaching me more than I'll ever know.

Love,
Erika.

FIVE

We Don't Do Nothin' In Here

My fifth-period eighth graders came in and sat down quietly on the first day of school. Warily, they waited for me to begin class. Nothing in particular about this group of thirteen- and fourteen-year-olds struck me. If anything, I was pleased that they weren't starting the year by acting out in the too common manner of resistant students.

Even Jermaine, whom I'd had the previous year, sat expectantly with his notorious sidekick, Chemon. Derrick seated himself behind them. Laurelia, whom I'd had in language arts during elementary school (and whose wonderful poem, which I'd submitted to *Language Arts,* was published) sat with Natachia; Nona and some of the other girls sat at the back of the room. Brandon and Tristin, the only white student in the class, sat together up front; both girls had been in one of my classes the previous year. Larry sat with DeSean, and Dwight and Erik sat together. Kim sat uncomfortably alone. So did Donald and big Jason, both of whom headed for the opposite corners of this large classroom, far from each other.

In contrast to other eighth-grade classes I'd had, where certain boys flexed their muscles and difficult girls flaunted their "attitudes," this group seemed content to be quiet. Little did I suspect, on that steamy day in late August, that this group would prove to be my nemesis, the class that made me question my worth as a teacher and as a person.

Launching the year

As with my other language arts classes, I began by dividing the class into pairs. I asked them to interview each other and collect information for brief introductions they would then make to the class. Most of their introductions were adequate but not distinguished; they were too general, bland, and unrevealing.

As was also customary in my classes, the students wrote letters of intention. Dwight wrote a strong, independent letter in which he told what he liked and disliked about reading and writing; from his perspective, there was no point in talking about books. Natachia, Laurelia, and Nona wrote acceptable letters about their intention to improve as well as their particular expectations for classroom fare, as did Brandon and Tristin. Derrick, a slow writer, expressed his desire to work in small groups and have class discussions, but he did not want to read and write unless absolutely necessary.

Dear Derrick,

Well for one I hope we don't do to much writing and reading unless we really have to. I would love to do more class discussion and working in groups rather doing it as a class that way every on will have more fun and participate. There is one book I would like to read and it is Autobiography of Miss Jane Pittman as a class.

Sincerly,

Derrick

In a second letter, Derrick spoke from the point of view of his parents, alluding to his difficulty ("messing up") in passing seventh grade.

Jermaine's letter to himself put me on notice that he didn't want me to read everything in his writing notebook. In another letter, he wrote from his parents' point of view indicating his own desire to improve. Chemon also expressed a mild willingness to move ahead, while Jason, Donald, Kim, and Larry wrote tentatively and sparsely, and DeSean wrote to please.

Dear Donald:

I hope to have a good school year. I hope to get all good grades and finish all my work.

sincerely,

Donald

Erik, a fine writer, conveyed his worst fears about trusting people. His letter ends on a pessimistic note.

Dear Erik,

I hope to improve on my reading skills. I really hope we don't do too much group activities. I never did like to do things with a group of people, because people make me feel nervous and uneasy. They never realise that people can make mistakes, and soon as you make one they're right there to criticize you. I love dog's, and I hope we read this dog book called White Fang. I think I like dogs more than I like people. Dogs don't criticize, they don't talk about you behind your back, and don't turn on you, (at least my dog, Champ doesn't). This year in school doesn't look too promising for me. But I hope for the best. See ya later.

Sincerely,

Erik

In their responses to a questionnaire I gave them, the students revealed their feelings about reading and writing: they disliked both of them. Reading took too long and was boring; writing was more palatable, but not their favorite subject (Figure 5-1 shows Jermaine's survey answers).

When I made my customary, first-week-of-school telephone calls to students' homes to introduce myself and encourage whoever was raising the child to call me any time, I sometimes heard suspicion—in one case, overt hostility—in their voices. The flat sound of some of their voices, so different from the voices of the other parents I'd called this year, began to make me realize this would be no ordinary class.

NAME *Jermaine*
DATE *8/30/89*
GRADE *8th*

FIRST WEEK OF SCHOOL SURVEY

. How do you feel about reading?

I hate reading books.
I only do it when I need to.

'. Do you consider yourself a reader? If so, tell which books you have enjoyed most
and which book(s) you've read recently.

no

3. If you don't like to read, tell what you don't like about it.

I get headach reading little words.

4. How do you feel about writing?

Its helpful to the brain

5. Do you consider yourself to be a writer? If so, tell why you like to write and
what all you have written.

sometimes I like to write stories and poems.

6. If you don't like to write, tell what you don't like about it.

(If you'd like to say more about any one of the issues, turn this paper over,
indicate the number of the question and write on!)

FIG. 5-1 *Jermaine's Survey Answers*

Facing facts

Perhaps my unwillingness to size up these students and assess them consciously, the way they were assessing me, got the year off to a bad start. Their behavior (with the exception of Jermaine and Chemon's notorious reputations) fooled me into believing that I could excite them with just a bit of coaxing. In my usual fervor to bring us together and engage us all in language learning, I overlooked or unconsciously chose to ignore obvious indicators that this apparently manageable class might prove my undoing. The dynamics of this group of adolescents, who had failed too long and too often and who had responded by becoming passive, would pose unimaginable challenges for me in the months to come.

The facts of their lives were sobering. Half the students in this class had been retained at least once. One was in therapy because of a stepparent's physical abuse. I suspected that another student was being abused by his father. Still another had been beaten by his natural parents before he was adopted as a toddler. One student had spent three years (an uncommonly long time) in a residential treatment center for seriously emotionally disturbed children.

More than half of the students came from one-parent homes. One girl and one boy lived with their grandmothers; their mothers had either fled the scene or been deemed unsuitable parents. Two boys had already had encounters with the law. I knew that these situations existed, and because a few of these kids—unguarded for a moment—let things slip out during class, I also knew that even more family pathology existed. But these students strongly denied their family problems out of loyalty to their parents. Thus, with good cause, they were not merely apprehensive. They were bereft of self-esteem, self-confidence, and self-respect—three ingredients essential for learning.

My reaction to them

Each particular mix of students creates its own classroom dynamic; the teacher's job is to get a handle on this intangible quality as soon as possible. But instead of reading the signals these students were sending out with their unusual stillness, I charged in with vigor and asked too much, too soon. Quite likely I terrified them with my energy and expectations. The contrast between the quiet, docile students and the expectant, enthusiastic teacher proved as unsettling to them as it did to me. The more they protected themselves with passive resistance, the more anxiously I tried to draw them out, wanting them to be generators of ideas rather than empty receptacles I would fill each day.

Soon I took to hanging out in the school library, seeking the solace of its atmosphere and of Esther Mathews, our library aide. "Esther, what do you think I should do with this bunch?" I asked her.

"Stick with them, Mary. They'll come around. Maybe not as fast as you would like. But these kids *will* come around." (I did not share Esther's confidence.)

By mid-September, the freshness of the new school year was gone and I was fast losing ground. Close to half the class took to sauntering in late. Explosive sneezes that erupted like Vesuvius occasionally rocked the silence. Jermaine and Chemon slouched in their seats and gave off silent signals, the kind that don't leave fingerprints, to sabotage whatever I'd start, whether it was a discussion about a piece of literature or a mini-lesson on the writing we were doing.

Like the kids in my other classes, certain of these young people came to class without even the simplest essentials—pencils and paper. Since a greater number of these kids enjoyed the sport of repeatedly smacking pencils on the edge of their tables until they splintered, those who did have pencils wrote with jagged, truncated stubs. Some kids, like Laurelia, rolled their eyes at their compatriots and muttered half-heard comments designed to crush vulnerable classmates (and occasionally me). Others greeted eager-to-please learners like Tristin with an embarrassing silence.

One day when the class bell rang at the end of fifth period, I heard Dwight call to Natachia, "You can leave now!" The temerity! Didn't they suppose that I, too, wanted to make a quick exit? My nerve ends were raw. I knew I'd have to back off to regain an adult perspective. As my friend Doris Blough put it during one of our hour-long phone calls, "These kids are performing Chinese water torture."

Mea culpa

I needed to assess my goals, my outlook, and my behavior and maybe jettison some naive idealism in the process. Without exonerating myself—or beating up on myself—

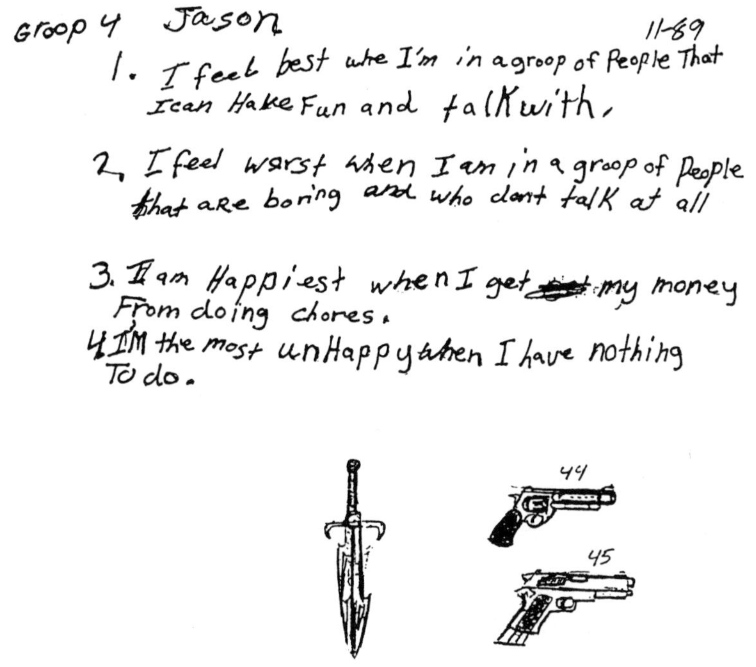

Groop 4   Jason   11-89
1. I feel best when I'm in a groop of People That
I can Hake Fun and talK with.

2. I feel worst when I am in a groop of people
that are boring and who dont talK at all

3. I am Happiest when I get my money
From doing chores.
4 IM the most unHappy when I have nothing
To do.

44

45

FIG. 5-2   *Jason's Response*

I began reflecting on my personal and emotional needs, squarely and objectively. I focused my attention and energy on standing up to the students' demands and figuring out how to lead them forward. I tried to modify any behavior that might be aggravating the problems: being too eager, too anxious, too expectant. I worked on relaxing myself, but not my standards.

While I was trying to relate literature to life, and engage my students in writing and conducting a schoolwide survey based on reading we'd done, Gail Rose, our department chair, was awarded a grant from The Martha Holden Jennings Foundation of Cleveland to improve the self-esteem of the underachieving kids in the language arts/reading program at Shaker Heights Middle School. The goal was to improve our individual and collective skills for dealing with students' emotional baggage and learning difficulties. Among other professionals, Mrs. Rose invited a black psychologist, Dr. Willie Williams, to work with the language arts teachers and our most difficult classes once a week for six weeks.

Dr. Williams devised a program to build self-awareness and self-esteem. During one session, for example, he asked each small group to mull over these questions: In what sort of group do you *most* like to work? In what sort of group do you *least* like to work? What makes you happy? What makes you unhappy? Groups of three wrote answers to these questions and then discussed their responses among themselves (Figures 5-2 and 5-3 show how Jason and Nona responded).

Sounds great, right? But with the exception of one session in which Dr. Williams engaged the students in a values clarification exercise, my fifth-period class greeted him and his assistant with a wall of silence. (Selfishly, I have to admit that I was glad to see Dr. Williams struggle with this crowd.) After nearly every class, Dr. Williams

①I feel best when I am in a group of people that know what I am talking aboud and if they understand me.

②I feel worst when I am in a group that blocks me out or doesn't care what I say.

③I am happiest when I get to do what I want and when I get good grades and my day is going well.

④ I am most unhappy when my day has gone bad and I am allways getting into trouble. & when someone else like my little sister gets me into trouble

GROUP 3
Chemon
Nona
Jermain

Nona 11-89

FIG. 5-3 *Nona's Response*

and I talked about ways I could bring these kids together: give them choices, put them in charge, remain constant, set reasonable limits. Everything he suggested sounded perfect, just my style. But when I offered my fifth-period students choices, they shrugged. When I put them in charge, they balked. When I remained constant, I lost my spontaneity. When I set reasonable limits, they found ways to create a struggle and distract us all from learning.

Each day I approached fifth period with bated breath and throbbing temples. Would they saunter in late to class, showing me who was in charge? Would Jermaine or Chemon deliver an unspoken signal that would start the cold war that day? Would Laurelia shift into reverse? Would Nona and Natachia tell me with their eyes that what we were doing was pointless? I almost longed for the disruptions of my other eighth-grade class; at least they gave me something substantial to rail about.

I took time to explain to my fifth-period students in detail *what* I expected from them and myself and *why* I was trying to operate in this way. But the leaders of this group weren't buying. Like silent dissidents, they sat and stared, especially when I said, "I want to hear from you." Some almost glowered. Others, like Kim, Brandon, Jason, and DeSean, looked frightened because I wasn't protecting them from the likes of Jermaine and Chemon.

Even Dwight, who still wanted, I was sure, to become involved in books and learning, silently showed signs of pulling away. Although he disapproved of Jermaine's and Chemon's sabotage tactics, he didn't want to be one of the few good guys who—like Jason and, on the surface, DeSean—actually followed the teacher's lead. Dwight went underground with the enthusiasm he felt for our class; he even stopped popping in after school for books and a chat. When I said one day that I missed seeing him, Dwight shifted uncomfortably and said, "I'm not around much anymore."

"But you're still in our class!" I smiled. "Maybe you need a little space. I'll give it to you, Dwight."

To a few close colleagues, I dubbed this class "subterranean." (I wonder how this bunch described me!) Almost everything they did or said was quiet and below the surface. They signaled each other without saying a word. They would not raise their hands to talk because getting into groups and discussing ideas was playing ball with the enemy.

Tristin, Brandon, and Jason continued to tough it out, but with more reserve. Using well-honed body language, Jermaine and Laurelia mocked Tristin's awkward but regular attempts to contribute in class. I think they went for her jugular because Tristin's speech impediment reminded them of their own grave shortcomings. When kids ganged up on Tristin, even Brandon, normally a kind and lovely girl, abandoned her in favor of sitting near Nona. Natachia, meanwhile, worked diligently and successfully, but she had difficulty deciding what kind of friends she wanted and what attitude she wanted to project. Natachia and Nona took to laughing secretively as they came down the corridor to Room 226.

The reading race

Toward the end of September, I had a flash of inspiration: I'd stage a month-long reading race. I'd give points (I really *was* desperate) for reading recipes, obituaries, directions, advertisements, poetry, picture books, prose, plays, newspaper articles, comic strips, comic books—anything except pornography and textbooks.

At the start of the contest, I gave each student a colorful pocket folder and an inventory sheet. Each day they'd meet in teams to record the titles and number of pages they'd read. The team and the individual who had read the most and thus earned the greatest number of points between September 26 and October 26 would be my guest for dinner at a restaurant. I was willing to try *anything* to inspire reading and camaraderie. Figures 5-4 and 5-5 illustrate Jermaine's and Nona's reading inventories.

Each day, as they added to their inventory sheets by entering the titles of articles, interest among some of the students was almost palpable. But when I asked teams to meet to talk about the reading they'd done and enjoyed, they sat and looked at each other.

I purposely didn't require my readers to write or make oral book reports, answer questions about their reading, or indulge in any other kind of foolproof evaluation scheme. (Remember, I was trying to hook them on reading, not make them back away from it even further.) Instead, I inventoried kids' outside reading in several ways. When I gave everyone ten minutes or so to read at the beginning or end of occasional class periods, I watched them intently. The *real* readers read. A few, like Dwight, Brandon, Tristin, and even Natachia, who claimed to hate reading books, became

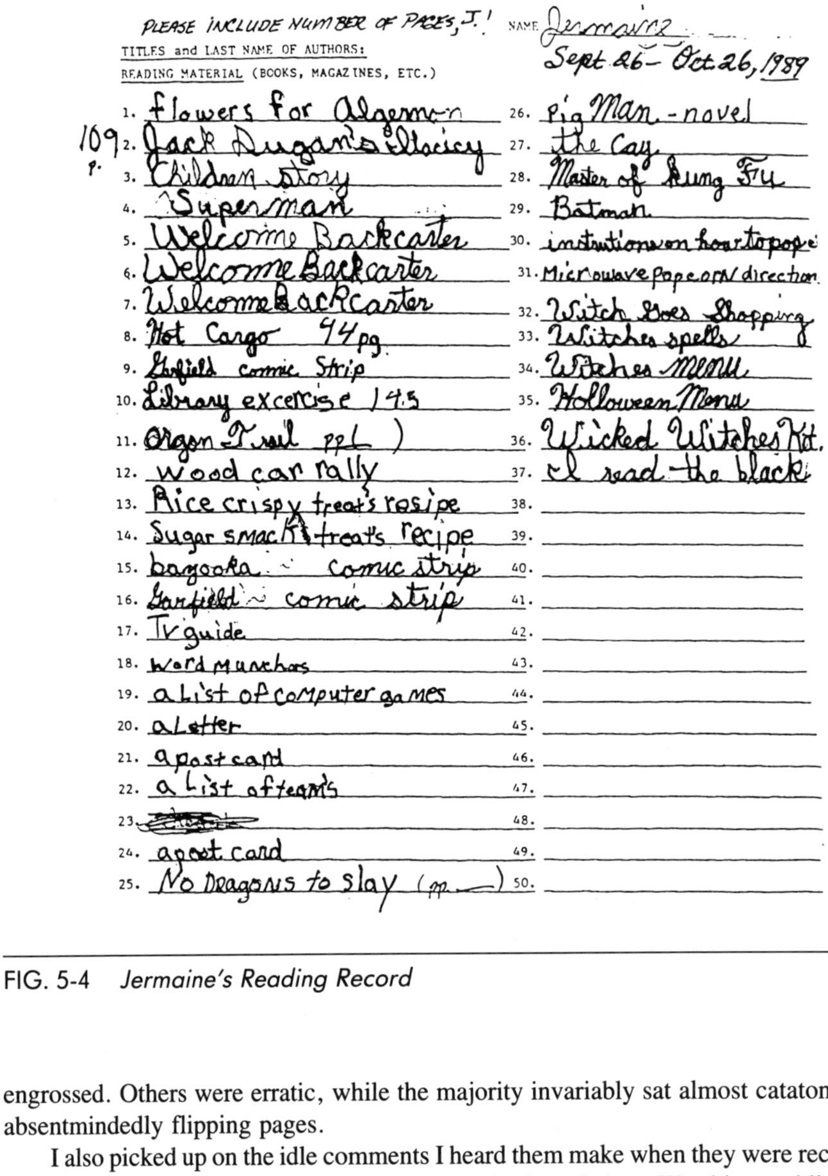

PLEASE INCLUDE NUMBER OF PAGES, J.! NAME Jermaine

TITLES and LAST NAME OF AUTHORS:

READING MATERIAL (BOOKS, MAGAZINES, ETC.) Sept 26– Oct. 26, 1989

1. flowers for Algernon	26. Pig Man.-novel
109 p. 2. Jack Dugan's Illacicy	27. the Cay
3. Children story	28. Master of Kung Fu
4. Superman	29. Batman
5. Welcome Backcarter	30. instructions on how to pop
6. Welcome Backcarter	31. Microwave popcorn direction
7. Welcome Backcarter	32. Witch Goes Shopping
8. Hot Cargo 74 pg.	33. Witches spells
9. Garfield comic Strip	34. Witches menu
10. Library excercise 145	35. Halloween Menu
11. Oregon Trail pp( )	36. Wicked Witches Kit.
12. wood car rally	37. I read the black
13. Rice crispy treat's resipe	38.
14. Sugar smack treat's recipe	39.
15. bazooka comic strip	40.
16. Garfield comic strip	41.
17. Tv guide	42.
18. Word munchers	43.
19. a List of computer games	44.
20. a Letter	45.
21. a post card	46.
22. a List of team's	47.
23.	48.
24. a post card	49.
25. No Dragons to slay (pp.)	50.

FIG. 5-4 *Jermaine's Reading Record*

engrossed. Others were erratic, while the majority invariably sat almost catatonically, absentmindedly flipping pages.

I also picked up on the idle comments I heard them make when they were recording titles from the previous day's reading at the beginning of class. Watching and listening carefully, as well as reading through their reading records, helped me tally their points and name the team and individual winners. Curiously, the kids never questioned my methods of assessing the validity of their reading records.

When the day came to announce the winners, anticipation ran surprisingly high. With much pomp and circumstance, I talked to the class about tallying their groups' points and noticing that certain students had achieved remarkable success. I passed out handwritten invitations congratulating the winners on their team's accomplishment (even though their winning didn't really reflect teamwork) and inviting them to accompany me to dinner on a mutually acceptable date. I also presented Dwight, the

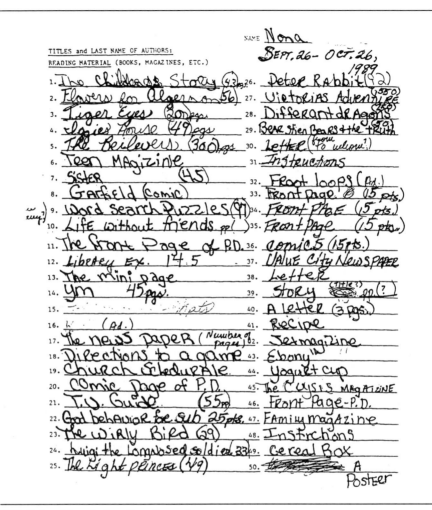

FIG. 5-5 *Nona's Reading Record*

individual who'd accumulated the most points, and Nona, the runner-up, with new hardback books.

Catch 22

Natachia, Dwight, Derrick, and Donald, the winning group, seemed very excited. But excitement didn't stop Derrick and Donald from challenging my authority and revealing their own ambivalence about winning first prize. My students, who had experienced mostly failure in school, were frightened by the thought of success. The day before our night on the town, the two boys sashayed into class late. Though their breaking school rules gave me cause to disqualify them from dinner out, I surveyed several adults whose judgment I trusted before I reneged. Renée Paige, one of our assistant principals, advised me to delay the treat, thereby giving the two gents an opportunity to square things with me. Bill Jarvie, the other assistant principal, suggested that I call the boys' parents and talk it out with them, thus leaving the decision in the parents' hands.

Dr. Williams advised me to fulfill my promise. Derrick and Donald had already won the contest, and Dr. Williams believed my using the Red Lobster restaurant as leverage in an unrelated incident wouldn't be fair; reneging on a promise would only confirm the students' mistrust of adults. But Dr. Williams did agree that I should telephone the boys and their parents.

When I called, I said that I had at first considered cancelling the boys' invitation to Red Lobster in view of their recent behavior. Both sets of parents cooperated, supporting any action I might decide to take; in fact, Donald's father encouraged me to withhold the privilege. I took this opportunity to explain that our *talking* openly about this situation, using language to clarify and crystallize it, was crucial to its resolution.

The Red Lobster evening was a success. Derrick thanked me profusely for the good dinner and noted my generosity in spending my money on him and his classmates. Donald actually talked during dinner, something he'd *never* done in class. Natachia and Dwight, whose voracious reading had carried Derrick and Donald in the contest, acknowledged that they'd read far more than usual because of the inducement.

The reading race had been successful for others, too. Nona, Brandon, and Tristin (who already was a voracious reader) had devoured reading material during that month. In a survey that I passed out to everyone, the kids wrote positive comments about the Reading Race, praising this opportunity to choose books on their own. Several wrote that they were reading faster, reading more, and enjoying the experience. Perhaps, I imagined, this was a new beginning.

To acknowledge everyone's reading, I threw a pizza party for the whole class. The kids sat and ate in utter silence. Until that day, I'd never been to a party where the guests didn't talk! The silence continued when I suggested that we stage another Reading Race. One kid responded: "One's enough!" I hoped my face hadn't revealed my feelings.

If at first you don't succeed

"We don't do nothin' in here," Jermaine said under his breath one day, just after many kids in the class had started on their rough drafts of personal stories.

"Wrong, Jermaine. *You* don't do nothin' in here!" I retorted. He and Chemon slouched down. Then, in customary fashion, the pair looked back over their shoulders to their receptive audience, who had aligned themselves with these two powerbrokers rather than chance standing up against them. Jermaine's hooded hazel eyes and Chemon's sneering smile told them what they, too, must do.

Chemon cut a wide swath when he proclaimed that he wanted to split from this boring class. As soon as this period was over, he said, he was going to meet with his counselor about switching to a section where they were really doing something. Instead of rejoicing about Chemon's plan, an action *I* should have taken weeks before, I felt vulnerable and numb with failure. That day I hit an all-time low. Then Liz Strickler, the supportive friend and colleague with whom I shared a classroom and daily conversation, asked to see my class list.

Colleague to the rescue

"If you're going to recover this class, you'll have to take strong action—and soon," Liz told me. "You'll have to separate the dynamic duo that is putting the kibosh on everything you try to do. Put the slow and the most resistant learners in harness; give them worksheets they can do within a class period. Siphon off the most able to do more challenging work. Don't worry so much about those kids who are resistant; it's likely too late for at least some of them. You've got to choose which ones you can really help. Good luck!"

During my free period that bleak November day, I went to the library and laid my plans. I would involve the most eager and able kids in reading *Hoops* by Walter Dean Myers. The larger group, the least able and most passive kids whom I'd put into harness, would, with my assistance, read Myers's *The Young Landlords,* an exceedingly easy book and one they might even enjoy. In writing, they would answer straightforward questions or do other short, prescribed activities that would be due by period's end.

Although this regimen was far from compatible with my usual way of running a class and quite against my democratic principles, it was a survival tactic. If *I* didn't survive, the class wouldn't survive. With renewed hope and vigor, I came into class the next day with two sets of books, *Hoops* and *The Young Landlords.* Calmly I explained what we would be doing, at least for a while. I was learning to spend adequate time explaining why we were doing such and such, rather than assuming that they'd made the connection. Their eyes and faces were immutable when I told them to meet in one of two groups.

To the "top" reading group (of course, I didn't label them as such), I handed out a lighthearted word puzzle (see the partially completed one in Figure 5-6) which I asked them to work on together, if they wished. While Dwight, Brandon, Tristin, Natachia, Laurelia, and later Nona quietly, almost happily, banded together to work on the puzzle, I introduced *The Young Landlords* to the "bottom" reading group, who sat around a table on the other side of the classroom.

"There were these kids who wanted to buy and restore an old and very dilapidated apartment building. . . . " I spoke quietly about Walter Dean Myers's book. Then I assigned only four or five pages of *silent* reading to Jermaine, Derrick, Chemon, DeSean, Jason, and Donald, allowing me to move back to the top reading group to launch *Hoops*.

For a few days, this plan seemed to work. The young people appeared to appreciate the predictability. The kids in the skills group worked their way through one sheet of thought questions, even though I knew that most of them hadn't really read even the few assigned pages of *The Young Landlords*. Several of the more able kids in this group seemed content to talk about or respond in writing to the literature, on their own and at their own pace. At least they felt they were accomplishing something.

Then Chemon and I got our wish: he was removed from my fifth-period class and placed in another section. (Liz's kind suggestion that I have Chemon removed from my class backfired. She inherited him for a few weeks until he landed in the Positive Behavior Class, the class for the most dysfunctional and disruptive kids in our school.) Things were looking up.

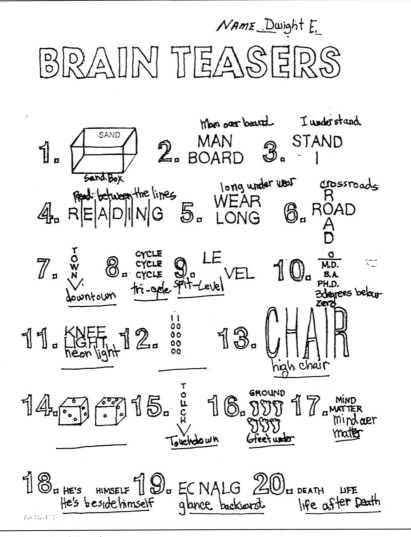

FIG. 5-6   *Word Puzzle*

"A bent spine is a bent mind"

At Gail Rose's invitation (and with her educational grant), Les Brown, a nationally acclaimed motivational expert, blew into town one snowy Saturday to spend the full day meeting with parents, kids, and teachers. Brown wowed everyone with his charisma and the powerful messages of his down-home stories. He spun off aphorisms at an impressive rate: "A bent spine is a bent mind." "If you're casual about life, you'll be a casualty." "If you worry, don't pray; if you pray, don't worry." "Tough times don't last; tough people do."

Brown exhibited a politician's charm, a comedian's timing, an orator's golden tongue, and a preacher's honor. He asked each of us to quickly jot ten personal goals. Then we were to collaborate with seven tablemates by sharing our dreams; they in turn

Les Brown, an internationally known motivational expert, inspires young people, their parents, and teachers.

were to affirm each of us publicly in pursuing those dreams. He required a mix of boys, girls, and adults to band together and become involved in small group activities, such as finding all the ways a simple belt might be used on a desert island. Electricity was in the air—especially when he unexpectedly handed out five-dollar bills to each member of the winning team.

"It's fun to see what a group of people can do together when they don't know that a reward will be offered!" Brown laughed impishly as he waved a handful of crisp new fives in the air.

A couple of my kids turned and winked at me knowingly because I had offered to put five A's in my grade book next to the name of anyone from my language arts classes who turned out for Les Brown on a Saturday. My enterprise had enticed twenty-six students from my five classes to attend the all-day session, nine from my nemesis class! Ten of the kids' parents accompanied their sons or daughters.

I felt proud when Dwight, Dameka, and Freddie stood up to speak their minds and hearts. Dwight's mother looked as if she would burst with pride when her son spoke passionately about his dreams for the future. At the end of the day, she came up to me and said, "I appreciate anyone who can inspire my child. Dwight talks about your class at home. I know how much he's enjoying it." Would wonders never cease!

I wasn't above hanging onto Les Brown's magic coattails for a day or two. At the least, I could milk the opportunity for informal classroom chatter about this appealing man come Monday. Les Brown's tape, which every participant in the Saturday seminar had received, would surely interest those who hadn't attended and affirm those who had, giving them status of the positive sort. The following Monday, Saturday's participants guardedly said a few words about the almost evangelical experience that had moved them more than they dared to reveal. While Les Brown's tape played, everyone listened to his insistent themes: Work on liking yourself. Make your own decisions after considering many possibilities. Stop blaming other people for your problems. Start investing in yourself by making positive changes in your life. The class listened intently, but they did not respond; they sat.

Batman in the bargain

That was our all-time high, but we couldn't sustain it. Between Thanksgiving and our winter holiday, the classroom atmosphere once again declined. The students looked and acted lethargic and uninvolved—until a week before school was to let out in December, when Laurelia announced that her uncle had brought her the movie *Batman*.

"Oh, Mrs. Krogness, please, can we see Batman right before we go home for the holidays?" Laurelia cooed. Many others jumped on the bandwagon. Showing more intensity and energy than usual, they alternately begged and coerced me.

"You're always telling us that *everything* relates to language and literature, so why *can't* we see Batman?" Natachia protested, more vigorously and persuasively than she had all year.

Librarian Pat Fagel reminded me that I could tie the gods and goddesses of Mount Olympus to this mini-lesson, and thus justify my decision to my kids, any doubtful parents, and most of all to myself. It was December, and I was exhausted, but that wasn't the main reason I agreed to show *Batman*. I felt some distant hope that showing the film would infuse them with energy. Better still, I could use *Batman* as collateral. If they were going to deal, so was I. And I knew exactly where I wanted to start.

Sitting down at the bargaining table

When Peter Lawson Jones, a successful black lawyer and city councilman whose ebullience had always captivated my classes, came to my fifth-period class shortly after Les Brown's visit, he encountered dead silence. When he asked the students to talk about their heroes, they stared glumly; many slouched uncomfortably in their chairs. Peter wasn't accustomed to a hostile crowd, and I was furious with my kids and mortified at their passivity, which seemed to reflect on me. Yet, once again, *I* was assuming too much of the responsibility, *their* responsibility! I took stock again. Was Peter out of their reach? Inaccessible? Overwhelming because of his obvious intelligence, professionalism, and accomplishments? I decided that his *joie de vivre* was simply too much for them. Also, many of these kids had just witnessed Les Brown, who, like many of them but unlike Peter, had come up the hard way and had not succeeded in school.

"Peter what's-his-name is boring," Nona dared to say within earshot.

"I like Les Brown better." Even Brandon, whose sweetness and good manners distinguished her, spoke out vehemently.

But in customary fashion, I insisted that everyone write thank-you letters to Peter. In fact, if these kids wanted to see *Batman* in the library the next day, they would have to write the letters on their own time, not during class, and the letters would have to follow the criteria I'd printed out for them: (1) thank Mr. Peter Lawson Jones for taking time to visit our class; (2) tell him what you observed, learned, or liked; (3) if you want, share with him dreams or goals that you have for your future. The printed instructions also included a model of a friendly letter. At the top of the directions, in large letters, I'd added: LETTER DUE TOMORROW, DECEMBER 18. In compliance with our deal about *Batman,* they agreed to fulfill this obligation.

Roll call

The next day, as the students filed into the library to watch the video, I stood by the door to collect their thank-you letters. DeSean and Dwight smiled as they entered the library. "Mrs. Krogness, DeSean and I will do our letters to Mr. Jones tonight and give them to you tomorrow." Dwight was the spokesman for the two. I shook my head, indicating that their plan wouldn't fly. The rest of the kids filed in. More than half the class hadn't prepared their letters, yet apparently they fully intended to sit down and see the first of three segments of the film.

Not rising to their bait, I feigned calmness and held up the slim sheaf of letters I'd collected. I said: "As you can see, only a few of you wrote thank-you letters to our guest speaker, Peter Lawson Jones." I waited quietly.

But before I had the opportunity to speak further, Dwight looked up from the letter to Peter Jones that he'd already begun composing and yelled out: "You expect too much from a *few* of us! You seem to think that *everything* revolves around this language arts class." The room was still. All eyes were on Dwight, boy wonder, who had the audacity to shout at the teacher. Dwight continued his diatribe.

"I have an English essay to finish, tests to take, and a bunch of other work to do—*all* before vacation starts," Dwight bellowed. Although his voice was strident, it eventually trailed off into a whisper. The room was like a tomb.

For a change, I kept my cool and remained the adult in charge of this class— this group of wayward, frightened teenagers. Rather than pounce on Dwight for insolent behavior, I seized upon his accusation and pulled off a dramatic roll call, Dorothy Heathcote fashion, that forced everyone's hand, yet put the kids in charge. Quietly I surveyed the scene. Quietly, in measured but not constricted tones, I spoke.

"Dwight says that I expect too much from a few of you. I'm wondering what *your* feelings are."

"Natachia, do you feel that my expectations of you are too high?" Natachia shook her head.

"Nona, do I expect too much from you? Jason, how about you?" I moved through the ranks, looking squarely at each student while quietly asking if she or he considered my expectations too high.

Only Derrick and Jermaine said I expected too much from them. When Jermaine took this opportunity to tell me again how boring our class was, I listened to his accusation and made no reply. I waited before I spoke again. "Is there anyone in here who feels that my expectations for her or him are too *low*?" No one made a sound, but some shook their heads no.

"Now about the letters. Everyone here knew that if you did not complete a thank-you letter to Peter Lawson Jones, one that was personal, specific, and well developed, you would automatically see me after school today. I made this clear yesterday, and you all agreed." By this time about fifteen minutes of class were left. I knew I'd made my point, so I showed the beginning of *Batman.*

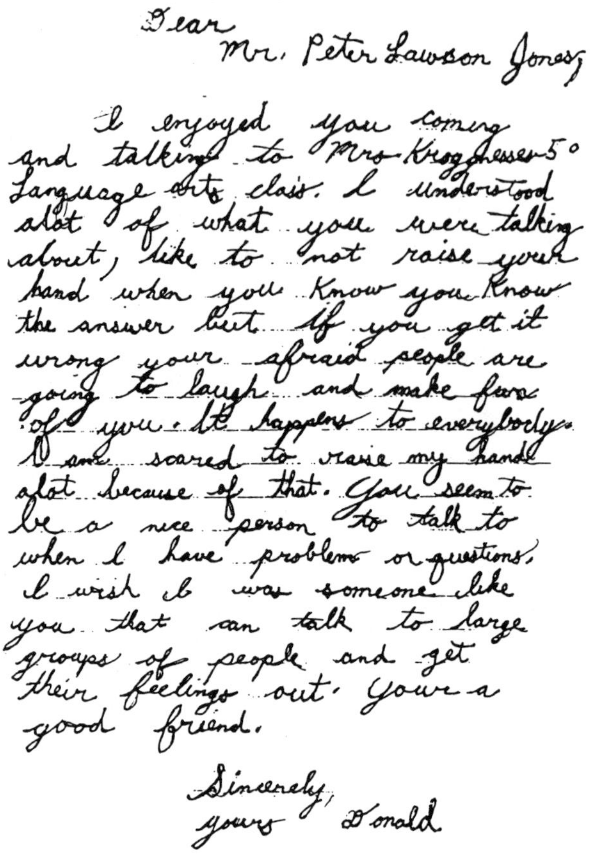

Dear
Mr. Peter Lawson Jones,

I enjoyed you coming and talking to Mrs. Krogesser's Language Arts class. I understood alot of what you were talking about, like to not raise your hand when you know you know the answer but. If you get it wrong your afraid people are going to laugh and make fun of you. It happens to everybody. I am scared to raise my hand alot because of that. You seem to be a nice person to talk to when I have problems or questions. I wish I was someone like you that can talk to large groups of people and get their feelings out. Youre a good friend.

Sincerely,
yours Donald

FIG. 5-7   *Donald's Letter*

In the end, all but one student came in after school that afternoon and wrote letters to Peter—not merely good letters but splendid letters that reflected genuine warmth, sadness, and beauty. It was his letter to Peter Lawson Jones that signaled Donald's blossoming (see Figure 5-7).

This episode had seemed like an unending roller coaster ride. Mercifully, *Batman* held their rapt attention for the three days immediately before winter holiday in December. Before any vacation, I steel myself against students' need to separate, which often makes them downright nasty. I figured this group of kids would skulk out of class on the last day without saying a word. Wrong! But then, this gang had kept me off balance all year. Several, like Derrick, warmly wished me a happy holiday season. Donald offered me an awkward, over-the-shoulder smile and a muffled holiday greeting as he loped out of the A.V. room. Dwight, who had engaged in animated conversations with me about all manner of subjects since the blow-up and before the last installment of *Batman,* wished me a happy vacation. Laurelia, who the previous day had rolled her eyes disapprovingly, carefully waited until the crowd had left, then handed me a lovely Christmas card on which she'd written a personal message.

Miracles and misgivings

Before I was ready, the new year brought the students back to school looking glum. "If a class hasn't come together by the end of first semester, there's not much chance that it will," I told fellow teacher, Ruth Blair. She empathized, but encouraged me by saying that I'd managed with other tough classes, and that maybe this one would just take longer to pull together.

"One thing about middle school kids," Ruth said, "they surprise you. Things change, too. Right now, what *was* my best class is my worst."

"*Nothing* remains static—not even the most horrendous difficulty," Sara Wasserman, art therapist, said, smiling her lovely smile. "Stand back and gain some emotional distance from these kids. By trying too hard and wanting too much to engage them, you're making yourself vulnerable," my husband, John, told me warmly.

I'd already gone through the stages: denying the problem, stewing in guilt, trying to bargain, letting off steam, engaging in self-examination. Now I recognized that this group, with whom I'd gotten off to a bad start, probably was frightened of me and my expectations; they'd likely gone underground to protect themselves. They had too little self-confidence to try what I wanted, and they buckled under the strain of negative forces within their own ranks.

Meanwhile, I had lost *my* confidence as the adult to whom they were supposed to look for stability and direction. I was too bent on pleasing them. I had lost my bearings, my security, and thus my perspective. One thing I did have, though: an unusual supply of tenacity. I kept hearing Esther's words: "*Stick* with them, Mary. They'll come around one of these days."

Fifth period and I were *stuck* with each other for a whole semester more.

The balance shifts

Like the tectonic plates that form the earth's crust, the dynamics of a class can change subtly or suddenly. Now that Chemon was gone, his pal Jermaine, a very savvy kid who lacked security, was free to become cooperative.

Out of the blue, and out of earshot of his classmates, Jermaine asked, "Mrs. K., do you think we could do some drama today?"

I didn't question why Jermaine wanted to do improvisation, something I'd tried unsuccessfully with this class from the start. I merely responded. "Fine, Jermaine. Why don't you lead us in improvisation?" He agreed. He said that he'd like to do "Pivotal Person," a theater game that I didn't use merely as a warm-up, but as a way to play out real situations.

Two people, sitting opposite each other, engage in a conversation that revolves around the pivotal person, who remains a constant character: a bank teller, a school counselor, a lawyer, a rock star, or any other character who has the power to engage a range of people. Members of the audience individually intervene (when they judge the timing is right), take the chair opposite the pivotal person, and carry on an impromptu dialogue with him.

Jermaine fondly remembered playing this improvisation game when he was in my seventh-grade class. He had played the part of a worker at the welfare office, where he'd counseled indigent people about their right to collect welfare money. So, much to the delight of the eighth-grade class, Jermaine announced that he would play the lead in this drama, the "welfare man."

He instructed everyone to form a large circle, and then he explained the game. Not surprisingly, they followed Jermaine's lead. They laughed admiringly at his easy-does-it style and perfect timing. I watched and waited until I found the right moment to get into the act. I sat down opposite Jermaine to play an older woman, a former school teacher of Jermaine's who had fallen on hard times and was now on the dole.

"Don't you remember me?" I asked Jermaine, the welfare officer. "You were once my student. Surely you remember me!" I pleaded with him: "Can't you do *me* a favor?"

I was already getting in a few licks in this safe and controlled setting. Jermaine played his role, the fellow in control, to the hilt, but never did he overdo it. He merely thumbed through my folder and asked me, as he'd already asked other welfare clients, probing questions about my need to receive a welfare check.

Jermaine's welfare improvisation engaged everyone. The next pivotal person was a psychiatrist, played by Jason. Erik, who was Jason's first client, got right into the act by saying that he had a cigar-smoking dog whom he loved, but the beast ate him and his family out of house and home. Erik had never been so free during our class. The audience laughed appreciatively at his witty improv. Jason engaged several more kids in the drama.

Jermaine's appointment with the psychiatrist proved to be very interesting, indeed. This is how he began: "There's this strange woman. She carries a pink and blue plastic lunch box for a purse." Jermaine turned and looked slyly at me, for of course I was the strange woman. "She pushed me out the window!" Again he looked at me. I couldn't miss this opportunity. I quickly jumped to my feet to intervene, taking Jermaine's place.

"Doctor, I saw this guy coming out of your office. *He's* the fellow who's been harassing me and accusing me of pushing him out of a window!" I shouted.

Suddenly Jermaine barged into the psychiatrist's office, pointed to me and yelled: "*She's* the one! *She's* the strange woman who carries the pink and blue lunch box! *She's* the one who pushed me out the window!"

I joined Jermaine "on stage." "Since we're talking about pushing . . ." I paused and looked around at the attentive audience.

"Just a minute here! You both will have to stop shouting. I won't have you acting like this in *my* office," Jason, the psychiatrist, shouted above Jermaine's and my voices.

"*She's* the one. *She's* the one who pushed me!" Jermaine persisted.

"Well, sir," I yelled, "this guy has pushed me very close to the edge, and . . ." At that moment, I took the liberty that one has *only* in an improvised dramatic situation: I not so gently shoved Jermaine backwards. The audience laughed, applauded, and cheered. Jermaine and I shook hands and sat down, both of us smiling!

Turning point

The improv proved a major turning point for the class and me. Jermaine had lifted the ban on talking in class. In a free but structured setting, Jermaine and I had played out our feelings of frustration and anger. Esther had been right about sticking with this enigmatic class.

That evening I wrote a letter to James Thornton, artistic director of our school system's remarkable theater department, on behalf of Jermaine and several other young people who not only expressed genuine pleasure in drama, but showed exceptional talent. Perhaps involvement in theater, as in athletics, would help Jermaine focus his life and redirect his energy. Several months later, Jermaine—without any prompting from me—included a theater class in his new ninth-grade schedule. I fantasized that this Spike Lee look-alike might just have a chance to pull his life together.

Along about March, after a highly successful Shakespeare experience that captured even passive kids like Derrick, we started to write again. First we wrote thank-you letters to Christy and Erik, the two young Shakespeare actors who had visited our class. Then we embarked on fable writing. In preparation, I dragged in armloads of fables by Aesop and others. I told stories that appealed because they were short and manageable; they challenged even the best writers to stay focused. As a class we brainstormed forty or fifty human qualities that one could hang a short story on.

And this is what happened. Nona, who was learning to assert herself, said, "I don't want to write a fable!"

"But that's what we're going to be doing," I said matter-of-factly.

"I don't *want* to write a fable," Nona insisted.

I decided to push. "What *do* you want to write, Nona?"

"A play," she replied.

"A play, huh?" I remembered that in Nona's letter of intention, written during that first week of eighth grade, she'd declared her interest in writing a play.

"What do you want to write a play about?" I asked.

"About a girl in this big family who gets stuck doing all the housework and never seems to have any fun," she said.

"Well, Nona, it looks like you ought to get started on that play right away." I smiled because for months I'd been trying to help Nona bust loose from her own fear and, I suspected, depression. Now I asked, "What do the rest of you want to do?" I tried not to let even a trace of my excitement show, although I was certain that every pore on my body was exuding delight.

Laurelia wanted to work on a play, too. Hers would be a teen romance, a love triangle. Brandon wanted to work on a fairy tale, Tristin on a story in diary form. One day after school, Dwight brought in a story that he'd started working on in the seventh grade, a fantasy story about a young hero, Quick Silver, who wants to take charge of his life and grow up to be someone. Dwight said that he wanted to continue working on his novella. His friend Erik opted to write a series of short stories about Champ, his dog and best friend. Natachia decided to write a fable with a modern twist. Jason, DeSean, Jermaine, and Derrick asked if they could create a little work center so that they might collaborate in writing funny fables. Donald, too, wanted to write a fable, but apart from the boys who wanted to collaborate.

I was careful not to speak of my pleasure with this newfound initiative. Using reverse psychology with Nona—insisting that she write a fable because that's what we were doing—had the positive effect I'd hoped for during the long months of first semester. But I feared that if they knew how happy I was, they'd scotch their plans for independence and retreat into their old mode. If they knew, they didn't acknowledge it.

The slow ascent

Indeed, Nona did write a play (an excerpt of which is in Chapter 10), though she stubbornly continued to claim that play writing was boring. Laurelia worked away on her play, too, an adolescent romance replete with seductions and rebuffs. Brandon and Tristin worked on their chosen writing, as did Dwight. When Erik was at school (he missed more than fifty days that year), he worked on several engaging pieces about Champ, which unfortunately he took out of the classroom and then misplaced.

Quietly, Natachia wrote and revised a modern-day fable. Jason, DeSean, Jermaine, and Derrick laughed and talked while they unabashedly enjoyed using bad words such as *damn* and *piss off* in their fables (words that paled in comparison to the ones I'd heard some of these guys use in everyday spoken language). Their bawdy little fables about "that damn dog" and the bear "that peeves his friends off" amused them.

Sensing my pleasure and knowing exactly which buttons to push, Jermaine asked, "Hey, Mrs. K., when are you going to bring in that good cheese and egg pie that you made for us last year? You could bring in those good brownies, too," he said. I shrugged noncommittally. "How *does* that boy know what a soft touch I am?" I wondered.

As all these exciting things were happening, only Donald sat and sat. Even after he and I talked about his plans for writing a fable, he wrote a sparse, lifeless piece (see Figure 5-8). Here was a boy who walked alone from one class to the next, who refused to eat lunch in the cafeteria and roamed the halls during the lunch hour, who sat apart from others in our class, who never uttered a word. He seemed ready to explode from anger and loneliness. What could jar this boy loose without unraveling him?

One day when most kids were writing and talking animatedly, Donald leaned back in his chair and let out a yawn that sounded almost like a lion's roar. He smiled. A few kids turned to notice where this noise had come from.

"Oh, so that's why I gave you a D on your interim report card!" My words shot out before I could stop them. Donald's face stiffened. I won't forget the hurt registered in his eyes. Some kids stopped working to look around and laugh. I walked back to where Donald was sitting and said very quietly, "I'm sorry, Donald. What I just said is terrible—unforgivable." Donald gazed out the window until the bell rang and then got up more quickly than usual and lumbered out the door.

The next day I began the class with a public apology to Donald. Dwight muttered something about Donald deserving my mean remark because "he doesn't do nothing anyhow." That evening I called Donald's parents and apologized to them, too. Not only were Donald's mother and father appreciative of my apology; they understood my frustration. Then I gave Donald simple pencil and paper activities rather than insisting that he get cracking on the listless fable in his writing spiral.

But one day, not long after I'd made that ghastly remark, Donald began to work almost feverishly (for him) on his meager little fable about Bear and Lion. He turned it into the best piece that he had written (see Figure 5-9), and then he wrote another little fable about Brutus, a cowardly dog who is afraid of cats. These animated fables came complete with dialogue and stories that held together nicely, especially after Donald *voluntarily* came in after school for a writing conference. I read them aloud to the class, and I made copies for Donald's family, his L.D. teacher, Gloria Fried, and the assistant principal, Bill Jarvie, one of Donald's friends. Donald enjoyed many moments of glory as a result of his effort.

Draft #1   Donald   Mar 7, 1990

This is a story about
a bear and a lion.
They are both tough and
strong animals. One day
the got angry at each other
they wanted to see who was the strongest
The both got into a
fight and they both
really hurt each other.
They both went away.
The next day they saw
Each other and they said
lets fight.

Soon after that they
approached each other and
made up and the live
Because it wasn't write
Happily ever after.

THE End
Donald

FIG. 5-8   *Donald's First Draft*

Final Draft

Donald   april 5, 1990

This story is about a bear and a lion. They were both tough and strong animals. One day they got angry at each other because they wanted to prove who was the toughest. The lion said, "I am king and I am the strongest."

The bear said "I am more powerful and bigger". They got angry and went home. The next day they met each other again and the lion said "We will call all the other animals in the forest to come watch and witness who is the strongest."

The bear said, "fine We will meet here at Noon tommorrow. I can't wait."

That night the bear and the lion thought to themselves. They both thought that they could both be the strongest animals and be best friends but they already made a bet and neither one wanted to chicken out. Until the time finally came and all the other animals from the forest gathered around in a big circle. The lion and the bear approached each other. They said nothing, all they had were angry looks on their faces. They walked around for a long time, somebody had to make a move. The bear finally charged at lion and

I love this detail!

FIG. 5-9   *Donald's Finished Fable*

the lion jumped back with a loud roar. The lion then jumped on the bear racking into claws into its back. Then the bear flipped the lion off its back in to the ground. The bear then jumped on the lion and said "I am the toughest." The lion then got angry and hit him on the face as hard as he could.

They were both tired. They both said to each other we don't have to do this, lets just be friends. The other animals of the forest agreed. Both the lion and the bear shook paws and made up. From that day on they played together and did all kinds of fun things like friends should do.

The End
by Donald

FIG. 5-9 *Continued*

A movable feast

Yes, this class was coming around. I was relaxing, too, and feeling utterly magnanimous at our coming together. One day late in March, right before spring break, I surprised the class by bringing in four homemade quiches, a big salad, brownies, and a jug of cider. During fourth period, when the room was empty, I pulled together several tables, threw on a paper cloth and set out paper plates, cups, and napkins.

When the fifth-period bell rang, the kids quietly walked into class. "What do I smell?" Dwight smiled.

"This class is like an eating club," Tristin remarked. "We just had Caesar salad on the Ides of March."

"But what *are* they?" Derrick asked, pointing to the quiches.

"They're called quiche, and they taste like an omelette, only better," I said.

"What's this all for?" Nona wondered.

The group gathered around the table while I explained the unexpected treat and cut wedges of quiche loaded with red peppers, parsley, mushrooms, bacon, onion, and various cheeses. I tossed the salad, poured the cider, and cut big brownies.

"This is my treat to you because you're engaging in learning. *You're* taking the lead, now. *You're* making important decisions; *you're* taking charge of your work and your lives. I imagine that you're feeling better about this class, too. I know I am."

It was as if the locusts had passed through. All of them except Jermaine ate, asked for seconds and even thirds, and talked happily. Jermaine was sitting down in ATS (Alternative to Suspension) because he'd cut after-school detention; he'd racked up nearly thirty as a result of a grand array of misdemeanors in many of his classes. Ironically, it was Jermaine who'd inquired about my bringing a quiche surprise to our class as I'd done for the class he'd been in the previous year. How often my kids missed out on the necessities as well as the pleasures of life.

How we all had changed

I wouldn't dream of saying that from the day Jermaine lifted the ban on silence, we all lived happily ever after. Of course we had setbacks. But looking at the big picture, we'd come a long way. All of us had made progress in our ability to work together amicably and productively, and the students had made good academic progress as well. Nona, who had often looked depressed, was asserting herself now and blaming others less often. She'd become a solid student and by year's end was just beginning to smile and voice her own opinions.

Laurelia, who might have made excellent academic progress had she not been so fearful of success, held her own but guarded against distinguishing herself academically or creatively. (For instance, Laurelia continued to balk at writing poetry even though I'd used her poem, published in *Language Arts* several years earlier, as a fine example of poetry.) Brandon opened up more and gained confidence. She could think more deeply and critically about literature and write with more feeling.

Tristin, who constantly worked to overcome her learning disabilities, had made lovely strides in feeling better and asserting herself without radiating anxiety. Clearly, Tristin aimed to achieve good grades in school, and she regularly accomplished this goal.

Although Derrick continued to do everything in slow motion, he showed more interest and involved himself more than he had during first semester. The visit of the young Shakespeare actors inspired him; unabashedly, Derrick spoke of this experience as the highlight. When it came time for final projects, Derrick thought of creating a picture book in which he would chart and illustrate the usual day of a typical teenager, and he got off to a splendid start. But he stored the rough draft in a friend's locker on the day that Dr. Peterjohn announced locker clean-out. Derrick's promising work was inadvertently trashed along with his friend's miscellany. I doubt the loss was accidental; such an act of destruction represents years of low self-esteem.

Jermaine, who was capable but not strong enough to fight the odds of a destructive life, behaved more acceptably by spring than he had earlier. But most of his written work showed a decline from the previous year. Knowing how and when to use simple conventions such as *an* and *and* escaped him.

Donald, though certainly still a loner and mute on most counts, had made strides in asserting himself, writing, and relating to people on a very limited basis. One day he said, "I'm asking three people to sign their names and telephone numbers on this job application. I picked three people who would say nice things about me." I felt happy that he'd been willing to set aside that unconscionable remark I'd made to him a few months earlier.

DeSean made good progress in his writing, finishing friendly letters, fables, and a poem. But he still resisted reading, and read as little as possible. Jason's verbal skill strikingly—even shockingly—outweighed his written skill. He avoided reading to the very end.

And enigmatic Erik, who almost always greeted me unctuously and who was undoubtedly very bright, carried such an assortment of complex emotional baggage that it was difficult to know and impossible to measure how much academic progress he had made. When I tried helping him study for science tests after school, he would gaze into the distance and merely go through the motions. Then he'd miss school the next day and, of course, miss the science test. But emotionally, Erik was far more comfortable. By year's end, he talked openly in class rather than sitting stone-faced, his light brown eyes shifting uneasily. When he was at school, he wrote nicely. Sadly, his series of short stories, which he'd decided to write in a spiral notebook other than the one he kept in the classroom, somehow got lost.

Holding their own

One May day I announced, "My husband, John, will be coming to class to take photographs for the book I'll be writing when I take a leave of absence next year from Shaker Middle School." At last, I felt safe saying that I was taking a sabbatical without fear of their silently (or not so silently) cheering.

"You're not coming back to teach at SMS?" Derrick asked.

"I won't be here anyway, so it won't matter." Dwight spoke quietly.

"You're writing a book? Will I be in it?" Jermaine called out.

"You'll be in it, Jermaine. And so will the rest of you."

"What's this book going to be about?" Dwight asked. He'd actually dared to ask me a personal question publicly.

"It's going to be about all of us, how we have learned to work together and use language to learn. I want to give each of you a contract and get your and your parents' permission to use samples of your writing—plays, letters, stories, and poems—in this book for middle school teachers."

"How much will I get paid for letting you use all my poetry and those dope fables I wrote?" Jermaine laughed.

"You mean royalties?" I laughed, too. "Your payment will be having your original work and your first name published in a best-seller!"

"If it's going to be a best-seller, will they make a movie out of it?" DeSean, who had opened up through improvisational drama, was trying out his humor in what was now a safe setting.

"Anyhow, what would you guys like to be doing when Mr. Krogness comes to class tomorrow to take pictures?"

"Drama," they chorused.

"What do you want to build a drama on?" I asked.

They all thought a moment. "Let's have a court scene," Tristin suggested. "How about a murder about a rich guy who owns a business?"

When at long last a classroom community develops.

"Yeah, a court scene. Let's make a drama about a murder—where a guy gets framed," Jermaine said. "I'll be the guy who gets framed. That's why I get into so much trouble. I always get framed."

"I'd like to be the prosecutor," Dwight offered.

"I would, too," Erik said.

"*If* you're in school, we'll take turns playing the prosecutor," Dwight chided his friend.

"I'll play the judge and bang—what's that thing called?" Derrick drawled.

"A gavel," answered Jason, who enjoyed using his good vocabulary.

"And I'll pay you off," Jermaine laughed.

"What about us girls?" Nona called out indignantly.

"What *about* you?" Erik challenged Nona.

"I'll play a witness," Brandon said. "Maybe I'll play Jermaine's girlfriend and be his alibi."

"And I'll be the daughter of the guy who gets murdered," Tristin said. "Maybe someone has murdered him for his money."

"The bell's about to ring. I hope you'll come in on time ready to start playing this drama."

And that they did, for not one but *three* class periods. In Heathcote fashion, the students first sat in a circle and planned their next scene, exchanged roles, revised the plot; then they played it out seriously until someone muddled the story by introducing evidence that contradicted what had already been introduced or made a surprising or witty comment. The rather complex drama was laced with laughter and brief but lighthearted arguments. Various students led planning discussions and played major roles, while others sat on the sidelines and prompted more willing and confident actors to get into the act. I sat quietly in the circle, almost a bystander, deferring to them. John unobtrusively moved about the classroom taking pictures.

Late in May, Sara Wasserman, art therapist, came in to talk about leaving the Middle School in preparation for the separation they would face when school let out in just a few weeks.

Moving around the circle of eighth graders about to be graduated, she asked, "What word describes the emotion you're feeling right now? Think about words that might describe the feeling."

Nona still relied on the word *bored,* while others used such words as *excitable, peaceful,* and *happy.* Predictably nobody in this class described himself or herself as being *frightened, sad, scared, tense, anxious* or any of the words that might characterize young people preparing to leave all they've known for two years and go to the big and unknown place called Shaker Heights High School. So Sara talked about natural concerns they'd probably have and doubts and anxiety they'd likely feel about leaving or separating.

When Sara asked my students to take a deep breath, inhaling peace and serenity, and then exhaling all tension, sadness, anger, and stress, they did so willingly. Then she asked them to close their eyes and relax while she took them on a journey along a clear river, up, up, up a steep mountain where they could look out. I realized that a couple of them had fallen asleep. When it came time to draw what they'd seen and experienced, many just wanted to sit and relax, to bask in the peace of this quiet moment before the bell rang.

All's well that ends well?

This fairy tale was not heading for a happy ending. During the last week of school, my kids were restless. To prepare for ending the year, many were distancing themselves again. Yet they wanted to celebrate. I wasn't sure *what* exactly, because lately they'd been drifting back to their old ways of behaving.

"Can we have a party?"

"Why not?" I answered. "You decide who'll be in charge and who'll bring cups, chips, pop."

Michael and Angelo, two former students of mine who were now high school sophomores, had asked to meet with my eighth graders to fill them in on the ways of the *seasoned* people my kids would soon meet. While Mike and Ange talked and answered an array of questions—about everything from high school teachers to Saturday School (detention for very serious misdemeanors), from studying to sports—I started getting ready for our end-of-school celebration. As I too quickly opened the first very warm liter bottle of pop, the thing exploded. The sticky stuff ran down my face and my glasses. My class—this quiet bunch of students—laughed out of control and applauded while I mopped my brow. "Well, this is the most action I've gotten from you for at least half of this school year," I muttered.

The next day, the last full day of school, they dragged into class, many looking and behaving as they had during those recalcitrant days of first semester. Even the obedient ones whined and groused about all the mean teachers in this awful place that they were only too glad to leave. They signed each other's yearbooks, and when the bell rang, everyone got up and left, saying scarcely a word.

"Good-bye. I'll see you around. And good luck." My words trailed off.

When they all had left Room 226 for the last time, I didn't indulge in feeling sorry for myself, even though I felt sad that our last day together had been so distant. I knew they needed to leave without looking back. Growing up is so hard—even for someone who is fifty years old!

I occupied myself by picking up scraps of paper, broken pencil stubs lying on the floor, and one writing spiral that had been left behind: Jermaine's. And I thought, "Planting seeds sure is hard work. I guess I'll just have to wait for rain."

SIX

Speaking Up
At the Heart of It All

Talk is not cheap

In my classroom, talk was *not* cheap! From the first day of school, I expected all my students to talk, for I firmly believe that the classroom is an ideal place for oral exchange. Although talking has always been central to every culture, the American classroom—especially the secondary school classroom—continues to be a strangely quiet place. The appalling statistics show that American students spend, on average, three hours of a five-hour school day sitting passively while their *teachers* talk.

My students and I started the school year by learning how to talk with one another. The long, difficult process of limbering up our minds and loosening our tongues eventually paid great dividends. During the first week of school we met in pairs to collect bits and pieces of information about each other and then report our findings to the class. More than a few students balked at this experience, fooling away the five or so minutes they were supposed to spend asking the questions we'd developed. Meager, superficial oral reports about peers' food preferences and favorite colors or weak attempts at slapstick comedy usually resulted.

But since I aimed to engage all of my students in daily classroom conversations, I pressed on. "I want to hear from you. I want to know your thoughts and feelings," I often said. That wouldn't seem to be a tall order for adolescents who spent many of their waking hours talking to their friends. For many resistant learners, however, the idea of talking *in class*—talking to learn—was daunting. Often my questions were greeted with an uncomfortable silence or sullen remarks. Through body language and under-the-breath comments, the students let me know that they hadn't come to class *just* to talk; they were in school to do *real* work.

The reason for my students' resistance to talking in class was simple: lack of experience. They had learned to rely on the teacher's words or prescribed pencil and paper work; they'd had little practice in trying on ideas publicly or exchanging insights with their peers. Consequently, many of them had not learned to value their own ideas or those of their classmates.

To change this attitude, I needed leadership, perseverance, and knowledge of language learning. I designed apparently casual conversations that I imagined would engage most students and created exercises that provided an incentive and a structure within which to talk. Class time offered ample and varied opportunities for students to practice conversing about all manner of subjects, but especially about their feelings and insights on literature and writing. Talking is the most important means of developing classroom camaraderie and trust, two essentials for an open forum.

The art of the matter

To free my students from their terrible anxiety about talking in school, I enlisted the help of my great friend and colleague, Sara Wasserman, a registered art therapist from the Shaker Heights Youth Center. Sara's specialty—using art to open kids up—became the first step of the process. During our sessions, she helped us deal with personal issues such as building self-esteem, developing and respecting people's boundaries, setting goals, and dreaming dreams.

First, Sara would ask us to breathe.

"Breathe deeply, then exhale all of the tension that you feel; let the anger, anxiety, and fear go."

"Now, slowly breathe in a peaceful feeling. Let go of the difficulties and fears that you've stored. Inhale good thoughts about yourself and the others around you."

Then Sara would ask us to close our eyes, let our bodies fall slack, and put our heads down on the tables while she took us on a mystical journey. Her voice soft, almost like a lullaby, she'd guide us along a pure and beautiful river, lead us up a craggy mountain path, and ask us to look out over the vast world from a new perspective. Although Sara's stories varied from class to class, all were archetypal and therefore symbolic. She asked us to draw what we had felt during our journey, expressing the images and emotions through art rather than words.

Again, some students expressed anxiety at what they believed they could not do: they weren't good artists; they couldn't draw a river or a mountain. Sara reassured them that their drawings didn't have to be representational. She wanted them to feel free to draw shapes, experiment with colors, use the pastels freely and without concern. Although many were determined to make their drawings representational, others were happy to shade and swirl colors over the blank sheets of paper until they melted together and swept from side to side.

Then we made a circle with our chairs and Sara moved around it, asking each student to talk about his or her picture. Sara would both comment on the student's insights and add her own interpretation, making sure to focus on the positive.

"Joe, you've drawn a small house next to the sparkling river. The trees in the background are lush and will shade you. The river will give you water for drinking and bathing; it will also give you peace. The sounds of water running and trees rustling in the wind are soothing. You seem to want to achieve a peaceful feeling. The sun is just rising; it must be dawn. Might you be thinking that this new day is offering you fresh chances and opportunities? I wonder about that dark and ominous cloud at the right. Are you worried that the freshly made day might be spoiled by something?"

"Mrs. Krogness, you've swirled hot colors—hot orange, magenta, yellow, red, and purple. The spirals of intense color are vibrant. There's a lot of energy in your picture; the energy seems to be directed, yet not tightly harnessed. You let the colors drift off the page. I sense that although you're feeling turbulence, you're usually not too uncomfortable with it. Mainly, you get caught up in the excitement of your life. I notice that you seem to feel differently than you did a few days ago, when you drew heavy, dark shapes. I guess you're feeling a lot freer and more in control of an exciting life."

Sara spent several sessions developing the complex concept of self-image or self-esteem. First, she asked questions.

"What is a person's self-image?" Once we had established a simple definition, she asked: "How does a child build a self-image or a picture of him- or herself? Who helps the young child develop a healthy image or picture of him- or herself? What if a person's family does not or cannot help the child develop a positive self-image?"

Sara spent time asking these important questions, then listening. A little at a time, my kids began to talk.

"You mean when I look in the mirror, I think, 'Now there's a nice dude and he's real handsome, too, ' " Jamar laughed.

Sara smiled and nodded affirmatively, then urged others to talk about their own feelings or worries.

"I think my self-image changes every day," Marie said. "Depends mostly on what kind of a day I be havin'. Like when I get along with my friends, pass tests, and stay outta trouble, I feel good. But when everything goes wrong, well, you know . . ."

Sara complimented Jamar and Marie for their insights and then explained that our feelings of self-worth are based on what *we* think of ourselves—Jamar looks in the mirror and sees a nice, handsome person. Our self-esteem is also based on how others view and respond to us—Marie says her self-image relies on how she's getting along with her friends and is doing in school. The following poem by Jermaine shows his feelings of self-worth are different from Jamar's:

Jermaine
Feb 27, 90
I wonder why when
I was born everybody
   Left me

When I look
in the mirror
   all I see
      is
         a big head
         a crucked mouth
         and my nose is on my cheek
         and my lips are Fat

         Why!!

Then Sara asked us to draw representations or symbols that would show how we see ourselves. Some kids drew likenesses of themselves, while others sketched their personalities, interests, or hobbies, using smiling faces, hearts, classy cars, football helmets, money, and fashion trends. They also printed the names of musical groups. While certain students drew bold, colorful, expansive representations, others cautiously made a few small, cramped, and primitive symbols on their large white sheets of art paper.

Sara asked for volunteers to show and then tell us about their symbolic pictures. When everyone had done so and Sara had commented on each picture, she asked the class to take a further step and think only of positive words to describe their classmates, since a person's self-esteem relies on the responses of others, too. Each student offered a compliment that was written next to each student's name.

I am acceptable. I am capable. I am forgivable. I am lovable.

Marcus definitely has dreams for himself.

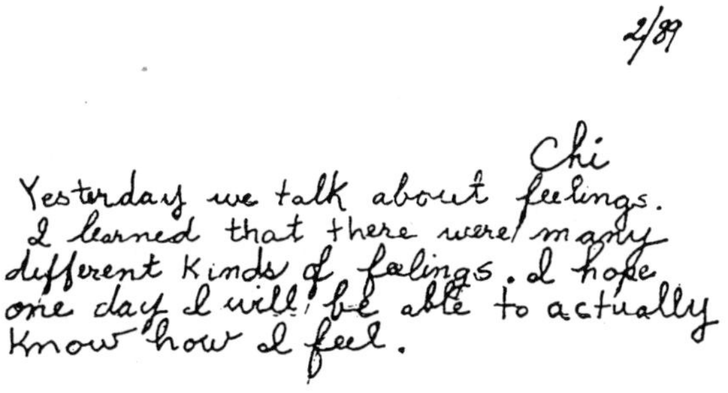

2/89

> Chi
> Yesterday we talk about feelings.
> I learned that there were many
> different kinds of felings. I hope
> one day I will be able to actually
> know how I feel.

FIG. 6-1   *Chi's Response*

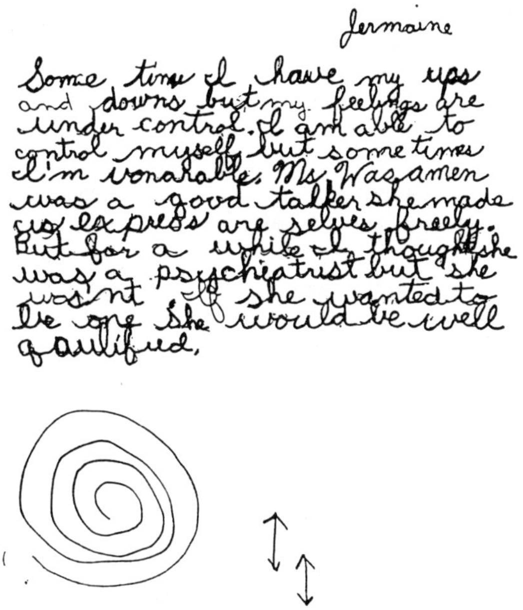

> Jermaine
> Some time I have my ups
> and downs but my feelings are
> under control. I am able to
> control myself but some times
> I'm vonarable. Ms. Wasamen
> was a good talker she made
> us express are selves freely.
> But for a while I thought she
> was a psychiatrist but she
> wasn't if she wanted to
> be one she would be well
> qaulified.

FIG. 6-2   *Jermaine's Response*

Our art therapist asked us to wrap up each of these sessions on self-esteem by repeating after her these four simple sentences: "I am acceptable. I am capable. I am forgivable. I am lovable." We did so willingly.

After this particular meeting with Sara, I asked everyone to respond in writing to the two big issues of our conversation: expressing feelings and building a positive self-image. Figures 6-1 and 6-2 show Chi's and Jermaine's responses, open and honest. This was a good beginning to other fruitful discussions and adventures into art that related directly to literature and to our own lives.

The art of asking questions

Just as Sara helped us to gain confidence through drawing, I gently pressed forward, challenging my students to take more responsibility for their own learning by talking and asking questions rather than relying on me to be the questioner and primary talker. Knowing that my students would likely become more invested in topics of their own choice, I invited them to ask questions that they had always wanted to ask.

The first five or ten questions posed by students were slow in coming and not very substantial:

"Is Marie's favorite food pizza?"

"Can we go on an all-day field trip Friday?"

"Do we have to have homework tomorrow?"

While I jotted their questions on the chalkboard, I coached them:

"What is the answer to each of these questions? Do you realize that these questions, which begin with *is, can,* or *do,* require only a *yes* or a *no* answer? Which other question-starter words might help you acquire better and more interesting information?" Lisa S. thought the question-starter word *what* would bring good information. Someone else thought that *where* and *when* were strong question-starters. These students were on the right track. Finally, Chris offered *why* and *how* as good question-starter words.

I directed the students to start generating questions beginning with *why* and *how,* the two words that inevitably evoke interesting responses. Exciting thinking began to result:

"How come parents have the right to be in charge of us teenagers?" Jawan asked.

"Why do some people (I won't mention any names) seem to get all the credit for having good ideas when other people have good ideas, too?" Jermaine wondered.

"Why do parents tell you not to do something like drink alcohol yet they would drink and say it's all right for adults to drink but not kids?" Jamar asked.

Jung wondered aloud why so many languages were spoken. Chi, our other ESL student, asked when she would *ever* learn to speak English.

I could hardly record all their other questions about racial conflict, nuclear war, poverty, disease, homelessness, child abuse, drugs, and family and school problems fast enough. After I'd read each of these questions aloud, I asked them which questions seemed the most interesting. We boiled the list of about thirty-five down to the three we thought had the most potential for discussion:

1. Why do adults have the right to be in charge of teenagers?
2. Why do blacks and whites have so many problems getting along?
3. Why are so many languages spoken?

For several days we spent class time discussing these pressing questions and their social, racial, ethical, linguistic, and developmental implications. Everyone had an opinion; everyone wanted to talk. Together we set guidelines for talking: Each person in the circle could give one opinion or response at a time; then it was the next speaker's turn. If someone interrupted, he or she lost a turn.

We sat in a circle. I gave everyone a number, explaining that when a student's number was called, he or she could express an opinion or insight or could ask another related question. After this student had had an opportunity to contribute, I'd call on the next student. If a student did not answer within a reasonable amount of time—maybe ten seconds—I would call the next number in sequence, thereby keeping the conversation moving and allowing everyone many turns.

As I moved around the circle quickly, this is what I said: "Student number one, do you have an opinion or insight about this issue?" Assuming that student number one contributed an idea, her turn was over until the next round. If student number two had nothing to say this time around, he simply passed. I noticed that attention increased because this activity was exciting and fast-paced but manageable. (Fast-paced and demanding exercises for kids at risk are critical.) More students talked because the topic affected everyone and everybody was guaranteed a turn. More students listened without interrupting because this guaranteed them more turns to speak.

The next day we relaxed this highly structured method in favor of a more natural one. Again I asked students to sit in a circle, but this time I asked them to watch the speaker carefully and find just the right moment to come forth with their responses, one at a time. One rule did still hold: the speaker was allowed to make one and only one comment about the subject. I monitored the speakers carefully so that no one would dominate and no one would be interrupted.

Being sensitive to the speaker and finding the appropriate time to enter a conversation are sophisticated skills that require practice. Both were especially difficult goals to achieve when so many students had customarily said nothing in class or blurted out derailing comments whenever they felt the urge. The majority of the kids experienced great difficulty managing the more loosely structured experience.

Sharpening our senses and sensibilities

Together, we analyzed what had happened at both of these talking and listening sessions. Here are some of the questions I asked and answers I received:

1. What do you like about the structured method of talking and listening?
   "Everyone *gets* to talk. Everyone *has* to say something!"
2. What have you learned about listening and talking?
   "You have to watch the talker so you don't interrupt them."
3. What have you learned about yourself as a listener and a talker?
   "Sometimes I don't talk 'cause I think my ideas are dumb and some people'll laugh."
   "I talk just to talk sometimes."
   "I'm worried that I'll forget what I'm gonna say when I have to wait."
   "I can't wait [to talk] so I cut in."
4. In what ways has the entire group improved its ability to listen and talk together?
   "Certain people in here are less scared to talk now."
   "Certain people are learning to talk *all* the time about any subject."
   "Other kids' ideas help me think of more ideas to talk about."

Next we considered the pros and cons of having full responsibility for listening and talking in a group:

1. What is challenging about having the full responsibility for listening and talking—without my calling on you?
   "I gotta be careful to come in on the conversation when it's time."
   "I have to learn to speak up, especially when *certain* people in here are talkin'."

2. What do you like about this more natural mode of conversing—where you are fully in charge of taking turns?
   "The teacher's not in charge; *we* are!"
   "It's more fun to say what's on our mind, you know, so we don't have to wait [to be called on]."

3. In what way have you improved your ability to listen and talk?
   "I'm thinking more about what I'm saying now."
   "I be worried about answerin'. Now, I just say it."
   "Now I know there's a lot of good answers to one little question."

4. Which of your classmates have improved in talking or listening? Why?
   "Chris is smart—especially when he talk, especially when Chris ask quesions."
   "Jawan. He have a whole lot to say—especially when he don't put his head down [on his desk]."

5. Who can generalize or tell us what the big issues of your questions are?
   "We was talkin' about peer pressure and things that bothers us."
   "Interesting subjects about all of us here—that's it."

At this point, I want to address the important and sensitive issue of black dialect and to convey my goals for the African American students, many of whom spoke black or nonstandard English dialect. I wanted my white students, most of whom spoke the standard English dialect, to understand and appreciate language variation. I told the kids that it's not a matter of speaking correct or incorrect English, because *every* dialect—whether standard or nonstandard English—hangs on a grammatical framework. I explained that *every* dialect has a set of rules (which, according to some linguists, such as Walt Wolfram, North Carolina State, are broken as frequently as the rules of standard English)! I informed my students that in addition to variations in grammatical structure certain words, such as *both, bathroom, birthday,* and *month* are pronounced in a nonstandard way. Probably included in nonstandard vernacular is what my kids referred to as slang, words such as those that appear in the boys' dictionary in Chapter 3, which are minted at a rapid rate on the street.

But first I got to know my students and they got to know me. When they felt free to talk in class, I showed them a few parallel grammatical constructions in both standard and nonstandard English. For example, I used the verb *be* according to standard usage and then according to the rules of nonstandard black dialect: "I be going to football practice," which connotes habitual behavior.

I took time to teach occasional brief linguistic lessons when appropriate to send all the kids the message that the language they'd learned to speak at home or in their neighborhood is a legitimate language that allows them to converse easily with their families and friends; for them it was also a good vehicle for thinking. However, we would talk about audience—the various people with whom my students communicated each day: families and friends at home and in the neighborhood, teachers and students in the classroom, and the general public—whom they occasionally met and would be meeting more frequently, especially when they would, one day, apply for jobs.

An easy explanation of different audiences went like this: "When you go to sports events—maybe a football game—you probably wear casual clothes suitable for the occasion; when you go to church or to a party, you wear dressy clothes appropriate for the occasion. When you talk with your family and friends, you feel free to talk in a nonstandard dialect; when you talk or write in school, you are expected to use the standard dialect—except when you write poetry or dialogue in a story. When you apply for jobs, you'll be expected to talk and write using the standard English form. It's up to you, the speakers, to judge which audience you are talking to."

My explanation of audience and language was clear to my students: The non-standard English dialect most students spoke is not wrong or inferior; in fact, it is rich and expressive. Second, society expects its members to be conversant in a standard dialect. Keeping these goals and attitudes in mind and knowing that I wanted to encourage talk, I refrained from "correcting" students, especially in midsentence. Rather, I relied on these discussions, the influence of our immersion in language, and my students' growing interest and confidence in using both oral and written language to lead them toward a kind of bilingualism.

The art of conversation: An easy give and take

An imaginative structure for engaging kids in talking is David Ignatow's poem, "Two Friends." Ruth Blair, the friend and colleague from the English department who gave it to me, also shared ways she's used it to give daily conversation the status it deserves. This little gem helped my kids and me to concentrate on conversing. We read the poem in unison and then used it as a point of departure for improvised conversation.

Two Friends
By David Ignatow

I have something to tell you.
I'm listening.
I'm dying.
I'm sorry to hear.
I'm growing old.
It's terrible.
It is, I thought you should know.
Of course, and I'm sorry. Keep in touch.
I will and you too.
And let me know what's new.
Certainly, though it can't be much.
And stay well.
And you too.
And go slow.
And you too.

After reading Ignatow's poem in unison several times *without* talking about its many possible meanings, we let the words touch us. Then I asked two student volunteers to face each other and read alternate lines to the other, using their voices in any way they wished. During the first couple of early readings, the two readers' voices were flat because they were still concentrating on deciphering the words and reading them aloud. After several more reading rehearsals (during which I coached them on how to use their voices), Marie and Jawan began speaking the lines of the poem to each other. Their voices told the rest of us that they were sympathetic; the readers realized that the occasion called for it. After they had read Ignatow's exact words to each other several more times, I asked Marie and Jawan if they would try improvising—making up their own conversation using the line-by-line pattern of Ignatow's poem. This is Marie's and Jawan's improvised conversation:

Marie: I have something to tell you! [*Marie spoke excitedly*]
Jawan: Go ahead, Girl, I'm listenin'! [*Jawan responded enthusiastically*]
Marie: I'm gonna hear L. L. Cool J. at the Coliseum tonight.
Jawan: Hey, that's live.
Marie: I never heard him before, have you, J?
Jawan: No man, but sure like to.
Marie: I just thought I should tell you because you are my friend.
Jawan: And you're my home girl, so I *should* know.
Marie: Tell you all about it in language arts, J.
Jawan: I bet you be telling me he baddddddd!
Marie: Sure will.
Jawan: Take care.
Marie: You, too.
Jawan: Chill.
Marie: And you, too.

We all applauded. Through this structured yet free-wheeling experience, my students focused on what constitutes conversation: a responsive give and take.

Analyzing our friendly conversations à la Ignatow

Here's how we analyzed other improvised conversations based on Ignatow's poem:

"Let's take time now to talk about what you noticed about these conversations."

Question No. 1: What happened between the two people who were talking?
"They looked at each other."
"They talked and laughed."
"The talkers seemed to enjoy talkin'."

Question No. 2: What was important about these conversations?
"Well, one person stopped talking and listened while the other person talked."
"They put feeling in their voice."

Question No. 3: Who was in charge of the conversation?
One student responded: "*Both* people was, but one usually led the way."

Question No. 4: Why did these conversations work well?
"Marie and Jawan, especially. They talked because talkin' come natural to *both* of them."
"Both Marie and Jawan quit talkin' and just listened."

Question No. 5: How would you define a good conversation? What are its characteristics?

Jermaine said, "It's when everybody don't talk at once!" We all agreed that a good conversation is people listening and then responding to others.

Question No. 6: Can we generalize about our own conversations in this class? What can each of us do to improve classroom discussions or conversations?
"We can say our opinions, then shut up," one student said.
"You can respond, too," I added.
"We can watch and listen to make sure the talker's done talkin' before we start up."

Through daily classroom practice, we were learning how to converse with one another about all manner of things. Our new confidence freed us to raise questions and bring to our daily forum the richness and complexity of our lives.

Seizing the moment

I'll never forget the day Jawan and a confrere steamed into class filled with righteous indignation that yet again, teachers and administrators had denied students their rights! He and other kids around our school were riled about the possibility that book bags might be outlawed. Members of the physical education and health departments were worried that carrying book bags crammed full of heavy tomes would cause backstrain; teachers and students had been knocked flat when they'd tripped over book bags in corridors or on steps; administrators imagined that book bags could become arsenals for concealed weapons. One faculty meeting had already been devoted to the pros and cons of allowing students to carry book bags.

Jawan and his friends were incensed that students had not been included in the debate. These kids would tell the principal and teachers a thing or two! Aha, I thought, here was a golden opportunity for me to engage the kids in classroom conversation. Every last one of them wanted to put in two cents' worth on this all-school topic. Scotching my other plans, I seized the moment to launch an informal debate on the pros and cons of book bags.

"Them teachers don't have no right to ban book bags," Jawan spoke emphatically.

"Yeah. They have no right 'cause the book bags—they our property," Marie sputtered.

"Book bags ain't none of them teachers' business, 'cause they ain't their property," Jermaine agreed with Marie.

The kids did realize that back problems could occur when book bags were too heavy; they amicably—even a tad self-righteously—acknowledged the problem of unattended book bags that often lay scattered in the corridors. They fumed, however, when I told them that administrators and teachers were worried that certain students would conceal weapons in their book bags. They were incensed that they'd been found guilty without a chance to prove their innocence.

"So, I 'spose they think they have the right to search our book bags," Jamar hissed.

I couldn't resist the temptation to add *my* two cents to this conversation: "Frankly, school officials—principals and teachers—*do* have the right to search students' book bags and lockers, because they are responsible for your safety and your lives."

"So, I guess we can just about forget *our* rights," Joe said.

"*What* rights?" Chris asked rhetorically.

Oh, what a good bout that one was!

Jawan

Book Bag Solutions   4-13-89

In my opinon the book bags shouldn't be ban because people have to carried books from class to class and if the staff take away the book bags people will be going to they lockers offing and will be late for Classes. when students go to the library they should not be aloud to carrly book bags to the library. and for the book bags In the class room book bags should be under the desk or In the back of the Class room and at lunch time, the stundents should keep book bags on the pyramd and [i.e, a large structure to leave books on] in class under the desk.

In the hallway stundents should carry the book bags by its hook. If one of the staff members see a student which a book bag on one shoulder the student should get a detention.

FIG. 6-3   *Jawan's Piece*

After we had debated the heated book bag issue, we wrote about it. In surely one of Jawan's most skillfully wrought pieces of writing, he sketched out guidelines for students carrying book bags at Shaker Heights Middle School (see Figure 6-3).

When talking is a matter of the heart

Talking helped my students come to grips with powerful emotions that often stood in the way of our coming together and learning. A language arts/English class is the ideal place for students to express and explore, explain and complain. We used precious class time to talk out our feelings and figure out ways to resolve personal and classroom conflicts.

Many members of one particularly difficult eighth-grade class alternately acted out disruptively or sat passively, playing with pencils. Nothing we did in class seemed to entice them. I decided to brave what I imagined might turn into a human sacrifice: letting them say out loud and in the presence of their classmates what they thought the problems were and how they proposed to solve them.

Very carefully I laid the groundwork: "Be serious and thoughtful when you assess our difficulty in working in this class. Be honest but not unkind when you speak your mind. Be fair; talk about *what* is wrong rather than *who* is at fault. Be a good listener when others are talking." I promised not to explain or defend my point of view during this discussion, but I would keep the conversation moving, act as a monitor, and record each speaker's thoughts on a big, yellow legal pad. (Recording what is said by whom is an ideal way to hold students accountable for what they say and a useful technique in managing a conflict-ridden classroom.) Difficult as it was, I held my tongue throughout.

At first the students uncomfortably shifted in their chairs, which were arranged in a circle. A couple of students cracked jokes, to which I quickly and firmly responded: "Either take this opportunity seriously or go to the office." Finally, one student began to talk about being bored. Even after many years in the classroom, the word "boring" from the mouth of even one student sends volts of electricity through my body. This group knew which buttons to push. I thought, but didn't say: "If many of you would only give a little during class and get involved, you wouldn't *be* bored." But just as teachers tend to call recalcitrant or tentative kids "lazy," disaffected young people resort to accusing teachers of conducting boring classes.

Despite my rules about not blaming people, Lisa M. laid the blame on me for moving too quickly from one project to another. In my desire to capture their interest, I *was* quite possibly casting about somewhat frenetically to find a subject that would shake them loose from their apathy. Another student complained, "We don't do any *real* work in *this* class." "Yeah," another responded, "all we do in here is read and write—and talk!" A couple of kids who weren't out for my jugular vein, and who seemed to be more confident than the rest, declared that too many students in this class weren't seriously committed to learning.

A roll call for responsibility

Meanwhile, I was jotting copious notes and recording the name of each speaker. Five minutes before the class bell rang, I called a halt to the meeting and read aloud the comments made by various class members. This roll call showed whether I'd recorded the speakers' intentions accurately; if not, I clarified their comments. It also allowed me to place the responsibility for analyzing the classroom climate squarely on the shoulders of each speaker.

The following day I requested that everyone gather together again. Then I asked, "Where do we go from here? Yesterday we identified what prevented our working hard together. Today, we should identify what each of us is responsible for doing to improve our working relationship." For several minutes, we all remained silent. At long last, one brave soul, Tammy, spoke about the necessity for everyone to come to class with a positive attitude rather than "an attitude." She detailed her own past course and the positive steps that she would begin taking to help correct a less than pleasant atmosphere. A couple more students asserted themselves by committing themselves to coming to class on time, settling down to work after the bell, and cutting the silly or hostile comments. But the majority just sat. I imagined that many kids were uncertain or worried that their peers would accuse them of appeasing the enemy.

I watched the immutable faces of those kids who were most responsible for our class problems but assumed no responsibility for their behavior. For too many years they had hidden behind a negative attitude; their disruptions deflected adult attention from their academic potential and deficiencies. Many resistant kids don't believe that they are worthy of positive attention; others fear the great unknown of success and will do almost anything to avoid achieving it because they fear losing friends.

On the second day, my aim was to engage the students in finding practical solutions for dealing with those who continued to arrive late, derail, and disrupt. The usual solutions were offered: send the offenders out to the hall or to the office, write referrals, and call their parents. I pointed out that, though these solutions were worthwhile, they fell, once again, on my shoulders.

On the third day, I asked everyone to respond in writing to our classroom caucus, and specifically to our suggested remedies. A few earnestly agreed to come in to Room 226 on time, ready to work. But certainly not all were bent on turning over a new leaf. Ameer, who could imitate entertainer Eddie Murphy to a T, wrote vehemently. Figure 6-4 shows his response.

I can't report that this group magically turned around and dug into learning. But the caucus had at least given everyone the experience of talking to resolve a common problem. At the suggestion of one of my seventh graders in the back-to-back class, we instituted a regular Friday morning class meeting, which we called "On the Spot." Jawan aptly described our twenty-minute discussion in a short bit of writing (see Figure 6-5).

For these meetings, I established three rules: (1) listen carefully to each person and don't interrupt; (2) don't "crack" on anyone, since a speaker has placed great trust in all of us; and (3) respond to what the person has said in helpful ways.

One day in February, when we knew one another well, Marie set the conversation in motion by saying she was tired of hearing remarks that classmates were making about her mother. "My mother—she's dead. Everybody in here know she died last year. So I'm gonna punch especially certain boys in this class because they always whisperin', 'yo mama'!"

Nearly everyone including Judith Bratt, our volunteer, and I responded to Marie.

"Marie has a right to be mad at certain people who talk about her mother. Maybe they should get a week of detentions," Lisa S. said, a smile appearing.

Marie smiled back and Lisa nodded approvingly.

Ameer   2-22

You (Mrs Knogness) ! They
to Press us to do so much
in so much time. We
have the whole year to go.
We are not wizz kids. So.
Why do you pressure us
so mush. I think the meeting
was a waste of time. These
rules shald of been out before.
we even started the second
Semester. We could of been
talking about the One Child
book, in stead of the meet
meeting. People have to
trust in ther seleves to
obey these rules not you.
You had got mad at me
for a comment that you
ask us. I prob probaly
did not understand the
question very well. But
you ask it.

I can understand the rules
but like I said, "the children
have to beilieve in there
selues to obey these rules.
The pressure that you put
on some of us makes us
irretated and the we just
Burst. You putting me over
all your problems about
me. You put so much pressure
on me, what is a person like
me going to do-hide under
a shade, no! I am a human
being. That what you call
emotions. Mark my words

FIG. 6-4   *Ameer's Response*

on tHE Spot   2-21-89
               Jawan

Once a week We have a meeting
It is call on the spot
The Truth comes out

and people startes to talk

Their are some Hot feeling

Some cold feeling

But the best of all my
class is feeling good.

FIG. 6-5   *Jawan's Piece*

Jamar 2-21-89

On febuary 16 a thursday Mrs. K.
had a very exciting meeting about
one of our local girls and
her feelings. I felt so bad
about the way when Marie was expressing
hersad feeling because
Speaking s Jermaine, Jawan and
Chris where laughing at her.
but Marie exopland her business
real good she just came out
with it and the meeting went
great but when I was talking
about how Jawan makes me
mad, and I just want to
hit him I going to do it before
spring break.
Mrs. K you handled the meeting
well you let us projėct
                    eachother in
our feelings toward the
feelings meeting.

FIG. 6-6   *Jamar's Response*

"But Mrs. Krogness, Marie—she always crackin' on other people in here. Maybe she need to keep her remarks to herself," Tiawan advised.

"I won't let any o' y'all crack on my mother, especially 'cause she dead." Marie again spoke passionately. "But, I will stop dissin' some other people if they promise to stop." Marie was conciliatory.

"Name calling *is* disrespectful—no matter who resorts to it, and it won't be tolerated in our class," I added.

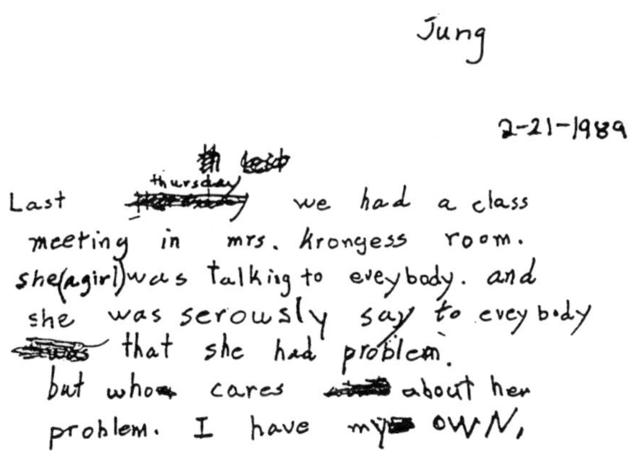

Jung

2-21-1989

Last ~~thursday~~ we had a class
meeting in mrs. Krongess room.
she(a girl) was talking to eveybody. and
she was serously say to evey body
~~that~~ that she had problem.
but who cares ~~that~~ about her
problem. I have my OWN,

FIG. 6-7 *Jung's Piece*

Then Judith spoke: "You're fortunate to be in a classroom in which you can air your grievances and feelings. It sounds to me as though you're learning how to use this privilege to your advantage."

The meeting was intense until Jamar, who was eager to be heard, spoke up. "Well, since we're talking about personal things and people getting on our nerves, I wanna say that Jawan's always doggin' me about my new suede shoes, and he keep it up too long!"

Big J. laughed and rolled his eyes in acknowledgment. We all laughed, not because we were unsympathetic to Jamar and his plight but because we were relieved that he had broken the tension. Jermaine's uncanny sense of timing and keen insight into his classmates' vulnerabilities prompted him to speak: "Tiawan's laugh [which Jermaine mimicked perfectly] gets on my nerves and other people's, too."

Tiawan, who usually hid behind his anxiety and hesitated to be straightforward, was gaining strength today. He shot back: "Well, Jermaine always has an attitude. Maybe that's why Mrs. K. calls him 'Spicy Meatball.' " He grinned knowingly.

I closed our classroom caucus by praising everyone for taking the three rules seriously. Judith commended Marie in particular for her courage to speak personally and take responsibility for her own actions. Joe, who had been silent throughout the meeting, announced suddenly that the meeting was boring. He continued to fidget and slap at kids who sat nearby. But the rest were enthusiastic—especially playful Jamar, who exclaimed on his way out of class: "I loved it [the meeting] because it was just like Judge Wapner's 'People's Court'!"

Because the time was ripe, we spent part of the next morning reflecting through our writing on what had happened during this last classroom conversation. Figure 6-6 shows Jamar's response.

Even Jung, who until this day in February had shown little emotion, let down his guard. He expressed his sadness and anger at being left behind by his mother, father, and sister who, after coming as a family from Japan to the United States one summer, left Jung in a new country and culture with a young uncle. Jung would live in the United States permanently. His feelings of abandonment were inescapable (see Figure 6-7).

Shortly after writing the piece about having his *own* problems, Jung created a lovely concrete poem about loneliness (see Figure 6-8). A few days later, he let down

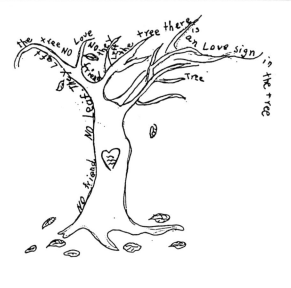

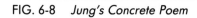

FIG. 6-8   *Jung's Concrete Poem*

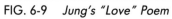

FIG. 6-9   *Jung's "Love" Poem*

his guard even more and wrote a typically adolescent little love poem that stopped us all (see Figure 6-9).

"I didn't know Jung thought *those* thoughts," Marie remarked. "I thought he only liked Nintendo games, not girls," she laughed appreciatively. In this case (and others), still waters ran deep.

Family folklore

Now that both my seventh and eighth graders were learning to use personal experience in the classroom, we were ready to move on to oral histories. At first the kids weren't at all intrigued with the idea of interviewing family members and neighbors. Most said that their families didn't have any famous people to investigate; some even worried that they might turn up notorious types lurking in their past.

But I pressed on, for I felt that such a venture was promising. With Americans so much on the move, few children today enjoy the benefit of knowing their family history.

First we spent several class periods brainstorming an array of questions that might bring interesting responses. Inevitably, the students wanted to know what life was like "back in the old days." They wanted to know how children were raised and disciplined by their parents and what sort of schoolwork their parents and grandparents had been expected to do. Entertainers, music, dances, fads and fashion, slang expressions, and sports stars whetted their curiosity, too.

I pressed them to think further: "What else is important in a person's life?" I became directive, because family folklore implied family values, family customs, family stories, family superstitions, favorite family recipes, and the like. Laron, a seventh grader, thought about the role religion might have played in his family's traditions. Lisa S. wondered about holiday traditions, and Chi asked about the languages families spoke, while others wondered about their families' occupations.

I jotted *all* the students' topics on the chalkboard; I didn't eliminate any or try to categorize them, for this job would be the focus of other lessons. Maybe it was Chris who wondered why so many people immigrated to America, a primary consideration when a student is investigating his family. I seized upon it because I could tie it to history.

"Why have people given up their homelands to immigrate to another country and join a new culture?"

We stopped to discuss major reasons people immigrated— religious, ethnic, or racial persecution, war, new opportunities and freedom, wanderlust and curiosity—and speculated about the difficulties of getting settled in a new land and culture. Finally, Cleo, a quiet eighth-grade girl, said: "But my people came to America to be slaves for the white man." In American history class, Cleo and many of her classmates, the majority of whom were African Americans, were watching and discussing tapes of Alex Haley's *Roots*. Now in language arts class we were discussing the significant difference between the immigration of most Europeans, Asians, and Latinos to the United States and that of African Americans: the Europeans, Asians, and Latinos had escaped to America or come freely, while black Africans had come as slaves in chains, against their will. We were getting to the heart of a matter that also was a matter of the heart; we were talking openly about an issue that affected not only my African American students, but my white students as well. During this month of preparing to become savvy interviewers, we were considering our own lives from different historical perspectives.

In another eighth-grade class, Erika and Radha expressed strong feeling that most history books pay little respect to African Americans and their contributions to America and therefore to American history. Radha spoke with conviction, "I feel that I know quite a lot about the white man's history, but I know very little about my own." Suddenly the prospect of interviewing family members about such monumental questions was exciting. Family folklore held a more immediate promise.

Asking more questions and building a framework

"What kinds of questions do you want to ask when you interview your relatives, neighbors, adult friends, or teachers?" I asked. I reviewed with my students the question-starter words that we'd already gained dexterity in using—words such as *how* and *why*—and then we added *when, where, who,* and *what.*

Twelve-year-old Joe was interested in the economics of past decades. Joe's interest prompted me to tell them that when I was young, a single-dip ice cream cone could be bought for a nickel! My students, who already believed that I'd been raised during the Dark Ages, looked incredulous. When I said that I could recall buying a good pair of shoes for five or six dollars in the 1940s, they gasped excitedly—until I mentioned that my allowance had been raised from twenty-five cents to fifty cents a week. Quite naturally this conversation led us to realize that the worth of the American dollar had declined significantly. And so the conversation went.

Categorizing our questions

It was time to begin thinking of general categories for our growing collection of interview questions. Again, we read through the list and thought about general titles. We found that most of our questions fell under Growing Up or Early Years; Family Values; Family Traditions; Family Stories, Folklore, Jokes, Sayings, and Superstitions; School/Education and Religion.

We thought of still more questions that went beyond the confines of the immediate family: world events such as The Great Depression, World War II, the Korean and Vietnam Wars, the civil rights and the women's movements. But even this final categorized list was not unchangeable. The questions had become points of departure for asking still more questions, broadening and deepening our language landscape. The list below would serve as a framework for interviewing our relatives and friends.

Oral history
Here are questions that all of us, together, brainstormed and finally categorized during class in preparation for our taped interviews of family members and friends. These are questions that we might ask our relatives whom we'll interview and tape.

Home life
1. How would you describe your life at home with your family?
2. What do you remember about growing up? Where were you born? When? Where did you live?

3. What do you remember about your mother, father, sisters, and brothers? Your grandmother and grandfather?
4. How did your parents raise you? Can you give examples?
5. What kinds of values did your family have? What did they expect of you and your siblings? How do you know?
6. What kind of discipline were you given?

Home and neighborhood
1. How would you describe your home?
2. What was your favorite room? Please describe it.
3. How would you describe your neighborhood? Your neighbors?
4. What do you remember about your neighborhood?

Family traditions
1. Family superstitions?
2. Family stories?
3. Family recipes?
4. Family expressions?
5. Family traditions on holidays such as Christmas or Easter or birthdays?

Religion and religious practices
1. What were your family's religious beliefs? Church attended? Where?
2. How would you describe a typical church service?
3. How did you and your family participate in the church? A minister? Member of the choir? Organist? A deacon?
4. In what ways did you raise your children in the church?

School
1. How would you describe school when you were growing up?
2. How would you describe your teachers?
3. What was expected of young people by all the adults?
4. What was your favorite subject? Why?
5. Who was your favorite teacher? Why?
6. What do you remember best about school?
7. What were the school's attitudes toward race?
8. Did you attend a "separate but equal" school or an integrated school?

Worries and concerns
1. What did you worry about when you were a teenager?
2. Whom did you talk to about your concerns?
3. What were the *big* problems that young people worried about when you were growing up?
4. What was the most serious problem in the world when you were young?

Fashions and styles
1. How did you wear your hair in, let's say, high school?
2. Please talk about the clothing styles when you were in high school.
3. What kind of music and dances were popular when you were growing up?
4. Who were the popular entertainers when you were young?
5. What kinds and models of cars were popular when you were young?

Economics
1. What was the cost of the following: an ice cream cone, a pair of shoes, a car, a house?
2. How much did you get for an allowance?
3. What was the minimum wage?
4. What did your parents do for a living?

World events
1. What were the big world events that affected everyone when you were growing up?
2. How did a war, the Great Depression, an earthquake, the civil rights movement, or whatever affect your family?
3. What did this big world event seem to do to the society?

If . . .
1. If you could be born during any period or era, which one would you choose? Why?

Classroom rehearsals

In preparation for interviewing, I staged a mock interview in which the kids practiced asking me questions based on our list. As my students inquired about my early years—about my parents, brother, growing up in a small Ohio town out in the country, riding horses and thriving outdoors—we stopped to analyze what was happening. They recognized that I was telling stories. By stopping briefly to side-coach my students while they interviewed me, I helped them dig more deeply. Inexperienced interviewers tend to jump from one subject to the next, letting a promising subject die as they move on to a fresh one. They also tend to ask superficial questions, the kind that automatically dead-end.

I was careful to praise the first student who asked a significant question which was not—as yet—on our list of interview questions: "Who had a big part in your life?" I stopped for a moment to talk about people and events that had shaped all of our lives. Then I talked specifically about my own parents' influence on my life.

I asked my young interviewers to think of other questions related to this important concept. "What other questions—especially *how* and *why* questions—might you ask me that are directly related to the influences in my life?" Here are their responses: "How did your mom and dad influence you?" "What goals did they have for you?" "How did they expect you to act?" "What did your parents do when/if you didn't do good—especially in school?"

Connecting questions

I encouraged the kids to build more questions from the interviewees' responses. We spent about twenty minutes talking about my life, all the while stopping to analyze the process of asking good questions and anticipating responses. Then I asked everyone to recall and reiterate what they remembered best about this conversation. It turned out that everyone had most enjoyed Marie's asking me if I liked school and had always done well in school.

Marie's classmates laughed apprehensively at first, then with great relief when I told them about my struggle with mathematics, particularly plane geometry in high

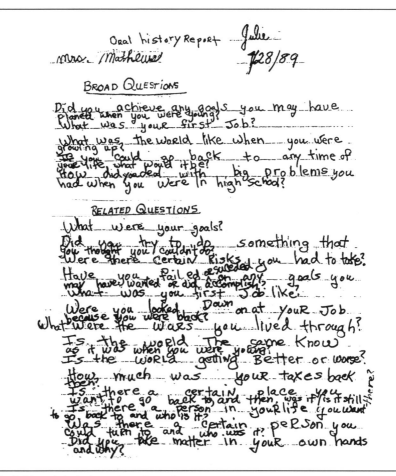

Oral history Report — Julie —
mrs. Mathews — 1/28/89

BROAD QUESTIONS

Did you achieve any goals you may have planed when you were young?
What was your first Job?
What was the world like when you were growing up?
If you could go back to any time of your life, what would it be?
How did you deal with big problems you had when you were in high school?

RELATED QUESTIONS

What were your goals?
Did you try to do something that you thought you couldn't do?
Were there certain Risks you had to take?
Have you failed or succeeded on any goals you may have wanted or did accomplish?
What was your first Job like?
Were you looked Down on at your Job because you were black?
What were the wars you lived through?
Is the world The same Know as it was when you were young?
Is the world getting Better or worse?
How much was your taxes back then?
Is there a certain place you want to go back to and then, was it/is it still there?
Is there a person in your life you want to go back to and who is it?
Was there a certain person you could turn to and who was it?
Did you take matter in your own hands and why?

FIG. 6-10   *Julie's Interview Questions*

school. I told them how my stomach had knotted when I opened my report card during homeroom and found a D next to the subject that positively unglued me.

"But I always thought teachers got all A's on their report cards," Jamar said quizzically. At that moment I let them see that I, too, had been a vulnerable student, an imperfect person who had survived school and life.

"What did your mom and dad say when you brought home that D, Mrs. K.?" Jawan wondered. Earlier I had explained that both of my parents set high expectations for me, and that because my mother was an English and Latin teacher, she especially regarded academic work.

"I guess they swallowed hard and took it in stride," I replied. "But they wanted me to continue working to improve my understanding of plane geometry. And every morning at 6 A.M. my mom *helped* me practice!"

After the practice interview, we further assessed our now overflowing bank of questions, taking time to consider the quality of each question before rewording and reordering. I retyped our question bank, a prototype that would guide my students' thinking during the interviews. But because every interview would be different, I asked students to write even more questions. Figure 6-10 shows the exceptional list of

---

Oral History of Joel W.
by Micah F.
5/10/89

PLEASE ANSWER THE FOLLOWING QUESTIONS:

1)   TELL ME ABOUT YOUR EARLY CHILDHOOD

1a) WHAT RELIGION WERE YOU BROUGHT UP IN?

1b) HOW DID YOUR RELIGION AFFECT YOU?

1c) DID YOU HAVE ANY ANIMALS? IF SO, TELL ME ABOUT THEM.

2)   WHEN DID YOU COME TO AMERICA? WHY?

2a) WHAT WAS DIFFICAULT ABOUT LEARNING THE LANGUAGE?

2b) WHAT WAS DIFFICAULT ABOUT AJUSTING TO A NEW COUNTRY, AND CULTURE?

2c) WHAT DO YOU LIKE BEST ABOUT THE USA?

2d) LEAST?

2e) WHAT DO YOU MISS ABOUT YOUR OLD COUNTRY?

PLEASE SEND BACK
5 copys

FIG. 6-11   *Micah's Interview Questions*

questions that Julie asked Mrs. Mathews, our library aide. Figure 6-11 shows Micah's excellent questions, which he never quite got around to asking his uncle.

Logistical considerations

After thinking of adults we might interview, we discussed the importance of making appointments with the interviewees having first asked their permission to interview and tape them. I emphasized the importance of establishing a *specific date, time,* and *location* for each interview. We estimated that conducting an interview would require one uninterrupted hour in a quiet setting. In some cases, telephones were turned off and quiet signs posted to ensure privacy. In one case, however, a seventh-grade boy competed with a blaring television that nearly drowned out his elderly, soft-spoken grandmother.

Another important logistic: having access to portable tape recorders that were in good working order and simple to operate. I encouraged everyone to try out the tape recorders and test proper volume before attempting the actual taping.

We carefully considered how we would handle asking personal or possibly intrusive questions of our interviewees. For example, "In what ways did you experience racism when you were going to school?" or "Which part of your life would you least like to repeat?" We decided that we could ask personal questions if we treated the interviewees respectfully and let them know ahead of time that if they didn't want to respond to certain questions, they could merely say that they would rather pass on to the next question.

The kids and I also decided that starting out by introducing ourselves, our interviewees, the topic of discussion, and the current date would be important. After all, these tapes were for posterity! One student suggested that at the end of each interview, the interviewers should show appreciation by thanking their family members and friends who had generously given us their time. A word of appreciation was a good wrap-up for the taped interviews, too.

The seventh and eighth graders were nearly ready to conduct their interviews. But as could be expected, problems arose: some students couldn't find working tape recorders, while the family members of others backed out of the interviews. I suggested that students interview teachers, librarians, library aides, administrators, custodians, or secretaries in our school and use school taping equipment.

A voice from Vicksburg

Quite unexpectedly, Cleo brought her taped interview to class before the due date. Cleo's grandmother, Annie T., was born in Vicksburg, Mississippi, in 1919. We gathered around Cleo to listen as she asked her grandmother about the old days in the South. The young oral historian's voice showed us that she was very much in charge of the interview. She wondered about her grandmother's dreams, her girlhood, and her life as an adult. Skillfully, Cleo asked one question after the other from our class question bank and her own list; skillfully, she built impromptu questions from comments that her grandmother made—responses related to the Great Depression, education, religion, civil rights, and of course Mrs. T.'s own family life. When Cleo asked, "Grandma, will you tell me about an experience that you will never forget?" Mrs. T. told her granddaughter to pass on to the next question. And Cleo gracefully moved on.

Cleo's and Annie T.'s voices rose and fell. Laughter occasionally punctuated their conversation. For much of the class period, my kids and I huddled around Cleo to hear every word. Annie T.'s voice, sad, deliberate, and resigned, held their attention; so did her philosophy of education and life: that people should be God-loving and take charge of their lives. But hearing that you could buy a pair of shoes in the 1920s for the price you now pay for a large pop at McDonald's brought gasps of disbelief.

We were touched by the personal quality of this, the first family portrait on tape. Cleo's interview gave all of us courage to ask our own questions and document our own family histories. For her part, Cleo decided to go beyond the original assignment and write a history of her grandmother as if her grandmother were writing it. Here is Cleo's diary, "The Files and Trials of My Life" written by Cleo T., story by Annie T:

The files and trials of my life

written by Cleo T. about my grandmother life story told by Annie T., my grandmother

Introduction

My name is Annie T. I was born in Vicksburg, Mississippi in the year 1919. My life as a young girl was very fascinating. I was a quick observer who paid close attention.

Although I was never an expert in school, I did learn about the world outside of me, considering I never went to college, or even finished high school for that matter.

As a young girl, I spent most of my life playing and meeting new objects, trying to learn about life and the wonders of life, about people and why they did the things they did. Most of the time, my mother (Elizabeth T.) wanted me to finish school, and do the best possible job I could in school and at home around the house. Not only did my mother want me to do good in school, but my parents, both of them wanted me to succeed in life.

Sometimes I would wonder about life in general, as most kids do. I would wonder would I make it and would I succeed. Trying to make it was a big thing to my family, for if I didn't succeed in life I would be branded as the dumb child. The child who never got good grades or the child who didn't try hard enough. So I kept my grades up until I finally quit school, which was one of the biggest problems of all time.

After I quit school, there was no hope at all left in my mother for me. She kept telling me to go back before it was too late, but I never did and I really lost contact with my school work which enabled me not to be able to go and make it in life. Part of my life went to caring for children (three of them) while the other went to trying to see if I would ever make it in life and crying some nights to myself for not finishing school.

By the time I was only 16 years old and I had already started to wonder about death and how my life would end up, In the ghetto, or in the high life. This led to danger and fear and totally not trusting myself to even go on.

I later found a way to overcome my fears of not being able to make it and I started going to church and learning more about our heavenly father, Jehovah God.

This fear had totally left me and now I was thinking about how I would not end up in the ghetto, but about what I could do to help my self and my children.

I never did go back to school or learn about accounting like I had always wanted to do, but what I did was even better. I began to develop a sense of understanding about how life was and that I could never make it in life sitting on my behind waiting for someone else to do it, but all I had to do was trust in God and he would show me the way . . . and so I did.

Revelations through oral history

The language came alive each time we listened to our family and friends speak. My students began to realize that people didn't have to appear in history books to be great and memorable. Through these oral histories, the kids learned about their own lives; they learned history firsthand. World events such as the Great Depression had brought hardship to their families, yet in the face of great adversity, their loved ones had survived. The students learned, too, about the civil rights movement, a moment in history that remained vivid to many of the interviewees. They became knowledgable about the Reverend Martin Luther King, Jr., Malcolm X, Rosa Parks, and other strong black leaders.

Through their interviews, my students recognized the gap between generations. They heard grandmothers in their fifties or sixties say that when they were coming up, racial prejudice did not exist in their segregated schools. Yet the daughters of these women emphatically spoke of the slights and slurs they had experienced in racially mixed public schools during the 1960s.

One boy brought a beautiful tape of his father, who had been a sharecropper in Texas. He told us about living in a small shack with a dirt floor, no electricity or indoor plumbing; about catching rain water that ran off the roof into a barrel; about the hard labor of picking cotton and cutting tobacco for a pittance.

Each day there was a new family story that brought us in closer touch with our country, our families, and ourselves. Through story telling, we learned about America and its diversity; we learned more about our language and how it works and sounds. When I asked the kids to fill out an evaluation form to assess our Family Folklore project, which had stretched into four or more weeks, this is what one student said: "Now I know what Alex Haley was doing when he went back to Africa to find out where his life started. In a way, I did the same thing."

Acting Out

Improvised Classroom Drama

"**H**ow about doing drama today, Mrs. K.?" my seventh and eighth graders often asked as they came into class. They had learned to like improvisational drama, or improv, as much as I did; it was an integral part of our language arts/reading curriculum. Drama without scripts or sets freed my most self-conscious or passive youngsters to become active participants; for those who wanted to "act out," it provided a positive means of expression. Improv not only enticed students to climb inside a character and figure out important issues, it also helped the class develop spirited camaraderie.

You don't need a degree in theater to involve kids in classroom drama. Attending drama workshops and reading professional articles and books helped me see its value and understand how to go about using it in my classroom. Through constant practice, I learned, and I'm still learning.

During the late 1960s and early 1970s, drama was brought into the classroom by Britain's remarkable Dorothy Heathcote, who believed that any improvised drama boiled down to "a man in a mess." I was fortunate to study with Heathcote for one intense week at Northwestern University in 1972; this is when I learned what it meant to climb into a character's shoes. As a member of Heathcote's troupe of teachers, I learned not to be completely cowed when, during a performance, we stopped to talk with fellow actors and regroup for the next scene, then got back into character and started up again.

After that seminar, I read and practiced Heathcote's principles—timidly, at first. As a point of departure, I eventually became skilled enough to use a provocative piece of literature or a character's motive or a historic event or a dramatic newspaper head-line. I learned how to coach my kids by asking one or two questions to focus our think-ing before we began acting. By taking a major character role, I indirectly led my students through an improvised play. But I also learned when to relinquish control, step out of character, and allow the students to carry on.

I continued to read and attend drama workshops conducted by many of Heathcote's disciples, Cecily O'Neill and others who have carried on in the Heathcote tradition. Like Heathcote, these artist-teachers use drama, not theater, to plumb the depth of a piece of literature, a period in history, or a current event. Drama helps students em-pathize with characters and understand their needs, vulnerabilities, motives, and points of view.

In theater, actors are assigned character roles, then read, interpret, and finally memorize a script. But when students and their teacher are involved in classroom drama, they sit down together and invent a play. For example, if students and their teacher meet a baffling moral dilemma in a story they're reading, they might want to find out how they feel about this dilemma. They sit down and identify the focus of their improvised play; they determine what the play will be about and who will be in it.

The goal is not to reenact the story, but to find out what the issues or emotions are. Of course, students who are engaged in classroom drama of this sort learn to understand themselves and others better through the process. After being involved in classroom drama, play-acting feels superficial.

Laying the groundwork

Here is how I began to use classroom drama, which takes place inside the classroom. I started with simple theater games, warm-ups that actors use to limber up before going on stage. For me, theater games were security blankets, because they were manageable and focused; they inspired my confidence and the confidence of my students. Viola Spolin's *Improvisation for the Theater* was one of my mainstays. I adapted theater games she described; I pirated warm-up games and techniques demonstrated by actors who visited my classroom; and the students and I created games of our own.

Before we started improvisation, I provided a firm structure for our work. I set down rules:

"Rule number one. From now on, when you hear the word *freeze,* you will stop whatever you're doing and stop talking. Let's practice." I asked everyone to stand and start moving within the circle, making noise. I called "freeze" several times, until they could instantly obey.

"Rule number two applies to the audience, anyone who is not 'on stage.' No one in the audience will talk, or distract the players while a warm-up game or drama is in process."

"Rule number three. Everyone should try to risk getting up and becoming part of the theater game or improvised drama. However, no one will be forced to participate." This rule usually freed even the most reticent student to get on her feet, for she knew ahead of time that she wouldn't be called on to act.

Laying the groundwork the first day of doing classroom drama was imperative for future sessions. With one class I made the lethal mistake of being too casual about stating and practicing my three rules. As you have already guessed, the results were disastrous.

Next, we shoved our tables to the side of the classroom to form a large circle with chairs. We called this space our "theater in the round." (Isn't it surprising how long it takes some seventh and eighth graders to perform such a simple, familiar task as forming a circle with their chairs?)

Warming up on theater games

All the theater games I will describe are simple and manageable. Each is unthreatening, yet has the power to engage even reticent players and exercise their imaginations.

No. 1: Shaff-loff

Shaff-loff, an easy, unthreatening theater game I learned from one of my students, comes in handy during the first few days of school. It not only gets the students' attention but helps me learn their names.

A leader moves about inside the circle, the stage area. She points to a classmate and says, "Shaff-loff." The classmate responds by saying his or her first name. Or, if the leader points to a classmate and says that person's name, the student must reply, "Shaff-loff." As the leader moves quickly and randomly inside the circle, pointing to students and either calling them by name or shouting "Shaff-loff," he or she tries to catch a classmate off guard, thus eliminating that person from the game.

No. 2: Just imagine

For the next game, you need a bandanna or an ordinary scarf. (These days I prefer the scarf, as bandannas have become gang insignia.) I begin by standing inside the circle, holding the scarf and saying: "What might this simple scarf become?" In past attempts, I have fashioned it into a blindfold and felt my way from one side of the circle to the other. Everyone guessed this use of the scarf. Next, I lay the scarf on the ground and pantomime a picnic—unwrapping sandwiches and pouring drinks.

The kids giggle, especially the eighth graders, who think this playing is for babies. But creative play was a mainstay in my language arts program.

As we sat around the circle, I asked, "Who will get down on the floor and play a game with me?" I said nothing to give a hint to the student volunteer, just moved a hypothetical checker on the bandanna "board," then sat back and waited. My partner took my cue, picked his checker up, and then "kinged" me. The first of many warm-ups had officially begun. We checker players stood up after our game, shook hands, and sat down in the circle, giving someone else a chance to use the scarf inventively.

During the early stages of any warm-up game, the ideas tend to be obvious and slow in coming. E. Paul Torrance, a creativity expert, believes that the players who spin off ideas fast, without judging their worth, will finally wind up with more electrifying ones. Thus, spending just ten minutes using the bandanna wouldn't fully tap the inner resources of these kids. So we played and played, probably the whole period, or at least until we had moved from making the bandanna into the usual blindfolds, aprons, and headbands to fashioning it into a tourniquet for a broken arm. Jamar folded the scarf into a propeller and put it into motion while creating the ticking sound of a low-flying chopper. Time allowed us to realize that the ordinary can become extraordinary.

No. 3: The elephant's trunk

This exercise, taught by the Great Lakes Shakespeare actors, is fast and fun. The class stands and forms a large circle, leaving a little space between each player. The leader, who stands inside the circle, points to someone and calls out, "Elephant's Trunk!" The designated student forms a trunk by making two fists and placing them in tandem on her own nose. The students who stand on either side of the "elephant" create the ears by placing a cupped hand at the side of the elephant's head.

I always engaged my students in several practice rounds before we played for keeps, allowing everyone to feel comfortable about a new game. Then we'd play slowly. As the youngsters became more sure of themselves, I quickened the pace,

Jamar twirling a bandana and making like a helicopter.

eliminating those who weren't attentive or who'd forgotten to make the elephant's trunk or ears. Each game became more challenging; after a while we added a new twist.

If the leader calls, "Rabbit's Nose" and points to a student, the student quickly points to his or her nose and sets it twitching. The students on either side of the "rabbit" create the ears by holding two V-ed fingers at either side of the "rabbit's" head. Some kids experienced great difficulty both processing the simple but fast directions and then putting their minds and bodies into action, especially after we added the rabbit's nose. This game helps the most scattered thinkers listen, concentrate, respond to directions, and develop better eye-hand coordination.

I played the leader during the early weeks of school, unless the class had shown unusual self-control or leadership qualities. When most students had mastered the rabbit and elephant, I added yet another twist: "1776." I called "1776" and pointed to a student in the circle; he or she was expected to respond quickly by pretending to hold a long rifle at attention in front of his or her body. The student to the right of the soldier plays a fife, and the student to the left beats a drum.

After a few slow practice sessions doing "1776," we added "Elephant's Trunk" and "Rabbit's Nose" to the array of commands the leader could call out at any time. As the pace quickens and ranks dwindle, the alert players learn to close in quickly and adjust the circle in preparation for more concentrated and faster play. The faster the game went, the more students were eliminated and sat down, until finally only two or three remained.

No. 4: Mime and voice

Mime and Voice involves only two participants at a time. One person, who remains seated in the circle, slowly and in an animated voice tells a story with plenty of action. The second person pantomimes the story as the storyteller tells it.

I went first, creating a story about someone named Fred who was taking his big, playful Great Dane, Ruff, for a walk. Jamar played Fred, miming the story as I told it. My tale, with extended pauses to allow Fred and his imaginary dog to play their parts, went something like this:

"So, Ruff, you want to take a run! Now you'll have to wait a minute until I get my coat and your leash." (Fred reached down and scratched his dog's ear.)

"Now, just be patient, Ruff. Let me put on your leash so that we can take a walk." (Fred opened the door, and the two started on a calm, delightful walk until . . .)

"Uh oh, Ruff sees a squirrel four trees away. The big dog pulls the leash with a jerk and yanks poor Fred pell-mell down the street." As the storyteller, I paused, allowing Fred to respond. Fred's outstretched arm conveyed the action: Ruff was pulling poor Fred down the street. Suddenly, the leash went slack when I said: "Oh, so now you want to see that squirrel who disappeared in the oak tree!" Fred and Ruff moved on down the street.

"I'm sure you'll notice that red fire hydrant down by the Hemmings' driveway, won't you?" I asked. And sure enough, Ruff made a beeline, galloping off and pulling poor Fred along. Jamar played the role of Fred to a T.

Mime and Voice offered my students and me infinite opportunities to use our imaginations and our storytelling ability, to interact with each other and be members of an audience. The storytellers were able to create simple, action-packed stories on the spot; the mimes used their bodies, not words, to convey the mood. My kids and I discovered that sports stories or stories based on cooking, baking, or cleaning were ideal for the Mime and Voice exercise. Making a pizza, for example, was a good exercise because of its built-in action. *Kneading* the dough, *rolling* it, *pressing* it into a pan, *chopping* the green peppers, *slicing* the pepperoni, *sprinkling* the cheese; then *setting* the dial and *popping* the pizza into the oven gave the actors a full range of action.

No. 5: A way with words

For A Way with Words, the only prop is a piece of blank paper. Each player transforms this blank paper into a newspaper account, an invitation, a letter, or some other message that he or she reads aloud.

I usually started this exercise by "reading" a letter from a perplexed or angry parent of one of my students. After several rounds to warm up, my students and I turned a sheet of notebook paper into a lively party invitation, a summons to court, a want ad in the newspaper, a Dear John letter, and a test. Creative thinking flourishes when kids and their teacher work together.

No. 6: Props from the prop box

Simple props can serve as excellent prompts for improvisation. An ordinary small cardboard box that I'd dug out of my closet became a box lunch, the P.A. system over

Bikers revving their creative motors.

which our principal, Dr. Peterjohn, boomed our morning announcements, a bomb planted in a hotel room and then defused by the hero, a present at a surprise party, and a boom-box that one boy held up close to his ear in order to get the full effect of a current rap artist.

No. 7: Pass it

In Pass It, one person in the circle begins by throwing an imaginary object in a manner that suggests its characteristics: feather-light, bulky, heavy, hot, cold, prickly, slippery, microscopic, sticky, or whatever.

Let's say that the object is microscopic. If I were the player who was trying to suggest the size of this minuscule object, I might reach deep into my pocket and slowly pull out the tiny thing, then hold it up between my index finger and thumb for closer scrutiny. Then I'd flick it off my palm to someone else in the circle, who would verify its minute size by catching it, perhaps, on her tongue. The recipient of the microscopic object would then change the object's size and perhaps its texture by sending it off in such a way that everyone would know that it was now hot or prickly or lightweight.

No. 8: What are you doing?

"What Are You Doing?" demands concentration and fast, imaginative responses. Two players, A and B, stand facing each other. Player A begins by miming, let's say, brushing her teeth. Player B asks, "What are you doing?" The first player, A, then names an action that is *not* what she is actually doing: for example, "I'm riding my bike."

Player B responds by riding her bike. Player B (who has just ridden her bike) performs a new task such as typing a story. Player A asks, "What are you doing?" Player B says, "I'm watching TV." Player A then watches TV. And so goes this game. If players stall or repeat an activity, or if they show bad taste (such as going to the bathroom), they are out of the game. (Make these three rules known ahead of time.) As players become more experienced, the game can move more quickly and imaginatively.

A Heathcote-style drama

After the class and I had spent six or eight weeks warming up by playing games a couple of times a week, *and* after the students became familiar with the rules for improvising, I gently led them to create a serious drama. For perhaps two class periods, we moved the improvised story forward, careful not to simply reenact.

Khalilah had brought to class a newspaper story about a dock worker who had been charged with murdering a friend, a charge he emphatically denied. The accused man and his lawyer found important witnesses to testify on his behalf; unfortunately, one of the key witnesses disappeared just before the trial. The accused man's life hung in the balance.

This authentic case served as a perfect point of departure for our classroom drama, *not* merely an event that we would recreate as if to photograph it.

Structuring an improvised drama

First I made sure that everyone was thoroughly familiar with the facts of the case. We speculated, too, about potential motives and witnesses.

Establishing guidelines in the beginning of this potentially chaotic operation was key. I explained that this improvised drama would have no clear direction at the start. The only facts before us were that a man had been murdered, and that another man, ostensibly the dead man's friend, had been accused of the crime. I explained that I would play two very different roles: the man who discovers the body and the coach who steps out of character to help the other actors.

I began playing the first scene by playing the lead role: I walked around the stage until suddenly I spotted what looked like a human body. "My God, what's this? Oh, no. Oh, God . . . it's a . . . dead man!" Speechless, I stood looking in horror. Then I ran back to the warehouse to tell my fellow dock workers what I'd just seen.

"There's . . . there's a body near the water—next to the big dock! A man, I think. Couldn't tell exactly. Face was down. (Pause) Didn't get too close." Then I spoke in a commanding tone: "You gotta come with me and decide what we should do about the body."

The roll call technique

I used Dorothy Heathcote's famous roll call technique to involve everyone, moving from player to player to get their responses to the question "What do you think we should do?"

Each player looked at the dead man's body. Tristin gasped, "I can't stand the sight of blood. I can't look."

Brandon declared: "We should report this murder now."

Louis said, "Probably we should report it, but . . ." As an actor and the coach, I capitalized on Louis's hesitancy.

"Louis, why are you hesitating? Are you afraid of something?" I asked. Louis nodded.

Carlton interrupted, "Yeah, we probably should report this to the police, but I don't wanna get involved."

Danny spoke up: "If we report this crime, I'm afraid they'll accuse one or all of us."

Danny's excellent comment signaled me to engage the actors in weighing a difficult moral question, allowing me to move the drama forward. Playing the man who had discovered the body, I took the lead again. "We've gotta do something. I think maybe we should report it. But I see Danny's point. The police might accuse one—maybe all—of us of the crime. What should we do?"

I moved around the circle asking each player to consider again what we should do: report the body or not? "If we don't report the death, we'll have to swear not to mention this thing to anyone. But if the police find out that one or all of us knew about it, we'll be in deep trouble. What do you think?" Again, each player had to think on his or her feet and decide what was morally right or prudent under the circumstances. My students remained in character—letting their personalities and points of view develop.

"One thing is sure," I said, "we're all in this thing together. We got to make a decision now." I was pushing my students to come together and make a decision. Although this drama could have continued to unfold for several days longer—including a trial, newspaper accounts, and so on—we wrapped it up. Speculating about the legal and moral implications of reporting or not reporting a serious crime was our final act. By this time, my students, who had sustained their interest for two days, were running out of steam.

Stepping out of character

When the improv was done, we speculated about *what* had really happened, *when* the deed had been done, *where* the murder might have taken place, *how* it probably was committed, and *why*. Motives for such a dastardly deed led us to hypothesize that the murderer must have been desperate. Was he (or she) angry? Jealous? Greedy? Deranged? Spiteful or vengeful? As Dorothy Heathcote says about classroom drama: "It's about a man in a mess."

Everyone agreed that reading the newspaper had taken on new meaning. "I liked getting into this crime through improvisation," Danny said. "You really feel as if you was right there at the scene." He and his classmates were excited about what had just happened to them in language arts class.

Although I continued to use theater games to warm us up, I knew these games had limitations. I wanted the reading that we were doing in class to serve as points of departure for dramas that would help us understand ourselves and others.

Moving from literature into drama

One day I read aloud Mildred Taylor's *The Gold Cadillac,* a gift sent by two guests who'd recently visited my classes. Everyone was moved by this story (and, for that matter, all of Taylor's stories). They were especially touched when they realized that the delicious food that Mother Dear and the other women in the family were preparing for the auto trip from Ohio to Mississippi to visit grandparents wasn't merely for pleasure. This was no picnic, for the year was 1950. No restaurants were available to black people then; no hotels would accommodate them. Public drinking fountains and toilets were marked to separate black people from white. Any black man driving a shiny gold Cadillac was suspect, too.

I decided to use classroom drama as a means of connecting with Taylor's characters and learning more about racism in America during the 1950s. Certainly racism still existed, but now it often took a different form. Things *had* changed since the emergence of the Civil Rights movement and Martin Luther King, Black Power and the Black Panthers, the leadership of Malcolm X and other revolutionary thinkers. But this story, *The Gold Cadillac,* had aroused many feelings among my black students, who didn't really know firsthand about Jim Crow laws. My white students were indignant, too. How might we start with our own vehement feelings and move beyond them to the universal?

Building a framework

I started preparing for our drama, which lasted two class periods, by asking my students how this story had affected them. Maybe it was Jermaine who acknowledged that although blacks enjoyed more rights and opportunities, racial prejudice still existed. Jermaine told us that nearly every time he walked into a certain small neighborhood deli, he felt the eyes of the proprietor on him. Others remarked that they, too, had experienced such scrutiny and had even been followed when they shopped at the mall.

In school, Jermaine said, black kids were punished more often than white kids. Many chorused their agreement of Jermaine's charge. He slouched in his chair, cut his eyes at Jamar and laughed: "Who fills up detention after school?" Jermaine knew firsthand, for he was a chronic offender.

Marie looked around the room and observed that Lisa and Joe were the only white students in our class. Chi smiled and pointed out that she and Jung were yellow or light brown. I recalled Quinn's telling me that certain of his teachers and many white classmates dismissed his responses in class and expressed surprise when Quinn received an A on a math test.

I remembered Lisa M.'s description of eighth-grade socials, where white kids clustered together and didn't seem to want to dance with black kids. Chris M. reminded us that when he and several other black boys walked down the sidewalk, several white boys on bikes suddenly turned and headed in a different direction. "I guess they're afraid of us," Chris said.

How could I use these experiences to help black kids come to grips with their long-standing hurt and feelings of rejection, and help the handful of white students in our class empathize but not patronize? Ultimately, I wanted my students to move beyond stereotypes and take responsibility for their lives. I wondered what Dorothy Heathcote would do.

Pivotal person

This is how I built a structure within which we could work comfortably and successfully. We sat in a circle. Inside the circle I placed two chairs about two feet apart, facing each other. I explained that throughout this drama, my role—which I called the pivotal

Cutting to the heart of issues through improv.

role—would remain constant. I would sit in one of the chairs and play the role of a biased white teacher. The other chair would be occupied by a variety of students, both black and white, who would play such roles as angry or indignant students, concerned parents, a school board member, and another teacher. These characters took turns interacting with me about my problem. Here is how we played out this improvisation. I spoke first.

"*Some* people in this class *never* get their homework done. The same ones (my eyes were riveted first on one black student, then on others) do poorly in class and on tests." Momentarily I stepped out of character to briefly explain the word, *innuendo*. Then I asked someone to assume a role and play opposite me.

Marie was the first to volunteer. "Marie, I'm talking about you and uh . . . your friends." Marie assumed her role quickly and easily. Her eyes were downcast and her already husky voice became huskier when she responded to my harsh words.

"You know, Mrs. Krogness, I'm doing the best I can in this class."

"Well, your best, Marie, is far from acceptable." I glared at Marie.

At that moment—just as we were getting started—I stepped out of character and asked someone else to intervene (a new word for my kids) and take Marie's place opposite me. Marie returned to her seat in the circle, and Joe volunteered. I briefly stepped out of character and coached Joe a little.

"How might you, a white student, react to this teacher's harsh words to Marie? What might you say?" I resumed playing the role of the inflexible teacher who responded to her students in a judgmental way.

"Well, Joe, what is it that you want? Did I overhear you whispering to Marie? She doesn't need your help. She needs your sympathy!" My remarks were intentionally provocative.

"You're not being fair to Marie," Joe said. "My mother says she's glad I'm not a black kid in here because everyone knows that you're . . ." When Joe stopped talking, his face actually reddened slightly. The kids laughed appreciatively when Joe stopped talking, implying the punch line. Once again, I was directive. I invited Chi, who wanted to play an angry parent, to sit opposite me after Joe sat down.

"Mrs. Lim, what can I do for you?" I snapped.

In a halting cadence, Chi spoke: "My son is having hard time doing work. He say you help everybody, not him."

"Mrs. Lim, I help *all* of my students—I help your son who can't *even* speak English yet! But I've certainly noticed that your boy isn't the *only* one around here who can't speak standard English!" Then I leered at everyone in the class.

"What's *that* supposed to mean?" Jawan yelled out from his chair in the circle.

"If you haven't figured out by this time what I mean . . ."

Even though certain students wanted to continue the drama, we stopped and got out of character to talk about what had happened thus far. My choice to play the cruel teacher was deliberate, because I wanted my students to take the high ground—to play good characters who were entitled to vent their rage in a safe setting. In addition, my playing the pivotal character kept the drama moving.

Once we were comfortable with this drama structure, I rarely needed to prompt members of the audience to take part. I suggested that when one actor was engaging in conversation with me, the rest should remain quiet and determine an appropriate time to come up and stand by the young actor's side as a signal that they wanted a turn in the second chair.

Most of the students watched intently but didn't volunteer to play opposite me during this initial improv; it was a vicarious experience for them this time. But the succeeding drama experiences, in which members of the audience played every role, brought forth authentic feeling and fresh understanding.

The pivotal person changed from being a rigid teacher to a hostile and suspicious storekeeper, played by Jermaine. The ensuing dramas, based on the young people's own experiences with prejudice, paralleled but did not copy Mildred Taylor's story. They allowed us to get in touch with our feelings and bring broader experience to the literature we were reading.

A shot of adrenaline: Cecily O'Neill

With my English department colleagues, I had the great good fortune to work with dramatist-teacher Cecily O'Neill, who came to Shaker Heights Middle School to involve secondary faculty in drama in the classroom. Not only is O'Neill a gifted teacher, but she has mastered the art of reassuring anxious adults like me, who are comfortable leading impromptu dramas with kids but tense about improvising in the presence of peers.

Cecily slid us all into an unthreatening mixer that not only blasted us out of our chairs and onto our feet, but limbered us up emotionally. She asked us to mingle, and while we mingled each of us was to name or give away the title of a poem, play, or novel. As we received a title, we'd give it away to others. For instance, I gave away "To P.J. (2 yrs old who sed write a poem for me in Portland, Oregon)" by Sonia Sanchez. In return, I collected and then gave away "MacBeth," and a host of other titles. After we had mingled for several minutes (this was a brief warm-up), we sat in a circle and shared what we'd received.

Certain titles were offered over and over again. "The Tell-Tale Heart" by Poe, for example, was one title that we later used as the basis for our classroom drama. In addition to naming story and poetry titles, O'Neill suggested that students might give away important objects, items of clothing, or vocabulary. (I've since asked my kids to give away symbolic words that capture the essence of a story.) This easy warm-up exercise generates a wealth of material that can be the basis for dramas not yet conceived.

Improvisation: A tool for teaching and learning

Next, O'Neill asked each teacher to pair up with someone sitting close by. The pairs were to write headlines that would capture the essence of the dastardly deed in "The Tell-Tale Heart." O'Neill specifically asked us to include strong verbs in our headlines, which we wrote on paper strips and shared with the group. This exercise, again manageable and safe, led us to the next phase of our classroom drama: building an authentic improvised play.

O'Neill asked the pairs of teachers to play the roles of investigative reporters and story characters. (By letting the pairs continue working together, O'Neill was building trust and commitment, probably the two most important ingredients of classroom drama.) One partner would play the investigative reporter who would ask questions about the old man's murder, while the other partner, who was more familiar with the story, would play a specific story character or a bystander.

In the process, all of us teachers-students-actors became experts, whether or not we were familiar with this particular story. O'Neill reminded us that while many of our students don't read the literature assignments that we give them, improvisation is a way to include everyone in learning.

After we had spent no more than five minutes interviewing and being interviewed by our partners, O'Neill asked all of the investigative reporters to interview other characters and collect still more information. Thus, the reporters broadened their understanding of the old man's murder and gained insight into possible motives for this heinous crime.

Then she asked the actors who played character roles to stand apart from the rest of us. We, the investigative reporters, were to take turns ranking the characters in terms of their knowledge of the old man who'd been murdered. "Who knew the old man best? Second best? Least well?" O'Neill asked us. She wanted us to understand that certain witnesses' accounts would be more reliable than others. Then, finally, the journalists reported the results of their investigation to the entire group, substantiating their insights by quoting the most credible witnesses.

O'Neill offered an easier, more manageable alternative for staging an interview: putting just one character in the "hot seat" for the entire class to interrogate. I have done this with excellent results. By first putting myself in the position of the story character whom my students would interview, I anchor the drama. However, when students become strong enough to play the role of the interviewee, even more exciting exchanges develop!

Returning to my own classroom

I returned to my classroom that day filled with new enthusiasm and fresh approaches and asked my kids to sit theater-in-the-round style. Just as we teachers had done, my students were going to create newspaper headlines—this time about Cinderella's fall from grace. We spent twenty-five minutes discussing the characteristics of headlines (short, powerful, attention-getting) and generating strong words that they might use in their headlines: *forgotten, abandoned, left out, thrown away, cast out,* and *gutsy.*

Here are a few of their headlines: "Poor Girl Sent to Basement by Stepmom"; "Princess Sits by Hearth Waiting"; "Beautiful Girl Finally Gets Her Prince"; "Stepmother Found Guilty of Cruelty." One grabbed our attention: "Stepmother Fined for Child Abuse." After sharing our newspaper headlines, my kids and I were ready for the next day, when we'd create a classroom drama.

I established the structure for our drama when I said: "I want you to find out *why* Cinderella was relegated to the hearth and wound up being a servant for her stepmother and two stepsisters. If you are an investigative reporter (we talked about the verb *to investigate* and its meaning), you will ask questions that you think might help you determine just why the poor girl was dismissed by her family." I coached my students briefly by reminding them that *how* and *why* questions usually elicited the most interesting information. I encouraged the kids who would play character roles to infuse their responses with personal opinions.

Before the investigation, we quickly recalled the characters in the fairy tale: Cinderella, the evil stepmother, the two stepsisters, the fairy godmother, the prince, and yes, Cinderella's absentee or dead father (depending on the version)! At last we were ready to begin our drama. A few kids opted to play bystanders who observed the plight of the young girl while the story characters and the investigative reporters started the improvised interview.

The students who played interviewers (some of whom had the greatest difficulty listening under normal circumstances) had their antennae up, for they knew ahead of time that they would be reporting to us all about their findings. They were interested in hearing the scuttlebutt about poor Cinderella, which in certain cases they made juicy!

After the interview, my students and I stepped out of character and took stock of the information we'd gathered. The reporters found that Cinderella had been mistreated by a jealous stepmother and envious stepsisters, and had wanted to "dump the brat" because they thought she was a snob. One investigator believed that Cinderella was doing her darndest to keep her father for her very own. Certain reporters surmised that the stepmother *did* have cause to put the girl in her place.

Even though a couple of the reporters did stray from the main issue, they uncovered revealing information. Some believed the fairy godmother's motives were less than honorable when she provided the poor waif with clothing fit for a princess and set her up in a carriage to go to the ball. They thought the fairy godmother expected to get a "cut" as a result of all her good deeds—maybe even get to live with Cinderella and the prince in the palace after they were married!

Probably most interesting was the information that came from Cinderella's father, who many of my kids assumed had died or neglected his daughter. The reporters who interviewed Cinderella's dad offered this information: if Cinderella's father were alive, he should have stood up for his daughter instead of being dominated by his new, mean wife. One boy insisted that the father's failure to protect his daughter from his cruel wife was, indeed, child abuse! He volunteered further that he'd experienced the same sort of treatment from his own stepmother, and that his father had ignored the ugly epithets and demeaning accusations that the boy's stepmother had made about him. A painful revelation, yes. But a safe and healthy means for him to come to grips with a real-life situation and then have the opportunity, through traditional literature and classroom drama, to let some of his feelings go. I talked to this boy privately and conferred with his counselor about his home situation. The boy's father was called, and a conference scheduled.

Parallel dramas

Parallel classroom drama might also accompany such a literature study. This exercise, "The Inside/Outside Self," is played by *two* students (or a student and a teacher) who act as foils in the improvisation.

The inside self and the outside self struggle. Cinderella's father, for instance, has an inside self that perhaps is vulnerable, doubting, perplexed, and unsure. Like all of us, the man presents an outside self to the world by his actions and reactions to a difficult situation, the complex family dynamics that develop when his new wife and her two daughters join Cinderella and her father. The household has changed, and perhaps Cinderella's father doesn't know how to handle it. So he melts into the woodwork, into oblivion and anonymity.

Here is how this exercise works: the two actors, who face each other, represent the inside self and the outside self of a *single* person. Here is Cinderella's father, engaged in a personal struggle:

Inside Self: "*What* have I gotten myself into? This woman is making me crazy. And those two girls of hers! What was I thinking when I married *her*? (*Pause*) And I never imagined that my poor little girl would take such a beating from those three evil women."

Outside Self: "Cinderella's just going to have to adjust to my new wife and her daughters. That's all. I love my new wife. And I'm getting to like her girls, too. Cinderella's just going to have to adjust to them and even make sacrifices . . ."

Inside Self: "But will my darling daughter have to sacrifice her life for those sinful women? I'm a total failure as her father. I've done absolutely nothing to protect my child. I'm helpless, all right. What kind of father am I?"

Outside Self: "Get a hold of yourself, man. Cinderella's just jealous of all the attention you're giving her new stepmother and stepsisters. That's to be expected—especially because of the years that she's had *me* all to herself. A girl needs a mother; I married this woman for Cinderella's sake. Anyhow, a man needs a wife. Cinderella's just jealous and resents her new mom. She'll adjust. All she needs is . . . time."

To further involve young people in understanding that more than one point of view exists, I asked the actors playing the inside and outside selves to switch roles. Although this is a challenging improvisation, it is exciting to watch two young people act as foils and play off each other, impromptu. The possibilities are infinite: actors experience and deepen their understanding of the range of human feelings and see the contrast between the private self and the self we allow the world to see.

Connecting literature with life: Nancy Bush and Jay Indik

Nancy Bush and Jay Indik, the actors from the Great Lakes Theatre Festival, spent the first full week of February with all eighth-grade classes in the language arts/reading department engaging our students first in classic theater, then in improvisation. After ten or so minutes of warm-up exercises like the ones I've described, teachers and students took turns casting, directing, and blocking scenes from *Romeo and Juliet,* practicing reading and interpreting lines, and assuming characters' roles in authentic Elizabethan costume. For the street brawl, Nancy and Jay spent time schooling all of us in the art of fencing, wisely using daggers made of rolled-newspapers! A few of us had the opportunity to use real swords as we became the love-sick Romeo, hot-headed Mercutio, kindly Benvolio, and Juliet's cousin, the stealthy Tybalt. We took turns playing the roles of Romeo and Juliet, their parents, Friar Lawrence, Paris, and Juliet's nurse.

We played out the scenes that lead to the teenage lovers' deaths, too. The majority of eighth graders were captivated by the intricate chain of events that drive the exiled Romeo to plan his suicide when he hears news of his young bride's death. The kids empathized with Juliet, who awakens in a tomb from the sleeping potion only to find her beloved husband lying dead beside her. Electricity was in the air in Room 226!

Students and teachers were not just the actors and the directors but the audience as well. In traditional Elizabethan costume, Nancy and Jay enacted the famous balcony scene by standing on chairs and leaning over a makeshift balcony fashioned from a wooden room divider. They played the intense scene in which Juliet refuses to marry the young count, Paris, whom her father has chosen for her. Finally, Nancy and Jay created breath-taking suspense when they arranged the clandestine meeting between Juliet and Friar Lawrence. All of this high drama took place in an ordinary classroom, *not* on a stage, making the theater experience accessible to students and teachers alike.

Improvisation on a theme

Without question, the most exciting and moving part of the week was Nancy and Jay's involvment of the students in improvisations based on contemporary situations that paralleled Romeo and Juliet's forbidden marriage. First, the actors set the stage by talking with the students about teenage dilemmas, many of which were suggested by the budding thespians: parents arguing and divorcing; parents not understanding their teenage children; teenagers not heeding their parents' warnings about drugs or pregnancy.

Two eighth graders, Carl and Jasper, volunteered to improvise a one-act play. During a brief planning session, they decided that Carl would talk with his parents about a highly charged dilemma. Jasper would respond to Carl's problem from the point of view of a younger brother. This is how the improvised drama began:

"They'll find out sooner or later," Jasper warned Carl, who looked tense and acted anxious.

The rest of us, seated around the players, watched and waited for Carl to broach the delicate subject with his parents, played by Nancy and Jay, one night after dinner. Carl gingerly led up to the subject, a forbidden one that closely resembled Romeo and Juliet's secret marriage.

"Mom? Dad? Cherise and I plan to go to the movies this Saturday night," Carl bravely announced.

"Uh, Carl, you and Cherise have been seeing an awful lot of each other lately." Dad looked concerned as he spoke to his older son.

"But, Dad, when you care about someone, you want to spend time with that person."

"Carl, shouldn't both you and Cherise be seeing other people? I mean, after all, you're both so young." Carl's mother spoke softly.

"Mom, you're hinting again that I should take other people out. But I don't want to go out with Felicia, Dubonay, and Leticia. They're nice girls and all. I just don't want to go out with anyone else but Cherise. You see, Mom . . ." Carl hesitated. The young actor was growing more and more believable as he increasingly became invested in playing his role.

"Your mother's right, Carl. You're too young to see just one girl exclusively—even Cherise," Carl's father said with a good deal of intensity and finality.

"Carl, it's not that your father and I disapprove of Cherise. It's just that . . ." Mother's voice trailed off; she looked at the floor as she spoke.

"There's something that I need to talk with you two about." Carl looked first at Jasper, who was muttering something under his breath. (Jasper was using his habit of muttering and making asides to great advantage on this occasion.) "Oh, boy, wait till Mom and Dad hear *this* news!" Jasper made this aside to his receptive live audience. A hint of sibling rivalry could be detected in Jasper's voice and seen in the ambivalent smile that crossed his face.

Finally, Carl spoke. "Ya see . . . Mom and Dad. Uh, you'd better sit down." He gestured for his parents to sit down. And then Carl blurted out the news: "I have something to tell you. Cherise is, uh . . . Cherise-is-pregnant!" Carl's words rushed out.

The household that had been deadly silent blew apart. The father paced and raged, while his wife, who remained seated, wept softly. Jasper, the younger brother, looked on. The audience (the rest of us now perched precariously on tables pushed to the sides of the classroom) was riveted to the actors as their voices rose and fell and their faces contorted and relaxed. One girl in the audience who was plagued with personal problems wept openly during the improvised drama; another wrung her hands. *This* improvisation was real.

Carl, the errant son, stood face to face with his father, who loomed over the boy like an ominous thunder cloud. Silence gripped the audience.

"Dad, I know that I've disappointed you and Mom." Carl paused, turned away from his father and looked tenderly at his mother, who still wept. "But I have a responsibility now to Cherise and . . . our baby." Carl spoke the last two words quickly and very softly. He looked up. "And maybe there's something you don't understand. I love her. I *love* Cherise."

Now that was a response to literature! When Carl left the center of our classroom, the improvised stage, we all cheered. For all of us, improvised drama had become a compelling way to climb into the skin of the characters we were reading about.

EIGHT
Meeting Literature Head On

Winning them over and turning kids on to print

During that first semester at Shaker Heights Middle School, I asked my seventh and eighth graders to tell me which magazines they most enjoyed reading, whereupon I promptly went out and bought an enticing selection. I was bent on whetting their appetites for reading, and I wanted to drive home several more important messages: reading can be done strictly for pleasure; reading for information doesn't always lead to taking a test later; and reading during class is an important use of school time. I firmly believe that the good stuff should be saved for school, where the teacher and students can help one another. Intellectual assignments done during class build camaraderie, too.

I wanted to make clear—especially to my eighth graders, who were considerably less tractable than the scared seventh graders—that our reading class would be varied, rich, and exciting. Need I say that the kids were overwhelmed that I had spent my own money, *not* on the dreaded books but on everything from *Popular Mechanics* to *Gentlemen's Quarterly,* for our language arts class?

Unfortunately, in my furious desire to captivate my students' interest, I neglected to take the time to assess my new audience. My timing (the first weeks of school) and lack of overall structure condemned this potentially enticing project to fail. Mostly the students leafed through magazines and begged me to let them cut out pictures. The magazine supply quickly dwindled as students surreptitiously slipped them out of the classroom. The competition to locate tantalizing advertisements for dirt bikes and the like was great, and most of the colorful posters were gone before everyone had had an opportunity to see them.

Because I handed out the slick new magazines without taking the proper steps to initiate this project, I suspect that the kids misunderstood my intentions. I *wasn't* the easygoing, "cheery little laid-back lady" that Virgil, an eighth-grade boy, described! Introducing a variety of popular magazines was a nice idea but one that frankly didn't work.

However, I was undaunted by my faux pas, for I was intent on hooking my kids on reading. (Looking back, I think I should have felt ecstatic about my students' enthusiasm.) I continued to search for appropriate literature, reading that was exciting but manageable, challenging, and current without being Steven King-slick. Our school librarians supported my quest, as did friends and the owners of a bookstore where I'd bought hundreds of paperbacks for previous classes.

Throughout the year, I kept asking my kids what kinds of books they wanted to read. They usually shrugged or answered, "I don't like books!" or, as fourteen-year-old Kenny wrote, "I don't like to read because I do not know how to read." Although most of my students never did tell me their desires directly, I watched and listened to them carefully, then tried to bring in articles, poems, and stories that seemed to match their preferences.

Appealing but difficult YA novels such as Sue Ellen Bridgers's *Home Before Dark* or Virginia Hamilton's *Sweet Whispers, Brother Rush* were suitable only if I read them aloud five minutes each day during class, or in certain cases if we read together. Books like these were on my students' age, interest, and grade level but they were much too long and difficult for all but a few students to read independently. Thus, I was constantly on the lookout for easy-to-read articles from *Sports Illustrated* or *Time* as well as manageable novels and poetry.

The imperative of reading aloud to older students

I knew that if I could tantalize my students, I could gently bring them to literature. One day early in the school year, I brought Sue Ellen Bridgers's *Home Before Dark* to my most recalcitrant, passive eighth-grade, eighth-period class—a time in the school day when even the most ardent students slump tiredly. Before I read aloud, we talked about migrant workers. Few had heard about them even though men, women, and children picked grapes, apples, and other crops just north of Cleveland. As I made this connection, I slid in a brief vocabulary lesson: "Which words do you know that have the same root as *migrant*?" Cleo offered *migration*; Jon thought about *immigration*, and Stephanie connected another word-relative, *immigrant*. I jotted these words on the chalkboard along with their common root, *migrate*.

We talked briefly about the collection of related words, connecting their general meaning to migrating birds and then to the routine movement of workers who followed the crops. I mentioned Steinbeck's *Grapes of Wrath* and talked a little about Caesar Chavez and how he organized the farm workers to achieve better wages and living conditions. I created a sketchy backdrop before I began reading aloud Bridgers's moving story:

"The dusty white station wagon turned off the highway onto a narrow asphalt road that shimmered with steam and sunlight, then lurched at the downshift and, sucking air under its belly, roared into third."

Quite a few kids put their heads down on their desks. Others groaned because I was reading to them as if they were babies. But a few, like Cleo, sat quietly alert and expectant; they wanted to hear more. Each day I read to this class for the first five minutes after everyone was seated. And each day a few more kids quickly settled down, ready to listen to the next installment.

After two weeks of reading for five or ten minutes of our forty-two minute period, many kids were hooked. One day when an assembly shortened the class time, I broke routine and didn't read *Home Before Dark*. The next day, Jon said: "Ah, come on, Mrs. Krogness, you *never, ever* read that book to us anymore." Mind you, Jon had been one of the students who'd accused me of treating them "like kindergartners" because I was reading aloud!

Reading aloud to my students daily brought us together and hooked them on literature.

Everyone loves to hear a good story. Because many of the kids hadn't been read bedtime stories by their parents when they were little, my reading *Home Before Dark* or sometimes telling them parts of a story fulfilled several needs: it allowed us to start class quickly and it invited everyone to settle *down* and settle *into* language, to savor the easy rhythm of the story setting, and to picture the characters. Listening to the book made reading seem accessible to these young people, who often declared themselves nonreaders.

The luxury of hearing a story freed my kids to step out of their own lives and know another young person's dreams and disappointments. Stella, a girl about their age in the story, was hungry for love and life. She was, in some respects, a lot like them; life hadn't been served up to her on a silver platter, either.

Small victories

Although few overtly expressed pleasure in *Home Before Dark,* my students regularly asked me how long I would read. They listened intently. One day Mokita brought along a copy of *Home Before Dark* that she'd gotten from our school library and silently read along with me in class. "I love this story," Mokita confided to me after class. "I couldn't wait to hear what was going to happen next, so I got my own copy." Mokita paused. "Mrs. Krogness, do you mind if I read a little bit ahead?"

"You must really like this book," I smiled, barely able to contain my excitement. "Of course I don't mind. I'm pleased as peaches."

"My mom can't believe that I'm actually reading a book that I don't *have* to read for class. She knows how much I hate to read—how much I *usually* hate to read. But this book is different," Mokita added. She completed *Home Before Dark* on her own in several weeks. Based on her pleasure with Bridgers's novel, I gave her another story I thought she would like, *One Child* by Torey L. Hayden. Mokita didn't finish it. Conversion doesn't happen overnight, but the seed for pleasurable reading had been planted.

Hearing a novel read aloud became an intoxicating experience for more than just Mokita, Jon, and Cleo. Others went to the library and checked out their own copies so that they could read along with me each day.

Bringing young people to literature

Hooking seventh and especially eighth graders on literature was a challenge, and I constantly searched to find inviting ways to bring my kids to it. As Thanksgiving approached, I looked for a piece of literature that would parallel the intentions of the founders of our country and one that would have meaning for my students.

Martin Luther King Jr.'s "I Have A Dream Speech," provided exactly what I was looking for. Pat Baird, head librarian par excellence, found a complete tape of King's speech and an unabridged script of what happened in Washington, D.C., on August 28, 1963. My seventh- and eighth-grade students were riveted to photocopied scripts as they listened to that eventful moment in history unfold.

Together we listened (and read) as folk singer Joan Baez led the crowd in "We Shall Overcome." We heard Ralph Abernathy and other members of the Southern Christian Leadership Conference speak to supporters, both black and white, rich and poor, old and young, who had come together, two hundred thousand strong, before the Lincoln Memorial.

President John F. Kennedy spoke to the crowd, too, just three months before he died. Finally, Martin Luther King, Jr. spoke passionately and poetically about his dreams for America. I was moved by my students' rapt attention; the man became a living symbol to all of them.

In preparation for listening to the tape, I had made several preliminary remarks: "This important speech is similar in tone and intent to the dreams of early American settlers who fled oppressive governments to find freedom of speech and religion and to seek opportunity. Like the Pilgrims, Dr. King and the civil rights workers had a mission—that every American, regardless of race, color, nationality, or religious belief, would be free to make choices and enjoy equal opportunity and respect."

After we had heard King's stirring speech, I asked the students to respond in writing. I provided two assignments broad enough to give each writer latitude, yet specific enough to help him or her to focus: (1) write a paragraph about the dreams you have for yourself; (2) write a second paragraph about the dreams you have for the world. Figure 8-1 shows Erik's, Nona's, and Kenetta's.

My students had begun the difficult transition from mostly working their way through packaged reading kits, filling in blanks, and writing short answers to questions to thinking independently. But the process would take time. Each experience that engaged them in real inquiry contributed to changing their perceptions of themselves as well.

Erik

11-89

One of my dreams that I am determined to make come true for myself, is to become a very successful Veterinarian. I am willing to work hard and make a lot of sacrifices to do so. With the help of family and friends, to make me strive, I know I can be one. I am determined to be the best at what I want to be.

The dream I have for the world is that the entire human race establish a common trust and friendship among ourselves. We must break down the walls of racism, prejudice of Nationality or our cultures. We are all on this earth together. So why not love and get along with each other. We're not animals, we have minds to talk out our problems. There is no reason for war and violence between man.

FIG. 8-1A   *Erik's Dreams*

Nona

11-89

In the near Future I have a dream to be a F.B.I. agent or a Sergon. I want to be a middle aged woman living in a comfortable house owened by me and designed by me. I would like to be married with two children and be comfortable in money. I would like to have a Nice Looking husband who would take care of me. and who loves me. and who would Never leave me ★ I would like the world to stop the drugs by the time I grow up and have children. My dream for this world is to stop the drug wars and have all the abandoned children in the world to be Happy AND have good parents and living safely in Nice homes.

★ and who has a sence of humor and is fun to be with.

FIG. 8-1B   *Nona's Dreams*

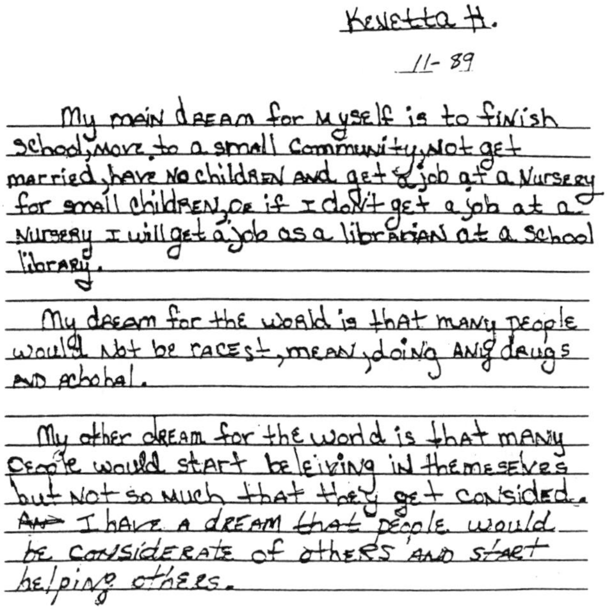

Kenetta H.

11-89

My main dream for myself is to finish school, move to a small community, not get married, have no children and get a job at a nursery for small children, or if I don't get a job at a nursery I will get a job as a librarian at a school library.

My dream for the world is that many people would not be racest, mean, doing any drugs and achohal.

My other dream for the world is that many people would start beleiving in themeselves but not so much that they get consided. And I have a dream that people would be considerate of others and start helping others.

FIG. 8-1C *Kenetta's Dreams*

Necessity is the mother of invention: Plan A

A question I eventually figured out was this: how would I introduce my eighth graders to Shakespeare to prepare them for a week of working with professional actors from the Great Lakes Theatre Festival? The year before I'd tried reading *Enchanted Island* aloud to them, Ian Serraillier's excellent story version of major Shakespeare plays, and followed it with discussion. But I wasn't satisfied. I felt driven to find a more exciting approach to *Julius Caesar*. I wanted my most persistent readers to come face to face with the philosophical and moral dilemmas of the play before we read the story version and a few key lines and speeches in Elizabethan English from the play.

My idea was to get my students to speculate about possible motives for Caesar's brutal murder by his friends. Since at this point my students knew nothing about the story, I had to invent a way of conveying the first part to them. I decided to try using three newspaper headlines to lure them into this intense story.

1. SOOTHSAYER WARNS CAESAR OF OWN ASSASSINATION ON MARCH 15
2. CAESAR BRUTALLY MURDERED ON IDES OF MARCH BY FRIENDS
3. CAESAR: ALLY TO THE PEOPLE OR GREEDY TYRANT?

Before we divided into teams of five to make conjectures about possible reasons for Caesar's murder, we read the three newspaper headlines *aloud* and discussed the meaning of *soothsayer* and *Ides of March*. Then I pointed to a map of Caesar's empire, talking informally about him, the heir-apparent to the throne, a Roman who lived before Christ and a man who would, according to a fortune teller, die by the swords of men who ostensibly were his friends. I asked my students to consider *why* friends of Julius Caesar might be *motivated* to kill this great leader who, by going to battle, had accumulated masses of land and many spoils of war for Rome. He'd given parks to the people and left the coffers, or treasury, full. What might Caesar have done to cause his friends to commit such a deed?

With this scant information, each group brainstormed a minimum of twenty-five possible reasons for Caesar's demise. I gave them a limit of fifteen minutes to talk and briefly jot their one-word speculations. Not only did every group exceed the minimum of twenty-five motives for Caesar's murder, but they were electrified in the process!

Derrick, normally passive, was an enthusiastic contributor to his group's list. So were Natachia, Laurelia, Jason, Dwight, Nona, Brandon, and Tristin. The group who collected forty-five motives, the highest point winners, and the group with the least, thirty-six, all worked feverishly for the greater good. Taking a cue from Les Brown, the nationally known motivational expert who'd come to our school to work with these students and their parents and teachers, I gave unexpected rewards: I tossed chocolate kisses to the winners.

The reporter in each group (whom I'd appointed when I assigned the groups) read the group's list to the class. Here are the more plausible motives generated by the teams:

Sample motives generated by student groups
1. Caesar—power hungry and greedy
2. Corrupt
3. Played favorites and gave good jobs to a few (I later labeled this practice *nepotism*)
4. Jealousy of his position
5. Ambitious friends
6. Womanizer
7. Senile
8. Paranoid
9. Stingy
10. Lazy now that he knew he would soon become king
11. Cruel
12. Crazy
13. Cowardly
14. Superstitious
15. Afraid of death
16. Suicide wish, so J.C. hired one of his friends to kill him
17. Love affair (a love affair between Caesar's wife and one of her husband's friends)
18. Prediction (the fortune teller predicted Caesar's death because the soothsayer wanted to become king)
19. Gang war
20. Caesar—unpopular (during the discussion that followed the small-group work, I added to this one by suggesting that J.C. might have wanted to become a martyr and thus, through death, to become popular again)

What extraordinary ideas these students, who customarily slouched in their seats during class projects, had generated—working together *without* my intervention.

Through this exercise, my students were starting to piece together the story line of Julius Caesar, too. I was ecstatic. So were they, in an offhanded way.

Their excitement freed them to discuss some real-life situations that motivated people—even honorable people—to become corrupt. This was the logical time to weave in more of the play and tell them about the honorable Brutus, his friendship with and misgivings about Caesar, and his conspiracy with Cassius and other senators to kill the ruler. This naturally led to my weaving in the avarice of Cassius, the man with "a lean and hungry look." I introduced them to the smooth Marc Antony, whose persuasive speech, along with that of Brutus, we chanted each day during class. Thus, we'd generated a profusion of ideas, interacted with the text and each other, and collaborated in our richest literary conversation to date.

A bit of jocularity ensued when I told this class that according to my experience with the Great Lakes Shakespeare actors, we very likely would learn to use real swords.

"What if a kid *accidentally* is clipped by a sword?" Jermaine wondered.

"What's one kid? There's a population problem in the world, anyhow." My face and voice were deadpan. A few kids laughed.

Jermaine momentarily looked puzzled. Then he quickly recovered and countered, "But what if a *teacher* gets it?"

"That's wishful thinking, Jermaine," I laughed.

Necessity is the mother of invention: Plan B

My next written plan went like this. Each newly formed team of five read along silently while I read this introductory piece aloud: "The date is March 14, the day before Julius Caesar is murdered. You and your teammates are investigative reporters. You have just heard rumors that Julius Caesar, the prospective emperor of Rome, will be assassinated on the Ides of March, March 15. The five of you are to interview various people who might have *feelings, opinions, knowledge,* or *concerns* about the death threat."

I talked briefly with my students about being reporters, preparing them for the work of formulating provocative interview questions. Then I presented another printout listing six important facts, which I read aloud slowly for the benefit of group members:

Facts about Caesar's assassination

1. A *soothsayer* or fortune-teller warns that Caesar will be murdered on March 15, *the Ides of March.*
2. *Cassius,* a jealous and crafty man and a senator, talks to *Brutus,* a fair and honest man who is Caesar's best friend, about the problems with their next ruler. Cassius tries to persuade Brutus of Caesar's growing desire to become king.
3. *Brutus* is concerned about Caesar's apparent desire for power. Brutus, a senator, wants to protect Rome at all cost—even if it means that his friend's life is sacrificed.
4. *Cassius* tries to persuade the honorable Brutus to be a part of his conspiracy (plot) to murder Caesar.
5. Cassius anonymously slips letters that praise Caesar, yet hint of his driving ambition, through an open window of Brutus's home the night before Caesar's murder.

6. *Calpurnia,* Caesar's wife, dreams that her husband will be murdered. She begs her husband not to go to the Senate the following day, but Caesar dismisses his wife's warnings and goes anyway.

Before the newly formed teams met to develop their interview questions, we talked about the people they might wish to interview: Caesar himself; Calpurnia, Caesar's wife; Brutus, Caesar's best friend; Portia, Brutus's wife; Cassius, who like Caesar was a general and is now a senator; the soothsayer; the senators Casca, Decius, Cinna, Metellus, and Trebonius; and perhaps Titinius, Caesar's slave boy who had accompanied the general during battle. I wrote the characters' names (all of them new to my students) on the chalkboard, pronouncing each.

Next, I reminded them that *how* and *why* questions (which we'd spent many earlier class periods learning how to ask) generally evoked the most interesting responses. I also instructed the recorder/reporter for each group to address the character being questioned and thus write his or her name at the beginning of each question. For example, "Brutus, if Caesar is such a dear friend, why are you helping to plan his murder?" Or, "Calpurnia, how do you feel about the soothsayer's prophecy about your husband's death?"

Each team would generate as many questions as it could in fifteen minutes. When I turned the teams loose, they were off and running. The sound of students' animated voices was music to my ears.

Sample interview questions generated by student groups
1. Brutus, what is your relationship with Caesar?
2. Soothsayer, how do you know that Julius will be murdered tomorrow?
3. Cassius, why do you want Caesar dead? Explain.
4. Calpurnia, are you going to be a partner in your husband's murder? If so, why?
5. Cassius, where will you be tomorrow (the Ides of March)?
6. Brutus, if you're really a good friend of Caesar, will you allow the murder? Why? How will you feel when your best friend is dead, Brutus?
7. Caesar, why do people want to overthrow you and want you dead?
8. Caesar, who do you think your worst enemies are? Why?
9. Caesar, what are your fears about dying?
10. Caesar, if you say that you are not superstitious, why are you worried about what the soothsayer says?
11. Calpurnia, what are your plans (for yourself) since you've found out that your husband is going to die?

Each reporter read his or her group's questions to the class. For the next two days, the class and I identified and then discussed the implications of the most promising questions. On the third day, I played the part of Julius Caesar and invited anyone in the class to interview me. I also determined the winning team by assessing the quantity and the quality of its questions. (One team didn't stipulate the character to whom each question was directed and thus was out of the running.) This time the award was a privilege: to go to the library during one class period and browse or read for pleasure. At moments like this, I felt that I was helping my students develop new habits of mind.

The uses of enchantment

Because my seventh and eighth graders told me in any number of ways that they were interested in human relationships, success stories, and issues like truth and justice, I decided to bring fairy tales to a seventh-grade class. My idea was not to fill in what they'd missed as kids but to use the fairy tales as vehicles for gaining access to the human condition.

But wouldn't middle school students perceive fairy tales as beneath them? Depending on the group of kids and the ways in which fairy tales are introduced and woven into the curriculum, I've found they can be used to great advantage. With the expert help of our librarian, Pat Fagel, I used traditional literature in one seventh-grade class as the core of a reading experience that stretched over six weeks and quite naturally encompassed all the language arts—listening, talking, reading, writing, improvising, and viewing.

During Pat's and my initial planning, I explained that I wanted to build a series of library and classroom lessons around fairy tales, especially the familiar ones such as "Hansel and Gretel," "Cinderella," "Beauty and the Beast," and "Rapunzel." I wanted this to be an excursion into literature, an intellectual and creative experience that would prompt my seventh graders to notice different writers' ways of interpreting an old, familiar story. I wanted my students to realize an author's power in determining the personality and motives of, let's say, Hansel and Gretel's stepmother or the witch.

We "read" many illustrators' artistic renderings of a single fairy tale and noticed the differences. For example, some illustrators imagined the witch in "Hansel and Gretel" as a sweet-looking little dumpling who lived in a candy-covered cottage, while other artists envisioned her as a wizened hag who lived in a thatched hut. Pat Fagel ordered an interesting and rather nontraditional film version of the story, a Davenport film produced in the hills of West Virginia; the Appalachian setting added yet another flavor to this familiar tale. In particular, the language and the attitude toward men's and women's roles stimulated our thinking. Cylenthia observed: "*This* stepmother seems real scared of her husband. She's being sort of sneaky about getting rid of *his* kids." This stepmother and her new husband obviously hadn't been liberated!

Pat Fagel, a voracious reader, exciting storyteller, and imaginative teacher, collected through interschool library loan versions of *Cinderella* from the United States, France, China, Vietnam, and Korea (where two of my students come from). Pat created simple library lessons that helped us identify such universal themes as good struggling to overcome evil or the weak and downtrodden struggling to prevail. Together we learned about important motifs or symbols from different countries: the crystal slipper from France, the red brocade one from Vietnam, the white silk slipper from China, and the reddish-gold gilded slipper from Egypt, which symbolized what each culture valued. Pat Fagel also explained the symbolic meaning of recurring numbers, such as the number three in traditional literature: the three billy goats gruff, the three little kittens, the three blind mice, the three bears who take in Goldilocks.

Here is an outline of Pat's library lessons on fairy tales:

I. Introduction to the genre.
II. Comparison of different authors' versions of one fairy tale, for instance *Cinderella*.

III. Analysis of illustrations in different versions of one fairy tale.
IV. A study of recurring motifs or symbolic patterns, such as the evil stepmother, and important numbers, such as three.

Using the gifts that kids give

For two weeks we had heard about evil witches and wizards, marauding giants and beasts, cruel stepmothers and stepsisters. Then it happened. One Wednesday morning during our regularly scheduled library period, we focused on "Hansel and Gretel," and specifically one of the most common motifs in traditional literature: the stepmother (I hesitate to call her an *evil* stepmother because so many women in our contemporary society are stepmothers).

I raised this question: "Why do you believe that Hansel and Gretel's stepmother abandoned them in the forest?"

"She didn't like 'em!" Marie called out with conviction.

"How many of you believe that the stepmother planned to get rid of the children because she didn't like them?" I asked. Everyone except Chris M. raised a hand.

"In other words, all of you except for Chris believe that the stepmother is an evil, selfish woman who hates children?" They nodded affirmatively.

"Chris, I notice that you don't agree with the others. Might you have other ideas about the stepmother in 'Hansel and Gretel'?"

"Well, I have a stepmom, and she's one of the nicest people I've ever met. She's kind to me, too." Chris, an usually perceptive boy, generalized about stepmothers on the basis of his own experience. Several more students in the class had stepmothers or stepfathers; one student had foster parents. Tiawan's father had recently remarried, but Tiawan wasn't sure yet how his new stepmother would work out. "So far she's nice," Tiawan said.

"So if not all stepmothers are cruel, do you think that stepmothers get a bum rap in fairy tales?"

Chris smiled and nodded. Here was a moment not to be missed. I wanted to push this point further and hear what other students thought; I wanted to show them that a good question can evoke *many* exciting responses as well as more questions. "Why *else* might the stepmother be motivated to 'lose' her stepchildren in the forest?" Although I used words such as *motivated* that might be unfamiliar, I didn't always take the time to inquire whether my students understood the new word. A teacher should use rich language to broaden young people's repertoire and grant them the dignity they deserve; anyhow, most kids can figure out what's being said from the context.

The question "Why else might the stepmother be motivated to 'lose' her stepchildren in the forest?" prompted a grand variety of hypothesizing. "Maybe she didn't know what she was getting into." I pressed shy Tiawan to elaborate on this interesting comment. "I mean, maybe the woodcutter didn't tell his new wife that he had two kids *before* he proposed to her. I bet she was surprised to find them."

"What do the rest of you think?" Several kids commented that Tiawan might be right. I pressed on. "How might a woman (or a man) feel when she (or he) is surprised about something as major as getting new stepchildren?" Most of the kids expressed a bit of passing empathy toward the stepmother, but they thought she'd resorted to unusually harsh measures. "Doesn't each person in here have the capacity to be cruel and harsh if and when she or he feels desperate?" I wanted to plant a seed, to connect reality with the truths expressed in this fairy tale. "When we're pushed beyond the limit of our capacity to cope, our desperation often leads us to react in extraordinary ways." But I didn't want to digress for too long from the important issues we were discussing: possible motives for the stepmother's cruelty.

"Besides the fact that she might not like kids or that she might not have known what she was getting into, what other reasons might she have had for abandoning the children in the forest?"

"Maybe the stepkids weren't nice to their new stepmother. Maybe they ganged up on her and whispered behind her back and did snotty little things to get on her nerves and make her feel bad," Jamar said. Everyone could relate to this possibility. They knew all too well what happened when *little* children (certainly not grown-up children like them) resented or disliked an adult!

"Why might the kids dislike the stepmother, though?" I asked. Jamar volunteered another good idea: "Maybe the kids were real mean to the stepmother because they missed their real mother." Jamar's subtle insight gave us a glorious opportunity to talk about Hansel and Gretel's bereavement. Of course these children would resent this intruder! Marie, whose own mother had died the year before, smiled knowingly as she spoke.

"You *can* feel real angry—besides feeling sad—when your mom dies," Marie said with authority.

Then Jermaine charged in: "Maybe the stepmother thought, 'Shoot, these brats aren't *my* kids! Why should *I* have to put up with them?' "

We were plumbing the depth of a simple fairy tale that brought life's truths to us. In *The Uses of Enchantment,* Bruno Bettelheim says, "Fairy tales get across to the child in manifold form: that a struggle against severe difficulties in life is unavoidable, is an intrinsic part of existence—but that if one does not shy away, but steadfastly meets unexpected and often unjust hardship, one masters all obstacles and at the end emerges victorious" (p. 8).

I continued prodding my students to think further: "So, you think that other circumstances might play into the stepmother's abandoning Hansel and Gretel in the forest?" My kids needed an opportunity to think before they responded to essentially the same question we'd begun to consider thirty-five minutes earlier. Time is an important commodity when people are grappling with a heady idea. So are patience and tenacity. I am learning to be patient, to endure the space of silence and not to toe-tap while a student is thinking through a problem. Occasionally, I give a student time by saying, "I'll get back to you after you've had a chance to think this idea through."

A purposeful summarizing

When no one offered new ideas for our list, I summarized our conversation: "So far, we've talked about the stepmother's possible motives or reasons for treating her stepchildren cruelly: (1) she might not like kids, specifically Hansel and Gretel; (2) perhaps she didn't know what she was getting into; (3) probably the kids miss their natural mother; (4) the stepchildren might have treated her unkindly because they resented her intrusion into their family; (5) the stepmother, on the other hand, might resent her two stepchildren because they aren't her children.

"We've uncovered five possible motives for her behavior. But on an even larger scale, we're talking about point of view. A person's point of view about something is the way he or she sees the issue. Each one of us sees and feels strongly about this issue from a different angle because our life experiences have been different. For example, Chris's stepmother is a nice person, so his experience with stepmothers is positive. Other kids whose stepmothers or stepfathers aren't kind might think of all stepparents negatively. Do you see that our life experiences help determine how we feel in various situations?"

Moving from the personal to the general

Finally, we returned to the key question: "Besides the stepmother's not liking children, what are other possible motives or reasons for the stepmother behaving so cruelly?" Lisa S., who often was preoccupied during discussions, entered into this one.

"Maybe the children's father didn't really help the stepmother. I mean, she was new to the household. Maybe he sided with his kids and didn't take sides with her." Lisa was getting at another important and subtle issue: the changing dynamics of a reconstituted family.

"In other words, Lisa, the balance of this family unit has been tipped since the stepmother has moved in. The old ways of doing things have shifted, but maybe the woodcutter *is* acting as if nothing has changed."

Pat Fagel asked another question: "In what ways do you think this household has changed since the stepmother joined it?"

"Well, maybe the new stepmom went out and bought a lot of new stuff for the house—new curtains and lamps, tables and furniture and stuff. My new stepmom's doing that!" Tiawan smiled. Nontraditional learners lean heavily on personal experiences, but it's our job to help them make generalizations and recognize other points of view.

"What might be happening if the stepmother is going out and buying lots of new furniture and so forth?" I asked.

"Maybe the stepfather was getting upset. I don't know how much [money] wood-cutters make, but maybe he sees his Master Card bill going up," Jawan remarked. We laughed.

"Maybe she's spending so much money that the family doesn't even have enough to eat, so the stepmother's gotta take those kids to the woods and lose 'em," Chris observed.

I quickly picked up on Chris's observation. "In other words, not having enough money can cause people to feel frightened, so frightened that they resort to doing desperate, even terrible things."

Again, I summarized our conversation. "Today we've talked about people's feelings and how they react when they acquire children who aren't their own; how children react when stepparents join households; we've talked about the difficulties of creating new families when adults remarry. We've also discussed kids losing their mothers or fathers through death and divorce, and feeling rejected, sad, abandoned, and angry as a result.

"Do you realize that having considered 'Hansel and Gretel,' an old and familiar fairy tale, we have come to understand ourselves and real life right now in the twentieth century better? And Chris, you gave us all a present when you started this conversation by declaring not *all* stepmothers are cruel!"

Pat Fagel, a new stepmother herself, smiled and told us that she was glad that we'd come to some positive conclusions about stepmothers!

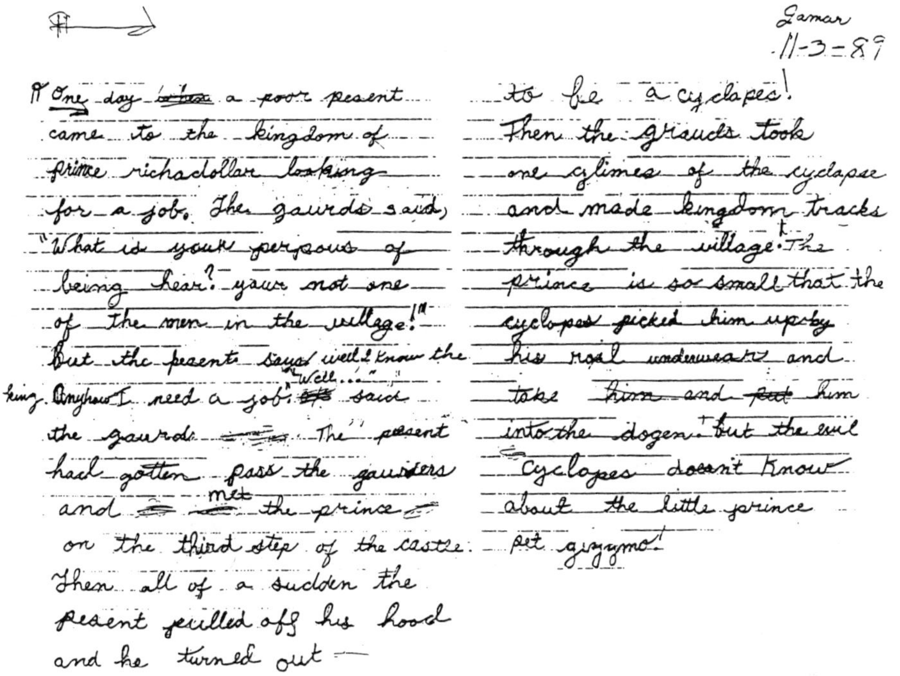
Jamar
11-3-89

One day ~~when~~ a poor pesent came to the kingdom of prince richadollar looking for a job. The gaurds said, "What is your perpous of being hear? your not one of the men in the village!" But the pesent says well I know the king. Anyhow I need a job." "Well..." said the gaurds. The pesent had gotten pass the gauiders and met the prince on the third step of the castle. Then all of a sudden the pesent pulled off his hood and he turned out — to be a cyclapes! Then the grauds took one glimes of the cyclapse and made kingdom tracks through the village. The prince is so small that the cyclopes picked him up by his roal underwears and take ~~him and put~~ him into the dogen. but the evil cyclopes doesn't know about the little prince pet gizzymo!

FIG. 8-2 *Excerpt from Jamar's Fairy Tale*

A springboard to understanding

Such a simple story had been a springboard to a highly intellectual and psychological discussion that ignited our imaginations and included all of us. It encouraged students to draw on their experiences and provided a manageable structure for moving beyond our experiences to generalize about human nature. This part of our literary excursion was from the inside out. Indeed, a magic moment.

In *Literature as Exploration,* Louise Rosenblatt says:

> The word *exploration* is designed to suggest primarily that the experience of literature, far from being for the reader a passive process of absorption, is a form of intense personal activity. (p. 54)

We also responded to fairy tales by creating our own. In class we contemplated typical fairy tale themes: good struggling to overcome evil, generosity struggling to overcome greed, humility struggling to overcome arrogance, and so forth. Through discussion, and later through writing, we created heroic and malevolent characters who confronted each other on all sorts of issues. Through brainstorming sessions in class, we imagined the personalities and appearances of wizards, genies, and gremlins in elaborate disguises. Figures 8-2 and 8-3 show excerpts from two students' fairy tales in rough draft form.

According to Bruno Bettelheim, the simple characters and clear conflicts in traditional literature allow young people to work through their own emotions. As they read

The Legend of Karist   11 — '38 =
                                Chris M.

It was a dark stormy night. every one was in there huts shivering exsept me and some friend were playing rocal chess and pesants run. We were having fun, the then the weather was worming up it got so warm that all the rain cleared up, that WAS uzen the people started back. the Dark Over lord was seen in the distance the people got back to their huts and they got their wepans and stood in front of the passage way the people with the Dark over Lord went sharging on an inogent village, they were swinging balls and chains we were runing around and my friend Jaken got captured my mother was snached to!

Marco

, My cousin and I were Making arrangements to get my mother back. As we were walking through the Halls of the forest we saw an aband hut it

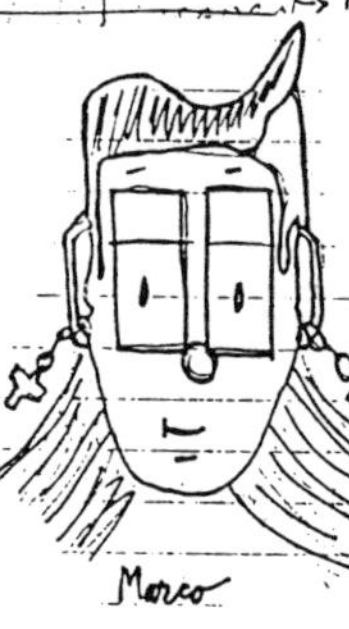

was pretty big it had two

. Now to get some

sleep and start are incredibable

Torney tomorrow. Good sleep
                                Marco
Tamarie "said Marco" You to, (Next morning)

Let get going Tamarie" look

at the sky look its so dark

if we go when its

dark the gards of the parimid

will not see us "O.K!" -- ok.

So what is the plan?

The two young warios ran through the coridors of

the forest the cricts are

creeking, the fly are Buzzing

the wind is smacking there
                        desratly
faces they run

through the forest to save marco's

mother and his frend.

FIG. 8-3   Chris M.'s Fairy Tale

about goodness struggling to prevail, young people recognize their own power to take charge even in the face of crisis.

The successful fairy tale experience made me pause to consider the ways we'd been engaged in thinking and reading. Here is how I finally defined the process: prereading, reading, reflecting, rereading, reassessing.

The thinking/reading process

The first step in the interactive reading process is *prereading,* building a common landscape with young readers that can mean finding out what students bring to the literary experience and helping them use that knowledge and experience to approach the text. Before reading, the teacher introduces the students to the historical events, vocabulary, motives, and people they'll need to know about to understand the literature and encourages them to hypothesize about the characters' actions and reactions. Raising questions is also an essential component of prereading.

The second step, *reading* the text, has various meanings depending on the reader's expertise. Experienced readers might read the whole piece quickly (if it's short) or skim it to gain an overall understanding and appreciation of the author's intentions. With inexperienced readers—particularly readers who face extreme difficulty just decoding and understanding vocabulary—the teacher must assume some of the responsibility. For example, I often read aloud passages or whole pages to my students during the initial reading, while my students silently read along with me. In this way, students had the luxury of savoring the language and the story without the burden of decoding. By reading along with me silently, they were in effect practicing basic reading skills and feeling the tension of the story's climactic events. Later, the students read aloud short, manageable passages of the text we were reading together during class.

Thus, my students and I took turns reading aloud and discussing the story, and sometimes I told parts of it to generate interest, move the story along, or build in transitions. As time-consuming as all this may sound, years of experimenting have shown me it's the only combination that works. Curiously, my underprepared readers enjoyed reading aloud, even though they stalled and stumbled, reversed and mispronounced words. They begged me to let them read aloud, probably because it helped them direct their energy and focus their attention; perhaps it also gave them a feeling of accomplishment, for they could see their progress as we made our way through a novel. Through daily contact with print, many of my kids became more skillful decoders. When we stopped to reflect on a character's reaction, shed light on an issue, and give our opinions, everyone felt a part of the group, the literacy club that Frank Smith talks about in *Joining the Literacy Club.* The pleasure of the process was ours to savor.

In the third step of the reading process, *reflecting,* the reader steps back and assesses her thoughts about what she's read; through conversation or written response, the reader also gains understanding. Reflection allows readers to clarify and redefine their attitudes or convictions. They can test their suppositions on their teacher or peers, then return to the story to hone their thinking. The process of reflecting creates a state of change in which few things are absolute and linear.

My students and I reflected before, during, and after reading a text. We made observations and predictions; we raised questions that we considered and reconsidered before we drew conclusions. We reflected by talking, writing responses, and performing passages of a novel or a whole poem. Because I never worried that we were required to cover a certain amount of material within a particular time, we had the luxury of uncovering and discovering.

Ideally, a class should read a story or particular passages of a story more than once, the step of the reading process I'll call *rereading*. With each reading, the reader brings more understanding to the text and breaks free to consider larger issues and more subtle details.

During all this time, each reader is *reassessing,* according to the text's power of persuasion and the reader's own readiness for change. Asking students what they have figured out and how they came to those conclusions is another way of helping them to explore the text. My students found this step difficult because they were so accustomed to looking for *the* right answer. The ultimate goal, of course, is to hook kids on reading so that they will independently seek new material and embark on a continuous quest to explore literature.

Applying the process

Much of this interaction between the reader and the text takes place at a level below conscious thought. But the teacher, the architect of the thinking experience, consciously designs the opportunities. Here's how my students and I used the process I've just described to meet and interact with Natalie Babbitt's story *Tuck Everlasting*.

Prereading

First, I spent plenty of time laying the groundwork by talking about our philosophy or belief systems. To help everyone understand what I meant by a *personal philosophy,* I asked kids to describe their philosophy about such familiar subjects as having an after-school job and then about more complicated issues like selling drugs. Finally, I asked my students to contemplate the main issue in Babbitt's novel: immortality (a word I explained). "How many of you would like to live forever?" I asked. All but one or two seventh graders raised his or her hand enthusiastically.

"Why?" I asked. "What *advantages* might there be to living forever?" (I paused to explain the word *advantages.*)

Roslind said that she'd like to live forever because she could meet lots of famous people. Greg responded that one could remain young, energetic, and healthy forever if he were immortal.

Chris K., new to our class because of a schedule change, quickly thought about all of the dreams every person could fulfill if an infinite amount of time were available. Greg picked up on Chris's response and said that if he could live forever, he could be certain if his children and his children's children had fulfilled their dreams.

Danyell imagined that immortality would allow a person to know her entire family. We talked about people's need to find their roots, to achieve a feeling of belonging, continuity, and connection. Kenya reasoned that if a person lived forever, she would surely know all that the future offered—cures for AIDS and cancer, solutions to pollution and drug addiction, new knowledge about our universe.

One of the most poignant responses was Rayshon's: "If I could live forever, I won't lose my gramma. Then I won't be afraid of losing people I love." (Rayshon had lost his beloved grandmother within the last year and was still in mourning.) Ryan, too, spoke seriously: "If we lived forever, no one would have to worry about wars and weapons. There would be no reason to try killing anyone because no one could die."

We spent the whole class period talking philosophically about the advantages of living forever, and I recorded everyone's responses on the chalkboard. I emphasized that almost every philosophical question had at *least* two sides. The next day I planned to continue laying the groundwork before we began reading the novel: asking my students to consider the disadvantages of living forever. Considering the liabilities of eternal life would, I imagined, challenge our thinking even more powerfully. I started class by saying: "What new thoughts do you have today about immortality? Could we consider the disadvantages of immortality?" Fred quickly responded, "I can think of disadvantages of living forever: one is, there wouldn't be enough room on this earth." Thus began a lively discussion of overpopulation and its attendant problems: pollution, unwanted children, poverty, and crime. Greg imagined that if people lived forever, they would run out of space, water, and oxygen.

Chris K. thought living forever would get awfully boring: what would there be to look forward to? My students' insights into the difficulties of immortality seemed to me unusually imaginative and perceptive. Maybe it was Kenya who said: "Just think, you couldn't grow up and you couldn't grow old either."

Fred, who became impatient whenever things didn't move along in a snappy fashion, thought that it would be awful to be always waiting around. Greg, who enjoyed daydreaming and procrastinating, recognized the possibilities: "I wouldn't have to do my homework for years, even centuries!" "And by that time, you be forgetting what the assignment was," Freddie quipped.

Danyell considered that living forever would preclude dying, denying a person the opportunity to know "the other half of life: heaven." Danyell's comment prompted Rayshon to say that religion would be nonexistent because if one could live forever, he wouldn't need a higher being from whom to seek comfort and guidance. Ryan wondered if people would even care about being good or think about right and wrong.

It was time to repeat the key question: "All right, *now* how many of you want to be immortal and live forever?" This time, no one but Roslind wanted to live forever. It was April, and we'd been practicing long enough that we all felt free to talk easily with one another and change our minds.

Now we were nearly ready to read *Tuck Everlasting,* the story of a family who accidentally drinks the water of everlasting life. But first we spent two more class periods reading the prologue, which is only one and a half pages long but demands careful thinking. (Curiously, no one grumbled about delaying the gratification of reading the story.)

The prologue reveals three apparently unrelated incidents that happen on a day in early August when the air is still and the heat oppressive:

1. At dawn, Mae Tuck leaves home for the wood near the town of Treegap to meet her sons, Miles and Jesse, something she does every ten years.
2. At noon, eleven-year-old Winnie Foster thinks about running away because she's bored by her life with her parents and grandmother.
3. At sunset, a man in a yellow suit stops by Winnie Foster's house to inquire about a person whose name he doesn't mention.

My students and I talked about the circular nature of these three events. We considered what besides this story was circular: a full day, when the earth makes one complete rotation on its axis; a calendar year, when the earth revolves completely around the sun. Kids mentioned that the sun, moon, and the planets themselves are circular, that clocks' hands move around and around, that a wedding ring is circular. The word, *cycle,* prompted us to talk about the life cycle of a butterfly or moth.

Only one student, Chris K., realized that this entire story would take place within one day. We would be considering the profound implications of all eternity within the span of twenty-four hours. After all this warming up, everyone was hooked.

Reading

We started reading *Tuck Everlasting* aloud: "The road that led to Treegap had been trod out long before by a herd of cows who were, to say the least, relaxed." We took turns reading passages aloud, then laid our paperbacks down. We discussed the plight of Winnie Foster, who rarely is permitted to go beyond the "capable iron fence" that defined the yard of her family's "touch-me-not" cottage. We wondered why the Tucks had drunk the water that imprisoned them. We wondered how the three apparently separate events would connect. Several kids speculated that Winnie Foster's fussy grandmother was somehow connected to the mysterious man in the yellow suit—perhaps he had been her lover from long ago. A few hoped that Winnie, who was abducted by the Tucks because she knew their deadly secret, would drink from the spring beneath the Ash tree, become immortal, and marry Jesse Tuck.

My students and I took turns reading most of the text. When readers became weary—although they had built up their endurance for reading throughout the school year—I read aloud to them or, better yet, told them parts of the story. Mostly I told them the parts that served as bridges or transitions to the mysterious happenings. The happenings themselves we read with zest and enthusiasm together.

Reflecting

Throughout our reading of the story, we reflected on four key questions: What might this story be about? In what ways are the Tucks "sentenced to life"? (I used the powerful metaphor Greg had developed and made it into a question.) What might Angus Tuck mean when he tells Winnie "Life is heavy work"? What might Angus Tuck mean when he says to Winnie, "But it [life] is passing us by, us Tucks. But off to one side, it is useless, too. It don't make sense. If I knowed how to get back on the wheel, I'd do it in a minute. You can't have living without dying. So you can't call it living what we got. We just are, we just be, like rocks beside the road."

Rereading

Besides raising questions, speculating, and talking, we used improvisational drama to help us engage in and with the text. For instance, I played the role of the reporter who had gotten wind of the Tucks's dilemma: living forever. The kids played the story's characters or bystanders who notice that the Tucks haven't aged. We wrote responses to the various characters' comments and insights. We also used important conversations between Winnie Foster and the Tucks in a readers' theater—using our voices to interpret possible meanings.

Reassessing

Finally, it was the kids' turn to take the lead. I asked them to think about big questions that they might discuss among themselves in small groups. While we prepared questions that would provide a framework for their thinking and talking, we realized that we'd *already* considered very personal considerations and questions of ethics. For instance, Kenya remarked that she knew someone who was on a life-support system and had been kept alive for more than a year. She compared her grandmother's friend to the Tucks.

Here are the questions the students asked during a large group discussion in preparation for working in small groups:

- Why do you think Mae Tuck visits her sons every ten years? (Roslind)
- How did the Tucks find out they were immortal? (Ryan)
- Why did the Tucks drink spring water in the first place? (Rayshon)
- Why did the man in the yellow suit follow the Tucks? (Chris K.)
- Why did Tuck talk to Winnie Foster about the cycle? (Rayshon)
- How did Winnie feel about staying with the procrastinating Tucks? (Greg)
- Why are the Fosters so overprotective of Winnie? (Fred)
- What did the Tucks ask God to do for them since they had to live forever? (Danyell)
- How does the ferris wheel fit into the story? (Kenya)
- What does this story have to do with us? (Chris K.)

Before dividing into groups to discuss these questions, we practiced taking turns responding, listening, and building new questions from various students' responses. We also came to an understanding of what constituted appropriate behavior in a small group: (1) taking turns listening and talking; (2) finding the best moment to respond to another member's comment; (3) listening quietly, but actively.

When all the students seemed to be ready, I assigned them to discussion groups and appointed group leaders to lead and then report the results of their conversations. Groups worked together for about twelve minutes. While most of the groups discussed their questions successfully, one group could only fidget, laugh, and poke at one another until I sat down with them.

Some interesting ideas resulted from the group discussions. They represent fresh thinking that was stirred by reading and discussing *Tuck Everlasting*. One group speculated that the mysterious stranger in the yellow suit might not only be a man that Winnie's grandmother had once loved, but was, perhaps, Winnie's grandfather. Because this unusual fellow was doing his best to purchase the woods where the spring of eternal life was located, certain students were convinced that the man in the yellow suit wanted to sell the water to others and make a profit. This thought led one group to worry that the man in the yellow suit didn't realize the dire consequences of selling water that made people live forever.

The small group discussions also led to more questions: What is important about the little toad, Winnie Foster's only friend? How does the toad fit into the whole story? Another group asked the big existential question: What is the purpose of life? This group focused its entire discussion on the life cycle, which brings purpose and meaning to human existence. As Danyell said, "You've got to die if you have lived because that's in the plan. Look at the Tucks; they're just kinda hanging out with nowhere to go."

After our small-group discussions, we came together to talk about their significance. Greg said, "We are learning how to cooperate."

"Our discussion was pretty good, and we also got along good," Rayshon said of his group.

Ryan observed: "Our group was real serious about discussing. We answered just one question. We stuck to Rayshon's question about Tuck explaining the life cycle to Winnie—we stuck mainly with that question because it was a good one."

"Except for *one* person in our group, we did fine asking each other questions and answering them," Kenya said as she coolly eyed a less-than-responsible group member.

I asked the class what they viewed as the specific advantages of group work without the teacher's direct leadership.

"We should be independent at our age," Kenya said.

"Kids understand kids better than adults," Chris K. observed.

"I think that *teacher*-led talks are better because the teacher might understand our questions better than students. After all, teachers have more experience in making questions than we have." Rayshon spoke with conviction. But everyone agreed that it was important to have experienced the responsibility for a discussion. They also felt that creating excellent questions was a challenge.

It's up to us, the adults, to find ways to hook our students on literature. Then it's up to them to become invested in the experience. By turning reading into an adventure, we bring our students and ourselves together for the common good. By reading aloud to our students and spending time responding to what we read, we can, as Freddie said about writing, engage in "a new sport."

NINE

Writing for Our Lives

For several days, Damion had been searching for a topic for his final writing project. He'd toyed with a factual report on cheetahs, a description of an ugly brawl at school, and an admiring story about his favorite athlete. Nothing had inspired him to push further than a paragraph or two, and Damion was growing more frustrated by the minute. Finally he scribbled an intense note in his writing spiral (see Figure 9-1).

Finding the story poses huge challenges for both students and teacher. Many seventh and eighth graders think they have nothing to say, and even if they believe they've found something worth saying, they fear they don't know how to say it. It's up to the teacher to guide students through each anxious step of the writing process: finding an idea, developing the focus, tightening and clarifying to present one clear, sharply wrought piece that carries the writer's individual voice. At each stage the teacher and the other students provide advice and encouragement.

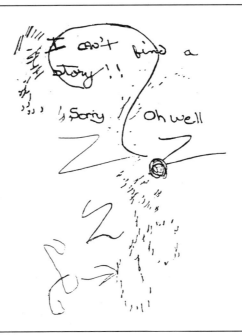

FIG. 9-1   *Damion's Frustration*

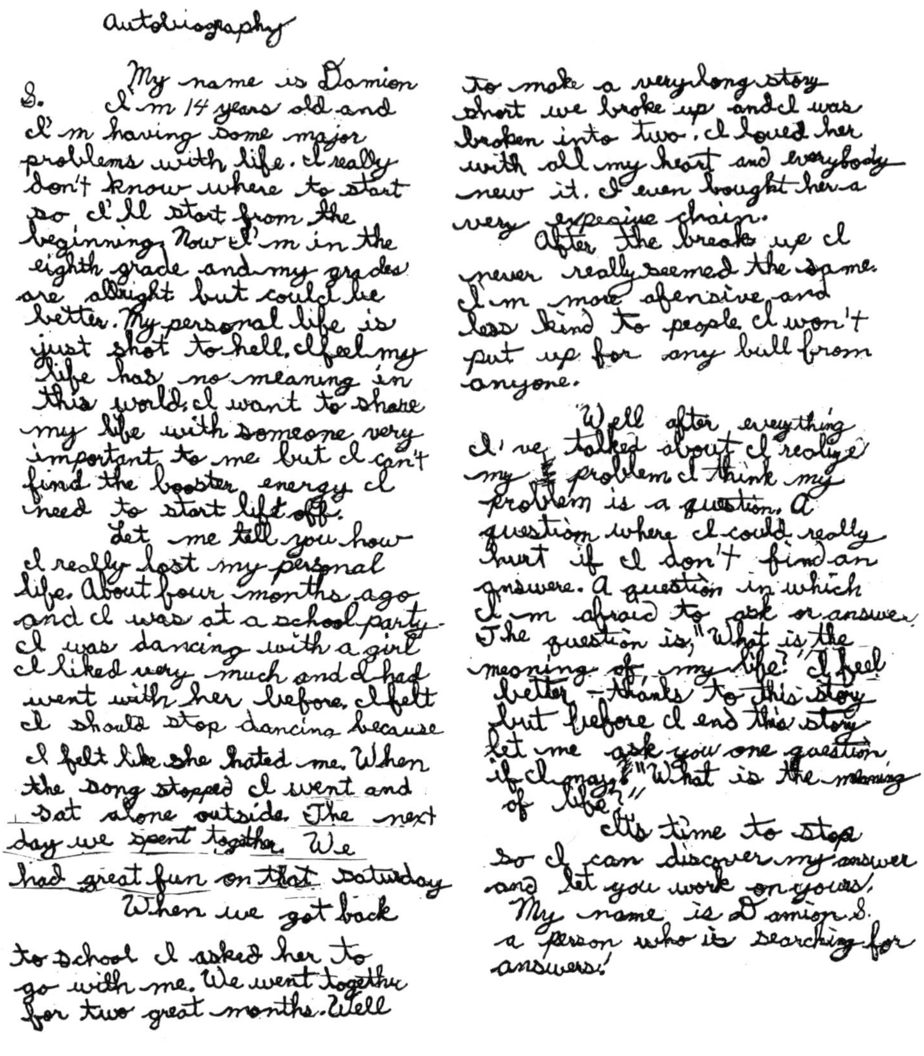

FIG. 9-2   *Damion's Autobiography*

Damion might have continued picking up and discarding half-formed ideas forever if I had not helped him break the cycle. By the time I got to him, he had given up on the cheetah, the school incident, and the sports star; instead, he was considering writing an autobiography. Aha! I thought. At least he's giving himself a chance to write about someone he knows well, someone to whom he feels committed: himself.

But starting the first draft stopped Damion. I quickly sat down with him and asked three important questions, which I jotted down: On which part of your life do you want to focus? Which incident(s) will show the reader how your life is going? How do you want to start your autobiography? We took several minutes to discuss them. This time Damion, a boy in search of himself, got busy writing. Figure 9-2 shows an excerpt from his autobiography. Notice his passionate use of language: "I can't find the booster

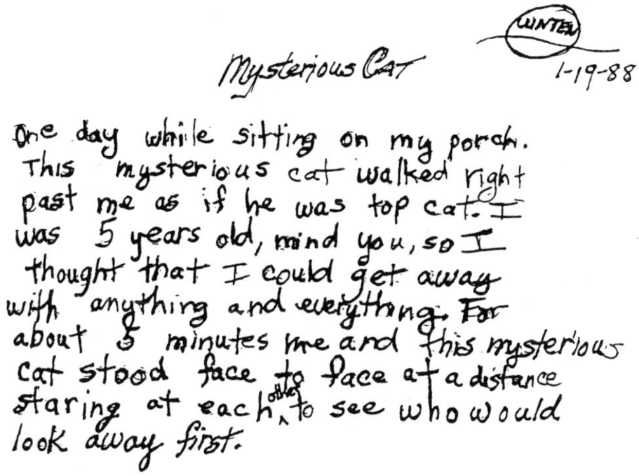

Mysterious Cat   ⟨WINTE⟩
1-19-88

One day while sitting on my porch.
This mysterious cat walked right
past me as if he was top cat. I
was 5 years old, mind you, so I
thought that I could get away
with anything and everything. For
about 3 minutes me and this mysterious
cat stood face to face at a distance
staring at each other to see who would
look away first.

FIG. 9-3   *Quinten's Paragraph*

energy I need to start lift off." Notice that Damion raises the big, existential question: "What is the meaning of my life?"

Helping Quinten find his poem

A teacher must have the sensitivity of a Geiger counter when helping young people find their way through writing. Take, for example, Quinten's paragraph about a mysterious cat (see Figure 9-3). After I read it aloud, I said, "You've got a poem hiding here in this paragraph, Quinten." He looked at me, incredulous because he still believed poems had to rhyme and have meter.

The clean, simple lines and deceptively commonplace language begged to be arranged in poetic form, one line under the other. His piece reminded me of William Carlos Williams's "Poem," which I yanked off my book shelf and read aloud to Quinten to illustrate my point.

As the cat
climbed over
the top of

the jamcloset
first the right
forefoot

carefully
then the hind
stepped down

into the pit of
the empty
flowerpot.

The cadence, spareness, and everyday quality of the two pieces were strikingly similar.

As a result of a brief one-on-one writing conference, Quinten's paragraph became a full-fledged poem, which he rearranged à la William Carlos Williams.

A Mysterious Cat
by Quinten

One day while sitting on my porch
this mysterious cat walked right
past me as if he was top cat.
I was 5 years old, mind you, so I
thought that I could get away
with anything and everything.
For about 5 minutes me and this mysterious
cat stood
face to face
at a distance
staring
at each other
to see
who
would look away
first.

He made no other changes. That year Quinten's poem was chosen for publication in *Kaleidoscope,* our school's literary magazine.

Early in the fall, I spent four class periods on prewriting activities designed to launch my students into the writing process. I didn't impose a schedule: Monday is for prewriting; Tuesday for rough drafting; Wednesday for conferring; Thursday for revising; Friday for proofreading. Rather, I allowed the students as much time as they needed to visit and revisit each step.

First we told anecdotes about significant people and events in our lives. We recalled memorable incidents, embarrassing moments, big decisions—general kinds of subjects to which each of us could respond. In other words, to limber our imaginations and stockpile ideas, we took the time to talk. We spent what many educators would consider an inordinate amount of class time preventing or getting over what fourteen-year-old Nona called "writers' cramp."

Resistant writers do experience "writers' cramp" in the most extreme way. Because they're unsure what to write about or where to start, they use their considerable energy unproductively. If they do get started drafting, their beginnings usually are meager, tight, lackluster, and vague. Typically, these are the kids who obsess over spelling and other mechanical problems, so they start over and over and over again. But telling one another stories in class launched nearly all of us into writing rough drafts.

After we had shared our lively and colorful stories, I showed them the next step: jotting an important event or vignette briefly, in chronological order, on an idea-collection sheet. The sheet was divided into three columns headed with broad, everyday, every-person titles. To model what I was asking my students to do, I stood at the overhead projector and filled one column of an idea-collection sheet as I told a personal story about my Grandfather Mercer (see Figure 9-4). Then many of the seventh-graders (though not all) set about filling in their sheets in preparation for more conversation and finally rough drafting.

A VERY IMPORTANT PERSON	A BIG DECISION	WHEN I WAS VERY YOUNG
1. GRANDPA MERCER: 1863 – 1956 (92½ YRS.)	11. SPIRIT OF ADVENTURE: A. WENT OFF ON EXTENDED TRIP – FAMILY FAREWELL;	C. SNAKES: BLACK SNAKES THAT COILED AROUND HIS NECK; KING SNAKES THAT LOOPED AROUND HIS WAIST; RATTLE SNAKES THAT MADE THE SOUND OF CASTANETS — WE STOOD BACK—AGAPE!
2. FATHER of 7; GRANDFATHER 18; RAW-BONED APPEAR;	B. REVVED MOTOR of ANCIENT CHEVROLET;	
3. FOUR (4) WIVES IN 92½YRS.	C. HIS OLDEST DAUGHTER GAVE HER FATHER SELF ADDRESSED POST CARDS TO KEEP HER INFORMED of HIS WHEREABOUTS;	D. OUR PARENTS STOOD HUNG BACK—NERVOUSLY
4. FARMER (OHIO);	D. FIRST POST CARD—MAILED FROM LITTLE OH TOWN — 20 Mi. FROM HIS FAMILY'S HOME!	
5. CARPENTER—BUILT OWN HOUSE & BIG BARN;		
6. NATURALIST: TRACKED OTTERS, POSSUMS, RACCOONS, FOXES, DEER + KNEW BIRDS + THEIR CALLS + EGGS;	12. CHEVY'S TRUNK = TREASURE TROVE	
7. TAXIDERMIST	A. GRANDPA'S MYSTERIOUS CAR TRUNK;	
8. TRAVELER—DROVE TO OREGON & WASH. IN HIS LATE 70's;		
9. STORY TELLER & SNAKE COLLECTOR;	B. GRANDCHILDREN GATHERED 'ROUND TO SEE HIM OPEN MYSTERIOUS BAGS — GUNNY SACKS WITH...	
10. TOOK LIBERTIES w/ THE LANGUAGE! "HARRY-di-tary" for hereditary;		

FIG. 9-4   Mrs. K.'s Idea-Collection Sheet

Micah's idea-collection sheet (see Figure 9-5) was excellent for several reasons: first, he'd *filled* it! Micah further distinguished himself because he'd recorded rich details that illuminated the essence of several possible stories. He identified the major issues in each story and arranged these details in logical order.

Thus, Micah had the choice of writing a story in any one of four categories: "A Most Important Person," "When I Was Very Young," "An Embarrassing Moment," and "A Big Decision." When Micah and I conferred, he indicated that the story about his mother going into the Satellite Cleaners to pick up her skirt was, for him, an exciting and funny idea, mainly because Micah loved talking about his cocker spaniel, Rocky, a central figure in this story as in others.

But I was also interested in his reaction to the embarrassing moment—when his watch slipped from his wrist to the floor, setting off a beeping alarm as he walked down the aisle during his sister's wedding. For some reason, Micah wasn't as attached to this story, although he could see the humor of it. He liked the story about putting one of his beloved dogs (not Rocky) to sleep after he'd found a lump on the pet's side. Putting the dog down was, as Micah told us, "like cutting off my own leg. And as you can see, cutting off one of *my* legs would be a *big* loss!" (Micah, so often self-deprecating, usually found a way to laugh, even if at his own expense.)

Micah had done a good job collecting ideas under the heading "A Big Decision." One senses the tension building when his mom asked him to make the decision about his pet. This was a monumental decision, for Micah knew that his dog would surely suffer from the spreading tumor, yet he had already experienced many losses during his

Most Important person	When I was young	A Enbarrasing Moment	A big Desision
① my mother is most Important person	① I Remeber sitting on Porch	① A sisters wedding.	putting Little fellow down
② Saved my life	② Dad said "you ought to be a doctor.	② walking sister down Asle.	① wouldn't eat
③ at Satilite cleaners	③ I looked at him	③ Watch Yalls off my Rist	② found lam on side
④ dog saw mom got excited	④ Mom said I should be a Pilet	④ The alarm Gous of	④ Lump grew → vet
⑤ dog was jumping Pushed car out of PARK Rolling car Kinsman rd.	⑤ I said OK OK	⑤ Still walking	⑤ Tumor spread
⑥ Mom droped Items and gun to stop car Rolling down hill		⑥ ON of auclows Picks it up	⑥ Dog would suffer
⑦ MOM open door and pushed it into PARK		⑦ I Recive it After ... The ...	⑦ better Put him to sleep
⑧ It Stoped Proplu			⑧ mom Gave me the decision
⑨ I was Thankful			⑨ I'll sleep on it

FIG. 9-5   *Micah's Idea-Collection Sheet*

short life. I liked the last note: "I'll sleep on it." Micah never did say why he didn't pursue writing this story, but I suspect that it was too painful for him.

After considering all these possibilities, Micah decided to write about an important person in his life, his mother, and the incident at Satellite Cleaners. Unlike many of my students, Micah understood that writing about everyday matters was perfectly acceptable and even preferable to writing on far-out topics that young writers know little about.

Here is Micah's first draft, written in one class period:

First draft   10-28-87

It was a sunny day my mother pulled up to satilite cleaners. She said, "I'm going in to the cleaners to pick up my skirt. My sister replied, "Leave the keys so I can liston to my favorit station 92.Q. So she did. My sister Amber was lisoning to her favorite song "Casanova" and just dancin rocken the car. I was playing with my small dog. he's a cocker spanial, his name is Rocky. We call him that because he so fisty. We were playing with his snasiges geting the windows all greesy with little dog treets, suddenly my mom walks out, my dog cocks his head wag's his tail he wish he had, and write befor my mom reached the end of the car my dog JUMPS UP and knocks the geer out of park Imedely the car rolls back into Kinsman and my mom drops the her skirt and open the door shoves it into part. My sister amber still listioning to casanova. My sister was still listioning to the radio she never knew what happened.

See's my mom and turn off the raideo and says Whats wrong and my mother said "The car was rolling down the hil you guy could of got killed. I was unaware of it to. My dog was still chewing on a snasiges

The richness of his writing was due, in part, to its common quality, to which everyone could relate. The draft held together nicely and provided an excellent framework for weaving in details and dialogue later. Micah was pleased when his classmates and I begged him to read aloud his first draft before the bell rang.

He made no revisions directly on this draft, the way I'd instructed the students to revise. Instead, he produced a second draft, a fresh copy, in which he had made significant changes. This method worked for Micah, and I could see no reason to make him follow arbitrary "rules."

In the second draft, Micah acted on some of the questions I'd asked him in conferences: "What led to the dog's knocking the car into reverse? What was going on in the car right before the dog became so excited at seeing your mother? What caused the car to roll?" When he rewrote, Micah spent time building the story conflict more slowly. Contrast the slow building toward the climax in draft #2 with the hasty laundry list of events in the first draft. The first time he had simply tried to set the whole story down, before he forgot any of it or ran out of steam.

Second draft

It was a sunny day, my mom pulled up to satilite cleaners. She said, I'm going in and get my skirt. My sister said leave the keys so I can liston to my favorite radio station 92.Q, OK my mothr replied back. My sister Amber started up the car and pumpt the radio so loud I was viobrating. My dog Rocky is a cocker spanial was eating some sloppy dog treat. The song my sister loves came on Casa Nova then she played it as loud as the speaker could play.

The my dog whos in the front seat JUMPS UP waging his tale jumping on the windows steaming them up. He left greasy paw prints every where. He sees my mom coming out of the cleaners, he JUMP all over the car and tryed to climb over the seet, fell back and knocked the geer out of park into nutral. The car start rolling back the Raidio was so loud I could not tell if we were upside down. My mother dropped her skirt and ran and opened the door. Shoved the geer into park. My sister was still listioning to the raidio she never knew what happened.

In the second draft, Micah became more focused. He deleted the tangent about playing with his dog. The focus became the dog's eating dog biscuits sloppily and his sister Amber's complete absorption in listening to her favorite song, "Casanova." Micah also used more vigorous language, especially verbs: "My sister Amber started up the car and *pumped* the radio so loud I was *vibrating.*" The dog's jumping from the backseat into the front, wagging his tail (because he'd spotted Micah's mother coming from the dry cleaner's), steaming up the car windows, and leaving greasy paw prints everywhere, contributed to this frantic scene. Micah described the dog's antics, the blaring car radio, and Mother dropping her newly cleaned skirt when she saw the car with her children in it rolling down the street.

Here is Micah's final draft:

Final draft   11-13-87

It was a sunny day, the kind of day that's hot and stickey. My mom pulled up to Satilite Cleaners. She said, "I'm going in and get my skirt." My sister, Amber, said, "Leave the keys so I can listen to my favorite raidio station, 92.Q OK?" My mother replied" "But don't play it to the world!" Amber started up the car and pumped the radio so loud I was viobrating.

My dog Rockey who's a cocker spaniel and I did not like the music. My sister Amber whos in the front seet JUMPS! She said, "CASANOVA my favorite song." She blasted the raidio so loud I could not tell if we were upside down. My dog was chewing on a dog treat realy greasy and slopy, and I was covering my ears trying to block out at least 10% of the loud music.

Suddenly my dog looks up and cocks his head. Rocky looked realy cute with his long ears flapping. He started jumping on the windows really smearing them up. He was wagging his little tail I thought while he was trying to squeeze his body out through the narrowly cracked window. The I saw my mom coming out the store. "That's what your getting excited about," I thought.

Then the dog got so excited he pushed the geer into nutral. The car started rolling back into Kinsman. It was a nice size hill we were on. The raidio was so loud I could not tell if my sister was driving—and thats bad! My mother dropped her skirt and run, open the car door, and shoved the gear into park. The dog flew forword. My sister asked, "What happened."

In this third and final draft, Micah fine-tuned his piece by using even more dialogue and including specific details such as the ones in his lead sentence: "It was a sunny day, the kind of day that's hot and stickey." He referred to the street, Kinsman, where his mother had parked the car, as "a nice size hill." In staccato fashion, and in just one sentence, Micah presented the events that led to a near disaster: "My mother dropped her skirt and run, open the car door, and shoved the gear into park." In contrast, Micah's sister, Amber, who was still quite preoccupied while the radio blasted, asked, "What happened?" An ideal story ending! Micah's three drafts, done while conferring often with his classmates and me, bear testimony to the power of revision.

Different students, different starts

Not everyone used the idea-collection sheets as directly as Micah. Like all writers, students draw on the ultimate idea bank, their memories, from which ideas emerge on no predictable schedule. Maryalita had jotted a description of her grandfather in September, on her first idea-collection sheet. On another sheet she recalled her shock at hearing of her grandfather's death. But it wasn't until February, after we had watched several films about heroic people, that Maryalita felt inspired to write about Grandpa Freddie. The first draft rolled out easily, needing little revision; she had probably been rehearsing it subconsciously for months. My job was simply to help Maryalita fine-tune the draft, to make it as crisp and pungent as the old man she so lovingly brought to life.

Other students filled their idea-collection sheets but then took off in different directions. Figure 9-6 shows a sheet done by Michael, who resisted most rules and seemed so sad that I sometimes thought he might be clinically depressed. That he filled the sheet was itself a miracle, but then he couldn't decide which idea he wanted to pursue. In conference, Michael at first said he wanted to write about his older sister, Monica, his favorite person since his mother's death. His other ideas, he said, "wouldn't be interesting to anyone who would have to read them."

Michael did draft a sweet story about going to a rock concert with Monica and her friends, but he didn't feel committed to it. Instead, he decided that he wanted to write about his "old best friend Jon." This story didn't relate to any of the ideas Michael had developed during prewriting, but I didn't care. He had obviously benefited from the idea-generating and drafting he had done so far, and if his friend was what he wanted to write about, that was fine with me. I wanted my students to see our classroom as a laboratory where they could feel free to experiment and follow their instincts.

Embarssing Moment	When I was young	Big Desision	Impt Person
① gym show	① weird sounds in night	① If shoubl let dad marry Nancy	① Monica
② forgot white socks	② loud noises	② Hate her	② Sister
③ had to wair blue	③ scary	③ She hates me	③ Popuhr
④ got laughed at	④ make me crazy	④ Will never like	④ Edmire her
⑤ tried to ignore	⑤ like something ecoping louder + louder	⑤ She hates kids	⑤ Sincere
⑦ played soccer	⑥ dad ignored me	⑥ still thinking	⑥ Folous rules
⑧ sucked	⑦ couldn't sleep		⑦ Tall (5ft9)
⑨ Ignored them	⑧ put on ear phones with loud music		⑧ Blue eyes
⑩ SCORED A GOAL	⑨ watched tv		⑨ Blondish Brown hair
⑩ won game	⑩ LOUD NOISES		⑩ own Job
⑪ got medal	⑪ got over it		⑪ makes hundreds
	⑫ wasent serious		⑫ 17 years old
	⑬ emagination		⑬ going to Ohio State maybe
			⑭ be marine biologist
			⑮ takes me out to dinner
			⑯ going to live near each other in Flordia

FIG. 9-6   *Michael's Idea-Collection Sheet*

Michael's first draft about his friend was somber. He began it this way: "Jonathan, my best friends, *was* my best friend. I went over to his house across the street when I wanted to, and if he wasn't home, I'd wait. I'd always have fun there." The writing showed Michael's feelings of abandonment: "We have suddenly broke up because I've moved." Although underdeveloped, this draft served as a framework for the story. It also prompted Michael to telephone Jon that evening. He returned to class with feelings for his friend rekindled; he was ready to change the tone of the story.

During this time, we were talking in class about drafting strong leads, and about showing rather than telling. We all practiced writing leads, and we looked for examples of *showing* in books we read. Michael grasped the point more quickly than many of his classmates. He revised his wordy lead, a classic example of telling rather than showing, into this strong beginning: "My old best friend, Jon, let me come in the house whenever I wanted to without ringing the doorbell."

Now Michael was cooking! His new lead suggested, but didn't tell, the familiarity of the boys' friendship and of Michael's acceptance into Jon's family. Michael also peppered his second draft with dialogue that showed (again, didn't *tell*) the warmth this family had once demonstrated toward him. In his first draft, Michael had denied any estrangement between himself and Jon: "My friend Jonathan B. is probably the best friend I've ever had. We usually go mostly every where enless it has to do with personal reasons." The second draft, however, made it clear that the friendship had cooled since Michael moved, but that he was pinning great hopes on an upcoming visit.

Michael's particular approach to writing a story reminded me to let students follow their instincts (unless, of course, they never *stop* jumping from idea to idea), but it also taught me a more important lesson: the teacher isn't always right. In his final draft, Michael included dialogues like this one, a transcript of a recent phone conversation with Jon:

Jon: Hello.
Michael: What ya doin'?
Jon: Nothing.
Michael: Do ya mind if I come over?
Jon: I don't care.

In my final note to Michael, I said that he could have made Jon "a bit more talkative" in his story. I see now, however, what I failed to appreciate then. Jon's few words let the story show what Michael was not yet willing to admit: Jon did not want to be friends with Michael again. As a writer, Michael had found his own way of conveying that sad truth.

One student's work, from end to beginning

Dwight was a puzzle. Brighter than most of my other eighth graders, he ended up with us because he didn't fit the usual categories or follow the rules. Dwight performed erratically on standardized tests, and he didn't bother with homework. On one particular story, though, he worked—when he felt like it—as diligently as a sculptor shaping a rough piece of clay. Because Dwight's complex methods of revision nearly defy description, I will introduce his process, and my part in it, by showing the result. Here is the final draft of Dwight's story about himself and his cousin Thomas:

A Very Important Person
"Thomas, we'd better not go to East High or Daniel Morgan. If we get jumped, we won't have any help. So we'd better wait for Sid. This time, Thomas, don't start a fight."

"You get into more fights than I do. I always keep a cool head in the face of trouble."

"That's a laugh!" I remarked.

We headed for the side door of our grandmother's house because if we'd gone out the front door, we would have gotten the 3rd degree about where we were going. We made it into the kitchen, quietly opened the door and made a dash for it across the grass lot or field about forty yards long. Thomas and I ran until we came to an alley which led to the other side of the block where all the fun was.

It was Friday so everybody was outside having fun. Sid would be somewhere in the crowd. Sid, our older cousin, was the real level headed person out of the three of us. Thomas and I went out looking for a few friends named Junior and Client. Every time we got together it meant trouble with a capital T. The last time we got together, we broke a man's car window. When we started running, Thomas and I split up. Me and Thomas met at Bush's a little corner store. We got a couple of pops and Polish boys.

"Thomas, you want to play Mr. Do before we go?" I asked hopefully.

"Sure," Thomas replied with a vengeance in his voice and a facial expression that meant he wanted to win.

I slipped two quarters in the slot and hit the two player button. I decided early to wipe Thomas out, but that was harder than I thought. Thomas must have practiced while I had been with Darnail.

"You've practiced, haven't you?" I asked.

"You know that already," Thomas replied.

"Of course, *I'm* the natural at *this* game," I shot back.

There was one person who could beat me—a man. I never got his name. He could play the game for at least a half an hour before he lost his first man.

STORY COLLECTION SHEET - M. KROGNESS

NAME Dwight
DATE 10-18-89

A MEMORABLE MOMENT	WHEN I WAS VERY YOUNG	A VERY IMPT. PERSON
When I first learned to do gymnastic's I landed on my head all day before I got it right. The hardest flip I couldn't do was a "full" The only one next a "areal". Those were The only flips I could do at one point and time just about aveny other flip I could do except doubles.	I went to the meuseam but not to look at eneything. We menning Thomas, Darnal, Sid and I would do gymnastics in the grass because It was the best lawn eney.where. By the way Sid taught me and Thomas to do gymnastics before he coul do it.	My cousin Thomas a very important part of me even though I haven't seen him for three years. Thomas was like the Brother I never had when he was living in Ohio. Thomas and I were like glue you would always see us togather getting into trouble One example of how much trouble we got into is when we had a billow fight and were done gymnastics on the bed. The Pillows were torn and the bed was broke. I'm going to let you assume what happen when our grandmother came the stairs.

FIG. 9-7 *Dwight's Idea-Collection Sheet*

Back to the game. Thomas made his first mistake. And last! I took advantage when he lost his last man. I had two to go and was gaining fast. Thomas had to watch his lead get smaller and smaller by the second. When I got an extra man, I insured a victory unless a miracle happened. But unfortunately for Thomas, he had bad luck when playing video games. So, as they say, you win some, you lose some. In this case, you say Thomas definitely lost!

Thomas reminds me it is time to go. I don't have to ask where, but only follow. It was a short walk to East High where everybody was playing basketball. Sid was at home preparing food to be cooked by Grandmother so we wouldn't see him till we got home.

Later than night Thomas and I got the shock of our lives. Thomas's mother, who had been down South for the last two years, got off the bus, walked up to the house, rang the doorbell, walked in and started talking to our grandmother. Thomas's mother wanted Thomas to move down South with her. That night, Thomas and I were starting to talk about what it was going to be like with Thomas gone.

"Looks like it is time for Batman and Boy Wonder to split up for good!" Thomas said sadly.

"Don't talk as if you will never see me again. I'm coming South for a few days," I replied.

"Time to sleep," Thomas said with no emotion in his voice.

by Dwight
SMS, 1989

The long process that led to Dwight's story began with the idea-collection sheet (see Figure 9-7). Any one of Dwight's ideas could have become a good personal story

Working together for a common cause.

or stirred other recollections for writing. But the details about Dwight's cousin Thomas were dynamite!

When all the students had filled in idea sheets, they conferred to choose the most promising story ideas, the ones they were most committed to. With little discussion, Dwight chose to write about Thomas, "a very important part of me . . . like the brother I never had."

He got busy drafting his piece, which included a chronology of events and even bits of dialogue. In his first draft, Dwight built a solid scaffolding on which he could hang his warm, personal story. In less than two class periods he wrote a draft ending with this line: "That was the biggest challenge of my life—going on without Thomas."

Because a single class period didn't allow enough uninterrupted time for careful consideration of their evolving stories, and because many of the kids could not or would not work independently, I passed around a sign-up sheet, allowing them to choose after-school appointments for small-group writing conferences. (My friend and colleague Liz Strickler calls such a sign-up sheet her "guest list.") Thus, I provided a structure and helped my students set goals; I also let them take responsibility for coming in after school to do serious work.

Modified peer conferences

In conferring with my students, I devised an approach that was a combination of a one-on-one teacher-student conference and a peer conference with a group of students. I did this because so many resistant students suffer from inertia. They have not learned to focus or direct their energy productively; left alone, they will either sit passively or act out in all manner of destructive ways.

I didn't start with traditional peer conferences because I'd observed that few young writers know how to engage in the art of questioning. Because these young people were inexperienced questioners, they tended to notice only the most tangible and obvious aspects of writing, namely, mechanics. Instead of seeing the big picture—either the problems or the promise of a student's work—they would focus on a misspelled word or an unclear phrase.

If inexperienced writers and questioners are left to their own devices during a peer writing conference, the conference can become a superficial and somewhat useless meeting. Young writers need the benefit of informed leadership. So, when a group of between three and eight young people gathered around the conference table to read their writing and talk about it, I was very much present. The manner in which I led the conference differed according to the needs of the group assembled.

If the majority were just beginning their rough drafts, they usually wanted to read portions of their work aloud. The purpose of this particular conference, then, was for the writers to gain an appreciative audience and for me to ask them one or two questions: "How are you going to define the story conflict or problem?" "What events will likely lead up to the big action?"

If a student had reached an impasse in his or her drafting, then we were all there to help by asking questions or making suggestions. If a writer had completed a draft, however, our conference was much more complex and required a different kind of leadership. My role then was to help writers uncover the possibilities and the promise of their pieces.

During the *initial* stages of the conference, I acted as the primary questioner. Then, little by little, I turned the responsibility over to the students gathered around the table. Let me demonstrate by discussing a modified peer conference in which Dwight's story was the principal topic.

Helping Dwight

Dwight and three or four other eighth graders chose (with my insistence!) to come in after school to work on their stories, all of which were in different stages of development. After we had all gathered around the conference table, I asked everyone to read a portion of his or her story if it was fully drafted. Dwight read his piece about Thomas and himself aloud.

Because a modified peer conference requires that the teacher initially take the lead, I primed the pump. "What do you think is strong about your story, Dwight?" Dwight shrugged. I waited for several moments and then turned to the others. "What do the rest of you think is strong about Dwight's story?" Jason and Derrick thought the story was "good." I asked the same question again, this time pressing them to be more specific.

Erik, bright but tentative and also Dwight's good friend, said, "Dwight's story sounds real—like a real author wrote it."

"What's real about his story?" I asked.

"It's a story about real kids and what real kids do."

"Do you notice that real stories often come from everyday situations and events in our own lives?" I asked. "Dwight is writing about what he knows. Writers do use their own experience in their writing because that's what they know best."

Tristin commented on the dialogue sprinkled minimally throughout this first draft. Because few of the students wrote dialogue in their stories this early in the school year, Tristin's observation was an important one. Usually, students' rough drafts—when and if they had started writing them—consisted of events strung together chronologically; some wrote only a few meager lines. Because they usually didn't know how to write dialogue, they tended to *describe* their characters talking: *My cousin, Jared, told his mother that he was planning to go to the school social.* I've found that I usually have to teach students to write genuine dialogue, sometimes by letting them role-play their story characters and talk as the characters might talk.

We all appreciated Dwight's ability to write believable conversation, and we told him so. I kept that focus alive by asking Dwight to read aloud only the dialogue, this time omitting the narrative. This technique allows the writer and his listeners to hear what is happening in a story and provides a clear sense of the character's relationships.

Everyone who was sitting around our conference table that day wanted to hear more conversation between Dwight and Thomas. I was eager to hear Grandmother give these two guys, her grandsons, "the third degree" as well.

More questions

"Dwight, how might you be able to show the close relationship that you had with your cousin Thomas?" I asked. This was the second and last question I posed to him and the group. Although Dwight did not answer, I'd given him something to think about.

My questions prompted Laurelia to ask even more good questions. "Why did Thomas's mother come North without telling anyone ahead of time? Did your grandmother know she was coming? How did Thomas's mother explain to your grandmother why she had come?" Laurelia's questions urged Dwight to show the wrenching separation of the two cousins.

Dwight explained to us that Thomas lived with his grandmother during the two years that his mother lived down South. Now, Dwight explained, Thomas's mother was talking to Grandmother about taking Thomas back with her. But Dwight didn't reveal the nature of that conversation, and I didn't press him. Laurelia's questions, however, did prompt him to expand an important part of his story.

I kept wondering about the two cousins' closeness. How would Dwight *show*, not tell, how close he and Thomas were? I suggested that he recall incidents or events that would show the bond. As an example, I recalled the pillow fight between the cousins. Dwight was quiet but attentive.

Before this writing conference ended, someone sitting next to Dwight leaned over and noticed a number of misspelled words. I explained to the group our mission at this moment: to help Dwight take a fresh look at his rough draft as a whole. If we focused our attention too soon on the mechanics of writing, I said, Dwight would use all his energy to clean up misspelled words and might forget our suggestions for fleshing out his story.

Readers may be wondering, as I did, whether the other students who'd come prepared to get feedback on their own rough drafts felt cheated at having spent the bulk of this writing conference on Dwight's story. Interestingly, no one complained—either at this conference or others. I believe that because they were all involved in thinking and helping, they did not feel left out.

The ephemeral nature of the conference

Even when these modified peer conferences went well, the kids too often began revising only to ask, "What did Natachia tell me I could do about that gap in my story?" Or, "What was Jawan's suggestion about letting that character talk?" Confusion about conference suggestions was especially common when the conference and the revision time occurred on separate days.

So after our conferences, I wrote each student a letter, briefly summarizing the major points the group had discussed. I didn't ask the students to take their own notes during the conference because most had trouble doing more than one thing at a time. If they were busy taking notes, they wouldn't feel free to take part in the ongoing discussion. As Tyvonny once said, "All those ideas are going 'round and 'round in my head like a merry-go-round!"

From my point of view, little yellow stick-on notes don't work; they tend to peel off and disappear. For my students, who benefit from predictability and continuity, a short letter that was clear and specific, but also warm and personal, did the trick. I wrote the letters in their writing spirals, and watched with pleasure as they raced to the racks to read my latest comments.

My letter to Dwight

The letter I wrote to Dwight after that first conference certainly wasn't as brief a note as I advise! But I knew that Dwight, in contrast to nearly all of my other resistant students, could follow directions carefully; his interpretive skills were also better developed than those of the other students.

10-25-89

Dear Dwight,

Okay—you have a good framework for a story. The skeleton or outline of the story is here. Now you have to flesh out or develop it. Here are the suggestions that came from our writing conference:

(1) On your idea-collection sheet, you mention that Thomas "was like the brother I never had." This is a beautiful statement that *shows* (doesn't just tell) closeness. Maybe you could use it somewhere in your story.

(2) You refer to this closeness between you and your cousin as "sticking together like glue." This line, too, conveys closeness.

(3) I want you to think of specific occasions (in addition to getting into mischief) where Thomas does something *for* or *with* you that shows his fondness. How about the pillow fight you mention on the idea-collection sheet?

(4) Everyone agrees that you write believable conversation/dialogue. Everyone enjoyed hearing your characters talk. So let those characters like Thomas, Sid, and Dwight *talk* and tell their story. Let your grandmother grill you; or if that won't work in this story, then maybe let Dwight, the character, say out loud what she probably would have said.

Now start the job of changing or revising your story.

Mrs. Krogness

Perhaps my approach with Dwight was too directive; perhaps my letter seems heavy-handed. Early in the school year, Dwight (as well as many other students) told me that he worked best when the teacher gave him specific directions. He required a delicate balance of structure and freedom, and I offered leadership but left him to chart his own course. (In the end, Dwight ignored enough of my suggestions to absolve me of being too directive with him!)

A couple of days elapsed between Dwight's first after-school writing conference and his revision. While a couple of stable, motivated students started reshaping their rough drafts using suggestions from the conferences, others sat passively until I made my way around the classroom to help. As for Dwight, the two-day burst of energy he had used to write the rough draft was gone. He wanted to read.

"Anyway," he said, "I like my story the way it is."

When students make this statement (and they often do), they are not being lazy or recalcitrant. Rather, they are saying, "This is *my* writing; it represents me. I want to protect myself." Our job as writing teachers is to free students to take hold of their writing rather than hold on protectively. We help them develop psychological stamina for writing and rewriting and encourage them to make a personal investment in this venture. This requires time and sensitive guidance.

Dwight starts revising

The next day, immediately after a brief talk about rough drafts and a fifteen-minute practice session on developing strong story conflicts, I asked everyone to start revising while I worked with individuals and small groups. First, I stopped by Dwight's desk and asked him where he wanted to start.

"I like my story the way it *is*," he firmly insisted.

"Please read it aloud." I was insistent, too. I sat down next to him and listened, and when he'd read a few paragraphs of his draft, I suggested that he reread my four-point letter and reconsider the suggestions that his classmates and I had offered during the writing conference. I moved on to work with other students. I wondered what Dwight would do. This next stage was in his hands.

I'm always pleased when a student finds his own method of reworking a rough draft—adding, deleting inserting, and reorganizing even when it's difficult to decipher. Here is Dwight's revision:

> Later that night Tomas and I got the shock of our lives. Thomas's mother got off the cross-town bus, walked up to the door and rang the doorbell, Walked in and started talking to our Grandmother about Tomas moving down south with her. The last night Tomas and I was up all night talking about all the fun we had and what schools we liked and hated. While Tomas talked, you could tell he was filled with mixed emotions. He was happy to see his mother but sad because he had to move from the house he grew up in.
>
> "Dwight, are you coming down south for a couple of days?" Tomas asked.
> I replied, "If my mother lets me."
> "Time to sleep," Tomas saided with no emotion in his voice.

Dwight was beginning to take off! He'd added telling details that helped him build tension in his story: for example, Thomas's mother "got off the cross-town bus, walked up to the door and rang the doorbell," which gives the reader an ominous feeling. At the same time that Dwight discovered how to build tension he also found a beautiful

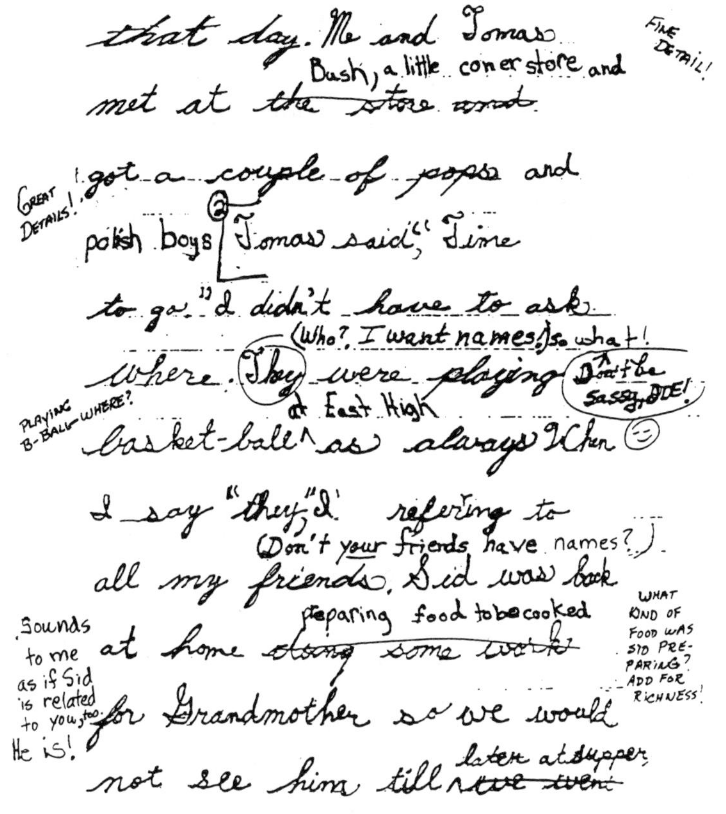

FIG. 9-8   *Excerpt from Dwight's Original Draft*

ending: the quiet goodnight. Dwight had brought his story full circle: it begins and ends with a conversation between the two cousins.

Cheering writers on

Besides raising important questions, I like to cheer writers on while they're revising. I wrote Dwight pithy notes in the margins of his manuscript (see Figure 9-8). I applauded his recent inclusion of the boys meeting at "Bush a little coner store," a sharpening of the original, "the store." I also was pleased that the boys and their friends were playing basketball "at East High." I was elated, too, with other rich details in the original draft ("got a couple of pops and Polish boys," deli food), which allowed me to picture the neighborhood, the boys' carefree existence, and the ease they felt in being together.

My marginal notes may seem to show a myopic preoccupation with details rather than the big picture, but I was trying to support Dwight's particular effort: adding dialogue and details. Each writer revises in his own way.

Beyond the cheering on, I was subtly trying to push Dwight to finish. But he seemed to be pulling away. He came to class subdued, wary, even sullen. His eyes and face told me not to come close, and not to make demands on him. When the class bell rang, he left quickly. His other teachers noticed that the quality of his work had slipped, and that he seemed preoccupied.

Meanwhile, the students and I agreed that they would submit final drafts of their personal stories to me in one week, using class time or after-school conferences to finish. Dwight still had a significant amount of work to do. When I asked him to come in after school for a writing conference, his face told me that he would not appear, and that I shouldn't push. But when I went to my mailbox later, I found a note from Dwight saying he had an-earlier-than-usual basketball practice after school and would come in for a conference the next day.

Room to revise

Anxious about the conference and the amount of work that lay ahead, Dwight paced around the classroom, reading his manuscript to himself.

"Don't you want to sit down to work?" I asked.

"Ideas circulate better when I walk!" He grinned sheepishly as he evaded my question. Then, with great aplomb, Dwight explained that he needed quiet, uninter-

---

Beginning

"Tomas, you want to play Mr. Do before we go?" I asked hopfully,

"Sure," Tomas replied with a vengence in his voice and face expression.

I sliped to couters in the slot and hit the 2 player button. I decided early to wipe Tomas out, but that was harder than I thought. Tomas must have practiced while I was with Darnail.

"You've practice, haven't you?" I asked.

"You know that already," Tomas replied.

"Of course I'm the natural at this game."

FIG. 9-9 *Dwight's Beginning*

End

2. There was one person who could
   bet me - a man I never got
   his name. He could play the
   game for at least a half an
   hour before he lost his
   First man. Back to the game.
   Tomas made his first mistake.
   And last, I took advantage when
   he lost his last man. I had
   two to go and was gaining fast,
   Tomas had to watch his
   lead get smaller and smaller
   by the second and when I got
   an extra I ensured a victory
   unless a miracle happened, but
   unfortunately for Tomas he
   has bad luck when playing
   video games, So as they say,
   you when some, you lose some, In
   this case you can say Tomas

   defenably lost!!

FIG. 9-10   *Dwight's Ending*

rupted time "to do solid revision." He asked my permission to take his writing spiral home over the weekend, a request I rarely granted. None of my students could afford to damage or lose their growing collection of writing; it would be like losing their history.

But so far, Dwight's track record with me had been good. He was reliable, and his reasonable explanation that he needed more time to tackle the big job of showing the boys' closeness prompted me to relent. Still, I had no illusions that he would actually do much work, especially over the weekend. Dwight had patently refused to do homework in most of his other classes.

To my delight, when Dwight came to class the following Monday, he'd done a rather monumental job of revising. He'd written three major inserts, two of which he labeled: "(2) Beginning" and "2. End," and a third unlabeled insert he numbered "(1)." His unorthodox (and from my point of view confusing) method of revising made good sense to him. After all, he was the author! Figures 9-9 to 9-11 show the three revisions.

① "Tomas, to bad you have to leave

because June gave my her number
and told me to give it to you!)

"How long did you have her number?"
Tomas asked politely.

"For about two days," I replied

"You had her number for two days,

and didn't give it to me? How

low can you go?" Tomas Bolted

"Alot lower," I replied,

" Shut-up before I make you a part
of the wall!")

FIG. 9-11   *Dwight's Unlabeled Insert*

Dwight was cookin'

Wheeew! I was ecstatic with Dwight's additions; he had finally given his first major piece of writing the effort it deserved.

I wrote Dwight a letter before he started the final draft. I'm ashamed to say that I asked him yet again to tell what his grandmother said. Only later did he tell me that his grandmother's language was unprintable.

November 13, 1989

Dear Dwight,

Good. Over the weekend you added a lot of information and wove in dialogue. Yeah! Many of the additions are good—especially the dialogue. *I'm *not* sure about addition (2) that you've marked Beginning and another labeled 2. End; nor do I understand the insert marked 1. Where these pieces go still isn't completely clear to me. Please refresh my memory.

I *still* want to hear your grandmother give you guys "the third degree!" I want to hear *her* talk and know her type, her attitudes and personality.

Mrs. Krogness

A final conference

In Dwight's third insert, marked (1), he is telling Thomas it's too bad he has to leave town because June wants to give him her telephone number. Here it is in context.

"Dwight, are you coming down for a couple of days?" Tomas asked.

I replied, "If my mother lets me."

"Tomas, to bad you have to leave because June gave my her number and told me to give it to you."

"How long did you have her number?" Tomas asked politely.

"For about two days," I replied.

"You had her number for two days and didn't give it to me? How *low can* you go?" Tomas Boulted.

"Alot lower." I replied.

"Shut-up before I make you a part of the wall!"

"Time to sleep," Tomas saided with no emotion in his voice.

Our final conference gave me an opportunity to reiterate to Dwight the beauty of his spare writing and the skill needed to create his fine ending. I asked whether he thought the teasing tone of the passage about June's phone number worked well with the solemn mood of his closing scene. He quietly acknowledged that writing requires decisions, and might even mean discarding a chunk of writing that had taken much work. "Treat your writing roughly," I told him. He decided to discard the insert about June. Finally, he was ready to make the final copy.

Dwight had given his best when revising and had done a masterful job on the cerebral part of the process. I felt certain he would bridle if I asked him to clean up all his mechanical problems, too. I've learned to choose carefully what I value most. Building intellectual muscle is a gradual, often painful, process. I have to keep reminding myself to seek a balance between high expectation and acceptance of my students' different stages of development. I usually know when they've had enough and when I should stop pushing.

I encouraged Dwight to come in after school to start the arduous process of recopying his story in ink or typing it on the computer, since the final draft was due the following day. But basketball practice prevailed, and Dwight refused to take the story home again. He planned to recopy the whole thing the next day during class.

Dwight wasted no time getting started; he pushed his ballpoint fast. Midway through the period, he looked up from his work and smiled.

"I've found an even better way to revise this story."

"Great!" I replied, but I wondered what sort of plan he was hatching at the eleventh hour. He worked feverishly throughout the period to finish the ink copy by the bell, and he succeeded. This is how his new version ended:

"Looks like it is time for Batman and Boy-Wonder to split up for good!" Thomas said sadly.

"Don't talk as if you will never see me agian. I'm coming South for a few days," I replied.

"Time to sleep," Tomas said with no emotion in his voice.

Yes, Dwight *had* developed and refined his story ending further. But he had also left out both of his important inserts, simply because he ran out of time. Still, from my point of view, he had succeeded admirably.

Ruth Blair, a colleague in our English department, thought Dwight wrote like S. E. Hinton, and promptly accepted his story (complete with the inserts that Dwight had omitted) for publication in *Kaleidoscope*.

Here is my final letter to Dwight:

November 27, 1989

Dear Dwight,

This is a powerful story—especially the final dialogue between the cousins. Very real and very poignant. Now I have a strong feeling for each of your characters, the main characters, especially because you let them talk and interact. I wish I could have heard Thomas's mother talk with Grandmother about taking Thomas back down South with her.

You did a remarkable job of revising this story, even though you didn't include the two big inserts in your final ink draft. (Was omitting these inserts "the even better way of revising?") You still get an A for revision because you did do the *real* rethinking when you took your writing spiral home.

I'm not going to lay anything heavy on you now, but some day before this school year is over, I want to talk with you about your future plans for yourself. OK? Keep on working.

MK

The art of fine-tuning

So far, I have examined the big issues of conferring and revising: focusing, developing, organizing, and giving voice. After all that comes fine-tuning. When a writer fine-tunes her writing, she operates as if she were a tree trimmer, excising all the dead wood. She prunes the flowery adjectives, those million-dollar words that weigh a piece down but rarely convey meaning (how big is "gigantic"?). I tell my students to draw a single line through verbiage, such as "I saw a *small little* girl standing alone." I tell them to draw a line through all deletions so that the history of the writing isn't destroyed. Seeing how a writer thinks and rethinks her writing is important for assessing growth—and it's interesting.

The writer who learns how to fine-tune stays on a word budget, choosing just the right words and putting them into just the right order to convey the ideas. Surprising words rub together, letting the reader enjoy the sound effects of language. In fine-tuning, the writer substitutes strong verbs for anemic ones (*dashed* for *went*) and chooses among various shades of meaning (*amble* vs. *trudge*). As Mark Twain said, "The difference between the right word and the almost right word is the difference between lightning and the lightning-bug" (p. 70).

The writer in the final stages of polishing understands another fine-tuning technique: varying sentence structure and length. She knows that beginning sentences with words like *when, because, since,* and *if* allow her to vary the structure, adding interest to her piece. As for length, a short, incisive sentence creates a very different mood than a long, leisurely one.

Mrs. K. talking with Crystal about fine-tuning her final draft.

Next, I talk with the students about the final step in the writing process: cleaning up the mechanics (spelling, punctuation, grammar, and so on). I compare proofreading to hitchhiking. The sloppy hitchhiker who doesn't bother cleaning up his act before he hits the road probably won't catch a ride. The writer who doesn't bother to proofread probably won't attract many readers.

The reason for proofreading, I emphasize, is to make a piece easy for the reader to read. But because my resistant students are bogged down by many writing difficulties and tire of the process more quickly than most mainstream students, I don't hammer them about proofreading. The cerebral part of writing—revising and reshaping—is the most important and demanding part of the process, the part I most want to engage my students in learning. So I tend to go easy on the proofreading stage.

I ask my young writers to put in the end marks while they read their pieces aloud; with colored pens in hand (usually red), they make sure that each sentence ends with a period, not a comma. Next, they put quotation marks around all quotations, something we practice throughout the school year. They can refer to a model of dialogue we keep permanently on the chalk board.

Because the students tend to run their characters' conversations all together in one extended paragraph, I ask them to write a backward P each time a different character talks. When they finally recopy or type their final drafts, the paragraph sign reminds them to indent.

I ask the students to capitalize the beginning letter of the first word in each sentence; then I ask them to capitalize only proper names and names of special buildings, holidays, cities, states, or countries. Since they tend to capitalize indiscriminately, I am specific about which kinds of words require capital letters. Finally, they clean up misspellings. If they haven't run out of steam, I ask them to exchange papers with partners who will give the drafts a final look over for mechanical errors.

Then they either recopy their pieces in ink or go to the computer lab and type the final draft.

In conclusion

Helping students find their stories and their unique voices is, from my perspective, our key role as writing teachers. When a student's first draft flows easily and apparently painlessly, we can rejoice with the young writer. But we'll be there, too, when a student struggles or stops dead in his tracks; or when she suffers from what Nona called "writers' cramp." Our job is to help kids find their way to and through writing. Whether young writers produce lumbering leviathans or stingy little morsels that give little promise for the future, we can find ways to lead them forward, to take hold of their writing and generate what Damion called the "booster energy . . . to start liftoff."

TEN
Becoming Playwrights

"Me and Passion got to be practically best friends 'cause we worked so close on our plays," Natalie observed. *"She listened to me read all the new parts I added, and Passion would always tell me how they sounded. And I did the same for her."*

"David helped me find a title," Nick said.

"Nick listened every time I changed an idea. He helped me with the dialogue," David responded.

"I wasn't sure how I was going to end my play until I talked with Keith about it," Halley said.

Playwriting was magical! Writing—or is it "wroughting"?— original plays brought my kids and me together as no other long-term writing project did. Plays tap into authentic feelings and uncork imaginations. They also beg to be read. During the course of more than two months, the least likely kids came together to read their works in progress. Their characters, who became our intimate friends, eventually walked and talked and came as close to being flesh and blood as anything these students had ever created.

Students collaborated to create. They helped one another breathe life into an array of original characters who could be fragile or strong, duplicitous or honest, weak or courageous. Their characters took charge and combatted evil. I suspect that these stories represented my young playwrights' highest ideals; their characters let them play out their dreams and voice some of their deepest doubts and fears. Here are a few of those voices, rooted in students' own lives.

When Chris R.'s father, a minister, accepted a difficult pastorship in Texas, Chris recognized the disease of racism. In his play, Chris fictionalized this experience by creating two boys, one black and one white, who bring a congregation in a small Ohio town together.

LISTEN TO THE CHILDREN by Chris R., eighth grade

Reverend Mr. Jones: (*Pulls up the driveway to new church. Reverend Jones sees three white deacons and asks them this question.*) Is this Shiloh Baptist Church?
Deacon Bailey: Yeah, this is Shiloh Baptist Church. But who are you?

Making characters come alive and good friends—all through playwriting.

Reverend Mr. Jones: Why, I'm Reverend Jones, your new pastor.
White Deacons: (*All chuckle.*)
Deacon Smith: There must be some mistake, Reverend. We didn't send for no *black* man.
Reverend Mr. Jones: Well, I am black and I am also *this* church's new pastor. Tomorrow is Sunday and I'll be here and so had you better be! (*Reverend Jones gets in his car and drives away. Reverend Jones gets back home and finds that his wife is in tears.*)
Reverend Mr. Jones: Sweetheart, what's the matter?
Mrs. Jones: Jason (the Jones's son) was playing outside. I don't know where he is now. But it's three o'clock and he's not back yet. Just a minute ago a rock flew through the window. Anything could have happened to him.

Figure 10-1 shows an excerpt from one of Chris R.'s early drafts.

Nona wrote about a large family that struggles, as every family does, to get along and work out differences. Tonya, a teenager, is the oldest child still at home and resents carrying the full responsibility since her older brother and sister have gone to college.

UNTITLED PLAY by Nona, eighth grade
(*In the kitchen Abigail Washington, the mom, is cooking supper.*)

Abigail: Tonya! Come here and help me with dinner.
Tonya: But Ma, Michael is not doing anything but watching t.v. and Dionna's playing in her room.
Abigail: Tonya, what did I tell you?
Tonya: (*Lets out a big sigh.*) Ohhhhhh, fine. What do you want me to do?
Abigail: Look in the cabinet and get some cinnamon for the sweet potatoes.

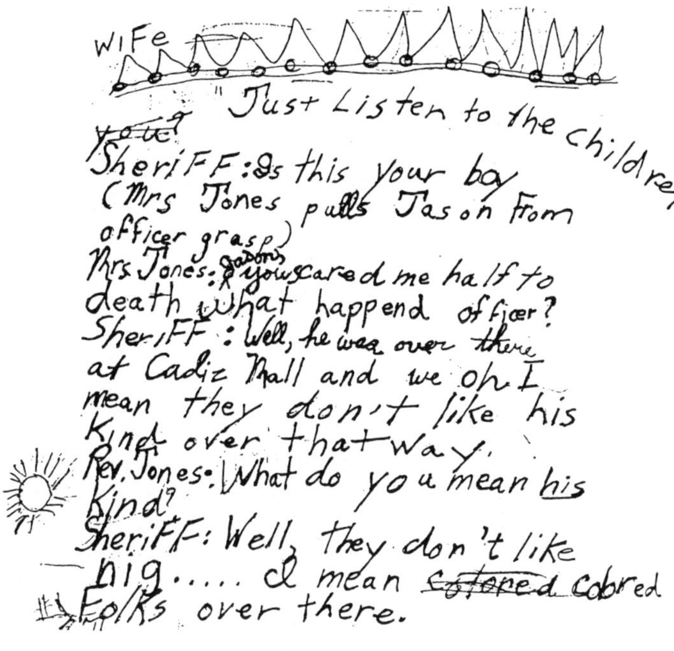
WIFE

"Just Listen to the children"

~~You?~~

SheriFF: Is this your boy

(Mrs Jones pulls Jason from officer grasp)

Mrs Jones: Jason's you scared me half to death what happend officer?

SheriFF: Well, he was over there at Cadiz Mall and we oh I mean they don't like his kind over that way.

Rev. Jones: What do you mean his kind?

SheriFF: Well, they don't like nig.... I mean ~~cotored~~ cobred folks over there.

FIG. 10-1 *Excerpt from Chris R.'s Draft*

Tonya: (*Closes cabinet very forcefully and says nothing.*)

Abigail: Tonya, close that cabinet door and open it like you have some sense.

Tonya: (*Mumbling under her breath.*) I hate her. She's always calling my name to do things around the house.

Abigail: What did you say, Tonya?

Tonya: Nothin'!

Abigail: If you have something to say, then say it out loud.

Countless more play characters took shape: exotic Madame Zara, a fortune teller; Liz, a lizard who is the best friend of a lonely boy; Mick, a handsome young dude who learns the hard way when he tries two-timing twin sisters. As my students struggled with the plays that contained these characters, they focused at first on the Dobama Theatre's Playwriting Festival For Kids. The winners of this all-city contest receive a savings bond and have their plays performed by professional actors and published in a book.

As it turned out, however, the prospect of being rich and published wasn't what sustained my students' energy when playwriting got tough. It was the excitement of working together and watching their characters and plots take miraculous shape that kept them going.

Generating ideas

We began the process of playwriting when I asked my seventh and eighth graders a few leading questions: What kinds of stories turn you on? What kinds of characters do you enjoy reading about most? What happens to these characters that makes an interesting story? What do you imagine that your play might be about?

These questions set our minds in motion during two weeks of brainstorming sessions before we ever put pencil to paper or touched the computer keyboard. We batted around the usual and sometimes sensational ideas that every twentieth-century teenager knows or has heard about: death and divorce, drugs and disease (mostly AIDS), abuse and abandonment, rejection and dejection, despair and depression, peer pressure, teen pregnancy and suicide, crime and punishment, sibling rivalry and, of course, complex teenage romance. I recorded every idea on the chalkboard; I knew that my students would have to be engaged in the whole process if they were going to write plays.

Creating characters

Next, we spent time picturing potential characters, such as a heroin addict who takes charge of his life, an unwed mother who manages on welfare, a superstar football hero or rock star whose life plummets when youth or popularity runs out. The kids conjured an ancient prophet who uttered exotic incantations and a dog who thought it was human. Dramatic and even melodramatic characters came to mind at first. Then less sensational ones began to evolve: a younger child in the family who feels her older sister is always more successful than she, and is favored by her parents; a slightly built middle school boy who dreams of making the first string basketball team at his school.

Each day I typed their lists of play ideas and characters. Each day we thought about these one-dimensional characters who were asking us to give them life and limb. We practiced speculating about their lives: What happened to the little sister who craved her parents' respect? How did the short adolescent fulfill his dream of playing first string on his school's basketball team?

After two weeks of setting the stage, most students were able to settle—if only for the moment—on their play topics. At this point in the school year (early January), we'd done a lot of writing in class, so they understood the importance of writing about what they knew. They realized that even fairy tales, mysteries, and science fiction could be based on their own experiences.

Chris N., for example, recognized that his first idea—a boy having a religious experience—wasn't a subject he knew well enough to write about and stay committed to. After working for almost two weeks on this play, Chris told me that he wanted to base his new play on a personal experience instead. Meanwhile, we spent class time identifying the conflicts in the others' tentative topics: Sabrina finds a mysterious note in her locker, Dalisha receives a curious Christmas package from her grandmother, Deone dreams of living with his father who's just moved out of the house. Conflict, after all, is the backbone of a traditional story.

Making blueprints

To begin plotting their plays, I asked my students to write a simple sentence or two in which they stated the *conflict,* the *climax,* and the *resolution.* I wanted them to make blueprints before rough-drafts because authors who have a plan are far less likely to write themselves into a corner—that is, find themselves unable to resolve the story conflict. A blueprint for a play or a story is never cast in iron; it serves merely as a framework on which a story *might* hang. As the writer becomes better and better acquainted with his characters, he will make significant changes. When the writer meets with his classmates and teacher in conferences, he hears still more ideas.

This process of blueprinting plot parts proved an incredible thinking exercise that asked each writer to focus on a conflict, build to a climax, and then find a plausible resolution. Play plotting was a deceptively difficult task. My writers had difficulty not only in coming up with authentically plausible conflicts but in finding strong resolutions that solved them. More than once, a student tried to settle for the classic solution: the protagonist wakes up; the whole problem was just a dream!

The process at work

When we all helped David, a reluctant writer, make a blueprint of his play, we helped ourselves learn the ropes. David wanted his play to be about a grandfather who suffers from Alzheimer's disease. I started the process of plotting by asking: "What might happen to an old man whose thinking has been impaired?" I wanted David and his classmates to begin thinking through David's story conflict. David imagined that Grandpa Joe, as he called him, had forgotten his name.

I asked, "What might Grandpa Joe's forgetting his name lead to?" Someone imagined that he might get lost and his family would be frantic. This plausible idea led us to think further: "What might happen if Grandpa Joe gets lost?" David and his classmates considered various consequences: Grandpa Joe is abducted and murdered by a gang; he falls down and is rushed to the hospital; he is never seen again. Then we speculated about these consequences. I wanted David and his classmates to consider the *real* issues of this budding story, so I asked: "Is the real issue Grandpa Joe's deteriorating mind and the terrible things that could happen to him? Or is it the effects of his impairment on the old man and his family?"

Many kids still wanted to pursue the gory details of Grandpa Joe's being lost. This is where my leadership came in. Without saying that the gory details were *not* really the primary issue, I asked the class to consider what would happen to the story if, let's say, Grandpa Joe is abducted, then murdered by a gang. Would the story be about Grandpa Joe or about a gang that picked on an elderly man with Alzheimer's? What would happen next if the old man were murdered by a gang?

We speculated about Grandpa Joe's falling and being rushed to the hospital. Would *that* story be about the old fellow? After his hospitalization, what would happen? And if the story was that Grandpa Joe wandered away, never to be found again, where would *that* story go? Eventually, some students realized that all of these stories would lead to dead-ends.

I pressed the students to continue thinking about David's plot: "Grandpa Joe has wandered away. What about his family? What are their thoughts and feelings when they discover that he has disappeared?" I was trying to show them that the forgetful old fellow was merely the writer's vehicle for telling a story about human relationships. From Grandpa Joe's disappearance, our thinking could proceed in many directions, away from the gory consequences.

I asked: "Who discovers Grandpa Joe's disappearance? Where might he have gone? What will his family do upon discovering that the old man has wandered off?" We continued speculating. David imagined that one of Grandpa Joe's grandchildren would be heroic and organize a search party to look for him. The grandchildren and their friends would find their grandfather and bring him back to the safety of his family, thus resolving the story conflict.

David's blueprint

Here is how David plotted his play:

1. *Conflict:* Grandpa Joe walks away from home and nobody knows he's gone.
2. *Climax:* Tom, Grandpa Joe's grandson, realizes he's missing. Nobody in the family knows where the old man has gone.
3. *Conflict Resolution:* Tom and his sister organize a search party.

This outline looked fine—for the moment. But such a scaffolding should be flexible, and David's plot did in fact change when he began writing a rough draft. During a conference with a few classmates and me, David realized that he couldn't simply start his play at the point when Grandpa Joe gets lost. Rather, he would first have to give the audience clues that Grandpa Joe's thinking is impaired and that his family is warm and supportive.

Like many young playwrights, David wanted to let a narrator do the work: describe Grandpa Joe's problem, tell the audience about Alzheimer's disease, and describe Joe's nurturing family. But I put my foot down on including narrators in the plays. Using a narrator, I told my students, was copping out; it was preventing the play's characters from doing the work of telling the story. When they argued that *other* plays had narrators, I still didn't budge. I told them that I, too, knew a play or two with a successful narrator—*Our Town,* for instance—but no one in this classroom had the writing experience of Thornton Wilder.

David reluctantly agreed that he would let his characters—*not* a narrator—do the work of showing the audience that Grandpa Joe was experiencing difficulty thinking and remembering. But David wasn't sure how to accomplish this task. How would he set the stage for Grandpa Joe's problem without giving a belabored and boring explanation of Alzheimer's disease? How would he show the family's concern?

One of David's classmates suggested that Joe's family might sit around a dinner table where all of them would witness Joe's mistaking chicken for hamburger. Someone else suggested that in addition to the old man's difficulty distinguishing chicken from hamburger, Grandpa Joe might have a headache, another clue. We talked about these clues being a foreshadowing of Joe's problem, the major conflict of this story.

David gets more help

Another classmate suggested that instead of having Joe merely wander off, as David originally had planned, his wife might ask him to drive to the local deli to buy ham for lunch the following day, setting the stage for yet another of his memory lapses. One student suggested that Joe might become confused and drive to the mall instead, and get lost. David liked our suggestions, but he wasn't sure what should happen next. I suggested that Joe's family might be concerned—especially if the old man had been gone an inordinate amount of time.

David liked this idea, too. He speculated that Joe's daughter, Sandy, might worry about her father's long absence. David recognized that we were helping him build tension into his play. But as David said, "I don't want it to be over *yet!* I mean, I don't want Joe's family to find him yet because then I'll have to write 'The End.' And it's too soon for my play to be over."

After David had worked on his rough draft for a while, a group of us banded together for another writing conference. When David's turn came, one of us suggested that Joe's going to the deli might be one of two examples of his getting lost. David decided that instead of a family member finding Joe, the family would receive a telephone call from the mall manager, who sees Joe walking around absent-mindedly. But then what? David wanted Joe's family to take him to the doctor, who diagnoses Joe as having Alzheimer's disease and tells them that they will have to keep an eye on him.

I pointed out to David that the audience would likely imagine that something more was going to happen. David, who was becoming more confident in deciding where *he* would take his play, imagined that Martha, Joe's wife, could be busy planting flowers in her garden. Joe follows her every step, throwing dirt on the tulips she's planting. When Martha goes to the tool shed for more sod, he disappears again.

David knew that he could use his original idea now: letting Joe's grandson, Tom, and granddaughter, Sarah, start looking for their grandfather. But just looking wouldn't do; the characters had to talk, not just walk. I asked more questions that I hoped would stir David's thinking: "What kinds of details might shed light on the whereabouts of Grandpa Joe?"

David wasn't sure. Nick, who sat next to David and was in on almost all of David's thinking and decision making, suggested that Sarah knows that Joe likes Big Macs and wonders if maybe the old fellow has gone to McDonald's for a burger. David liked Nick's idea, and I encouraged him to generate more details that would involve the audience in finding Joe.

I asked another question: "Where might the children find Joe?" The group thought of different locations that would move the play to its final scene and conclude it: the mall, his own home, the drugstore, the hospital, the amusement park. One student mentioned a retirement home that would be located next door to the McDonald's.

David took this suggestion, then imagined the final scene: Joe's two grandchildren find their grandfather sitting on a bench near the retirement home feeding squirrels. The doting grandchildren call their parents, who immediately come to take Joe home. But David wasn't satisfied. He thought that Joe should be placed in a nursing home, perhaps the one where his grandchildren have just found him.

Titles come last

But what about the title for David's play? I believe the title of any work should not be a major consideration of the writer until the piece is well underway or finished. The writer can't imagine a suitable title until he knows his characters intimately and has fully developed the story line. We left titling plays until the very end. Once again, we all got into the act by brainstorming ideas and helping each other find evocative titles that we called "grabbers." David's final title was "What's Wrong with Grandpa Joe?"

Playwriting was undoubtedly David's most satisfying writing experience. For the first time during the school year, writing sustained his interest and energy, and he saw a long-term project to a polished conclusion. As David said, "I really got into play-writing because I got plenty of support from everyone in this class—especially from Nick."

Other challenges

In addition to thinking through the plot, my writers faced a number of other challenges: keeping the story focused, figuring out plausible conflict resolutions, and writing dialogue. Some students strayed far from their original story conflict, letting the play run away. Others introduced more than one conflict, complicating the play and leaving it without a major focus. Michelle, for example, envisioned a typical teenage boy-meets-girl story. Her protagonist, Tony, a shy and awkward seventh-grade boy, admires the beautiful Sheila from afar. So far, so good.

But then, Sheila falls in love with Shawn, the star football player. Michelle's original story about shy Tony falling for Sheila has lost its focus. This is where the writing conference came in. I suggested that her story might be about Sheila and the star football player instead of the inexperienced, love-sick Tony. A classmate suggested that all three characters might become involved in a love triangle: Tony is hopelessly and silently in love with Sheila, while Sheila is hopelessly but less silently in love with Shawn. The new focus became the constant struggle of teenagers to survive love's labors lost.

Michelle, who was getting good suggestions, thought of a possible plot: Sheila goes with Shawn but finally decides that the "fast lane" isn't for her; she seeks a quieter, lower-profile man of her dreams. Then Tony becomes the central figure in the story. The important part of the conference was to engage her in imagining many ways her story might go—and then, finally, choosing *one* focus.

For nearly all my students, finding plausible endings was as difficult as finding a focus. They learned to conjure up wonderful conflicts, but then were stumped when it was time to resolve them. Take Crystal's story about a grandmother who is left to raise her deceased daughter's two teenage sons. Crystal imagines that the strong grand-mother raises the boys well, but that both of them—despite their grandmother's dire warnings—turn to drugs and drink.

Crystal couldn't think of a good way to wrap her story up. In a writing conference with a few classmates after school, I asked her, "What is the conflict in your story?" Crystal wasn't sure whether it was the grandsons' drug problems or the sixty-year-old grandmother's enormous responsibility in raising the boys. Crystal's classmates helped her sort out her difficulties. Lakiesha and Dominicque imagined that the grandmother, who loved the two boys and had given her life to them, finally recognized that she would have to take matters into her own hands. Reluctantly but bravely she stood up to the delinquent young men, called the police, and turned them in.

Certain stories or plays cannot be resolved in the traditional way because the issues are not resolvable. Jenni's play, for example, was about a teenage girl whose mother gave all her time and attention to her handicapped younger brother. Angry and de-pressed, the girl goes to her favorite teacher. The teacher acknowledges the teenager's feelings and advises her to find a good time to talk with her mother.

Jenni couldn't figure out a good resolution to this dilemma; clearly, the mother couldn't start ignoring her disabled son. Jenni talked with classmates, who helped her think of a plausible ending: the girl asks her mother to go to lunch on a Saturday, when

Writing believable dialogue challenges all young playwrights.

her dad is home and can care for her younger brother. Jenni allowed the audience to witness mother and daughter sitting down in a cozy booth and beginning to talk. This ending is not the they-lived-happily-ever-after kind but merely a suggestion that the characters are going to try to work out their difficulties.

Letting characters talk

Although playwriting freed my students to talk to one another easily and often, they had great difficulty writing believable, well-developed dialogue. Unlike prose, which allows a balance between narration and dialogue, the unfolding events in a play must be conveyed by the characters' actions and conversations. Early in playwriting, students filled page after page with short, stilted exchanges, such as, "Yes, I can go"; "No!"; and "I don't want to."

To resolve this problem, we took turns becoming the characters in the plays. We assumed the characters' points of view and talked as we imagined they might talk in various situations. The writer usually played the main character, while I or another student played the other parts, inventing dialogue to suit the situations the writer had devised. I wrote the conversations on the chalkboard, giving all of the stymied writers a sample of free-flowing, natural dialogue. We did this role-playing often and for long periods of time, until the most cautious writer had developed a feel for written conversation.

Just as with plot, however, a writer can get carried away writing dialogue and completely lose track of the story line. Taking time to read portions of their plays aloud helped these young writers figure out how to get back on track, to use dialogue to advance their stories. Teaching novice playwrights how to create believable dialogue that can advance the story and give characters life is a cerebral aspect of playwriting;

showing them the conventions of playwriting is easy. I show them the format: each character's name is written next to the margin and punctuated with a colon; the dialogue without quotation marks follows. Stage directions are within parentheses. Students referred to a permanent model on the chalkboard for writing dialogue. When the class bell rang, my students pulled their writing spirals from the racks, sat down, and began reading their revised conversations to classmates. The more we talked, took on characters' roles, and tightened the writing, the more our play plots thickened.

From the inside out

Play-making was a process that unfolded from the inside out; the students' plays came from their own lives and feelings. Danny, for example, burned with indignation at the slights and slurs that his African American brothers and sisters still endured. Feverishly he worked on his play—even during the nine days when he was suspended from school. When he returned and proudly handed me his first draft, I was struck by the passion of *"Heros Under Political Siege."* Here is Ricardo Valdez speaking at the funeral of Drake Manchester, the martyred young black revolutionary:

Ricardo Valdez: Today we celebrate Drake Manchester's life. The man who murdered Drake Manchester not only murdered a friend and loved one but he murdered a prophet of peace. He murdered a ring bearer of hope, of love, of joy and equality. (*Valdez looks at the coffin.*) Well, my friend, now you can sleep tight because as long as I live, your dream some day will become a reality. (*Valdez pauses.*) Drake Manchester: he came, he saw, he conquered.

Danny's feelings were close to the surface, especially in this part of the eulogy: "With as little education he [Drake] had after failing a grade and not being able to catch up wit [sic] his class, he was skilled in writing and speaking, and he used these skills to try to destroy the only man in which he held feelings of hatred."

The heroic Drake was Danny, the boy who was held back in seventh grade and could not go on to eighth grade with his classmates. For Danny, playwriting not only was intellectually and creatively satisfying, it was therapeutic.

Another student, Michael, used playwriting to explore his feelings about not being cool and "in" with the popular crowd. Merve, the leading character in Michael's play, was the seventh-grade nerd who mistakenly got locked in the school for the night. But Merve heroically made the most of his all-night incarceration: he learned his schedule and located all the classrooms that had eluded him during a school day fraught with anxiety. Here is a bit of Michael's first draft.

Merve: It was scary but . . . I thought of the best idea. I spent the whole night looking around and I memorized my schedule. The next day when all of the guys were lost, they came to me. Now I'm probably the most popular kid in the school.

In review, we rejoiced

After I'd mailed more than twenty-five polished, neatly typed plays, meeting Dobama Theatre's deadline, we rejoiced by forming small groups and performing our plays for our own pleasure. Loud huzzahs and applause buoyed us all.

Finally, after two-and-one-half months, we wrapped up playwriting when I conducted a taped interview of my young playwrights' experiences. They talked openly and frankly about what playwriting had meant to them, what they'd gained and how they'd grown.

Brandon: Playwriting was hard and it felt good!

Chris N.: I learned that writers don't like just sit around waiting for an idea to hit them. Writers have got to get going and write!

Tristin: I'm glad playwriting is over because it was really hard work. But if you [Mrs. Krogness] would have given us a list [of play ideas], it wouldn't have done much good. Our opinions are important. We wouldn't have felt so good.

Dawn: I can relate myself to my fairy tale and to the characters that tell their stories. Making plays helps you *feel* what you want your characters to say.

Keith: I like doing big projects instead of little ones because I really get into a big one. Just as I was hoping that we'd start another big project, you told us about playwriting.

Chris R.: Why is it that when you're done and have turned in your play, you think of a better idea? I've been thinking about a better way to start my play.

During these interviews, Rachel mused, "If only just *one* of us would win [the Dobama Theatre contest], then we'd all win." Rachel had her wish: Lonell's play, "A Death in the Family," was one of four winners among the 150 entries in the junior high/middle school category. I would add to Rachel's generous comment: Every student who participated in playwriting was a winner.

Here is an excerpt from Lonell's play:

A DEATH IN THE FAMILY by Lonell, eighth grade

"A Death in the Family," by Lonell, a prize-winning play in the all-city kids' playwrighting festival sponsored by Dobama Theatre, was based on fourteen-year-old Lonell's own personal family experience: His mother, grandfather, and uncle died all in one year, when Lonell was just six years old.

Grandma: Lonell, wake up. Lonell, honey, I need to talk to you.

Lonell (*age 6*): What is it, Grandma?

Grandma: Lonell, your mother died early this morning.

Lonell: Why is Mom lying there? (*At the funeral home.*)

Dennis (*a family member*): She's gone, Nel. She's gone to heaven where she will be peaceful.

As the play character, Lonell, says: "I don't think that anyone can stop me now because I have my family behind me—as my Uncle Earl says, 110 percent. The inspiration and momentum will continue." Grandma says: "I believe Lonell. When he says he's going to do something, he usually does it. I'm proud of him. So, I'm going to get out of Lonell's way and let him do what he has to do."

I joined Lonell and his family as their guest at opening night when the award-winning plays were performed by professional actors at Dobama Theatre. After Lonell introduced me to eight aunts, uncles, and cousins, who filled one row, he smiled in the direction of his family and said to me, "This is my support." Then he turned to me: "And without you, Mrs. K., I wouldn't be here tonight."

Playwriting had done for my students what I'd hoped it would do: engage them in writing fiction, teach them to develop clearly focused stories and believable characters, and build camaraderie. Playwriting did all of this and more.

ELEVEN

Making Poetry
Side by Side with Poets

Meeting up with a poem

"How many of you like poetry?" I ask.

"It sucks," I hear a boy mutter. This boy's remark prompts me to bring his and probably most of his classmates' old feelings about poetry out into the open.

"Okay, how many of you hate the stuff?" I ask.

Halfheartedly hands go up to indicate that they don't like it. But they know what's coming and they're already enervated.

"I only like Shel Silverstein," another kid says less than enthusiastically.

"Did you know," I ask, "that Shel Silverstein's books, such as *Where the Sidewalk Ends,* are more often stolen from public library shelves than practically any other book in print?"

I continue to survey my students. "How many of you believe that poetry is about beauty and bees and birds and trees?" Hands go up.

"Well, it's not," I say and immediately begin to recite Lucille Clifton's voluptuous poem, "Homage to My Hips":

Homage to My Hips
by Lucille Clifton

these hips are big hips
they need space to
move around in.
they don't fit into little
petty places. these hips
are free hips.
they don't like to be held back.
these hips have never been enslaved,
they go where they want to go
they do what they want to do.
these hips are mighty hips.
these hips are magic hips.
i have known them
to put a spell on a man and
spin him like a top!

This poem stopped them dead in their tracks. "*Now* what do you think poetry's about?" I asked (I like being provocative, too!).

"I've never heard a poem about some lady's hips!" An eighth-grade boy laughed sheepishly. "I wouldn't mind having a copy of *that* one."

"I just happen to have a copy," I answered, and handed him one. "Homage means to pay respect. Clifton is paying respect to a woman's hips that have the power to do a whole *lot* of things."

"But I don't know about that sentence—putting a spell on a man and spinnin' him around like a top," another boy countered. Several boys laughed in agreement.

"Let's read this poem together," I said as I passed out copies of Clifton's poem, which I had heard her recite at an NCTE conference. We read the poem together not once but several times. This reading or chanting aloud is crucial if kids are going to hook up with a poem.

"What do you think of this poem?" I asked everyone. The boys shrugged, almost embarrassed. The girls smiled knowingly.

"I really don't think this is a poem," Natachia whispered.

"How many of you agree with Tachia—that this isn't a poem?"

Many raised their hands.

"It's a poem, all right," I said. "But it's probably not what you're accustomed to hearing. Your ears are used to hearing poems with regular meters, or rhythms, like this: da, dee, da, dee, da, dee, da, dee; and rhyme patterns like Shel Silverstein's." I showed them what I meant by a regular, predictable pattern of rhymes at the end of lines. As Eve Merriam wrote, poetry doesn't always have to rhyme. I'm always glad when kids think they don't like poetry because then I have a degree of leverage, something to push against. A little push-pull is good when you're teaching eighth graders.

I read aloud two parodies of Mother Goose rhymes by Paul Dehn from *Reflections on a Gift of Watermelon Pickle,* an old but still wonderful anthology compiled by Stephen Dunning, Edward Lueders, and Hugh Smith.

Hey Diddle Diddle
by Paul Dehn

Hey diddle diddle,
The physicists fiddle,
    The bleep jumped over the moon.
The little dog laughed to see such fun
    And died the following June.

"Say that one again, Mrs. K.," Julius yelled out. I obliged (eighth graders are attracted to this sort of warped humor).

"I have another one of these takeoffs, called parodies," I said, then started reading "Little Miss Muffet."

Little Miss Muffet
by Paul Dehn

    Little Miss Muffet
    Crouched on a tuffet,
Collecting her shell-shocked wits.
    There dropped (from a glider)
    An H-bomb beside her—
Which frightened Miss Muffet to bits.

Many managed to laugh. One or two had caught the pun about Miss Muffet being frightened to bits. Without saying so, I was getting across the idea that poetry can come in many forms and concern almost any subject imaginable. I could see that poetry was beginning to achieve a little status in this group of eighth graders.

I read another poem from *Watermelon Pickle,* a sports poem I've always liked because the poet, Edwin Hoey, skillfully uses simple language and hard-driving verbs to bring readers to the edge of their seats.

Foul Shot

by Edwin A. Hoey

With two 60's stuck on the scoreboard
And two seconds hanging on the clock,
The solemn boy in the center of eyes,
Squeezed by silence,
Seeks out the line with his feet,
Soothes his hands along his uniform,
Gently drums the ball against the floor,
Then measures the waiting net,
Raises the ball on his right hand,
Balances it with his left,
Calms it with fingertips,
Breathes,
Crouches,
Waits,
And then through a stretching of stillness,
Nudges it upward.

The ball
Slides up and out,
Lands,
Leans,
Wobbles,
Wavers,
Hesitates,
Exasperates,
Plays it coy
Until every face begs with unsounding screams—
   And then
     And then
      And then
Right before ROAR-UP,
Dives down and through.

What a poem! It's not good only for boys who like sports; it's for anyone who likes language. Now something was happening: poetry was breaking down the barriers in my language arts classes. I wouldn't go so far as to say that everyone thought poetry was cool, but in the understated language of eighth graders, "poetry's OK."

Performing poetry

A Word Is Dead

by Emily Dickinson

A word is dead
When it is said,

Some say.
I say it just
Begins to live
That day.

Taking a cue from Emily Dickinson and from classmates like Joe Echle at Bread Loaf, I involved the kids in performing poems: chanting, singing, clapping, moving to poetry's cadences, and dramatizing its sound effects for an audience. My kids and I worked side by side with poets as we climbed inside their words and felt the rhythms and textures of language. Our minds and imaginations relaxed and opened up to possibilities as the words left the page and found their way to our central nervous systems.

Harlem Hopscotch
by Maya Angelou

One foot down, then hop! It's hot.
  Good things for the ones that's got.
Another jump, now to the left.
  Everybody for hisself.

In the air, now both feet down.
  Since you black, don't stick around.
Food is gone, the rent is due,
  Curse and cry and then jump two.

All the people out of work,
  Hold for three, then twist and jerk.
Cross the line, they count you out.
  That's what hopping's all about.

Both feet flat, the game is done.
They think I lost. I think I won.

When my kids and I chanted this poem six or eight times, we were preparing to perform it. "Harlem Hopscotch" is not about the simple childhood game. As Wandy said, "This poem's about life."

I talked with the kids briefly about using our voices to express the feelings that lay inside the words. Our voices were our instruments, and like jazz musicians we would use them to sing out the staccato sadness of this poem. I made a couple of suggestions: "If you want to, you can repeat a certain line or word. Or you can choose just one powerful word or words and use them like a pounding drum to emphasize a feeling. Use those words and your voices however you wish."

As a class, we practiced repeating lines in a variety of meters: an even, two/four tempo and a syncopated rhythm that we made up. We chose one word in each line to sing, and we sang it! We practiced screaming, purring, whispering, whining, trilling, and elongating words—all with our voices. We experimented, for instance, by interpreting the two words in line one: It's *hot*. We sang high and then swung low to sound sultry. The sound effects we produced caused a sensation, as poetry is supposed to do.

After we'd practiced using our voices for ten minutes or so, I divided the kids into groups of three and asked them to take five to ten minutes to figure out ways to perform this poem. Group members had to decide which lines they'd say in unison and which would be solo; they had to experiment with rhythm, pitch, and volume to achieve exciting effects.

Performance par excellence

Virgil, who was always on the move, asked if his group, which included Wandy and Malcolm, could use their bodies to interpret the poem as well. Their final performance was videotaped by Michael, who flatly refused to perform but thoroughly enjoyed playing cinematographer. The three performers captured the mood of the poem with their voices and bodies as they soloed and harmonized, dipped and twirled. With six-foot, three-inch Malcolm's bass voice (he sounded like the bass singer in The Spinners) coupled with Wandy's alto and Virgil's tenor, the three eighth graders sounded like a real jazz trio. Some lines they delivered in syncopation; others were as cool as John Coltrane's saxophone.

Although the other groups didn't want to follow this spectacular act, they did perform. Lisa M. remarked that trying to organize her group made her realize how tough teaching was. (An important insight!) We cheered appreciatively as each group spoke the rich words of Maya Angelou in different ways. When the seventh graders listened to their performances on tape, Rayshon exclaimed, "I love poetry! Saying it over and over makes me a better reader. Don't you remember how I used to read: 'Uh, uh, uh.' " Rayshon mimicked his old halting style of reading aloud.

For recalcitrant kids like Michael (who ran the video camera), I found or invented other types of artistic expression: interpreting a poem by creating a collage or working in clay, taping music, and collecting and copying more poems from the library. Sometimes I simply let the quiet ones sit on the sidelines and take part vicariously.

But what about the meaning?

I wanted to break down the barriers that stopped the kids from meeting poetry, and then I wanted to engage them in language: saying it, hearing it, moving to it. I didn't want to diminish the powerful effect of this introduction quite yet by asking them to find meaning in the poetry.

Northrop Frye said: "I think that the basis of literary education is poetry. Poetry is rhythm, movement. The entering of poetic rhythm into the body of the reader is important. It is something very close to the development of an athletic skill and, as such, it can't be rushed." I agree.

When my students and I had read lots of poems to each other, performed a few of them, and gotten to feel that poetry was made by real people, we took a hard look at one or two poems. I asked: "Which words grab you?" We focused on specific words that conveyed particular meaning to us or intrigued us with their sounds. We all spoke the chosen words or combination of words out loud; occasionally, we took turns miming or acting them out.

"Poetry comes in lines, not sentences," I said then. "Which lines do you especially like?" We read aloud the chosen lines and I asked the students to share what the particular lines did or said to them. Then we moved on to their thoughts or feelings about a whole poem.

I varied my approach, sometimes letting the poetry come to us and sometimes taking us to it. But I never formally explicated a poem for my students. Instead, we began creating our own poetry by writing, literally, side by side with poets. We wrote in the margins of copies of poems by Maya Angelou, Eve Merriam, Langston Hughes, and Myra Cohn Livingston, and through this proximity we developed a sense of companionship with them. I was exceedingly careful *not* to ask students, either explicitly or implicitly, to copy a model I had in mind. Then we turned to a poem by Bobbi Katz, a little jewel that Marlene Birkman introduced me to:

Samuel

by Bobbi Katz

I found this salamander
Near the pond in the woods.
Samuel, I called him—
Samuel, Samuel.

Right away I loved him.
He loved me too, I think.
Samuel, I called him—
Samuel, Samuel.

I took him home in a coffee can,
And at night
He slept in my bed.
In the morning
I took him to school.

He died very quietly during spelling.

Sometimes I think
I should have left him
Near the pond in the woods.
Samuel, I called him—
Samuel, Samuel.

After reading and rereading "Samuel" by Bobbi Katz and laughing gently about the line, "He died very quietly during spelling," I asked students to reflect back on the time when they were five or six years old: "What sorts of losses do you remember?" This question prompted them to recall precious grandmothers and other family members lost through death or divorce. Many kids had lost beloved pets: fish, rabbits, hamsters, turtles, dogs, cats, and birds. We spent thirty or more minutes just talking. What we were doing, of course, was rehearsing to write, stockpiling ideas, and limbering up our imaginations. This talking time was the second step toward making our own poetry. When I sensed that most of us were sufficiently warmed up, we started jotting down incidents from early childhood that we'd stored in our memory banks. Then, from our stacks of poetry by favorite poets, each of us chose one to write next to.

Side by side with poets

In the margins of the dozens of poems I had copied, my kids and I doodled, jotted, scribbled, and experimented with words of our own—*after* we'd chanted the poetry made by Bobbi Katz, Judith Thurman, Nikki Giovanni, and Valerie Worth. Developing a sense of companionship with these poets gave us confidence and freed most of us to play with words. We developed a feeling for the cadences and colors of Eloise Greenfield, Eve Merriam, Paul Janeczko, e. e. cummings, Zora Neale Hurston, Lucille Clifton, X. J. Kennedy, Sonia Sanchez, Haki Madhubuti (Donald Lee), and others whom we had discovered and adopted as our own.

SAMUEL

by Bobbi Katz

I found this salamander
Near the pond in the woods.
Samuel, I called him—
Samuel, Samuel.

Right away I loved him.
He loved me too, I think.
Samuel, I called him—
Samuel, Samuel.

I took him home in a coffee can,
And at night
He slept in my bed.
In the morning
I took him to school.

He died very quietly during spelling.

Sometimes I think
I should have left him
Near the pond in the woods.
Samuel, I called him—
Samuel, Samuel.

10/25/88

Doggie
By Chris M.

I slipped into
the garage and what
did I see, little puppies
my dog Bear had
them, As they grew
so did I. those
puppies were
cute untill
they had to
go, we got so
attached to each
outher we all
wimpered when
they had to
leave
"So Long"

FIG. 11-1 *Chris M.'s Dog Poem*

Chris M.'s dog poem, which he wrote in response to Bobbi Katz's poem "Samuel," is shown in Figure 11-1.

Lisa S. wrote a splendid little poem apropos Bobbi Katz's "Samuel."

A Long Time Ago

by Lisa S.

A long time ago,
I was too young to stay home alone.
I didn't know what to say when
I picked up the phone.
  A long time ago, maybe 5,
  Maybe 6 years ago,
I got scared of creatures that
  might walk in the night.
  A long time ago in the dark—

SAMUEL
by Bobbi Katz

2/3°

Chi
10-25-88

I found this salamander
Near the pond in the woods.
Samuel, I called him—
Samuel, Samuel.

Right away I loved him.
He loved me too, I think.
Samuel, I called him—
Samuel, Samuel.

I took him home in a coffee can,
And at night
He slept in my bed.
In the morning
I took him to school.

He died very quietly during spelling.

Sometimes I think
I should have left him
Near the pond in the woods.
Samuel, I called him—
Samuel, Samuel.

This is 8year ago
ME 5year old I am to
short I am not
really like go to
school I like new
dress I like new
sweateR I like
I have a wash
but my another
She not buy
For me she
is buy For
my sister
not FoR
me every
night I go
to bed I am
crying why
my mother
love my sisteR
now I don't like every
thing. but now I like how can't
I speak english very much that
is I am very happy

FIG. 11-2   *Chi's Piece*

Pitch Black.
Just a long time ago
I used to get scared of the dark.

Chi wrote a touching piece about feeling second-best to one of her older sisters. (See Figure 11-2.) This poem, written early in the school year when the language was still new to her, proved to be an embarrassment to Chi later. But the words that she set down reflect the freshness a newcomer brings to the language.

Erika and Twilla are making poetry side by side.

Modeling, not copying

In writing side by side with published poets, we did not try to pattern our poems after the poets' works. Although we spent a little time noticing that poets sometimes repeat words and sometimes whole lines and that repetition unifies poetry, I didn't say: "In the poem, 'Samuel,' the poet repeats lines, and I want you to do the same thing." Serious confusion exists between *modeling* and *copying*. I've seen teachers use Cynthia Rylant's poetic prose *When I Was Young in the Mountains* as a starter that students finish: "When I was young in the mountains, I . . ." Horrors!

The next two poems, written by Devon, an eighth grader, and Jamar, a seventh grader, illustrate what can happen quite naturally when kids read and hear a poem so often they absorb its cadence. With their classmates and me, both boys had read and heard Bobbi Katz's poem "Samuel" many times. Their poems about their grandmothers bear a striking resemblance to "Samuel" because the young poets wrote in similar rhythm and repeated key lines, but they were by no means copying.

First, read Bobbi Katz's poem (on page 204) aloud again.

Now, read Devon's and Jamar's poems, especially noticing the cadence and the repeated lines. (Figure 11-3 shows Jamar's handwritten poem.)

Jesus He Was, Jesus with the Eyes
by Devon

I went to Grandma's funeral
and saw a picture of Jesus.

SAMUEL

by Bobbi Katz

I found this salamander
Near the pond in the woods.
Samuel, I called him—
Samuel, Samuel.

Right away I loved him.
He loved me too, I think.
Samuel, I called him—
Samuel, Samuel.

I took him home in a coffee can,
And at night
He slept in my bed.
In the morning
I took him to school.

He died very quietly during spelling.

Sometimes I think
I should have left him
Near the pond in the woods.
Samuel, I called him—
Samuel, Samuel.

10/25/88
Jamar

I had a grandmother
named Mrs. Seay,
Sweat chariot the
Song played.
I was her best grand-
son so I called
her granny.
Sweat chariot the
Song played.
my mother told.
me that we will
be seeing granny
Soon. sweat
chariot the
Song play but
She would be
in a casket.
Sweat charoit
the song played
And every
Sents granny died
I still remember
the song
Swing low
Sweat chariot.

FIG. 11-3   *Jamar's Granny Seay Poem*

Jesus he was,
Jesus with the eyes.
Right away I ran to Mom
and told her of the sight.
Jesus he was,
Jesus with the eyes.

I looked at the picture up and down,
I looked at it 'round and 'round
to see how real it was.
I walked two steps up
and two steps back—
No matter, he was
Jesus with the eyes.
Sometimes I wonder if he was in the picture.

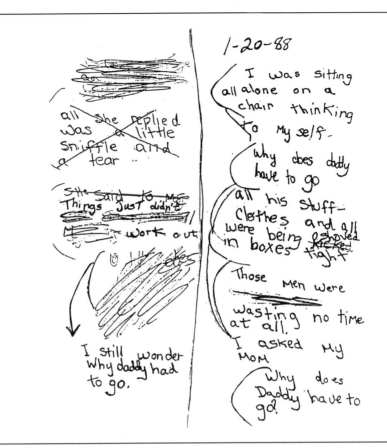

FIG. 11-4   *Marie's Poem*

(Is there really a Jesus? I don't know.)
Sometimes I wonder.
   Jesus he is,
   Jesus with the eyes.

Grandma Seay [pronounced "say"]

by Jamar

I had a grandmother
named Mrs. Seay
Sweet Chariot, the song played.
I was her best grandson
so I called her Granny.
Sweet Chariot the song played.
My mother told
me that we will
be seeing Granny
soon. Sweet Chariot
the song play but
she would be in a casket.
Sweet Chariot
the song played

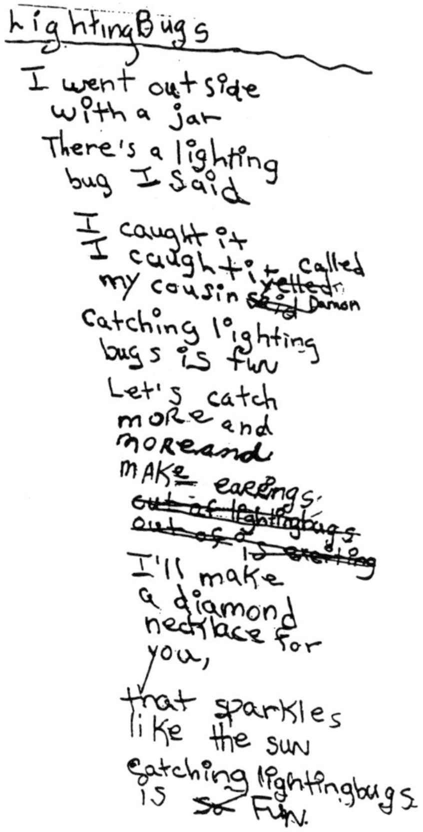

Lighting Bugs

I went outside
with a jar
There's a lighting
bug I said

I caught it
I caught it ~~yelled~~ called
my cousin ~~scott~~ Damon
Catching lighting
bugs is fun

Let's catch
more and
more and
make earrings.
~~out of lightingbugs~~
~~out of~~ ~~sterling~~

I'll make
a diamond
necklace for
you,

that sparkles
like the sun
catching lightingbugs
is ~~so~~ fun.

FIG. 11-5   *Sherry's Poem*

> And ever
> since Granny died
> I still remember
> the song
> Swing low
> Sweet chariot.

"Samuel" prompted Marie to express her loss in her poem "Daddy" (see Figure 11-4). Katz's poem stirred memories of Mississippi summers in Sherry (see Figure 11-5).

The trouble with paradigms

Teachers often want to provide some sort of structure for students who are making poetry. The danger is that the teacher and her students may feel bound to squeeze their words into that framework. For instance, the Japanese haiku form so beloved by elementary school teachers too often turns poetry writing into a syllable-counting exercise.

For me, form isn't a concern; I trust poetry to sing to my kids, to strum their emotional chords, and to play to their rhythms. I trust myself to lead them gently and help them recognize the gold nuggets in their early drafts. I seize on surprising juxtapositions of words or rhythms, fresh use of figurative language, strong images, and sound effects. I consider it my job to recognize the promise and then tell the young writer that he's got something wonderful to work with—or, really, to play with.

"Kisses" turned 'em on

One poem that fired up my seventh graders to write was Judith Thurman's "Kisses," from her collection *Flashlight*.

Kisses
by Judith Thurman

Two
kisses for hello,
pressed like snaps
onto each cheek.

One
kiss for sleep-tight,
planted on the forehead
like a flag.

A handful
of kisses for good-bye,
wind-blown
like seeds or bubbles.

A spidery
kiss that tickles
a sad feeling.

After we had read the poem several times, we talked endlessly and enthusiastically about the different kinds of kisses we'd gotten: sloppy and slippery smooches, pink lipsticked kisses smeared across our cheeks. Kids laughed when they recalled family members, mostly old aunties, who pinched their cheeks and kissed them repeatedly when they were little.

I let my students get started writing before I peeked. When I looked over Jamar's shoulder, I got tingly. As poet Denise Levertov said, "You can smell a poem before you see it." Jamar had quickly set down a dynamite little poem about his other grandmother, who quite literally captured her grandson with a mighty kiss (see Figure 11-6). I asked Jamar if I could read his poem aloud to the class. The only word he wanted to change was *guards,* for which he substituted *executioners.*

We all laughed, delighted with the wonderful poem that Jamar had written so quickly and easily. Lisa S., Joe, Chris M., Jermaine—everyone except big Jawan wanted to read their poems aloud. Jawan looked gloomy. "I can't write no poetry. I can't even get started." He slumped in his chair and put his head down. I pulled up a chair and asked him a few questions to prime the pump.

Jamar.
2/2/89

It to like When
I go over my
grandma Williams.
She says come
here honey bun
give me some
sugar. then
I feel like
a sweet role
all wrapped up
and tightened
up! but
when she
Pokes out
them lips
I am traped!
I don't have
any choice because
my parents are
looking over me like
gawds
executioers.

KISSES
by Judith Thurman

Two
kisses for hello,
pressed like snaps
onto each cheek.

One
kiss for sleep-tight,
planted on the forehead
like a flag.

A handful
of kisses for good-bye,
wind-blown
like seeds or bubbles.

A spidery
kiss that tickles
a sad feeling.

FIG. 11-6   *Jamar's Grandma Williams Poem*

"Jay, where do you mostly get kisses?" My question, a loaded one indeed, had slipped carelessly out of my mouth. A smooth smile crossed Jay's face.

"Forget that I asked you *that* question!" I laughed. But Jay answered: "I mostly get kisses when I go to church."

"That's the first line of your poem," I said. "Where do you go to church?" I asked this question quickly because I wanted to help Jawan create a mood.

"Holy Trinity Baptist Church at 131st," he replied.

"And that's your second line," I said. I wrote down the first two lines of Jawan's poem in the margin next to Thurman's "Kisses." Then he was free to finish his piece. Jawan's poem (shown on the left in Figure 11-7), in black dialect, nearly blew us all away when I read it aloud to the class. Again we laughed appreciatively. Marie

I mostly get kisses
when I go to
church — Holy
Trinity Baptist
Church at 131st
Sister Morrison
give me the water rain
puddle kiss of the
Sunday. And when she
pucker up, ~~it's it~~
~~go folk out her lips~~

~~It's~~ a rainfall.

KISSES
by Judith Thurman

Two
kisses for hello,
pressed like snaps
onto each cheek.

One
kiss for sleep-tight,
planted on the forehead
like a flag.

A handful
of kisses for good-bye,
wind-blown
like seeds or bubbles.

A spidery
kiss that tickles
a sad feeling.

I have a aant
name Annie
sis-sha give
me a kiss and
she have a mustache
When she kiss me It feel
like a brush
bristle and like
a dog kiss wet
and wild.

Jawan M.
2-2-89

FIG. 11-7 *Jawan's Poems*

smirked, "I bet Jay don't get *all* his kisses at Holy Trinity Baptist!" Jawan laughed in acknowledgment.

Quickly Jawan wrote another poem in the right margin (see Figure 11-7). And that is how it remained. Why work over a piece that's born good?

Again, I asked him if I could read his poem aloud, hot off the press and, like Jawan, earthy and graphic. We were now applauding anyone who read his or her poem aloud. The room was filled with excitement about poetry. As Marie said: "Poetry's *live!*"

"I guess I *can* write poetry." Jawan looked proud.

Everyone's poem was good, but a few, like Jamar's and Jawan's, were outstanding. I wanted to get more mileage from this poetry experience while my students were giddy with excitement. We talked briefly about what we liked about their poems: the humor, the words they chose, the naturalness of lines that resembled conversation.

Several kids commented on the black dialect used by Jamar and Jawan. We talked about the appropriateness of using nonstandard dialect in poetry. Here black dialect fit the occasion. It gave the poems richness and warmth. I commented on the "voice," or individuality, in these poems (for example, feeling "like a sweet roll all wrapped up and tightened up").

Danny and Khalilah are trying to put the best words in the best order.

Jawan's kiss from Sister Morrison that is "the water rain puddle kiss of the Sunday" demanded our careful attention. This run of words needed to be hyphenated, making seven words into one powerful word.

"What would happen, Jay, if you created a brand new word from seven separate words?" I asked.

I read aloud "water rain puddle kiss of the Sunday" as one word, heightening the image of one sloppy kiss and the sound effect of this rush of words. Jawan liked the result. So all we did was insert hyphens: water-rain-puddle-kiss-of-the-Sunday. Isn't this sound effect stunning?

Lisa S.'s piece, her first draft, stood up fine, too. And we all agreed that picturing Lisa balking when it came to being kissed wasn't hard. Here is Lisa's poem, which made us all laugh, especially the last five lines.

I Lost My Lips
by Lisa S.

I remember when
I had to go
out of town.
Everybody in my family
wanted to
KISS me.
I said NO.
I was little then
but I still
do not like being
KISSED.

I would say, "I have
no lips,
I lost them on the way,
and I haven't found them
yet!"

Thurman's poem, "Kisses," had touched off something wonderful in my seventh-grade classes, so I decided to hand it out and read it, along with other poems, to my eighth-grade classes. I reasoned that eighth graders were even more fond of the concept of kissing than seventh graders. Chris N., an exceedingly bright boy who was in our language arts class because he'd opted out of taking a foreign language, wrote about his Southern grandma. Here is his first draft.

Gramma—
One kiss
of days Gone.

Georgia—
a Dixie summer
Rosey powder
lemonade.

A Girl—
A parasoled beauty
My how I've grown
I've grown too fast.

A southern bell
A parasoled sweetie
Gramma grew too fast
The parasol broken.

Chris's first two stanzas are exquisite. Immediately he creates a picture of his lovely gramma's Georgia youth. His comparison of a "Dixie summer" to the imaginative "rosey powder lemonade" is as intoxicating as magnolias. The first two stanzas hold together because of the parallel construction: "Gramma— / One kiss of days Gone / Georgia— / a Dixie summer / Rosey powder / lemonade."

Chris started the third stanza the same way: "A girl— / A parasoled beauty." Then his little beauty took an unpromising turn: "My how I've grown / I've grown too fast." Chris said he didn't know how to finish this stanza. The last stanza, "A southern bell / A parasoled sweetie," was another promising start that rather petered out in the last two lines: "Gramma grew too fast / The parasol broken." I asked Chris what he meant by Gramma's growing too fast and her parasol breaking. Chris imagined his pretty grandmother blossoming, but becoming an awkward adolescent; the broken parasol represented her lack of the usual Southern femininity. During our writing conference, I tried hard to find out what Chris was trying to say in his poem. We concluded that the last two lines in stanzas three and four needed work. Chris fooled around with them, but he couldn't seem to write substitutes that matched the strength of the rest of his poem.

This is where I came in. "Why not use 'a parasoled beauty' and 'a parasoled sweetie' together to make stanza three?" Then I suggested that he go full circle by repeating the first stanza. Chris, who sometimes ran out of steam early, agreed whole-heartedly. Here is the final result:

Rosey Powder Lemonade
by Chris N.

Gramma—
One kiss
of days gone.

Georgia—
a Dixie summer,
rosey powder lemonade.

A girl—
a parasoled beauty,
a parasoled sweetie,

Gramma—
One kiss
of days gone.

Thurman's poem was a stimulus for fine writing. Ominicka warmed up by writing this short little rhyme:

Kiss me once
Kiss me twice
You can even
Kiss me three
Times cause
it feels just
right.

"Try another," I encouraged this spirited fourteen-year-old girl, who had just moved to our school district in the fall. This was the result:

Mama's Kisses
by Ominicka

Mama's kisses smell good
they smell like a baby
Mama's kisses smell good
like powder, maybe.
I hope Mama never runs
out of kisses for
her baby.

Chris R., always wearing a smile and filled with mirth, quickly wrote this one.

Old Aunt Ira
by Chris R.

Old Aunt Ira
does one nasty thing.
She sticks on your face
Like static cling!

Angelo

You know
when you
go over your
Aunts Hoose
And She gives
you A sloppy
Kiss on your
Cheek

V

It Be sitting there
On your cheek
Just as wet as rain.

KISSES
by Judith Thurman

Two
kisses for hello,
pressed like snaps
onto each cheek.

One
kiss for sleep-tight,
planted on the forehead
like a flag.

A handful
of kisses for good-bye,
wind-blown
like seeds or bubbles.

A spidery
kiss that tickles
a sad feeling.

FIG. 11-8   _Angelo's Poem_

Angelo, a slight, tentative boy with large brown eyes, frequently perched on the edge of his chair, his pencil poised. Rarely, however, did the pencil meet the paper that lay before him. Knowing that a watched pot doesn't boil, I laid off Angelo this day. Unexpectedly, he called me over to show me what he'd just written.

"It's not a poem," he said, preempting any comments I might make. I looked at the tiny writing scratched in the upper left margin of the paper (see Figure 11-8):

You know when you go over your
aunt's house and she gives
you a sloppy kiss on your cheek

"This is dynamite, Angelo! What do you mean this isn't a poem?"

"It just don't sound like one," he said, his eyes bigger than usual.

"This is a poem, all right. But it's begging you to finish it."

"I don't know how to finish it," he said anxiously.

"What happens when you go over your aunt's house and she gives you a big sloppy kiss on your cheek? What happens to that big sloppy kiss on your cheek?" I asked.

"It be sitting there," Angelo replied. He watched my reaction.

"How does it feel, just sitting there on your cheek?" I pressed Angelo to respond.

"It be sitting there just as wet as rain."

Everyone turned around because I had let out a scream that nearly sent poor Angelo into orbit. "That's the last line, Angelo. That's the last line of your wonderful little poem."

Angelo looked incredulous. "Now this is one fine poem, Angelo. It's the best piece of writing you've done." (I didn't say that it was practically the only real writing I'd gotten from Angelo this school year.) "Please let me say it to the class." Angelo agreed. And not only did I recite it to the class that day maybe three times, but on succeeding days I'd come blowing into our class reciting that wonderfully fresh small poem of Angelo's:

> You know when you go over your
> aunt's house and she gives
> you a sloppy kiss on your cheek? [Pause respectfully, now]
> It be sitting there just as wet as rain.

And Angelo would beam and fidget because he was pleased. After that day, the magical day when he made the poem, Angelo felt a little freer to put pencil to paper.

Poems like "Samuel," "Kisses," Nikki Giovanni's "Knoxville, Tennessee," and Valerie Worth's collections, *Small Poems Again* and *All the Small Poems,* had a way of getting under our skin and letting fireflies loose in our heads, maybe because the words are simple, not the least bit pompous or precious. We chanted and performed these poems, soaked up their rhythms and music, talked about how they had touched us. We wrote our own poems side by side with our favorites, not patterning ourselves after them but using the poems as springboards to take flight.

Julie's gifts

Some of my students went beyond Katz, Thurman, Giovanni, and Worth to make poems on their own. Julie wrote profusely and for her own pleasure. She listened intently when I played tapes or read aloud poetry by Langston Hughes and Paul Laurence Dunbar, Rita Dove, June Jordon, and Gwendolyn Brooks. I lent Julie poetry books from my own collection: William Blake, Robert Frost, e. e. cummings, T. S. Eliot (*Old Possum's Book of Practical Cats*), Vachel Lindsay, William Carlos Williams, Walt Whitman, and others. Between November and June, Julie wrote poetry outside of class and popped fifty-seven original poems ("poetry presents" she called them) into my mailbox. After having them typed, I enclosed them in a folder with cellophane pockets and presented the collection to her, since she would be leaving us to go to high school.

In trying to decide which of Julie's poems to include in this chapter, I did what a reader *should* do with poems: I read them all aloud many times. After much deliberation, I narrowed my selection to seven.

Poem
by Julie

Sometimes I wonder
and wonder
about my old shoes.
I got them about
a century ago

and they still shine
like new.
Sometimes I wonder
and wonder
about those
old shoes 'cause
At night they're
the light color
of blue.
I love my old shoes
that's the light
color of blue but
Sometimes I wonder
and wonder about
those old shoes!

Whispers

by Julie

Whispers are quiet.
Whispers can be
only heard in the
darkness but
if you are scared
at night of the
whispers, then
    TURN
      ON
        THE
          LIGHT!

Foggy Day

by Julie

A foggy day.
I can't see nothing but
streets of only shadows.
The air is kinda misty.
The air is blowing up
my nose. That's why I love
a foggy day.

A Tiger

by Julie

I watch the beautiful tiger.
The wind brushes its hair as it stares
out onto the wilderness.
Shhhhhhhhhhhhh
it's moving toward a deer
that is more than just a deer,
it's its dinner.

Jesse Jackson
by Julie

Last night I heard the
Real meaning of Rev.
Jesse Jackson. He speaked
of love, and what's right
for us black Americans. He's the
light of a star shining
in the night.

The Black Man In America
by Julie

Black man in America
strong-n-long
powerful-n-old
Black man in America.

I Wanna Be Something Spiritual
by Julie
I wanna be different.
I wanna be smooth
and sensitive, too, within
my mind.
I wanna be something
wise, or wonderful.
I wanna be something
spiritual.

Julie's poetry, though rough and uneven in places, had a sort of blues quality. Her keen eye and fresh view of the world gave her poems originality.

Poetry, the universal language

Kelly, a blond who wore sky-blue eye shadow and occasionally brought a teddy bear to class, could provoke a saint and often called classmates (girls *and* boys) heifers. Curiously, she took a fancy to poetry. Even more curiously, she liked poetry about *cows*! For her final project, Kelly decided to collect all the cow poems that had ever been written and make a few of her own. What an imaginative project, one that I'd certainly never run across in all my years of teaching. I must confess that when Kelly asked for a library pass and left the classroom with a handful of dimes for photocopying the cow poems she intended to find, I was relieved. This difficult girl was learning to use *Granger's Index to Poetry,* a resource she would never have bothered with otherwise. When she'd return to class, she'd beam beatifically and say, "Well, I just found some more cow poems in the library. Want me to read them to you?"

Like Kelly, Lisa M. was difficult. She didn't do much during class except act out inappropriately, make provocative remarks to Quinten, spit insults at me, and suck her thumb. So when Lisa M. asked permission to head for the library to read and then reprint favorite poems, I was pleased and, again, relieved. Black poets exerted a powerful influence on her writing. This stream-of-consciousness poem, "The World Goes Round," was part of her final project, a collection of her own poetry and that of favorite poets she'd encountered while browsing in the library.

The World Goes Round
by Lisa M.

The world goes round
so does my mind and
I'm sitting here writing poems
Not knowing how they sound.
We're all blind
But the world still
goes 'round.
I'm slow you're slow
They're fast but who
can be last not me
How about you
I told you we're not fast.
My house is full of fun
And my dreams are full of fantasy.
But my life is down and out.
My yard is full of beauty
But the beast in me still hasn't come to mind

Lisa M.'s poem is filled with conflict and turbulence; the last stanza is a mixture of chaos and beauty. The final line, "But the beast in me still hasn't come to mind," reminds me of Lisa's ambivalence about so many things. Did she imagine herself to be both Beauty and Beast? This autobiographical poem conveys the ambivalence of adolescence.

For a moment, poetry set a few other students free from the rage that seethed in them and sapped their energy. Erika, who, like Julie, wrote abundantly, handed me this poem at the end of class one day.

Thoughts of a Black Child
by Erika

I am a black child that has been scarred for life.
Just by the color of my skin, I've been cut with a knife
I try not to let my negativity show,
But the hatred for whites in me still grows.
I'm afraid to be like the others—
The neglected sisters
And forgotten brothers.

Maybe we should all get together
and join hands,
Finally forget the hatred
and make a stand.

Erika wanted to read aloud what probably was her best poem, "The Warriors," at one of our informal poetry readings.

The Warriors
by Erika

We are the warriors
Fighting the battle
of mass production.

So many temptations.
Riches, Greed, Jealousy
Are our seduction.

Death is no dare
Because you see, we
are already there—the
outside looking in,
or the inside looking out.

Nowhere to run
because Time has
Run Out!

One spring, Rowly Brucken, a former student of mine, came to class to talk about his experience of living in Zimbabwe during his junior year in college. He was there when Nelson Mandela was let out of prison after nearly thirty years. This conversation with Rowly prompted Crystal to write "Mandela," reflecting her heightened feelings about this great leader.

Mandela
by Crystal

As they raised their black fists
and cried Mandela,
they also cried for freedom.
Their black pride was taken away
from them, but they raised
their black fists and cried Mandela!
Even through the heat of oppression,
the Black Africans stood up—
sweat glistening,
they cried Mandela!
Through the tears of the Blacks
and the billy clubs of the whites,
they raised their Black fists
and cried Mandela!
They cried, "Freedom!"

We celebrated our first successes at writing poetry by holding poetry readings in our own coffee house, Room 226. Each person who volunteered to read his or her poem aloud sat in the chair reserved for the poet-in-residence. We all listened to the readings and applauded magnanimously. Many of these poems were published for all the world to read in *Kaleidoscope,* the school's literary magazine.

And now for making meaning

I had the extraordinary opportunity to participate in one of Patrick Dias's poetry response workshops at an NCTE conference. Dias, from McGill University in Canada, has created a simple but expansive and flexible procedure for students to use together while reading and responding to poetry. Dias's plan, which is certainly *not* a formula, works nicely with readers and writers of all ages, from upper elementary grades through graduate school. He recommends that five students work together, but the students, *not* the teacher, are in charge. Here is Dias's plan:

Groups of perhaps five students meet to read and talk about a poem. One member of each group is designated by the teacher or the group as the reader, one as the discussion leader, and another as the reporter. The reader begins by reading the poem aloud twice as the other group members silently read from their own copies.

Next, the leader of each group calls on the participants in clockwise order, asking each to respond to the poem. Students' responses may vary from profound insights to "I don't get it," but everyone is expected to say something about the poem during this first of several rounds of responses.

The reporter in each group, who is expected to participate and also listen attentively to everyone's response, gathers the thoughts of colleagues but does *not* write notes; he or she collects general insights as well as specific comments for reporting to the larger group later.

Next, the reader (or, for that matter, any other group member) reads a couple of lines of the poem aloud and then stops at a natural stopping place, asking for each member's insights. No one is prodded or coached; the participants merely reflect and respond. If the discussion bogs down, the reader rereads the poem from beginning to end. The group leader then asks for more comments about the whole poem, specific lines, or important or provocative words in the text.

For the last time, the reader reads the poem in its entirety so that the group members can hear the language spoken again. Everyone takes another turn, offering one last impression, insight, or understanding. The reporter summarizes the group's understanding of the poem for group members. The reporter also talks about lines and images that the group has identified as significant.

Finally, the reporter speaks to the other groups, reporting the impressions and insights of his or her group. Members of other groups can question or respond to the speaker. And so it goes.

After participating in a poetry response group led by Patrick Dias during that NCTE conference, I went home and adapted (mostly by abbreviating) Dias's procedure. Like him, I wanted to engage kids in reacting and responding to poetry *without* the teacher's intervention. First I handed each class member a printed set of directions, which I read aloud slowly while they read silently to themselves.

Written directions and goals

"I want you to respond to this poem, 'Hippopotamus' by Ron Wallace, by working with every member of your group." (Usually I assigned the groups and designated the readers to simplify matters and save time. I also wanted certain kids to work together.) "You can feel free to say how the poem affects you and what it seems to say to you. *Any* and *all* ideas are important. Your understanding probably will change as you read aloud, think about, and discuss this poem with members of your group.

"During this ten minute experience, I expect that each of you will participate by being quiet and listening to every other person's response, then expressing your insights and ideas when it's your turn.

"First, after I read aloud Ron Wallace's poem to all of you twice, I want group readers to read aloud the same poem two more times. I want every one of you to hear the language while reading silently along with your reader.

"Second, each one of you will be expected to say *something* about this poem. For instance, you might give a general impression or comment on a word that is striking or a vivid word picture. Please move from one person to another in a clockwise order.

"Third, the reader should read the poem aloud again, this time a couple of lines at a time (or wherever the poem naturally pauses).

"Fourth, moving clockwise around the circle, each group member should respond again. Everyone should listen to the sounds of the words, picture what the words say, and try to get a feeling for the poem.

"Fifth, the reader reads the poem one last time, giving everyone a final opportunity to speak.

"Sixth, one member of your group (or all members) can talk about your group's responses to the poem. Try making a big statement about the poem's possible meaning."

I asked if there were any questions, then reminded group members to follow Dias's procedure. As the students worked their way through "Hippopotamus," I quietly sat in on all the response groups to observe as well as to help certain members focus their attention. (A few kids chose to work alone, and I let them.) Each group certainly determined its own way of working together, and each brought a different understanding to the poem.

Hippopotamus
by Ron Wallace

I am tired of wallowing
in this mud and my own hide.
If I were a poet
and not a hippopotamus
I could be anything I wanted.
A gazelle, for instance.
The word springs from my mouth,
grows graceful
legs and muscles:
gazelle, gazelle
it dances on its syllables.
Excited by flies,
I waddled over to my thick wife,
full of secrets and poetry.

Malik, Kelly, and Ilanit reported their collective understanding: "A hippo pictured himself being a gazelle. The hippo is dragging along tired of living the way he does. He wants to become something exciting, beautiful, graceful, and full of passion: a gazelle with graceful legs and muscles. This can only happen if he is a great poet, full of imagination and enthusiasm. As the hippo realizes that he is not a poet, he waddles in self-pity to his wife to share his emotions." This interpretation, in which the group brought its ideas full circle, earned a round of well-deserved applause.

Mario, a highly imaginative boy with a contagious sense of humor and a gift for theater, said, "The hippo is tired of living in mud and its own hide. I bet if he was a poet and not a hippopotamus it would make its life a little easier, like a fly for instance, flying through the summer breeze with the different colored wings. It [the fly] dances on its syllables: f-l-y, f-l-y. The hippo waddles over to his thick wife full of beautiful secrets of poetry."

Big Brad, a solitary sort, worked through the poem earnestly and in different stages. First he carefully considered each line, looking for meaning. Finally he looked at the poem holistically: "A hippo gets tired of his life and he wants to be a poet so he can be anything he wants to be. And then he goes to his wife who is full of secrets of poetry because women are *supposed* to know everything in the world." All the young women in our class roundly applauded Brad's insight.

When I asked the kids their opinion about this activity, they generally felt positive about it (except for Jasper, who thought it was "a stupid waste of time"). They particularly liked not having to find "the right meaning" as determined by the teacher; they appreciated being free to say whatever they thought and felt. Certain kids, ones whom I wouldn't have expected to respond to poetry, made very astute comments about this whimsical poem.

Patrick Dias has tried giving certain poetry response groups teacher-prepared questions while asking other groups to read and interpret independently. His finding: students who were asked to answer teacher-made questions gave more predictable responses and produced fewer fresh insights. I performed the same experiment and got the same results.

Other response techniques

My eighth graders and I talked as a group about Eve Merriam's "I'm Sorry, Says the Machine," a poem about the impersonal nature of individuals, society, and the universe. The poem's cadence and repetitions set the tone for both discussion and the creation of original poems. First we read the poem aloud together four or five times.

I'm Sorry Says the Machine
by Eve Merriam

I'm sorry says the machine,
Thank you for waiting says the tape recording.
Trying to connect you says the voice in the
vacuum at the end of the line.

I'm sorry that sister is not in working order.
Please verify your brother and try him again.
I'm sorry that mother is out of service.
Thank you for waiting, that father you have
reached is not reachable at this time.

I'm sorry that water is not in drinking order.
Please verify that sunlight and try it later.
I'm sorry that blue sky is out of service.
Thank you for waiting, those flowers and trees
      are permanently disconnected.

I'm sorry that country is not in working order.
I'm sorry that planet is out of service.
Please verify that godhead and try much later.
Thank you for waiting, that universe has been dis . . .

"What does this first stanza say to you?" I asked my fourth-period eighth-grade class. I asked that question about each stanza. Together we considered the increased tension and seriousness of the last stanza: the country not in working order, the planet out of service, man unable to get in touch with a supreme being, and the definite implication that the universe has been disconnected. The poem, we discovered, took us from impersonal family life, to depersonalized society, to the final disconnectedness of the whole universe.

"Which depersonalizing, dehumanizing things in our society are you aware of?" (I'm certain that few of my students knew the meaning of either *depersonalizing* or *dehumanizing,* but they got the gist of my question.) "Can you think of mechanical things that make our lives easier but disconnect people?"

The kids immediately thought of telephone answering machines; they also thought about dialing Weather and Time and hearing the impersonal, robotlike messages. They identified the long-distance operator as sounding tape-recorded, distant and flat. I started jotting their ideas and imitations of these mechanical messages on the chalkboard.

"Give me a line that might be a tape-recorded message. Make it sound canned and like a robot," I said to the class. Various students offered lines based on familiar and generic machine messages: "At the tone, the time is . . . After the beep, please leave your name, number, and a brief message. We'll get back to you shortly."

After I'd jotted these mechanical lines on the board, we read them aloud and reordered them, then added others that unified our evolving group poem. Finally, we reworded, deleted unnecessary words, and substituted vivid action words for pale ones. Here is our response to Merriam's poem:

Information, Please

Information, please. What city are you calling?
HEAVEN!
Temporarily out of order.
Please hang up and try again.
Dial one before calling this number.
You have reached the residence of the Lord.
At the sound of the beep, leave your name and number.
The weather today is hot, too hot for humans.
Emergency break-through:
Will you accept this collect call from God?
At the tone, the Time will be . . .

Just as the bell was ringing to end the period, Virgil scribbled his own rap on a scrap of paper and promised to present it to us the next day as a performance. And that he did.

Virgil's Rap
by Virgil

This is information—
What city, please?

I said, "Heaven."
She said she could get that with ease.
Then she came back and said:
"Temporarily out of order."
So I dug into my pocket and pulled out another quarter.
She said, "Dial one."
And that was the end.
So I hung up the phone and tried my call again.
The last four digits ended with seven,
"You have reached the res-i-dence of Heaven."
I didn't know what was up,
But I knew it was wack,
"If you leave your name and number
We'll call you right back."
At the tone of the beep,
It came to my head—
I cleared my throat
And this is what I said:
"I'm Virgil B. and I'm from Earth, you see.
You can call me at 921-3593! Rock!"

Virgil's animated rap and dynamic performance led me once again to an insight that seems obvious but often goes unacknowledged: resistant learners deserve a good intellectual and creative workout even if they claim they do not want it. The teacher who pledges to give her best must stand up *to* the demands these kids make on her and stand up *for* the value of the creative process. Performing or creating poetry with passive or potentially out-of-control adolescents is a demanding challenge, but one well worth accepting.

TWELVE

Assessment
Measuring What Really Matters

A student's paper lay bleeding in the hall, slashed and circled with red ink by a frustrated teacher. At the top loomed the grade the teacher had assigned the paper: F+/D−. In pencil, the student had responded to his teacher's ambivalent grade by fashioning an A− from the F+; he'd made a B+ from the D−. With that transformation accomplished, the student had thrown the paper on the floor for someone like me to contemplate.

Neither the ambivalent grade nor the paper's fate surprised me. As far as I'm concerned, letter grades are essentially useless. They communicate little to students or parents about the student's strengths or promise; they don't even convey what's weak about his or her work. Grades seem even more absurd when applied to students' writing. What do letter grades tell young writers about ways to develop their ideas more fully, tighten their organization, clarify their thoughts, or give their writing voice?

Of course, I'm hardly the first teacher to decry the grading system. And like most of the system's critics, I faced a deeply embedded, institutionalized reality: no matter how I felt about grades, I had to give them. So I did, but in my own way and on my own terms. I did some long, hard thinking about the whole concept of assessment and what it really meant. Let me share some of that thinking and show how it applied to the progress of one of my students, a seventh grader named Fred, and how I graded him during the course of a school year. In Chapter 13 we'll examine other students, how their learning developed, how I (and they) assessed their progress, and finally how I arrived at the grades I gave them.

Important questions

Let me raise four important questions about assessing students' language learning and respond to them according to my philosophy and classroom practice: (1) What is assessment? (2) Who assesses students' work? (3) How—in what ways—are students and their work assessed? (4) When is students' work assessed?

1. What is assessment?

For my students and me, assessment was a habit, a way of thinking and behaving that eventually became a natural part of our day. We learned how to observe, to listen, and to respond to one another. We learned to ask good questions and then take time to reflect on what we'd noticed. By doing these things, we discovered what we valued most.

We were partners in this process of discovery. As the teacher, I realized that every time I made a comment or a suggestion, I was showing students what I valued. But I also showed them that my values changed, as theirs did, with each moment I read, wrote, talked, and lived. So each day we made decisions. We might reread part of a story to gain deeper insight into a character or spend more time asking questions about an issue we were discussing. We might decide to gather more data on our debate topics or to choose the novel or poem we liked best and figure out why. Consistent with my student-centered approach, my students and I worked as partners to converse and consider, weigh and measure, decide and then reconsider what about our conversations, our writing, and our reading was important, imaginative or interesting; what begged us to think and talk further, and what compelled us to ask more questions.

We treated every issue that came to our attention in this way. When my students and I listened to a guest speaker who came to our class, we responded by asking questions: "What did you mean when you said . . . ? How might we be sure? Why did you have such and such an attitude?" This process of observing, listening, responding, questioning, reflecting, and making decisions happened nearly every day my students and I spent together. As it did, we gained insight; we figured out what we valued.

When teacher and students take turns talking about situations that arise in class or their lives, when they discuss the literature they are reading and the writing they are doing, everyone is taking responsibility; everyone is a learner. In this kind of classroom setting, every student and every student's opinions is valued. And that's the way school is supposed to be. This process of evaluating and reevaluating invites students and teachers to come together for a common purpose thus achieving an even more informed understanding of what they know, believe, and care about.

When a teacher and her students are in the habit of weighing, debating, and making large and small decisions about intellectual and creative issues, they are naturally clarifying their own value system; together they are setting standards of excellence by figuring out what they are learning to value most (the root of *evaluate* is *value!*). From my point of view, what each of us learns to value is at the heart of assessment.

2. Who assesses students' work?

Let's take this ongoing and inclusive process of assessing a student's thinking and apply it to a discussion of a young writer's story. In assessing the successes or weaknesses of the story's ending, for example, a small group of students and their teacher would try out many possible ways to end the story. In the process, they would be raising important intellectual questions and making critical decisions that are constantly subject to change: How else might this story end? Which ending works best? Why? How does this new ending affect the characters' actions and interactions? If the teacher and her students agree to change the ending, still more decisions await: what other changes in the story must now be made? Finally, this involved team of thinkers must consider another important question: how can we make all the pieces of this story fit together?

Clearly, this meeting of minds differs strikingly from the traditional practice of having the teacher mark a set of papers or tests (often discrete entities), frequently with little thought to the students' past performance or future potential. Student-centered assessment also differs from a system in which the teacher records percentage points

Crystal is finding out that writing and rewriting add up to thinking and rethinking.

and calculates grades for report cards, and the students simply accept what the teacher decrees. (I still have trouble figuring out what constitutes an A, a B, a C, and so forth; not surprisingly, my perception of these letter grades changes nearly every day. I imagine that I'm not the only one who faces this dilemma. Giving letter grades makes it all the more difficult for me to be "fair" and "objective.") In this traditional way of assessing students' academic work, the teacher retains all the authority and, perhaps worse, all the responsibility for students' intellectual growth. The students play the role of passive bystanders, and even helpless recipients of their teacher's judgment calls. Endrico captures the feeling well in his poem, "Report Card" (see Figure 12-1).

When learning and assessment are so clearly in the hands of the teacher, students soon learn to rely on the teacher to dictate what and how to learn, and what to value. When learning and assessment are so clearly separated from each other, students soon deduce that the two are unrelated. A teacher-centered classroom encourages students to make achieving good grades their goal rather than learning how to be an inquirer and decision-maker—in other words, an authentic student.

It may sound as if my view of assessment produces a laissez-faire operation in which everyone and no one is in charge. But the teacher who acts as coach plays a crucial role in assessment, just as she does in all aspects of classroom operation. By bringing her knowledge to bear on her students' thinking, she is teaching. And as her understanding deepens and widens, her values change. The same thing is happening to her students.

The teacher, as model, shows students how to be prime movers, how to raise questions, make observations, and test their emerging thinking in the context of their laboratory, the classroom. In other words, teacher and students team up to gain competence in using language to learn.

Endrico H.

Report Card   January 3, 1990

Today is report card day,

I don't care about this particular day,

~~But~~ I got an F, F, D and D,

I know my mother's goin' to be mad at me,

I could solve this problem and throw it away,

but she'll find out on the next report card day.

FIG. 12-1   *Endrico's Poem*

3. How—in what ways—are students and their work assessed?

So if there's more to assessment than standardized tests and questions at the ends of chapters, then what's a teacher to do? First, understand that assessment can't be done in an instant. It requires both teacher and students to look at work over a long period of time. Assessing means developing perspective on where a student began, how far he or she has progressed, and where he or she might be going in the future.

To do this, the teacher uses a wide variety of assessment tools and applies them in different ways to different students and situations. For example, a teacher can explore students' attitudes and insights through taped interviews or specially designed written surveys. She can write personal notes to cheer her young writers on, helping them recognize the promise of their drafts and rethink the parts that still need work, and ask them to reply orally or in writing. Students' comments, too, help with assessment, showing the teacher their plans and goals, or their lack of direction, energy, or interest in a particular language arts project. The teacher considers the students' thinking as it emerges through formal assignments and class discussion but also by paying attention to a wide range of revealing assessment tools: the lists of books they've read; their idea-collection sheets done during prewriting; their writing spiral notebooks or folders; their outlines, jotted notes, and doodles. All these things reveal young people's growth and progress as thinkers and language learners.

Finally, conversations with families, whether by phone or in person, are important assessment tools. My students' families or caregivers and I often discuss the ways in which their young people are making progress, both personally and academically; during telephone conversations or face-to-face meetings, we evaluate what has happened so far and what still needs to be accomplished. Ideally, the parents or guardians become partners, along with the student and teacher, in the student's progress.

Rayshon reads and rereads a note of encouragement from his teacher.

4. When is students' work assessed?

By this time, it must be apparent that assessment—decision making and developing standards of excellence—is an ongoing, daily process that encompasses a wide range of criteria for judgment, not merely and exclusively quantitative measures derived from quizzes or tests. A student's personal growth can be judged in terms of his or her growing competence, confidence, and personal initiative; his or her academic growth might be demonstrated by an increased skill in using language in more and varied ways and as a tool for learning and creating. The *portfolio,* the *exhibition,* and the *writing archive* allow the teacher, the student, and parents an in-depth look at the young person's intellectual growth on a continuum. But as complete and revealing as these might be, they cannot be the only means of looking at a student's growth; a student's momentary insights, sporadic creations, and off-hand comments also shed light on his or her growing ability to tap heretofore unnoticed and unexplored reservoirs of talent and intelligence. Thus, I pay careful attention to the incidental, sometimes magical moments of each day that help me derive a complete and fair profile of a student along with the long-term portfolio, or what I call the students' writing archives. Another technique for judging especially the resistant adolescent learner is looking at the teen-ager during a time span of more than a few days, weeks, or even months. Assessing nonmainstream students on a continuum helps the students themselves and the adults in charge see where the young people were in the beginning of the school year and at various points along the way. Looking at young people's growth over time is not only more realistic and accurate, it sends a powerful message to students: learning takes time; it usually isn't accomplished in little snippets.

Although I usually do remember daily incidents, I cannot rely on memory alone; after all, I have close to one-hundred students. In my school journal, I jot notes—very brief ones about daily happenings—that help me develop a fuller profile of students who are emerging, a little at a time. Thus, I record (but not in a traditional grade book) the remarks and casual observations my students make. I record the information-giving and information-gathering telephone conversations I have with students' families in my telephone log. They also figure into the final grades I give my kids.

The unavoidable: Giving grades

In a perfect world, every school would issue narrative report cards, complete with respectful, specific, and informative remarks that would have the power to explain to the students and their families specific strengths and weaknesses in their work; or, better still, let students present portfolios or exhibits of their work. But in this world, no matter how much we resist, most of us have to conclude even the most student-centered assessment process by assigning grades. Here's how I worked within that system without feeling as if I'd sold out.

The letter grades I put on daily class work—kids' talking, inquiring, and informing as well as their reading, responding, and writing—and the final letter grades I put on their report cards reflected the wide range of assessments I've discussed. As I made a decision about a student's final grade, I considered his work from his stage of development when he entered my class and his current level of achievement. Two or more weeks before report cards were issued, I talked collectively, then individually with my students about their work during that grading period.

Together, we developed criteria that reflected their increased involvement and proficiency in language learning. I asked them to cite specific ways in which they had improved—in, for example, their ability to generate more and better ideas, develop ideas, focus on one thought at a time, cite examples or include telling details, use the language more richly and imaginatively, and express their ideas more clearly and with voice. During the conversations, I asked my students to give me examples of ways in which they'd improved their ability to listen more actively and responsively; to talk to try on ideas for deeper and broader understanding; to read to enjoy and respond as well as to merely acquire necessary information; to write to create and crystallize their thoughts and ideas. I asked them to identify the aspects of language learning to which they needed to give more effort and attention—skills such as asking more questions and looking for more answers, developing thoughts more substantively and systematically in their writing, and attending to the conventions or mechanics of writing.

By establishing these criteria, students could proceed on to the next phase of assessment: selecting samples, a collection of their best work that met these criteria. They looked for writing that showed their progress in talking, listening, reading, writing, and thinking; they also recalled instances when they were good talkers, questioners, and idea-generators. I made it clear to them that we were looking not only for grades on written quizzes and tests but for anything that demonstrated their investment in language learning—their developing ability to think and talk about ideas and the new discoveries they were making about themselves as language learners. Jamar, for example, noted that his imagination had "caught on fire" in our language arts/English class; Kenya realized that she was making excellent connections between literary characters when she said that "Naomi [survivor of Nazism] and Cassie [protagonist in *Roll of Thunder, Hear My Cry*] was both real heroes, and both of them is girls"; Lisa S. recognized that she was learning to become "an excellent writer—especially at revising my drafts"; Chris M. remarked that he hadn't realized what "dynamite questions" he asked until he started asking them in our back-to-back language arts/English class. Jawan said that he always believed he was "slow in school," but now he was recognizing what a strong class leader and "smart dude" he was. Even my students' ability to assess themselves factored into their final grades!

Students' work habits, such as their ability to use class time effectively, general organization, focus, stamina or endurance (commonly called attention span), and care in preparing their work figured into its general quality and therefore affected their growth and their grades, as did their behavior and attitude. During conversations about assessment, I asked students to discuss the ways in which they'd improved in developing good work habits, acceptable behavior, and positive attitudes, and how they planned to improve. This part of our discussion inevitably caused at least one student to yell out: "But it's not fair that you gradin' me on my behavior. If I do good work, it don't matter about the behavior. Just so I do the work." So I took time to help the kids make an important connection: good classroom behavior and a positive attitude are closely connected with academic growth and success. I pointed out that when someone walks into class late, yells out during class, makes comments and gets out of his or her seat during an important discussion, that person is *not* doing the work; furthermore the disruption prevents other students from learning; it also causes me to stop teaching to reprimand the disrupter, perhaps resulting in an unpleasant scene.

When I did finally put grades on the collections of work students had submitted as their best, I graded them holistically; that is, I gave a single letter grade to each collection according to criteria we had established, and also according to the purpose of the various assignments and the general quality of the papers. For instance, in grading collections of students' best written work (which, of course, had already been graded), I did a fast reading of all the papers, looking at the large picture to gain a broad perspective of the quality (or lack of quality) of the writing and the progress I noticed the writers making. Then I put these collections into three piles to quantify them in general terms. The papers in the first pile showed at least moments of original thinking. These writers had achieved at least partial success in developing an idea and organizing their thoughts; they'd revised their writing in significant ways; their writing often exhibited artistic or imaginative use of language, energy, and an authentic voice. The papers in the second pile were noticeably varied in quality, and the best of them could be described as being solid but not necessarily original, artistic, or carefully or fully developed, although varying degrees of revision were in evidence and ideas were presented clearly. The papers in the third pile were sparse and sorely lacked even the most basic development of an idea; and the writer had neglected the most basic and simple conventions of writing and spelling. Even though these collections tended not to be of high quality, I noted signs of progress, as meager and infrequent as they usually were.

Finally, after I had gained a general understanding of the overall quality of the students' papers, I reread them more carefully, writing comments and putting grades on each collection. The student who was gaining momentum—who actively and consistently contributed to our classroom conversations, asked probing questions, sought new avenues of expressing him- or herself and submitted an excellent collection or portfolio received an A, which only a few students—maybe a half-dozen—achieved. The student who was making strides in taking charge of his or her learning life, who was developing greater endurance in accomplishing work in our class, and who submitted a solid collection or portfolio that indicated fairly consistent progress received a B. I gave perhaps thirty percent of my students B's. A broad range and a large number of my students received C's. Most characteristic of C students was the erratic nature of their work and their lack of stamina. Sometimes their work held promise, while at other times it fell far short of our goals. The C student usually experienced backsliding because he or she had frequently missed class, had been inattentive or called to the office during class, had not completed assignments, or had not spent the extra time required to shape a piece of writing. Rarely did I give my students D's. With my insistent help, classmates' support, and family involvement, the backsliding student usually mustered the necessary perseverance and stamina to achieve a modicum of success according to the criteria we had developed. Of course, if our collective effort did not help, the student received a D.

As frustrated as I often became with certain malingering students, I tried never to punish them with bad grades; rather, I used grades to bolster confidence and reward improvements in attitude and work. I reasoned that if I gave a student a D accompanied by an unsatisfactory effort grade and a poor mark in citizenship or classroom behavior, and followed up with a telephone call to the family, I'd sent that young person and family members the message that he or she needed to work with me and seek more help during after-school conferences. I rarely, if ever, gave an F. If a student had missed many days of class, or for some other reason had made little progress, I wrote an I.E., an individual evaluation (specifically indicated on our school's report card), in which I candidly spelled out what I considered to be the student's progress, strengths, difficulties, and needs. This individual evaluation was supposed to take the place of an unsatisfactory letter grade. Then I called a conference with the student and his or her family to determine a plan of action.

"Mrs. K.—she easy," I sometimes heard my students say, especially at the beginning of the school year when they didn't yet understand my ways of assessing them and their work. For young people accustomed to receiving low grades—often D's and F's—receiving good, even excellent, grades is not only unbelievable, it is downright unsettling, for they feel so unworthy and unentitled to high achievement and excellent grades. But when I heard them say, "Mrs. K—she easy," I responded by saying one of two things: "It's just that I make learning easy" or "You're a lot smarter than you think you are. Do you notice how well you're achieving in our class?"

Advantages of looking from many angles

If we approach assessment from many points of view and measure what counts in real life, everyone can learn and everyone can achieve. Students discover what interests them, how to inquire, how to generate ideas, how to take responsibility for learning, how to work together and on their own—qualities that will prepare them to lead a productive life. And in this kind of school setting, they learn to feel free to do so. Led beyond what they know by a knowledgeable adult and getting to practice what they're learning, students experience excellence firsthand. They internalize these bench marks of excellence and begin to recognize the promise in their own work. They also understand what is below standard, both their own and that of their teacher. Finally, young people who participate in assessing their own progress and that of their peers learn what school is really meant to be.

Teachers learn, too. By observing, listening, asking questions, and reflecting, they come to appreciate what the young people in their charge bring to the learning occasion and the different ways that students learn. Teachers seek to find myriad ways to respond to their students' needs by paying close attention to what they say (and don't say), what they do (and don't do). Savvy teachers find out what worries their students; they attempt to understand what causes them to behave inappropriately (students' destructive behavior deflects attention away from their worry about themselves and the anxiety they feel about failing in school). The keen adult leader or coach tries to devise ways to alleviate students' anxiety and lead them to take increased charge of their learning—and their lives.

Certain schools—for instance, members of Theodore Sizer's Coalition of Essential Schools—are leading the way in valuing and evaluating students' work rather than quantifying it in percentage points and letter grades. Students in the Coalition Schools collect their work over time, then select their best work and present exhibitions. Together with their teachers and parents, the students witness their own changing abilities and assess their growth. When these means of assessing students' work take hold more widely, the future of America's school children will certainly brighten. In the meantime, I'm just one teacher taking my own steps in that direction. Let me demonstrate just how I put theory into practice with one particular seventh-grade student: Fred.

Metaphor man on the move

Fred arrived in my double-period language arts/English class feeling uncertain about school in general and language learning in particular. Oh how Fred fidgeted and fussed, complained and yelled out during those first weeks! This anxious boy played out his anxiety and worry by being in perpetual motion. Only seconds after the bell rang and he sat down, he'd turn around in his chair and make a provocative comment to Roslind, Danyell, or Greg, launching them into orbit. Roslind often burst into uncontrollable laughter, Danyell steamed silently, and Greg hurled an incendiary comment back. Fred called making this kind of chaos, "nappin' " or "pickin' " with his classmates. Although Fred treated me with respect, he blamed me for giving him too much work and not giving him better grades. He would tap his pencil on the edge of his table, pound out staccato rhythms with his fist, or sneeze explosively just as we were trying to settle into learning.

Here is Fred six-and-a-half months later, on March 16 (see Figure 12-2). In joyous disbelief he wrote about the progress he'd made: "I would had never belive how far I have came in writing in my note book." Then he pointed to the caution that he had demonstrated during the early weeks of school: "First week two sentence pargraph two mouth later have a page then full page then page in a half then two page. And Im still working on three pages."

Fred needed only to read through his writing spiral, his archive, to grasp the progress he'd made in language learning between late August and March. The more he wrote, the freer he felt to try out the language that had so intimidated him. At the end of the first two grading periods he received a C and a C+; but he wound up the third and last grading periods with a B+ and a B in language arts/English, for by this time he was working consistently and his oral and written work were of consistently high quality. By this time, too, he was reading independently during class and occasionally at home. Fred was positively elated with the tangible (and traditional) proof of his success in language arts/English; he sashayed around our classroom, waving his report card in the

A
Fred, this is an outstanding piece of
writing because you explain why
and in what ways you have improved
this year. 3/16/90 You express important
thoughts clearly.

I would had never believe
how far I have came in
writing in my note book.
First week two sentence pargraph
two mouth later have a page
then full page then page in a
half then two page. And I'm
still working on three pages.
But for some reason I'm starting
to like it to write with not
a lot of confusion. Reading
and writing are becoming a
sport to me I like it a
lot not ready that much but
writing.
One of the things I like to
write the most is respone to
literature. I also like to write
about what I have done
and Improved on. those are
the one I like the best.

FIG. 12-2   *Fred's Self-Evaluation*

NAME _Fred_

DATE _8-30-89_

GRADE _7 grade_

FIRST WEEK OF SCHOOL SURVEY

1. How do you feel about reading?

   I do Not like 'Reading.

2. Do you consider yourself a reader? If so, tell which books you have enjoyed most and which book(s) you've read recently.

   No I do not consider Myself A Reader.

3. If you don't like to read, tell what you don't like about it.

   Sitting down for A A long time.

4. How do you feel about writing?

   It is o.k At times.

5. Do you consider yourself to be a writer? If so, tell why you like to write and what all you have written.

   I like to write Jokes. I have written Jokes.

6. If you don't like to write, tell what you don't like about it.

(If you'd like to say more about any one of the issues, turn this paper over, indicate the number of the question and write on!)

8/31/89

Dear Fred,

Please give yourself a chance to read — many chances. We will all work together. As for sitting "a long time:" we will get out of our chairs and do drama. I'd like to see the jokes you've written. _Mrs. Krogness_

FIG. 12-3   *Fred's Survey*

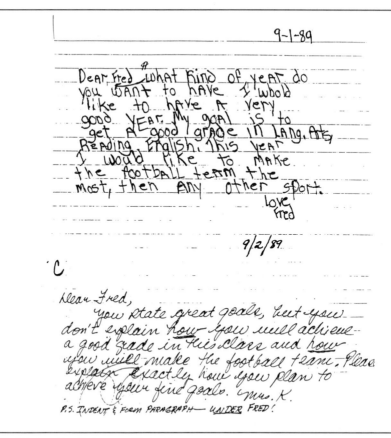

FIG. 12-4   *Fred's Letter of Intention*

air (Fred received not one, but *two* excellent grades, because both language arts and English were listed on our report card). His mother and father were delighted with their son's achievement. They also noticed that his behavior and general attitude at home were significantly improved, as they surely were at school.

"Reading and writing are becomeing a sport to me I like it a lot not reading that much but writing." I called Fred the Metaphor Man when he read aloud this line about reading and writing becoming a sport. By March, Fred had begun to grasp the magnitude of his own progress. But like all learning, changes happened slowly, one day at a time, and often they were imperceptible. However, school success had not always been so accessible for Fred.

On August 30, the beginning of the school year, Fred and his classmates filled out my First-Week-of-School Survey (Figure 12-3 shows Fred's survey). This sad, meager, dispirited piece of writing reflected Fred's feelings not just about reading but about himself. I didn't grade my students' responses to this survey; I merely looked at the quality of their responses and made note of it. Fred's letter of intention, written September 1, was an attempt to set goals for himself (see Figure 12-4). But the sound of commitment was absent; he had merely fulfilled an assignment. I gave him a grade of C and wrote a brief note. Fred's heart wasn't in language learning, but I was glad he liked football!

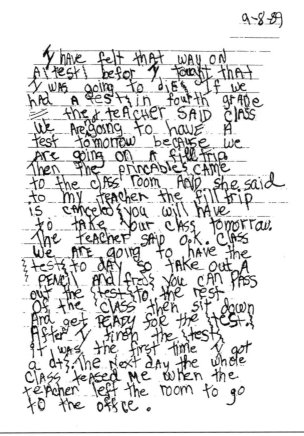

9-8-89

I have felt that way on
A test befor I tought that
I was going to die. If we
had A test in fourth grade
the teAcher SAID class
we Are going to have A
test tomorrow becAuse we
Are going on A fill trip
Then the princAbles cAme
to the class room And she said
to my teAcher the fill trip
is canceld you will have
to tAke your class tomorrow.
The teAcher SAid O.K. class
We Are going to have the
test to dAy so tAke out A
PENciL and fros you cAn PAss
out the test to the rest
of the class then sit down
And get REAdy for the test.
After I finsh the test
it was the first time I got
a d+. The next dAy the whole
class teAsed me when the
teAcher left the room to go
to the office .

FIG. 12-5   *Fred's Response*

Fred continued to go through the motions of reading and writing in our class, that is, when he wasn't feeling anxious and agitated and spending class time spinning his wheels. But slowly, and actually quite erratically, he began to take hold. After reading Susan Shreve's *The Flunking of Joshua T. Bates*, Fred responded to my question: "When have you felt like Joshua T. Bates?" (see Figure 12-5). Signs that Fred was beginning to rev his motor were evident: he wrote a whole page about a personal experience. In factual terms he set down telling events in the exact order in which they happened *until* he protectively wrote: "it was the first time I got a d+. The next day the whole class teased me when the teacher left the room to go to the office." Again, we pick up Fred's anxiety about school: the squiggly lines interspersed with script told me of his shakiness. In a note of encouragement, I praised him quite specifically for being successful and gave him a B (see Figure 12-6).

After reading about Joshua T. Bates, the boy who failed a grade, we all wrote about our feelings toward school (Fred's response is shown in Figure 12-7). Concern about the pressure and harshness of certain teachers (teachers are either "nice" or "mean") weighed heavily on Fred's heart. So far, his handwriting—a jangled mixture of rough-looking capital and lowercase letters—and the quality of his writ-

9-8-89

B

Dear Fred,

Today you were very successful. Why? You dived into this writing assignment and told a story about yourself. This story is a good one because it is real; you also include excellent conversation so that I know how the characters really feel and behave.

Mrs. Krogness

FIG. 12-6   Mrs. K.'s Note

ten expression seemed to reflect a lack of practice in writing, a worried resistance to using the language, and overall anxiety. I gave Fred a C and wrote him a short, encouraging letter in which I spelled out exactly what I liked about his piece and what he needed to work on. Fred still spent too much time and energy stewing about school. I knew that helping him relax during class would be my first challenge in freeing him to learn.

Late in September, I witnessed another example of Fred's fear. After I had modeled the process of collecting telling details in preparation for writing personal stories (see Chapter 9), Fred produced an idea-collection sheet, a lengthy chronological collection of events (thirty-two items) under the category "When I Was Very Young" (see Figure 12-8). Because he'd carefully recorded the details of an entire story in chronological order on his idea-collection sheet, I gave him a C+/B−, a combination grade I sometimes gave when the paper was neither one grade nor the other, and I wanted to send the message that with more work, the higher of the two might be attained. Fred then used these details in a story about himself as a three-year-old who crawled out of his crib, got his bottle from the fridge, and turned on the TV. After Fred had read the story aloud, a student who had been in his sixth-grade class recalled having heard this story before.

Fred sheepishly admitted to us that indeed he had written a story that was "something like this one" in sixth grade. Certainly I wasn't trying to catch this fragile boy in

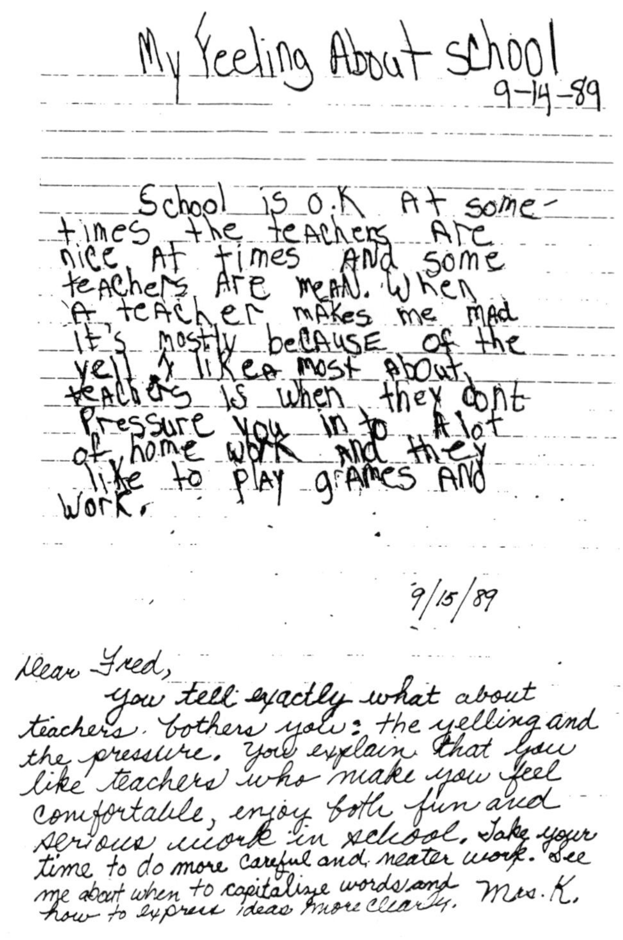

My feeling About school
9-14-89

School is O.K. At some-
times the teachers Are
nice At times ANd some
teachers Are meAN. When
A teacher mAkes me mAd
It's mostly beCAUSE of the
yell I likea most about,
teachers is when they dont
Pressure you in to A lot
of home work ANd they
like to PLAy gAmes ANd
work.

9/15/89

Dear Fred,
    You tell exactly what about
teachers bothers you: the yelling and
the pressure. You explain that you
like teachers who make you feel
comfortable, enjoy both fun and
serious work in school. Take your
time to do more careful and neater work. See
me about when to capitalize words and
how to express ideas more clearly. Mrs. K.

FIG. 12-7   *Fred's Response*

a protective bit of subterfuge. He was too scared, too cautious, to try writing a fresh, new story about his early life or, for that matter, another subject. He obviously felt that he needed to write about a familiar topic, thus repeating an experience that had been successful and safe. Of course, I let him, but I wondered how I could defuse his worry.

A striking change

By early October, Fred had really begun to change, though he still shot provocative comments at me and his classmates. For example, one day Fred looked up at me and said: "Mrs. Krogness, you know that fat hanging from under your chin? It makes you look kinda old." I replied: "Well, Fred, I seriously doubt if you'll live to be as old as I am—making comments like that!" We both laughed.

I knew, however, that Fred was starting to relax. I began—a little at a time—helping him set realistic and attainable goals: reading (anything from the sports page of the newspaper to a manageable section of a self-selected novel) for ten minutes at home

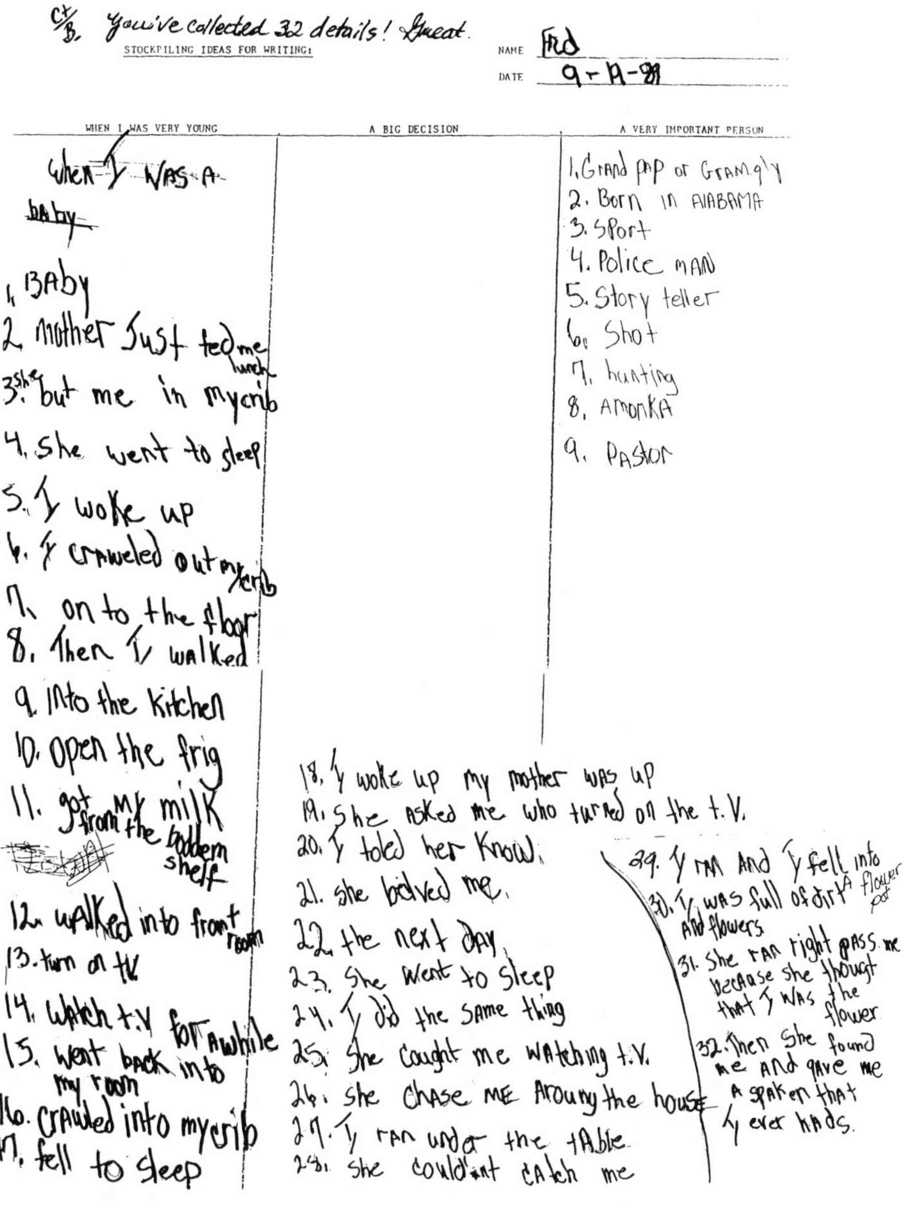

C+/8. *You've collected 32 details! Great.*

STOCKPILING IDEAS FOR WRITING:

NAME Fred
DATE 9-19-89

WHEN I WAS VERY YOUNG	A BIG DECISION	A VERY IMPORTANT PERSON

When I was a

baby

1. BAby
2. mother Just fed me lunch
3. She but me in my crib
4. She went to sleep
5. I woke up
6. I crawled out my crib
7. on to the floor
8. Then I walked
9. INto the kitchen
10. open the frig
11. got my milk from the bottom shelf
12. walked into front room
13. turn on tv
14. watch t.v for awhile
15. went back into my room
16. crawled into my crib
17. fell to sleep

18. I woke up my mother was up
19. She asked me who turned on the t.v.
20. I toled her know.
21. she boived me.
22. the next day,
23. She went to sleep
24. I did the same thing
25. She caught me watching t.v.
26. she chase me Arouny the house
27. I ran undr the tAble
28. she could'nt cAtch me
29. I rAn And I fell into a flower pot
30. I was full of dirt And flowers
31. She rAn right pass me because she thougt that I was the flower
32. Then she found me And gave me A spAken that I ever hAds.

1. GrAnd pAp or GrAmgly
2. Born in AlABAMA
3. Sport
4. Police mAN
5. Story teller
6. Shot
7. hunting
8. AmonkA
9. PAStor

FIG. 12-8   *Fred's Idea-Collection Sheet*

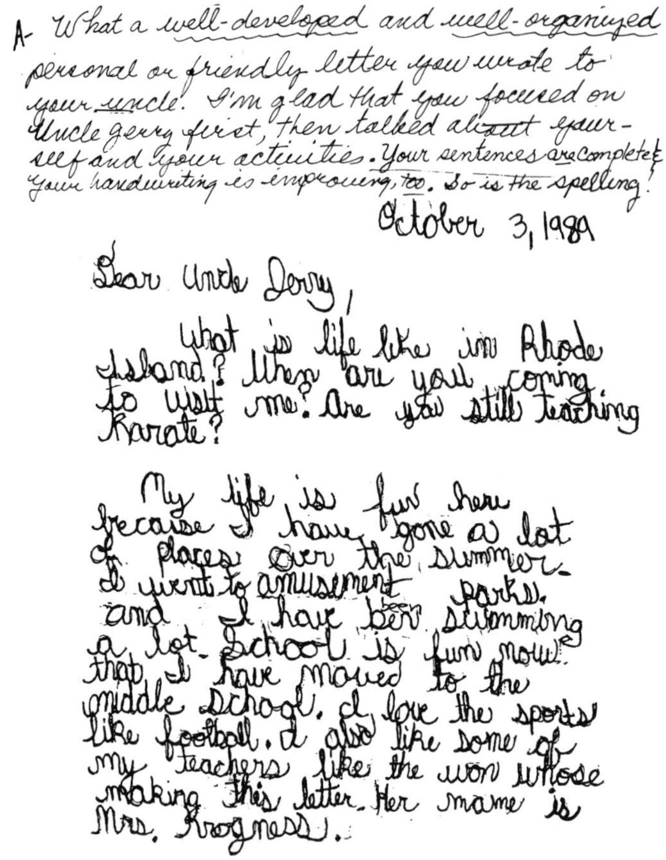

A ‑ *What a well-developed and well-organized personal or friendly letter you wrote to your uncle! I'm glad that you focused on Uncle Jerry first, then talked about yourself and your activities. Your sentences are complete! Your handwriting is improving, too. So is the spelling!*

October 3, 1989

Dear Uncle Jerry,

What is life like in Rhode Island? When are you coming to visit me? Are you still teaching Karate?

My life is fun here because I have gone a lot of places over the summer. I went to amusement parks, and I have been swimming a lot. School is fun now that I have moved to the middle school. I love the sports like football. I also like some of my teachers like the won whose making this letter. Her name is Mrs. Krogness.

FIG. 12-9   *Fred's Letter*

each night; reading a piece of children's literature aloud to his little brother; writing something every evening, such as a letter to a grandparent. Fred was trying to remain calm and focused during class so that he and the others around him could work. He was also working on liking reading better and expressing himself more clearly in writing.

The changes in Fred were apparent. He wrote more expansively and participated in the class's frequent conversations about developing ideas. As a result, the ideas in his writing held together better and were expressed with greater verve and vitality. He also began to demonstrate greater care and control over mechanics; his handwriting and spelling were far more standard than they had been. In a friendly letter to his uncle he made and developed two excellent paragraphs (see Figure 12-9). Of course I awarded Fred an A− for the warm and personal letter he'd written, one in which he'd carefully obeyed the protocol of letter-writing. When I called his home to report to Fred's parents the good news of their son's progress in recent weeks, he answered the phone and said somewhat breathlessly, "I know why you're calling: to tell my mom and dad I'm doing good. Right?"

For their next response to literature, I asked Fred and his classmates to recall a situation in their own lives or from literature in which a person appeared or seemed to

Fred, you are really making progress in lang. arts/English! Why? You just developed an excellent piece on Mrs. Goodman; you give specific examples of ways that Mrs. Goodman treats Josh nicely. Your sentences are fuller & clearer than earlier! Mrs. K.

B/ A+   Fred 10-6-89

Mrs. Goodwin WAS A big (rumor) rummer beCAUSE every body cAlled her "the tANK." So Josh hAd to go to her ClAss And he hAd herd she wAS BiG and very meAN. So he tought About the rummer so he wAS SCAred. Then After two weeKs he got AtAcHed to her ANd she wAS really nice. For exAmple, mrs. Goodwin wold have josh come Over to house for help on reAding & for cookies And teA. She Also cought (rotten) Tommy Wilhelm teAsing Josh becAuse he; wAS still in the third grAde. so she put Tommy bAcK in the third grAde so he would know how Josh feels. NeXt time he Knew Not to teAse Nobody

FIG. 12-10   *Fred's Piece About Mrs. Goodwin*

be something other than what he or she was. Fred still felt more secure analyzing the novel we'd read in September than he did with other stories we'd read more recently. He wrote about Mrs. Goodwin, the third-grade teacher who is known as "the tank" in *The Flunking of Joshua T. Bates.*

Although Fred expressed pleasure that he'd written more than a page, and I was pleased that he'd done the piece without a hassle—even giving *two* examples of Mrs. Goodwin's generosity, goodness, and protectiveness toward Josh—I knew that Fred needed to work toward greater clarity of expression (see Figure 12-10). His lead sentence, "Mrs. Goodwin was a big rummer because everybody called her 'the tank,' " heads in the right direction but is unclear. But toward the end of the first page, he gets a hold on the idea he wants to express and the language he wants to use to describe Mrs. Goodwin. Perhaps I was too extravagant in giving him a B+/A−, but I was thrilled with his new ability to be expansive and thoughtful.

After having read fairy tales and considered archetypal fairy-tale characters, the class and I talked about writing modern-day fairy tales in which real kids were the heroes. Fred energetically started a story—this time a brand new one—in which a heroic big brother by the name of Fred becomes the guardian of two younger siblings, whom he must support by working two jobs because the parents have either died in an auto accident or they were away because of family problems (Fred had not decided which conflict he wanted). Then Fred suddenly stopped writing. He was stuck. I sat down next to Fred, the writer, to talk with him about Fred, the hero, the big brother who is never home with his lonely younger brother and sister.

Building endurance

Fred and I talked about some of the ways that he might resolve the major conflict of his modern-day fairy tale. While he talked, I jotted down his ideas, for, as he said, "My fingers are getting cramps and my head's tired of thinking." Supporting a hesitant and inexperienced writer is important if he is to develop the necessary endurance for doing real intellectual work. And building endurance for thinking requires experience and time.

Fred finally decided that the two younger children would also become heroes and help their big brother out; each would get a job to earn extra money, allowing this newly formed family to spend more time with one another. This young author was becoming heroic: he was committing himself to his own learning and taking responsibility for himself. He was developing the stamina necessary for thinking.

A student can't make up for lost time in one great leap. Accepting students' current progress while expecting more from them is a difficult balance to maintain, but it's one of the most important aspects of the ongoing assessment process. By early November, Fred's energy and enthusiasm for school had flagged; he did not do several homework assignments and handed in others that were shoddy. He looked tired and was agitated.

When I asked him to come in after school during the regular after-school conference period to make up the missing work, Fred slumped in his chair, yawned, and said, "I'm working too hard these days." But, surprisingly, he showed up. To show my appreciation for this effort, I asked if he'd like me to record his answers to questions about Mildred Taylor's *The Friendship*. His face brightened. A little reciprocity goes a long way. But I knew that calling home and describing his lack of effort, his apparent lack of sleep, and his agitation would help him to regroup. That it did.

Growing competent, confident, and independent

By the end of November, Fred had gotten his second wind. The YA author Gordon Corman was to visit our school for a week, and in class Fred *independently* read Corman's *No Coins, Please,* a first! He reported the essence of this manageable mystery rather skillfully, too (see Figure 12-11). Fred wrote expansively, expressing

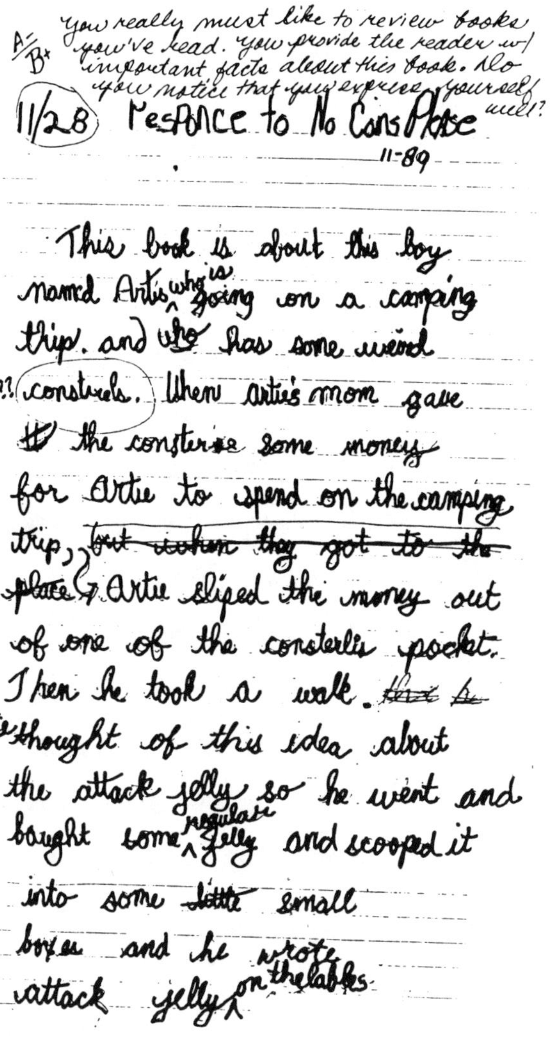
A-/B+ You really must like to review books you've read. You provide the reader w/ important facts about this book. Do you notice that you express yourself well?

11/28 Responce to No Cons Please

11-89

This book is about this boy named Artie who is going on a camping trip. and who has some weird ?? constuls. When artie's mom gave the consturse some money for Artie to spend on the camping trip, ~~but when they got to the place~~ Artie sliped the money out of one of the consterlls pocket. Then he took a walk. ~~then he~~ Artie thought of this idea about the attack jelly so he went and bought some regular jelly and scooped it into some ~~little~~ small boxes and he wrote attack jelly on the lables.

FIG. 12-11 *Fred's Book Review*

his ideas about Corman's book logically and clearly; the sophistication of his sentence structure also shows more maturity. I noted the complexity and construction of many of his sentences, the smooth development of his thought. With great pleasure, I read this piece aloud to the class and gave Fred an A−/B+.

Of all the writing experiences we had in class, Fred most enjoyed responding to literature. In early December, he again did himself proud by writing about Mildred Taylor's *The Gold Cadillac* (Figure 12-12 shows an excerpt from Fred's response). This story about a black family that wants to travel from Ohio down South in their brand-new 1950 Cadillac moved him. He especially loved listening to this story being read aloud, and he grasped at least part of the central issue: the shiny new Cadillac divided the adults. As he stated in his last sentence: "the car was separating

B You are learning how to write in
order to understand literature.
Writing *does* help us to understand. Mrs. K.

Fred,   The Gold Cadillac   12/1/89
I think this book was
pretty good because they
had a a nice Cadillac
but the mother did not like
the new car she liked the old
car and that made the
book very interesting. Then
it went later in the book
when she made the lesson
she was going to ride
in the car because she
did not want any thing to
happen to her husbon.

FIG. 12-12   *Excerpt from Fred's Response*

the family." His interpretation stopped just short of the larger societal issue: the shiny new car would make a black family living in America during the 1950s vulnerable to racism in its most vicious and violent form. But Fred was learning how to interpret literature.

Through early December, the class and I continued to work on our modern-day fairy tales. We spent a lot of class time practicing believable conversations. By reading only the dialogue spoken by fairy-tale characters from *Cinderella*, *Jack and the Beanstalk*, or *Hansel and Gretel* we tried becoming our own emerging characters and talking as we imagined they would talk. This is how we learned to create authentic dialogue. We also practiced the conventions of writing conversation: indenting each time a different character spoke and using quotation marks.

But when it came time for Fred to prepare the final draft of his modern-day fairy tale, he balked. He had breathed more life into his little story than he could have a month earlier, and he had obeyed the conventions of writing dialogue, but he couldn't bring himself to make a final copy. "I just can't make my pen move no more; and you know how slow I am at typing [at the computer]. I probably won't never get this story done." I assessed this particular situation and decided to type "A Family of Three" for him. I explained my reasoning to Fred this way: "You've come a long way in your writing during the past several months. You've brought this fairy tale a long way, too. Because you've given full effort to this long-term writing project and brought your characters alive, I've decided to type it for you." Of course, I didn't type everyone's story, and Fred knew it; so did the rest of my kids. I understood that Fred, like other resistant students, couldn't build intellectual muscle over night. Seeing a typed version of his well-developed story, the completion of a big project, would, I was sure, give him new energy to continue giving his best.

I hope I'm not painting a too-perfect picture of my pal Fred. He did not instantly or consistently work toward shaping up and taking charge of language learning. He still did some backsliding, mostly in the form of anxious behavior that momentarily stopped him—and his classmates—from moving ahead, but these incidents occurred less and less often. I want to focus instead on the *big* picture: Fred's long-range achievement.

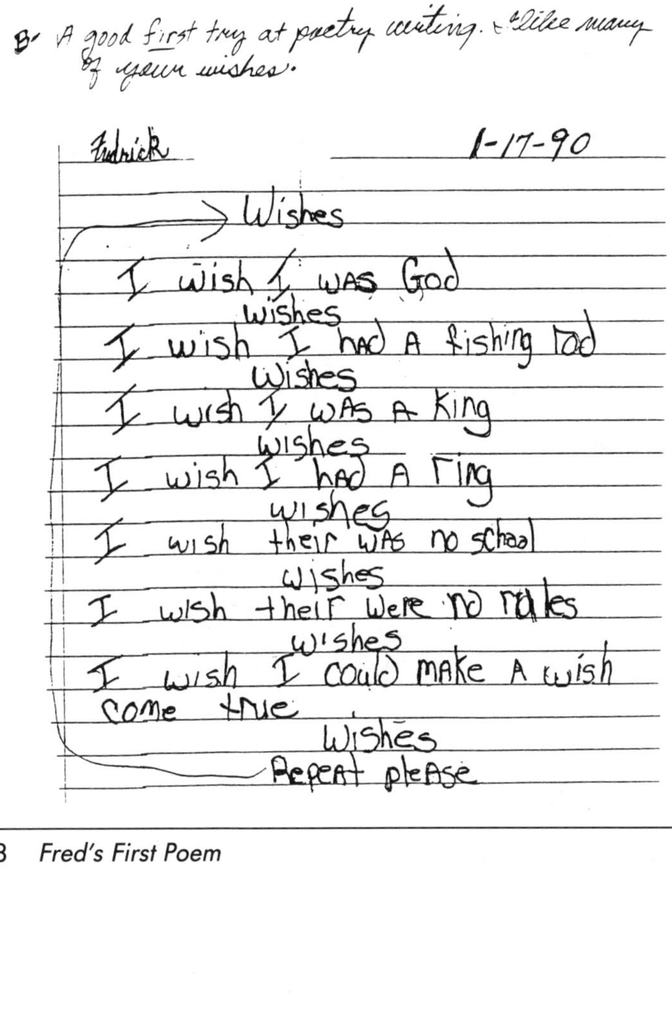
B A good first try at poetry writing. I like many of your wishes.

Fredrick 1-17-90

Wishes

I wish I was God
wishes
I wish I had a fishing rod
wishes
I wish I was a King
wishes
I wish I had a ring
wishes
I wish their was no school
wishes
I wish their were no rules
wishes
I wish I could make a wish come true
wishes
Repeat please

FIG. 12-13 *Fred's First Poem*

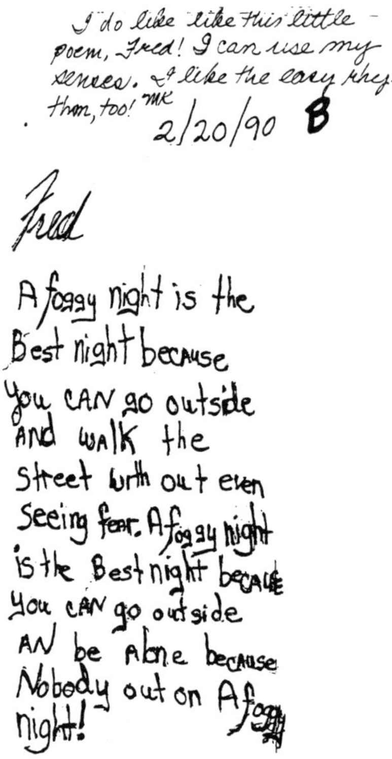

I do like like this little poem, Fred! I can use my senses. I like the easy rhythm, too! MK
2/20/90 **B**

Fred

A foggy night is the
Best night because
you can go outside
And walk the
street with out even
seeing fear. A foggy night
is the Best night because
You can go outside
AN be Alone because
Nobody out on A foggy
night!

FIG. 12-14   *Fred's Second Poem*

Risking new challenges

Although writing poetry was not Fred's forte, by January he felt free to try something new (see Figure 12-13). About a month later, Fred wrote another poem, this one about a foggy night; its repetition and easy cadence work nicely (see Figure 12-14). Fred was beginning to show some daring, and his confidence extended to more traditional areas as well.

During the time that we were reading aloud and discussing Beverley Naidoo's *Journey to Jo'Burg*, a short but powerful novel about apartheid in South Africa, we raised many questions in our group discussions. Individual readers raised questions, too. Figure 12-15 shows Fred's list of questions. Questions 3 and 4 reveal original thinking on his part. "I'm getting about as good as Mrs. K. at asking questions," Fred quipped one day in class. He also realized (and I hope internalized) the value of asking questions—to gain information, to test theories, to weigh difficult issues.

Hitting his stride

By March, Fred had hit his stride. He was learning to control his impulses and govern himself during class, thus using his energy productively. His growing competence and

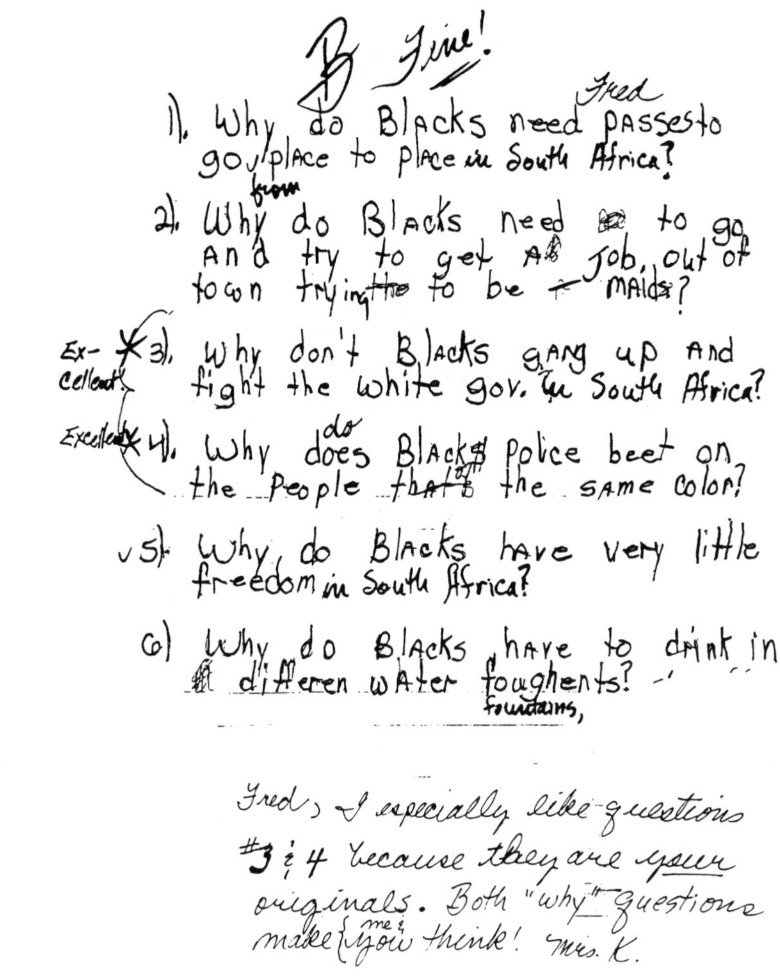

B Fine!

1). Why do Blacks need ~Fred~ passes to go place to place in South Africa?

2). Why do Blacks need from to go And try to get A job, out of town trying the to be + Maids?

Ex-Excellent ★3). Why don't Blacks gang up And fight the white gov. in South Africa?

Excellent ★4). Why does Blacks police beet on the People that's the same color?

✓5) Why do Blacks have very little freedom in South Africa?

6) Why do Blacks have to drink in different wAter toughents? — foundains,

Fred, I especially like questions #3 & 4 because they are your originals. Both "why" questions make me & you think! Mrs. K.

FIG. 12-15   *Fred's Questions*

confidence in language learning were evident to everyone, especially him. The following writing samples substantiate both his personal and his academic growth.

First he wrote a self-assessment about his own behavior and that of his classmates (see Figure 12-16). Then he wrote a strong response to Naidoo's novel. I asked Fred and his cronies to take out paper and pencil; we were going to have an old-fashioned test because, in their words, they'd been "nappin' " or fussing with each other too long! Fred's was the best paper I received that day (see Figure 12-17). In a note I praised his outstanding work and gave him an A−.

By our class standards, Fred had gained remarkable control of himself and of language. His oral and written work were receiving regular commendations from his classmates and me. He was learning, for example, how to vary his sentence structure, starting some sentences with prepositional phrases and adverb clauses, and becoming much more daring in choosing precise, colorful vocabulary. I was struck by the complexity and clarity of one sentence especially in reference to *Journey to Jo'Burg*:

3-6-90 Fred

I think I need to improve By Not talking out in class when the teacher is talking or any other person in the class is talking.

I think I need to improve by not turning Around so much.

I think I need to improve by not talking back after the teacher says something.

Mrs Krogness I think those are the goals I think I need to work on if I have any other problems I straten them up on the way

I think we as a group need to not talk when somebody is talking I think we should not "nap" to each so much I think We should work as a group and act like a group.

3/8/90

Dear Fred,

You are learning how to control yourself better than earlier in year. But you (and your classmates) have improvements to make.

Your ideas and plans for a more orderly classroom are excellent. Now practice putting plans into action! Mrs. Krogness

FIG. 12-16 *Fred's Self-Assessment*

"If a Black wanted to marrie a white person the white would have to refuse the quation [question] maybe not because she did not like him maybe because black and white could not marrie."

Why was Fred growing and changing intellectually? He was surer and, therefore, calmer. In his own words: "I'm getting good at language arts and English because I don't act crazy and wound up no more. I guess I'm growing up." When I asked him why he thought he was acting more grown up and not wound up, he answered: "Well, I'm not worried that I'll get bad grades in this class. Matter of fact, I know how to get

3-12 Test.   Fred

Explain the Real Meaning
<u>Of Journey to Jo'burg?</u>

I think the real meaning that
there showing you is that if you
[they're]
were black you had no freedom
at all. Whites had every think
that black had and a whole
lot more! ~~And~~ It was better
polished. In South Africa ~~the~~
the real meaning of the word
apartheid is separation of Blacks
and whites.

Blacks could not vote, publish, speak
aloud to a crowd, go to a white hospital
could not drink from the same
[They]
water fountain, could not go
to white school only Blacks
school

A'   3/14/90

Dear Freddie,

       This analysis is excellent because
you explain exactly the critical problem in S. Africa: no freedom. Then
after your 1st sentence or lead
you explain the specifics. I noticed
what black S. Africans cannot do
so that the reader knows the problem
immediately. (See where I put the arrow.)

       You also are writing more
complex and sophisticated sentences: "I
think the real meaning that they're showing is that
if you were black you had no freedom at all."

                              Mrs. Krogness

FIG. 12-17   *Fred's Test*

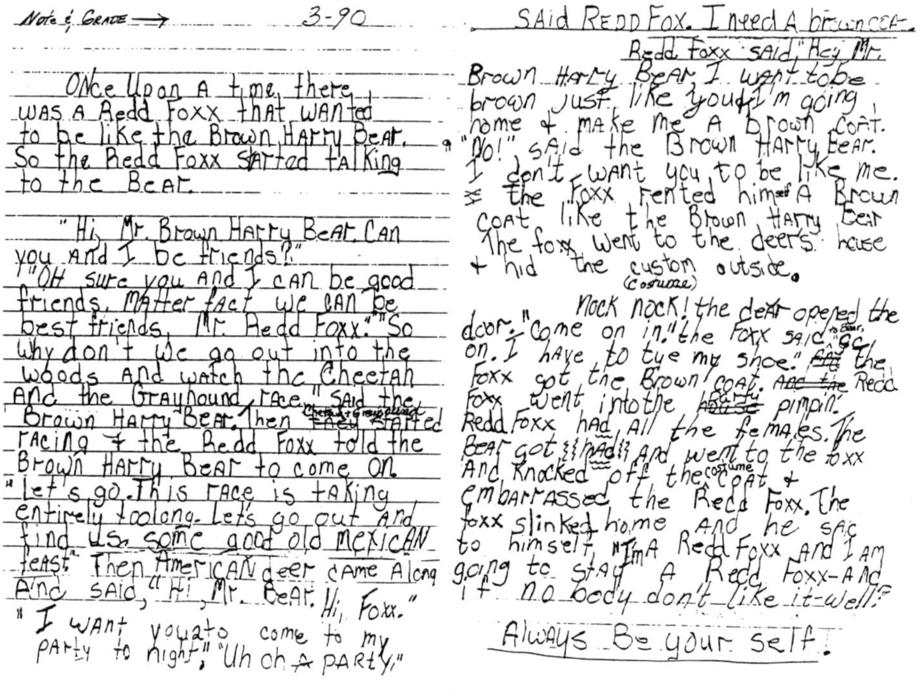

Note & Grade → 3-90

Once Upon A time, there was A Redd Foxx that wanted to be like the Brown Harry Bear. So the Redd Foxx started talking to the Bear.

"Hi, Mr. Brown Harry Bear. Can you and I be friends?"
"OH sure you and I can be good friends. Matter fact we can be best friends, Mr. Redd Foxx." "So why don't we go out into the woods and watch the Cheetah and the Grayhound race," said the Brown Harry Bear. Then ~~they~~ Cheetah + Grayhound started racing & the Redd Foxx told the Brown Harry Bear to come on. "Let's go. This race is taking entirely toolong. Let's go out and find us some good old Mexican feast." Then American deer came along and said, "Hi, Mr. Bear. Hi, Foxx." "I want you to come to my party to night." "Uh oh a party," said Redd Fox. I need A brown coat. Redd Foxx said, "Hey Mr. Brown Harry Bear I want to be brown just like you. I'm going home & make me A brown coat."
"No!" said the Brown Harry Bear. I don't want you to be like me.
The Foxx rented himself A Brown coat like the Brown Harry Bear. The foxx went to the deer's house + hid the custon (costume) outside.

Nock nock! the dear opened the door. "Come on in." the Foxx said to Bear, "go on. I have to tye my shoe." ~~And~~ the Foxx got the Brown coat. ~~And the~~ Redd Foxx went into the ~~house~~ party pimpin'. Redd Foxx had all the females. The Bear got "mad" and went to the foxx and knocked off the costume coat & embarrassed the Redd Foxx. The foxx slinked home and he said to himself, "I'm A Redd Foxx and I am going to stay A Redd Foxx - And if no body don't like it - well!"

Always Be your self!

FIG. 12-18 *Fred's Final Draft*

good ones. Oh yeah, I know grades aren't the important thing. You [Mrs. Krogness] keep saying learning is. But I like getting the grades—especially when they're good." Fred had assessed himself accurately: he was more focused and more able to listen to instruction and to apply what he heard. Most important, Fred was feeling good about himself, thus more free to learn and to be responsible for his learning. In Fred's words: "Now I come into this class happy 'cause I know I can do the work. I also think I'm settling down 'cause I feel proud of all the other work I've did in here."

Toward the end of the year, after we'd read and I'd told a quantity of Aesop's fables, Fred wrote another story, a short fable, rich in conversation and Fred-style humor. Although he might have focused more clearly and tightened the major conflict (Mr. Brown Hairy Bear's overwhelming desire to be like Mr. Redd Fox), he wrote exuberantly and imaginatively—in striking contrast to the first writing he'd done in our class when he felt compelled to resurrect a story he'd written the year before. By the final draft of his fable, Fred had begun to conquer the conventions of writing dialogue, indenting each time a different character spoke and placing quotation marks around the conversation. He was able to hang in there and finish the final draft, too. (See Figure 12-18.) I told him, "You've come a long way, baby!" and he smiled and said, "I know."

THIRTEEN

Many Students,
Many Measuring Sticks

It would have been wonderful if all my students had shown the kind of progress Fred did, but of course that didn't happen. In every class in every school, each student's academic journey is different. Those differences pose big challenges for teachers doing assessment. What kinds of cues will the student respond to? What kinds of feedback will nudge him or her to new heights? The teacher can never be sure. But within the general framework of my belief in a long-term, student-centered assessment process, I've found a variety of ways to assess individuals, and even give them letter grades. Here are the stories of five students, and the kinds of responses and support that worked or didn't work—or at least not permanently—for them.

The loss of two bright boys

Jawan

Jawan, whom we've met many times in these pages, brought with him a nefarious past. He had come to Shaker Heights Middle School from a Cleveland junior high school and was moved to my double-period language arts/English class from another English class in early October. Turning fifteen during his seventh-grade year, Jawan was typical of a large number of urban youth—often African American males—who are overage, educationally deprived, and headed in the wrong direction. They suffer from a lack of language background, disrupted home lives, unsupervised free time, negative peer pressure, poverty, hopelessness, and despair. For many of these young people, school (when they attend) has been a steady diet of isolated skill builders and homogenized literature.

I didn't obsess over Jawan's lack of skill in using language or the gaping holes in his storehouse of knowledge. I imagined that if I could persuade this teenager to trust me, maybe we could redirect his aggressive behavior, stretch his short attention span, and help him develop enough self-discipline and esteem to work toward success in school—at least in this class.

Jawan and I could not erase the statistics that portend a shockingly high drop-out rate among young people who have been retained once or more. But Jawan was quick and bright, though not according to traditional school standards, and surprisingly, he was still curious. For various reasons—many of which I didn't fully understand— Jawan and I got on famously after a rocky beginning. (For instance, when he was

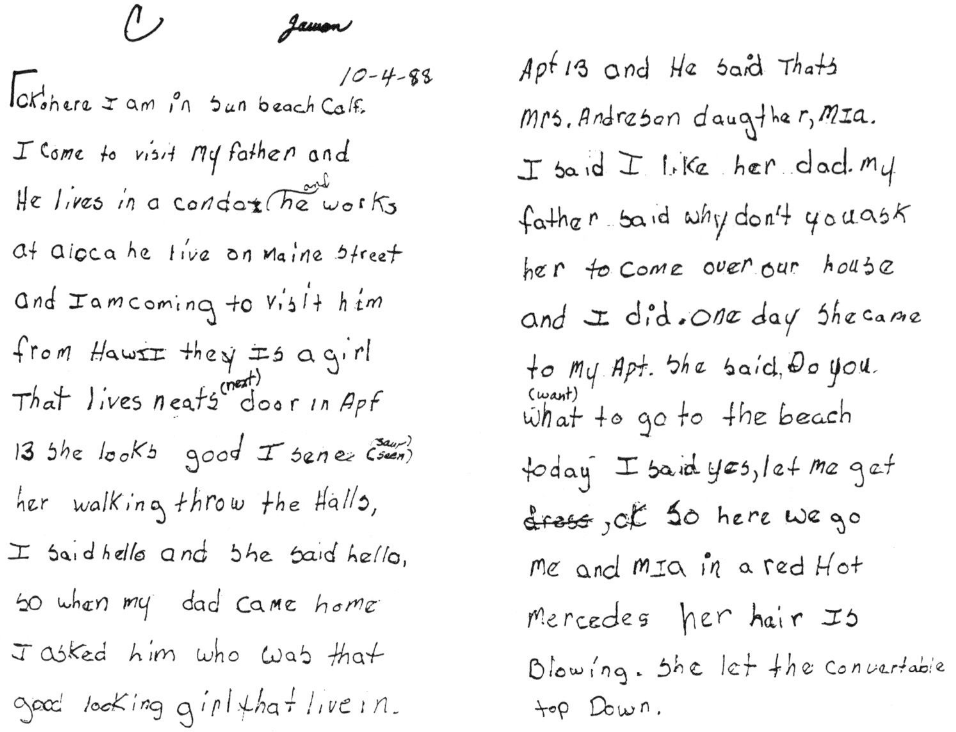

Jawan

10-4-88

Ok here I am in sun beach Calf. I come to visit my father and He lives in a condot (he works at aioca he live on maine Street and I am coming to visit him from Hawii they is a girl That lives neats (next) door in Apf 13 she looks good I senee (saw) (seen) her walking throw the Halls, I said hello and she said hello, so when my dad came home I asked him who was that good looking girl that live in.

Apf 13 and He said Thats mrs. Andreson daugther, MIa. I said I like her dad. my father said why don't you ask her to come over our house and I did. One day she came to my Apt. she said, Do you (want) what to go to the beach today I said yes, let me get dress, or So here we go me and MIa in a red Hot Mercedes her hair Is Blowing. she let the convartable top Down.

FIG. 13-1 *Excerpts from Jawan's First Draft*

disciplined and put into "Alternative to Suspension" [ATS], he would ask Bonnie Painter, the teacher in charge, to please let him out for language arts/English class. In the spring, he invited me to accompany his mother and him to the sports banquet.) Somehow, despite his bouts of pouting and putting his head down on his desk and my feeling and acting impatient, we got along. One day in class, Jawan smiled and said, "Chill, Mrs. K. Y'all gettin' too stressed out!"

Shortly after Jawan, along with three other boys and one girl, was transferred into my double period language arts/English class, the newcomers and I quickly talked about and plotted short stories, because the rest of the class was already well into drafting. Then Jawan began drafting. Figure 13-1 shows an excerpt from Jawan's long, episodic first draft.

Looking back on Jawan's first attempt at writing a story, I am struck by this boy's wishes: to be loved by a beautiful girl, to have plenty of money, to be accomplished, and to have a father at home. I am also struck by his inability to develop ideas or use the most basic writing and spelling conventions. For example, he almost never placed periods at the ends of sentences, and he indiscriminately capitalized words. He used *what* instead of *want; throw* instead of *through; form* instead of *from*. Lack of continuity in his schooling and a colossal lack of practice were holding him back.

Jawan and I spent little time honing this first story draft, mainly because the other students were already polishing final drafts when he arrived; we were about to tackle another class project. But this first story, into which Jawan *did* put good effort, gives a clear picture of his start. He'd stuck with his first project in our class, tried hard, and usually listened to Jeannine's, Judith's, and my suggestions. I wrote him a brief but encouraging note and gave him a C. (I aimed to encourage, not discourage kids like Jawan, who already knew what D's and F's were.)

10/7/88

Dear Jawan,

    I congratulate you for drafting a story—a love story. I can see that your characters have feelings. If you had had more time to revise, you could have let the characters tell more of their (and your) story; you could have polished the wording, too. You also didn't have enough time to clean up the spelling, punctuation, and other mechanical errors.

    We will work on written expression this year, and you will make good improvement in writing and all of language arts, *if* you come along with me and everyone in our class.

    I'm glad you joined us. I'm (we're) here to help you, Jawan.

Mrs. Krogness

During the early weeks in my class, Jawan was erratic. His desire to work—and the work itself—fluctuated dramatically. For the first three weeks, most of his writing was of about the same quality as his first story. His oral reading was halting; his understanding of the text needed to be teased out. He usually earned C's—sometimes D's—for his efforts. At the end of the first grading period, Jawan received a C and satisfactory grades for effort and citizenship, too.

But by late October, Jawan began to take off. Maybe coming from the city to the suburbs, a sacrifice for his mother, inspired him to turn over a new leaf in a new school where he'd have a fresh start. Maybe beginning to feel good about being able to do a satisfactory job in our class spurred him on. The mid-November test on *Roll of Thunder, Hear My Cry* is revealing (see Figure 13-2). Although we *always* read questions aloud before answering them, two-part questions often caused my resistant students difficulty. But Jawan read and answered both parts of question 1 satisfactorily. I was interested in his perspective: that white kids are smarter than black kids because one group had the advantage of getting the textbooks first, while the second group of students received cast-offs. Of course, Jawan didn't explain that because the black children received hand-me-down text books, they suffered from a psychological disadvantage. By this time, I had already noticed that his ability to infer meaning was better than that of many other students. For instance, he interpreted question 3, an inferential question, correctly: "A White woman can not work In a black school and a Black woman can not work in a white school." Jawan received an A− on that paper, the first A he'd received in our class. He jumped out of his chair, waving the A− paper in his hand. What a victory this was for him.

If it seems that I was extravagant in giving him an A− for a piece of writing in which he did not follow many conventions, it is because I was grading him on the content of his thinking at this point—showing him that I respected his ability as a thinker. I was also showing him that spelling, punctuation, and capitalization—while important—are not the essence of writing (which most of my kids had come to believe).

NAME *Jawan*

DATE *11-16-88*

A−

1. Choose <u>one</u> example of <u>racial injustice</u> that we have met in this powerful story.
   First, describe the racial incident.
   Next, explain how this incident affects the people involved.

My first racial injustice is the white kids can get some new books like text books or something and then the white kids will give the old dirted rip pages book to the black kid. I think the white kids was smarter than the blacks. Because the white kids had the books first than after the white kids was final done, they pased it down to the black kids.

−1   2. True or False questions: please write out TRUE or FALSE. Do NOT write T
        or F for these two letters can easily be confused!

True a. Miss Crocker is an obedient person.

True b. Little Man is proud—especially when he refuses to accept out-dated text books.

True c. Mary Logan feels indignant that her own children and students must use hand-me-down books.

True d. Mary Logan is not the usual black woman. She is an independent woman.
        She asks questions and asserts herself on many issues.

False e. The Logan family asks questions and challenge authority—the white man's
        authority.

True f. The white boy, Jeremy, feels safe and accepted by black children; therefore,
        he'd rather walk with the black kids such as the Logans than ride the school
        bus with the rest of the white children.

True g. Possibly, Jeremy feels as if he's an out-cast among the whites.

3. How can you be perfectly sure that the teacher, Miss Crocker, is a black woman?

Because a White woman can not work In a black school and a Black woman can not Work in a white school.

Very Good

4. Why do you imagine that Miss Crocker is so obedient? Why does she act as though
   the white people are perfectly right in handing down those old text books?

                                            Write on back!

FIG. 13-2   *Jawan's Early-November Test*

I felt certain that in time I could help Jawan overcome many of these mechanical problems. By giving him an A− and explaining in my note the strengths of his piece, I was showing him what I valued.

By the end of November, Jawan more often than not was putting forth effort. When faced with open-ended questions, he provided thoughtful, carefully phrased answers in which he made a valiant attempt to obey mechanical conventions. With increased practice, he often succeeded. Often he asked Judith, Jeannine, or me how to spell words he wanted to use. (Research tells us that constant practice in using conventions and vigilance in correctly using the mechanics of writing in daily work help young people to improve their spelling, punctuation, and capitalization.) Best of all, Jawan was learning to develop an argument and supply supporting evidence in the form of telling

Jawan,

A   This is a pretty darn good piece! You are trying to learn, to improve, to express ideas. Great. Mrs. K.

1. My favorite character is Little Man because he's willing to stand up for his rights and he likes to be neat and clothes ~~wear~~ ?

2. Mrs. Logan trimmed ~~the~~ the paper to size of the books, looking [pouring?] glue from the brown bottle onto the inside cover of one of the books. Then she took the paper and placed it over the glue. (But, what is ~~her purpose of~~ cutting brown paper + gluing it in books?)

3. The nightriders was ~~at~~ white men who tar and feather black people ~~say~~ like if a black man said something to a whitewoman the black man would get tar and feather.

4. Stacy disobey his ~~her~~ mama by going up to that store and Ma ~~a~~ told him not to go.

5. No I would have ~~be~~ [been] too scared to fight him because his family is ~~crazy~~ ~~they~~ don't like black people.

6. Mr. Morrison is living ~~which~~ (with) the Logan family because he got into a fight ~~which~~ (with) a white man and beat the white man up bad ~~and Mr. Morrison~~ need a ~~place~~ to ~~sleep~~ and Mr. Logan him he ~~couldn't~~ told could move in (with) his family ~~to~~ to watch over his family and ~~to~~ help around the ~~family~~ house while he (David Logan) is down in Louisiana laying R.R. tracks.

FIG. 13-3 *Jawan's Late-November Test*

details, facts, examples, and inferences from the text. Figure 13-3 shows an end-of-November test. Jawan took great care in preparing his answers to this test on Taylor's *Roll of Thunder, Hear My Cry*. He wrote in cursive instead of printing. His sentence structure had greatly improved as had his spelling.

Maybe the best part of these reponses is Jawan's strong voice. I applauded his informed opinions, which are authentically expressed. For example, in answer 5, this husky, muscular boy admits: "I would have been too scared to fight him [T. J. Avery] because his family is *crazy.*" I wonder if any literature before had touched this non-reader so powerfully as Mildred Taylor's classic.

I gave Jawan an A and wrote a note to him specifically identifying and labeling what was excellent about this most recent piece of exposition. I felt certain that if he could get into the habit of redirecting his energy and use it to succeed in school, he might yet succeed. Here is my response to Jawan's essay test:

11/28/88

Dear Jawan,

Congratulations! You have earned an A on this difficult test that Mrs. Rajewski [Jeannine] gave. Let me explain why:

(1) you answered each question fully and clearly, and you explained your point of view; you showed your endurance (staying power) by giving even the last questions your best—you didn't hurry;

(2) you gave proof or supporting evidence (examples and details) from the story, helping you prove your point;

(3) you made every attempt to create clear, complete sentences; you also tried hard to punctuate and spell correctly;

(4) I heard your "voice" each time I read one of your answers; in other words, you put *your* own ideas and insights down on paper!

I hope this excellent piece of work encourages you to keep up the fine work you're capable of doing.

Mrs. Krogness

Although Jawan was taking more risks in using the written language (see, for instance, his poems in Chapter 11 about getting kisses at church and Annie Sis, which he wrote in late October, each receiving an A), he still usually spoke and wrote in nonstandard dialect. He said things like "His mom bought *they* clothes at the department store" or "He *be* going to school." He almost always used a plural subject with a singular verb: "He *have* a nice father" and rarely put the past tense ending *-ed* on verbs. As is true of all dialects, the speaker obeys particular grammatical rules. Jawan was doing just that.

Mrs. K. helps Jawan tighten his fairy tale and breathe life into his characters.

Linguists have been telling us for years that no one dialect helps language users to think better, and Jawan certainly demonstrated that point. Because he was working more diligently during class and making noticeable strides, I was not about to penalize him for using nonstandard dialect. I felt sure that by constantly reading standard dialect and hearing it spoken, he would in time pick up at least a few of the conventions.

Sometime in November, after we'd read and heard Pat Fagel tell many classic fairy tales, we wrote our own (see Chapter 8). The rough draft of Jawan's fairy tale is more complex than his earlier story; it's full of archetypal characters and the classic plot of good versus evil.

This time Jawan did have an opportunity to hone his tale of a heroic prince who comes face to face with loss and fear. Jeannine spent time talking with him about ways to fit all the pieces of his story together, deal with discrepancies and contradictions, and fill the usual gaps that exist in most writers' rough drafts. In the last phase of writing, she guided Jawan to correct spelling errors and punctuate his story correctly while he (or she) read it aloud. His classmates, who eagerly listened to everything Jawan said, loved giving him advice about his story. Sometimes he even listened. (Figure 13-4 shows the beginning of Jawan's fairy tale.) I wrote him another letter assessing this most recent creation.

11/28/88

Dear Jawan,

You have done a great job writing another fairy tale, the second draft of this one. I am pleased with the quality of work, because you've developed an interesting plot and characters.

While you *re*read your story out loud, do the following with your pen in hand: (1) let your characters tell a little more of your/their story; write more dialogue/conversation; (2) cross out all the *thens* that you use—usually at the beginning of sentences; (3) correct all the spelling errors that you can, then let Mrs. Rajewski correct any other misspelled words with you. Also, put in periods at ends of sentences *while* you're reading the tale out loud.

You have a C+/B− on this story—so far. Good luck. And keep on working, Jawan.

Mrs. Krogness

Before Jawan typed his story on the computer, he and I sat down to assess his increased desire to take responsibility for his academic work and his actions. We made note of the following: Jawan was demonstrating greater responsibility for attending to academic work; he was becoming more responsible for his actions, and thus could probably be responsible enough to work effectively in the library; he deserved the opportunity to prove himself. His eagerness to excel and his need to take charge of his own learning earned him the privilege of using class time to type the final draft of his fairy tale on the computer in the library. After checking in with me at the beginning of class, he headed for the library.

Although Jawan continued to have bad days, his general attitude and achievement were quite solid because of a combination of circumstances. Able to attend class more regularly because he wasn't being hauled out so often for misdemeanors, he arrived on time and was ready to work. Each day, he was immersed in using the language in many different ways and for many different reasons, in a place where he felt safe and valued. The more competent he became, the more comfortable he felt. He was becoming a most respected class leader. To his relief and his mother's delight, my telephone calls home

Prince & Cyclops   ¶

Cx/B.   ¶

IL-88

Once aporid of time there was
a prince and the Prince AVERL who liked to
travel. once a month, the prince went
to England and the prince went
to visit his uncle, the duke, and he
stayed with his uncle for three → Good
#3 is a magic number
days. The prince went(walked?) to dinner at
King fazae Castel. On the way he the young prince
found a voodoo doll. But he didn't
know it was a vodoo doll. He thought when he picked it up + put it in his pouch.
it was a good luck charm. So when
three days was(were) up the prince Aveal
returned to his own Castle. the prince He
walked in the house, the Madd(maid) said
"Your father, the King, died your "majesty".

He Prince Aveal Thought to himself Self "I have been
Having Bad luck since I bought That good
luck charm home. I am going to take
It to the pond deep in the
woods. And throw it away forever!"

FIG. 13-4   *Excerpt from Jawan's Fairy Tale*

B

Shaker Hts middle Schod
20600 Shaker Boulevard
Shaker Heights OH 44122
January 20, 1989

Dear Laura & John,

I like the way you two guys worked together—

With the hands and finger communication

So that John my good buddy can

understand and he can follow

along.

Laura, I like the way you followed

along with us. I like the way

you teaches and I think you should

Come back real soon!

Sincerely,
Jawan

P.S. I was the big guy that you couldn't
Beat! Remember?

FIG. 13-5   *Jawan's Letter*

were increasingly positive. Jawan earned a B— for the second grading period (at the end of first semester) because the body of writing he chose to submit showed noticeable improvement in content, style, and command of the conventions of writing. His ability to perceive important issues and raise thoughtful questions distinguished him. His effort grade was satisfactory (when his moods fluctuated, it affected his effort). He earned a 3 (average) in citizenship during these two grading periods.

By January, after the three actors from the Theatre of the Deaf had visited all the seventh-grade language arts classes, Jawan was more and more often writing and talking in standard English dialect. (In Chapter 3 we saw that Jawan's cousins from Cleveland had noticed that their cousin was "talking fancy" since he'd moved to Shaker Heights.) Jawan expressed his appreciation to Laura and John, the two actors, in a warm and friendly letter (see Figure 13-5) in which he obeyed the standard letter-writing conventions, wrote personally rather than perfunctorily, and presented a neat final draft, which earned him a B.

Their, There, They're

you often do not listen when I am teaching!

NAME: *Jawan*

DATE: *2-9-84*   F F12

1. When ~~there~~ *They're* working on *their* homework, you shouldn't disturb them.

2. *They're* only trying to do *their* best on the writing exercise that X *there* / *their* teacher, Mrs. Krogness, gave them to do.

3. Alison sat over *there*, next to Pete, Noah, and Jeremy. The four students did the work of sixty students while they chatted and ate X *they're* / *their* lunches. *whose lunches?*

4. Many of *their* families were *there* at the school to honor them and X they're (*their*) classmates. *they're = they are*

5. *There* they are– all those students who work *their* buns off to achieve and learn.

6. When X *there* / *they're* practicing, X *their* / *they're* learning how to do X *They're* (*their*) own work without the constant assistance of X *there* (*their*) parents and teachers.

7. "Where are *their* books, pencils, papers and book bags?" the teacher asked. "X *There* (*They're*) all over X *they're* / *there*," called out Drake.

8. Three of us will sit together *there* in the second row, first aisle.

9. If X *There* / *they're* looking for us, tell them we'll be sitting over X *there* / *their* next to Peter and the rest of X *they're* / *their* families.

10. Tell me where X *Their* (*there*) are some violets, daffodils and iris.

FIG. 13-6   *Jawan's Skills Sheet*

Jawan was learning to express ideas and use mechanics more skillfully, but occasionally he reverted back to old habits and stopped listening. Using *there, their,* and *they're,* for example, continued to cause Jawan (and some of his classmates) trouble despite regular usage drills and daily practice writing. My scribbled note at the top of the skills sheet shown in Figure 13-6 indicates that Jawan had tuned me out when it came to practicing the standard use of these tricky words. I didn't hesitate to give him an F, a grade I rarely gave!

But looking at the *big* picture is important in gaining a clear perspective. He earned a B during the first grading period, second semester, an E for excellent effort, and a 3 for citizenship; because he'd gotten weary and ready for school to be over, he'd gotten a C at year's end. Jawan and I knew where he'd been before coming to our school. We knew where he was currently and how he was doing during seventh-grade language arts/English class. But neither of us was sure where he was going.

At the end of seventh grade, the administrators let Jawan, who wanted to join his peers, skip eighth grade and move up to the high school—not because of his academic performance but because of his size and social maturity. The next year I heard reports from Jawan's high school teachers that he was experiencing difficulty in and out of his new school, a large school of close to two-thousand students where a boy like Jawan (who needs to be monitored daily, nurtured regularly, and helped to achieve) can get lost. Finally, the statistics caught up with him: I understand that the school authorities expelled him.

Jermaine

A teacher gains an interesting—sometimes a disheartening—perspective when she has a student for two consecutive years. Jermaine, whom we've also met before, was a member of a large and growing group of young people—often minority students—who become disaffected about school. These are the young people whom society risks losing. In my seventh-grade class, though he was often in various kinds of trouble in and out of school, Jermaine set real goals and made real progress in our back-to-back language arts/English class. (I wish that had been the case in his other classes.) But in our eighth-grade language arts class, Jermaine plummeted so far that I was in despair. Let me trace Jermaine's seventh- and eighth-grade journey.

In seventh grade, Jermaine, who wrote about feeling vulnerable and learned to enjoy talking about feelings as well as literature and writing, seemed to feel accepted and successful in our class. Although he spent a quantity of time in "Alternative to Suspension" (ATS), he often tackled work in our class with imagination and care. Samples of his writing show his effort to develop ideas, use strong vocabulary, and obey the mechanical conventions, although by that time (like many of my kids) he had "mispracticed" them for too many years.

First, Jermaine worked earnestly on a complex fairy tale. Set on the Hulagon River, his tale is rife with avarice; it smokes with revenge, the kind that kindled Jermaine's own desire to pay back a world that had dealt him a bad hand. He earned an A−/B+ on this first story. Ambitiously, he started another, "The Determined Droul [Ghoul] vs. Mysterious Elf," a very dense tale about a clumsy cyclops, an elf trapped in a crystal, and an ambitious ghoul disguised as a fair maiden. Jermaine worked intermittently on this piece between October and early January. The handwritten draft (see Figure 13-7) reveals pungent lines of dialogue: " 'I can feel the power already,' " said the ghoul, disguised as a fair maiden. " 'If you can feel the power, then get me out!' " yelled the elf. One of the characters mused, " 'The eyes sure can play tricks on the mind! If that woman is a fair maiden, then I'm Merlin the magician!' " Jermaine's dialogue was fluid, spirited, and authentic. This boy was not incapable of making quantum leaps forward *if* he could only hang in there. Even better, if he could use his brain power for personal power, he might have a chance to succeed. I wrote him a lengthy letter to encourage him and give him suggestions for reworking his story. (It might seem that the letter I wrote to Jermaine in response to this story is

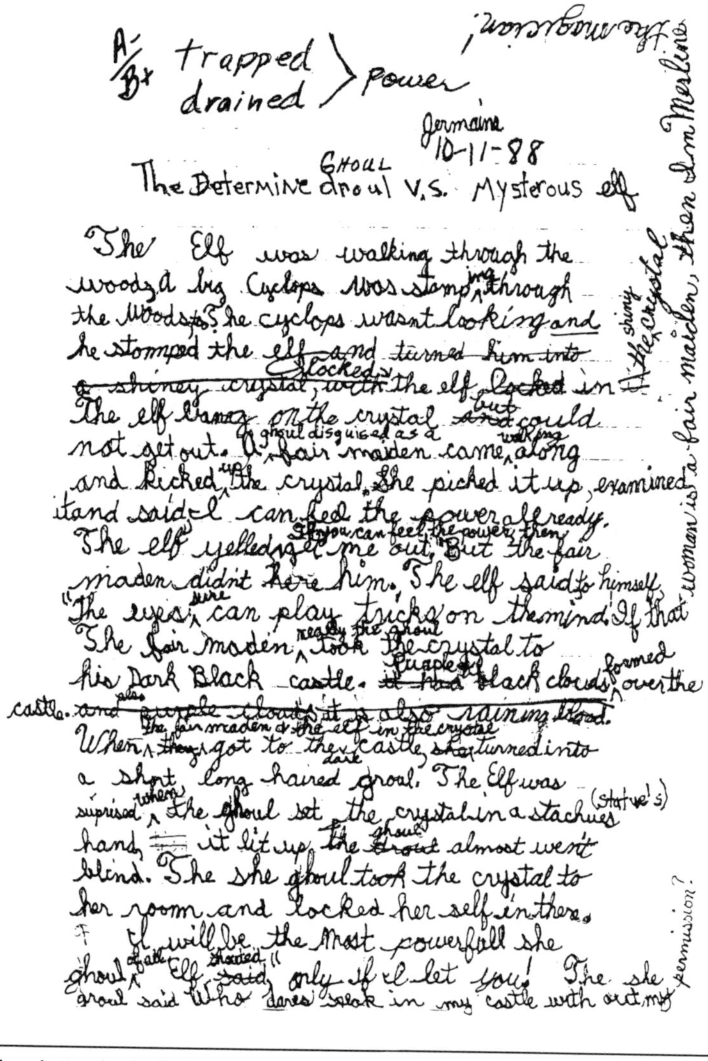

FIG. 13-7   *Jermaine's Fairy Tale*

too long and sophisticated for him to read and absorb. Perhaps. But when my kids had trouble reading or understanding my letters, I read them aloud and further explained the meaning. When I knew they were ready for a challenge, I stretched their thinking in my conversations with them and my letters to them. I also wanted to accord these young people the same respect and belief in their ability that I showed my students in regular or advanced classes, all the while modeling other ways to use language.)

10/12/88

Dear Jermaine,

I am thrilled with the rough draft of your second story. It is very interesting because you have woven together a tension-filled plot. An ambitious and evil ghoul, disguised as a fair maiden, masterminds a plan to trick the queen and king. Then he tries to make off with the crown jewels. (By the way, I think you mean a *ghoul* not a droul.) But the evil ghoul is foiled (stopped) when he accidentally breaks the crystal, allowing the elf to escape and catch the ghoul in the act. This is a very complex plot that generally holds together.

Here are my suggestions for revision: (1) Now that you have a good story plot or plan, I would suggest allowing the characters to tell more of your story. For example, I would let the ghoul, who meets the queen in the forest, talk with her so that the reader understands how much the two women look alike. (This clue is important to the rest of the story—when the evil ghoul entraps the innocent queen in the powerful crystal.) (2) How does the evil ghoul (disguised as a fair maiden) gain entry to the king's castle? This must be explained. (3) It seems too easy for the evil ghoul, a thief, to pause to listen to the elf who says, "Drop the gold and jewels." The ghoul obeys the elf's orders much too easily. How can you rethink the ending?

See Mrs. Rajewski or me about your story. I want to compliment you on the high quality of thinking and writing you're doing in here. In general, your attitude and behavior are acceptable now; sometimes they're excellent.

Mrs. Krogness

I gave Jermaine an A−/B+ on this draft, which at the moment seemed to fire him to polish it and maybe earn an A. But I suspect that the lapses in his behavior (less frequent now in our class), his frequent incarceration in ATS due to multiple referrals in other classes and the halls, the discouragement he felt in school and in his personal life generally, sapped his psychic energy, which carried over to this latest writing project. However, I reasoned that one double-period class, for him a colossal success,

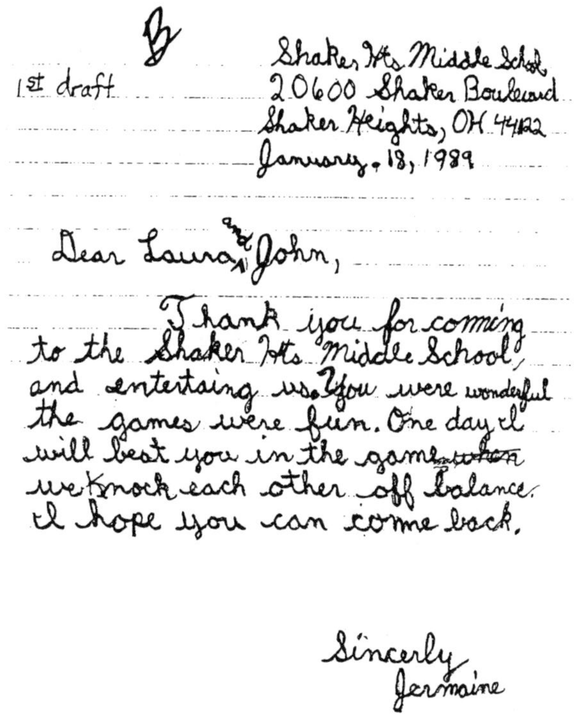

B

1st draft

Shaker Hts Middle Schol
20600 Shaker Boulevard
Shaker Heights, OH 44122
January, 18, 1989

Dear Laura and John,

Thank you for coming to the Shaker Hts Middle School, and entertaing us. You were wonderful the games were fun. One day I will beat you in the game ~~when~~ we knock each other off balance. I hope you can come back.

Sincerly
Jermaine

FIG. 13-8 *Jermaine's First Draft*

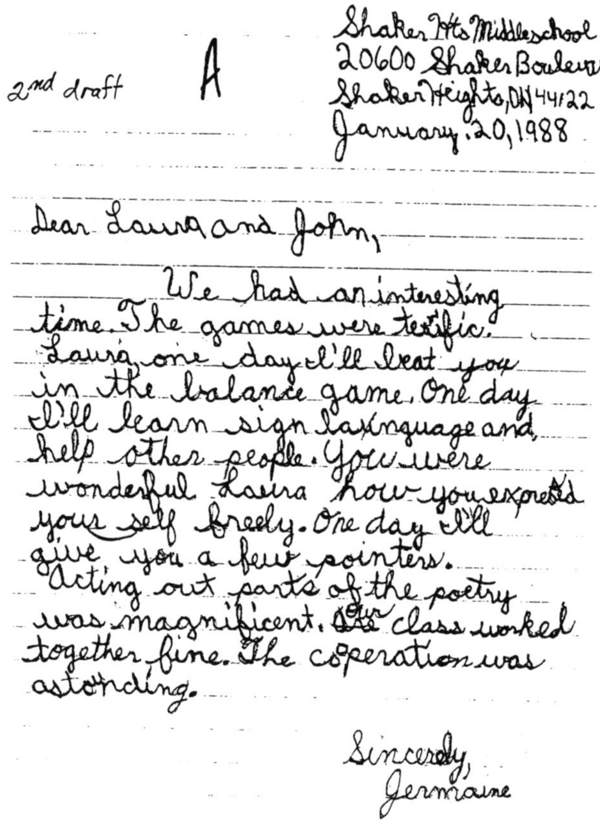

2nd draft   A   Shaker Hts Middleschool
                              20600 Shaker Boulevard
                              Shaker Heights, OH 44122
                              January 20, 1988

Dear Laura and John,

    We had an interesting time. The games were terrific. Laura one day I'll beat you in the balance game. One day I'll learn sign language and help other people. You were wonderful Laura how you expressd your self freely. One day I'll give you a few pointers. Acting out parts of the poetry was magnificent. The class worked together fine. The coperation was astonding.

            Sincerely,
            Jermaine

FIG. 13-9   *Jermaine's Second Draft*

might be ballast enough to keep him focused; maybe he would internalize a successful year in our class, letting it motivate him in other classes. I even mused that sustained success in language arts class might keep him focused on school instead of the activity in the streets. At the end of the first grading period, Jermaine's grade hovered between a C and a B; he certainly would have gotten a B had he not missed so many classes and so much in-class work. Although he was improving, his effort was still somewhat erratic, as was his behavior, thus earning him average grades in both.

    By January, Jermaine's growing desire to cooperate and his obvious investment in working hard were expressed not only in his class work and his efforts to seek extra help even after school, but in his willingness to write a *second* draft of a thank-you letter to Laura and John, the two actors from the Theatre of the Deaf. He and I talked about his first draft (on which he earned a B) being a little distant rather than warm and personal (see Figure 13-8). Without further ado, Jermaine rewrote and more fully developed his letter, congratulating Laura on her ability to express herself freely (see Figure 13-9). This letter earned him an A. How perceptive he was in observing one of Laura's strengths as an actress and a person. Jermaine had enjoyed working with Laura and John in improv, particularly Laura, a petite young woman whose exuberance, warmth, and joy spilled over to him and his classmates. He outdid himself when he extravagantly referred to our class's ability to perform poetry "magnificently"; he

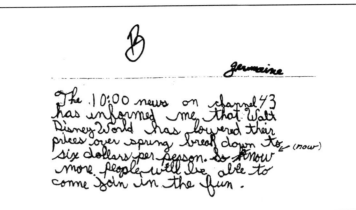

FIG. 13-10 *Jermaine's News Account*

was downright hyperbolic when he applauded the classroom cooperation that he termed "astounding." Though wary, Jermaine was receptive to the appreciation and respect he was receiving in our class. At the end of the second grading period he earned a B; he received an E for excellent effort and a 3 in citizenship.

Jermaine had a knack for getting to the heart of an issue, whether it was finding someone's Achilles' heel—or summing up a news report for homework. In just two well-developed sentences, Jermaine explained Disney World's new admission fee policy (see Figure 13-10). Although he certainly might have developed the news account more specifically—for instance, the types of fun and entertainment Disney World offers (and would have included them had he done the in-class work)—he did a nice job. And he had *done* the viewing and writing homework!

He also thought through the book bag situation—giving warnings about stray book bags and advice on where to put them and explaining the dangers and liabilities of taking book bags into the school library—which earned him an A−/B+ (see Figure 13-11). His impressive collection of writing and his increased oral responses in class and literary involvement earned Jermaine a B at the end of the first grading period, second semester, an E for excellent effort and a 3 for citizenship; Jermaine received a C+, S, 3 at the end of the second semester. Because he was tired of school, his grade had dropped.

Both Jermaine and I were satisfied with the progress he'd made during seventh grade. So I was delighted, if only for a day or two, when Jermaine asked to have his schedule changed so that he could join one of my eighth-grade language arts classes. After all, couldn't Jermaine make excellent progress with a teacher he liked and with whom he felt safe? Couldn't he sustain the positive feelings about his ability to do well in school that he'd developed during seventh grade? Couldn't we just pick up where we'd left off?

I may never know all the variables that sent Jermaine on a downward spiral that eighth-grade year. He seemed in terrible conflict about succeeding. His attitude was negative and the quality of his writing erratic; even the best did not measure up to his seventh-grade work. He often missed class because so many of his teachers were writing referrals in response to his disruptive behavior. At one point, he'd accumulated more than thirty referrals, which put him in ATS or, worse, got him suspended.

When he *was* in class, Jermaine usually slumped in his chair, silently sabotaging my efforts, and those of his more eager but timid classmates, to engage in conversation. His sly and slothful ways resulted in flat, unimaginative prose that he cranked out

A⁻/B⁺

Solutions for Book Bag Problem: *Jermaine*

1. Keep book pack out of traffic. (~~flood!~~)
2. ~~stop using back packes~~
3. In class put them on the rack ~~under~~ ~~on~~ the chairs.
4. carry them at all times
5. put them in lockers so they can't be stolen.

6. I don't think we should ~~stop~~ carrying back packs. If ~~they would~~ people would haft to carry loads of books which could spill.

7. people should put back packs on both sholders so that they wont have bad posture.

8. people should clean back packs every week ~~so that they could stay clean.~~

(lunch) 9. People should not go through the line with ~~out their~~ back packs because they might try to ~~still~~ steal food.

10. Don't put back packs on top of the desks; put them on a shelf or under desks.

11. Ms. Krogness was salty because we didn't have are homework! (A solution? ↗)

12. Don't ~~go~~ through peoples backpacks
13. Organise back packs.
14. Don't throw back packs (around or use them to push people around)

15. don't take backpacks to library ~~back~~ Someone might still steal

16. people put games in there (their) bags and then they are stolen (ex check b.b. for inappropriate items)

⌐ 1̄7. people put weapons in bookbag

⌐ 18. (our) they also carry drugs in are back pack.

└→ These 2 are dangers of kids carrying b.b. What are the solutions?

FIG. 13-11   *Jermaine's Solutions*

quickly and sloppily—if he bothered to do them (his earlier, more accomplished work had been neatly prepared). Although he did improve after January of his eighth-grade year, his final body of work was slim; many pieces were missing because of his frequent absences and failure to make up the missing assignments.

Samples of Jermaine's eighth-grade work may hold clues to what was happening to him. Curiously, he ripped from his writing spiral his very early letter of intention, which tellingly said little about his goals except for a wish "that Mrs. Krogness won't read everything in my writing spiral." He also tore out the letter of goals and expectations that he wrote from his parents' point of view. My responses to these two early letters indicated my encouragement but also my insistence that Jermaine come to class on time and get with the program.

In preparation for conducting a schoolwide survey on a popular clothing manufacturer (which connected nicely with literature we were reading), I asked Jermaine and his classmates to create possible survey questions. On this particular day, he attended to business for reasons that I can't explain. Here are his questions, thoughtful and well-phrased: (1) What does (name of clothing manufacturer) stand for? (2) Have you ever supported (name of clothing manufacturer)? (3) If you heard the Ku Klux Klan was supported by (name of clothing manufacturer), would you buy their products? (4) Do you know what the Ku Klux Klan does? (5) Do you know the rumor about (name of the clothing manufacturer)?

In a note, I praised him for his thinking and gave him a B+. Of course I wanted to remain constant and honest; I wanted to convey my acceptance of him at all times, but also realistic expectations.

9/13/89

Dear Jermaine,
    You worked well today. The good results reflect your effort. You ask on-target survey questions. You get at the real issues, but don't do what I warned against: "load" your questions so they bring the kinds of answers we want to hear.
    I think you'll enjoy actually conducting the survey throughout SMS.

Mrs. Krogness

Nothing that had worked the previous year to bring him along on a consistent basis seemed to matter to him during eighth grade: my help and support; honest praise when he did put forth effort; choices, expectation, and structure. Of course I took into account that an eighth grader (animal? vegetable? mineral?) is entirely different from a seventh grader. I believe that eighth grade is a pivotal year, the year we lose many marginal kids, unless they have strong families behind them or mysteriously see the light. I also imagined that Jermaine's self-esteem had so deteriorated because of a lifetime of sadness that he simply had no more tolerance for school failure. I also knew that during the unsupervised, unplanned summer months, he'd had a brush or two with the law.

This ambivalent boy waxed and waned. He did poorly on the test (D−) I gave on *The Children's Story* (see Figure 13-12). In the note I jotted at the top of the test, I offered Jermaine an opportunity to redo the essay questions, but he refused. Not long afterward, however, we watched about a dozen short films and then responded to them briefly. Jermaine's insights about the mimed film *Neighbors* reflected his ability to incisively cut to the heart of universal issues, a quality I'd observed in him during seventh grade. Jermaine jotted the following notes about *Neighbors:* "share with your

See note on back.

The Children's Story by James Clavell   September 22, 1989

60 pts.

Mrs. Krogness, language arts/reading   NAME *Jermaine J.*

Would you like the oppor... DATE 9/22/89

Each of the 3 essay questions = 25 points.

funity to redo the essay questions — except for #1?

I. Essay questions (to be answered fully and in complete sentences as well
with full support in the form of examples, details from the story):
Choose three (3) of the five (5) questions to answer in detail.

A. Explain the meaning of The Children's Story.

Fine! (The) *Children' Story means taking over
and taking charge by brain washing
and discrediting people, getting people on
your side getting people to agree
with them/you.*   **+20 pts.**

B. Explain, in detail, the importance of each of the three main characters—
New Teacher, Johnny and Sandra. Who/what does each character represent?

*New Teacher was an infiltrator (who...)
Johnny had never believed what New Teacher
said, because he new there was something
suspicious about her.
Sandra is a follower (because) she doesn't
know what's going on.*   **+18 pts.**

C. What is the importance of TIME and VULNERABILITY in this novel?

?

D. Name three tactics that New Teacher uses to overtake the children.
Explain each one by giving an example from the story.

*Tactics? She always (make) them agree with her
She sang to them.
an always put bad thoughts into mind*   **+10 pts.**

FIG. 13-12   *Jermaine's Test*

neighbor; fighting gets you nowhere; if it doesn't belong to either person, let it be." His
last point, "War doesn't decide who wins but who's left," is an example of Jermaine's
unusual ability to synthesize subtle and sophisticated information. These sharp insights
brought me hope and him a B. (He would have gotten an A on this paper if he hadn't
skipped one of the questions.) I wrote a brief and somewhat bland note to him—brief
and bland because his negative behavior, body language, and erratic work indicated to
me that *this* year he felt ambivalent about school success.

9/30/89

Dear Jermaine,

You're a good thinker. I especially like the way you size up the film, *Neighbors*.
The last insight, "War doesn't decide who wins but who's left," tells me how much and

E. Even though the print is big, the words are easy, there's plenty of space and no page numbers, how do you know this little book is not meant for little children?

Because it has some "kind of" symbolic meaning to it.

II. True and False Section: please write out the words, TRUE and FALSE.

True A. Johnny is a skeptic, a person who doubts and questions New Teacher's motives.

True B. Sandra is a crowd follower; she is like many German people who blindly and fearfully followed A. Hitler

True C. New Teacher might be compared to any number of well-trained infiltrators who seep into a vulnerable society.

True D. Rote learning is the best way for young people to learn.

False E. Johnny's father was sent away to "school" because he had learned wrong ideas.

True F. New Teacher destroyed the children's values in just 25 minutes.

True G. Miss Worden is intimidated by New Teacher.

True H. Miss Worden is discredited by New Teacher.

True I. Johnny is flattered by New Teacher.

False J. Time really isn't such an important element in this little story.

III. Matching: read all of the choices on both sides before you begin.

8 A. People who are most vulnerable in a society.

7 B. People who are most dangerous in a society.

C. A person who stands up.

D. A tactic used by someone who is taking over a group or a country.

2 E. The turning point in this story.

5 F. Clavell's reason for writing this story--his motives for writing it.

9 G. The Skinheads and the KKK.

10 H. Apartheid in South Africa.

1. Infiltration
2. Johnny's accepting New Teacher's principles.
3. **The least educated; the least questioning; the least strongly principled people in a society.**
4. An enlightened, thoughtful person who reads, thinks, listens, weighs issues and thinks for her/himself; a person who is strong inside.
5. Rote learning.
6. Our Leader
7. Desire to make people become aware of the dangers that lurk in society
8. People who dream of power.
9. Biased people who pre-judge.
10. Oppression
11. Twenty-five minutes

IV. Create a list of societies where oppression exists. Number each society and list on the back of this paper.

FIG. 13-12 (*continued*)

how clearly you understood this eight-minute film about humanity. I hope you'll continue thinking so smart.

Mrs. Krogness

By late October, when most students are getting in the groove and settling into their work, Jermaine was sinking fast. His idea sheet revealed a lackluster and meager collection of story ideas, which earned him a D; and in direct contrast to his seventh-grade stories, the rough draft showed little promise. Because Jermaine barely fulfilled this assignment, and because I knew what exciting work he was capable of doing, I gave him a D on his rough draft (see Figure 13-13).

Shortly thereafter, Jermaine, Mr. Jarvie, the skillful assistant principal, and I had a serious talk about what Jermaine, by this time a chronic disrupter and tardy to nearly every class, would have to do to remain in my class. I took this opportunity to reaffirm my belief in him and his ability, but I was adamant that he shape up. (Kids like Jermaine are quick to judge kindness and support as signs of weakness.) Jermaine insisted that

10-19-89
Jermaine.

One hot day me my cousin and grandfather
went downtown he bought us anything
we wanted. But on the way home my
grandfather almost had a hot flash.
So he ~~push~~ tried to push open a vent
on Top of the bus, he put to much
strenth into ~~pushing it open~~ _ _ _ _ _ _
when he pushed it open, he felt so imbarras
These 3 girls laught at him and so did
me and my cousin, but not outloud
Then we went back to Jermaine's
house an told everyone ~~what happen~~
What happend an they crackd up.
My grandfather ate then went
home, before he left me and
shawn said bye-bye thankyou
for taking us down town. He
said okay bye-bye,

FIG. 13-13   *Jermaine's Rough Draft of His Story*

he wanted to stay and promised to be on time, be respectful, and do his work. He wrote the final draft of his story, making a few revisions as he prepared a clean final copy. By adding a little conversation to the slim piece, Jermaine gave it only a scant bit more life, meaning, and structure. The final story, which I graded C−, wasn't nearly up to the quality of work he had done the previous year. A dearth of good writing, many missing assignments, no classroom conversation (except the exploitative kind), and a refusal to read aloud in class earned him a D at the end of the first grading period; I gave him a 5 (the lowest citizenship grade) because he undermined our class, and an unsatisfactory effort grade for erratic—often poor—effort.

Even though I frequently called his neighbor, who, I believe, conveyed my messages to Jermaine's parents (they had no telephone), Jermaine's behavior, attitude, and

---

A YEAR IN REVIEW: 1989

NAME *Jermaine*
DATE *1990 Jan.*

Finish! D−

Idea Collection Sheet

Explain!

1. A moment you wish to remember: *Back in 5th and 6th grade it was fun*
2. A conversation you recall having: *With Mr Jarvie about me coming back to school*
3. A personal victory: *Basket Ball game outside*
4. A personal failure: *Last year in math but somehow I past*
5. A person you'll remember: *Toby*
6. A moment you DO NOT want to remember: *When my father — 1st*
7. An exciting moment in your life: *When I went to geugalake*
8. A major disappointment (i.e., in a person, in yourself, in a situation etc.) *I let Jeff borrow money about 6 day's ago and he didn't pay me back yet*
? 9. A recent understanding of a situation: _____
? 10. A new insight about yourself: _____
? 11. A world event that you'll remember: _____
? 12. A song of the '80's that you'll remember: _____
13. A movie that you'll remember: *Harlem Nights*
14. A big dream (goal): *to be a basketball player (or) psychiatrist*
? 15. A monumental decision (to do/not do something): _____

16. The hardest part about growing up: *taking order's from parents*
17. The best/most important part about growing up: *got a Lisence*

18. Your most important New Year's resolution (promise): *To stay out of trouble.*
19. The funniest incident you can recall in '89: *When Jason and Donald had a fight*
? 20. The sadest incident in '89: _____

FIG. 13-14   *Jermaine's Year in Review*

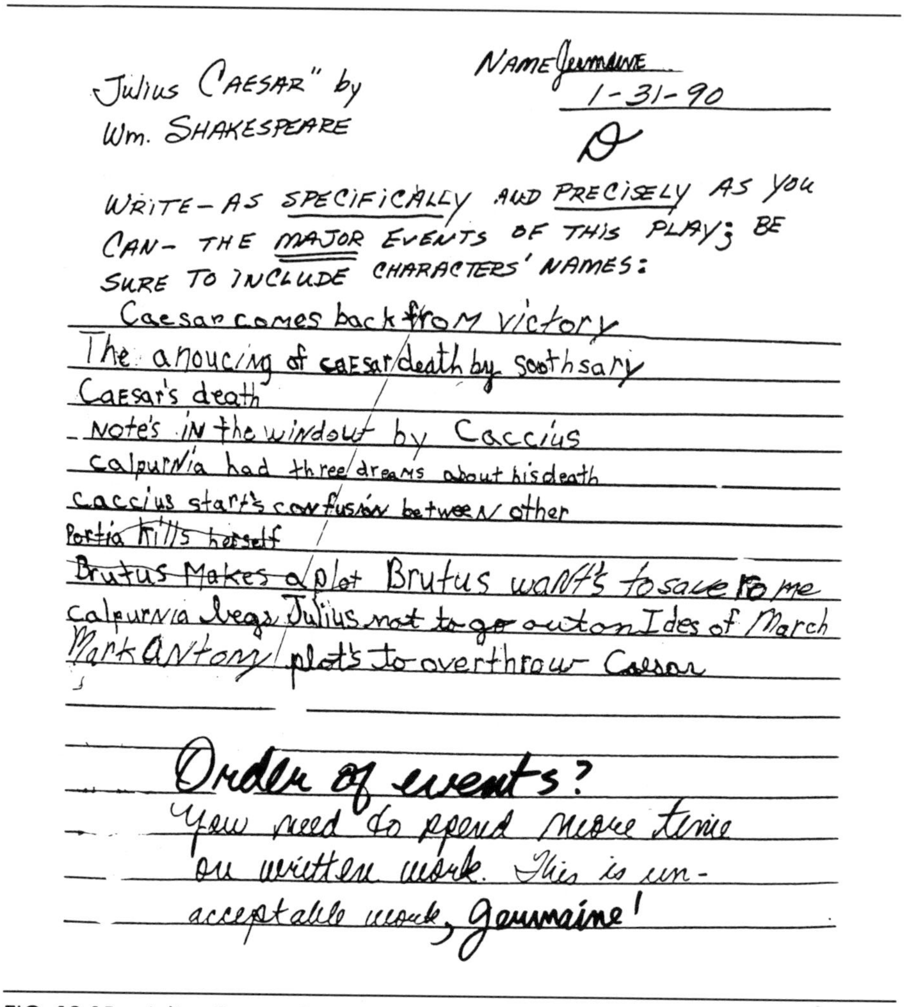

"Julius Caesar" by
Wm. Shakespeare

NAME Jermaine
1-31-90

D

WRITE — AS SPECIFICALLY AND PRECISELY AS YOU
CAN — THE MAJOR EVENTS OF THIS PLAY; BE
SURE TO INCLUDE CHARACTERS' NAMES:

Caesar comes back from victory
The anoucing of Caesar death by soothsary
Caesar's death
Note's in the window by Caccius
Calpurnia had three dreams about his death
Caccius start's confusion between other
Portia kills herself
Brutus Makes a plot Brutus want's to save Rome
Calpurnia begs Julius not to go out on Ides of March
Mark Antony plot's to overthrow Caesar

Order of events?
*You need to spend more time
on written work. This is un-
acceptable work, Jermaine!*

FIG. 13-15   Julius Caesar *Exercise*

work remained poor. My letters requesting parent-teacher conferences were sent home, but to no avail. During first semester, Jermaine was suspended more than once from school for increasingly serious misdemeanors. At those times, his parents were required to appear at school.

The remainder of first semester was a series of roller coaster rides with Jermaine. He often refused to fulfill assignments, or he'd do the bare minimum. His behavior often caused his classmates and me serious disruptions, contributing to a negative classroom atmosphere. His Year in Review reveals his lethargy (see Figure 13-14). He balked at doing at least one of the thinking/writing exercises in preparation for the Shakespeare experience. For one paper, he used most of class time to sit, stir the pot, and make uncalled-for comments, though he managed to finish the assignment. I gave him a D and wrote him a sharp note (see Figure 13-15). (Looking at Jermaine's list of major events in *Julius Caeser* afresh causes me to reconsider his grade; I'd probably give him a C, not a D, if I were grading his paper today. Alas, my depleted supply of energy and patience skewed my judgment.) Once again, I gave him a D on his report card.

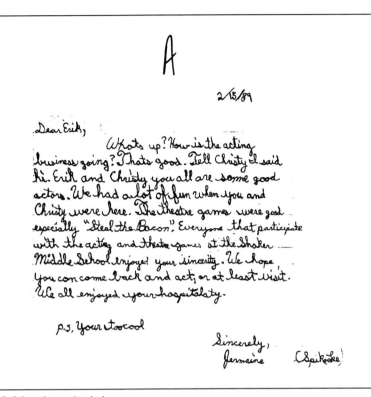

FIG. 13-16   *Jermaine's Letter*

Following the Shakespeare experience in February, however, he was willing to revise his thank-you letter to Erik, the cavalier young Shakespeare actor who visited our class, and, whom Jermaine admired immensely (see Figure 13-16). This piece, which earned Jermaine an A, was a striking improvement in both content and general quality from what he'd been turning in most of the year; it probably was his best piece of written work to date. My hope (and maybe his) was, at least for the moment, renewed.

By March of the second semester, Jermaine was putting forth more and more sustained effort to behave in class and get down to work (probably because Chemon, his erstwhile sidekick had been removed from our class), and he was emerging once again as a class leader. The general climate of this class had also improved to the point that being a successful class participant was generally acceptable. Jermaine and several other boys sat at a table and wrote short fables they read aloud to each other and laughed over. His fable about the old, worn-out rabbit with no money and the gullible-looking turtle was tangible evidence of his modestly renewed interest in language arts class. The final and *third* draft of his acceptably bawdy second fable, "The Mingle Between the Dog and the Cat," is further indication of greater and sustained interest (all three drafts appear in Figure 13-17). Jermaine received a B on the final draft of his fable; he earned a C for his work during the March grading period and satisfactory effort and citizenship grades.

But Jermaine's list of plans for spring break (sleeping, going over to his cousin's house, playing Nintendo, partying, and gambling) made me faint of heart; his list of summer plans (getting a paying job, traveling to California, Disneyland, and Holly-wood) seemed to be pipe dreams. I suspected that the lack of structure and direction in

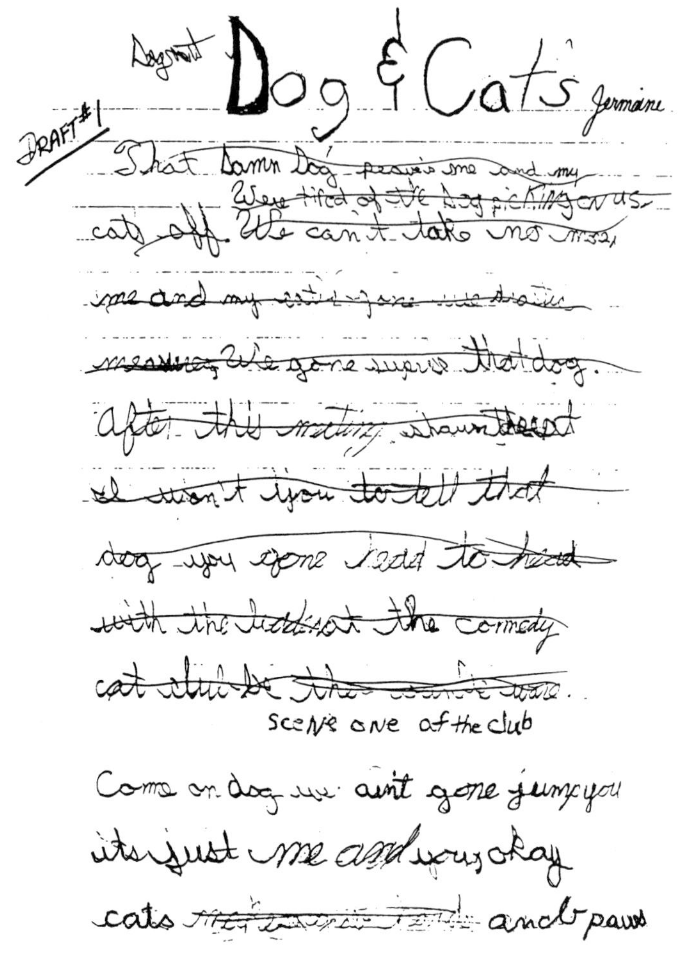

FIG. 13-17A   *Jermaine's First Draft*

Jermaine's life and his plans for the future were more accurately conveyed in the rest of his summer list: "party most of the summer, play basketball, go shopping."

By mid-April, Jermaine's energy for language work and his ability to sustain what seemed to me a miraculous effort almost until the end of school caused me to hold my breath. Although he made scathing remarks about Sue Ellen Bridgers' YA novel, *Home Before Dark,* he seemed to enjoy reading it aloud during class; he also wrote knowledgeably about the characters: "I choose Stella because she has a mind of her own. Stella wants to become something in her life other than being a low life. I know that Stella mother wants her to have the things she didn't have. But how could she get these things if her mother wan't let Stella live her own life. She's depressed because she wants to lead her life the way she want." I gave Jermaine a B on this exercise and wrote him a brief letter of commendation.

The depth and quality of Jermaine's thinking and writing had greatly improved from his earlier work. He continued to sustain his effort while maintaining a reasonable attitude, and he wrote without hassling me, too. Figure 13-8 shows Jermaine's response to *Malcolm Takes a Shot,* a film we viewed. His lead sentence is fully developed and

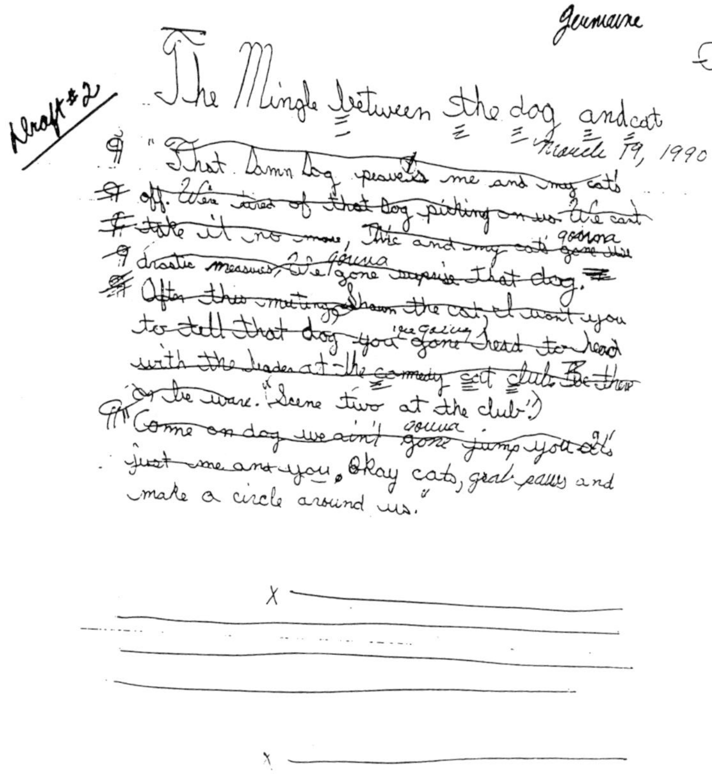
Jermaine

Draft #2 The Mingle between the dog and cat
March 19, 1990

"That Damn Dog peaves me and my cats off. Were tired of that dog picking on us. We cant take it no more, Me and my cats gonna drastic measures, We gonna surprise that dog. After this meeting Shawn the cat, I want you to tell that dog you're going head to head with the leader at the comedy cat club. Be there or be ware. (Scene two at the club")

"Come on dog we ain't gonna jump you it's just me and you, Okay cats, grab paws and make a circle around us."

FIG. 13-17B *Jermaine's Second Draft*

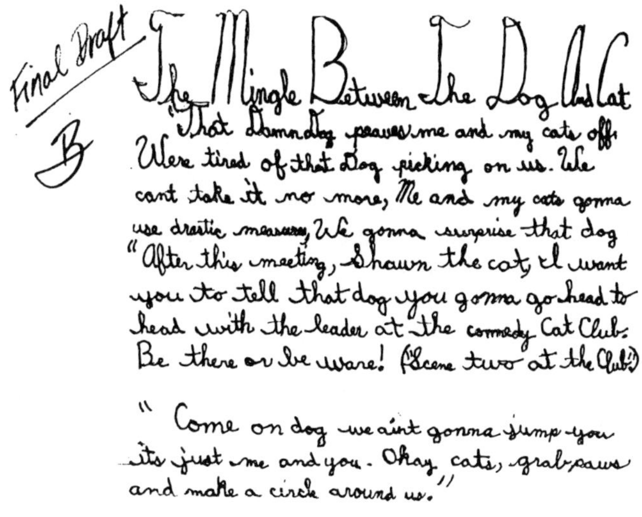
Final Draft

B

The Mingle Between The Dog And Cat

"That Damn Dog peaves me and my cats off. Were tired of that Dog picking on us. We cant take it no more, Me and my cats gonna use drastic measures, We gonna surprise that dog "After this meeting, Shawn the cat, I want you to tell that dog you gonna go head to head with the leader at the comedy Cat Club. Be there or be ware! (Scene two at the Club!)

" Come on dog we aint gonna jump you its just me and you. Okay cats, grab paws and make a circle around us."

FIG. 13-17C *Jermaine's Final Draft*

RESPONSE TO "MALCOLM TAKES A SHOT"

B+/A-

NAME *Jermaine*

DATE *5/3/90*

I want you to respond to Malcolm's dilemma (problem) in any way that you see fit.
You can discuss (in writing) his <u>denial</u> of being an epileptic; you can discuss
Malcolm's shattered dreams; maybe you can identify or understand exactly how
Malcolm feels when faced with this possibly debilitating problem that might
prevent him from playing basketball. Perhaps you have been faced with a similar
problem that stops you at least temporarily.

*Malcolm was scared to play basketball because
he thought he would have a nother freak
accident such an epileptic seasure. Malcolm felt
terrible when he found out he was an epileptic
Malcolm was very dissapointed. Malcolm felt
as if he couldn't have this. It was
almost that Malcolm thought he was too
good to be an epileptic. I have never
felt this problem or had something like it.*

FIG. 13-18   *Jermaine's Response to a Film*

informative. He deftly described Malcolm, the basketball star who is suddenly downed
by epileptic seizures. His understanding of the essence of this film, a teenager's stiff
denial of his vulnerability, earned him a B+/A−, and I wrote him the following note:

5/7/90

I especially like your last statement. You are saying, in effect, that this boy felt he was
beyond such flaws. He was therefore *not* vulnerable—*could not* be vulnerable! SMART
THINKING.

MK

Jermaine probably did his most revealing piece of thinking and writing on the
student-designed essay test. Like everyone else, he worked feverishly on this exam
until the end of the class period. The results are wonderful, particularly his answer to
question 6: "Think of the qualities (positive or negative) in any of the characters in
Home Before Dark. Identify the quality in the character, then explain the fact that you
also have this quality." Jermaine earned a B−/C+ on this essay test and applause from
his classmates and me. I was sorry he had relatively few pieces of work from which to
choose for his end-of-the-year grade—especially because he'd been energized during
the last few months of school. Although he casually resisted certain discussions and
small-group work, at least he'd worked effectively enough to wind up with a better than
passing grade. I felt sad that it probably wouldn't do much good in the end.

But I never gave up! My last shot at helping Jermaine was to guide him in the
direction of James Thornton's remarkable theater program at our high school. I felt sure
an involvement in Thornton's extraordinary theater community might help Jermaine,
who'd expressed interest in drama, to save himself, and I made a point of writing a

letter to James on the boy's behalf. Jermaine was invited to join the theater department. But the last I heard, he'd dropped out of theater; he'd also signed up and dropped out of sports that might have given him what Damion called "the booster energy" to survive.

Losing bright young people like Jawan and Jermaine gave me another good reason to reconsider our schools', and therefore society's complex challenges. While it reconfirmed my own feeling that this place called school must change, I also understood more clearly the need for much earlier community intervention for endangered children—between the time of conception and the age of three.

Good kids who fall through the cracks

Good students get attention for being good. No-so-good students get attention for their misdeeds. And the rest of the students, the large group in the middle and lower middle, may get little attention at all. These are the young people who neither wow their teachers with brilliance nor inundate them with problems; they just come in every day and settle down to work. In the average classroom, these quiet students—especially those who have learning problems and don't meet certain school requirements, such as achieving certain levels of proficiency on standardized tests or passing proficiency tests—can easily get lost. Because they usually don't make noise, they don't get acknowledgment or support, and without these they can lose momentum and interest. Next thing you know, they have quietly fallen through the cracks.

The teachers who deal with these students must be attentive to and vigilant about buoying their spirits and helping them stay interested in learning. My ways of doing this include talking with the students often about their plans, helping them with the particular types of work that cause them trouble, and encouraging them to find and pursue new interests both in and out of school. As I've said before, I encourage them to seek out adults who can guide them in addition to interested family members.

Unlike Jawan, who was overage and underprepared, and Jermaine, who was ambivalent about succeeding and who didn't feel strong enough to use his talent in productive ways, the young people I am about to introduce have the desire and are psychologically ready to excel in school. But they don't always have the background, backup, know-how, and skill to achieve academic success. They can become discouraged when they don't measure up to traditional school standards and measures of excellence. I think of Kenetta and Tequila. Both of these eighth-grade girls made giant strides in talking, reading, writing, and thinking during their eighth-grade year. They were solid but vulnerable kids who had to rely primarily on themselves for dreaming dreams, setting goals, and keeping those dreams and goals alive.

Kenetta

Kenetta had attended nine different schools before she came to Shaker Heights Middle School, not the first week of school, but sometime during the autumn. She'd come to live with her father, a new stepmother, a sister, and a new baby half-sister. This quiet, attentive, and obedient eighth-grade girl expressed dreams of finishing school, being a children's librarian (because she loved to read), living in a peaceful small town, *not* getting married and *not* having children. Kenetta felt comfortable in our class; she achieved B's and A's in language arts while maintaining average and below-average grades in her other classes, mainly, I think, because she often did poorly on tests. She didn't know how to read the heavy textbooks or study for the tests that followed. When she and I worked to master the texts and the tests, she fared well and felt good.

Early in the school year I was impressed with Kenetta's love for reading, a rarity among my students. I capitalized on this pleasure when I introduced the famous Reading Race (see Chapter 5). During the race, Kenetta burned the midnight oil devouring books of all subjects, sizes, and difficulty—not only because she wanted to win a supper out with the other winners and me, but simply because she loved books. Each day when we'd tally the number of points students had earned for the reading they'd done the day or night before, Kenetta would grin broadly and present an impressive array of reading material. Quietly she'd regale us with the stories that she liked best, informing her classmates and me about the types of plots and characters she most enjoyed. Kenetta carefully listed two-hundred entries on her Reading Record during the month-long contest! Her Reading Record, a running inventory of all the print she'd read, reflected the gains that she believed she'd made: "I have read more variety of books since the Race. I have also improved my reading skills. I notice that I stay up late sometimes just to finish a book. I noticed I sometimes read three or five books a day."

This self-evaluation prompted me to inquire about the variety of books Kenetta was reading. I also asked her in what ways her skill in reading had improved and why certain books wouldn't let her turn off the light and go to sleep. I found out that Kenetta, who especially enjoyed teen romances and what I call teen-talk books along with family stories, was also reading mysteries and nonfiction books about animals. She realized that her vocabulary had grown, her speed and understanding had increased, and she loved to read even more now than before the Reading Race. She emphasized that usually the books that "kept me up late at night" were the ones that "touched my heart."

I was also impressed with Kenetta's ability to gather ideas for stories she wanted to write. She thought of promising story material, collected telling details, and developed interesting characters with minds of their own. I noted, too, that Kenetta had a keen sense of story and timing, she demonstrated a good ability to create tension, as in her story, "Shot Gun," for which she earned an A− (see the excerpt in Figure 13-19). As I indicated in the following note, too many details bogged this story down and, toward the end of her story, deflected attention away from the plot. Otherwise it would have received an A.

12-4-89

Dear Kenetta,

This is a *fine* story! It's scary. I can picture this crazy old man and hear him laughing a cruel laugh after he shoots Bobbie.

I love the part where you're standing looking this cute boy over and Monica gets on your case because this man's shooting and you're flirting w/*her* boyfriend.

Not every detail is important—you must choose the most important details. Avoid one-word conversations like "OK."

Mrs. Krogness

Kenetta flourished in our class, which was composed mostly of girls who by second semester had developed camaraderie, independence, and self-discipline. Thus, I was able to give this class freedom that I wasn't able to give to my other classes. I encouraged these students to take increasing responsibility for deciding how they would spend class time, which books they would read, what kinds of writing projects they would embark on, and how class discussions would be handled. Kenetta expressed her

Note & grade on back.

KENETTA
10/89

Shot Gun

Monica stoped for a minute in front of a big green and white house. She said, "Darn. I lost my stupid earring. It must have fallen into the grass somewhere." She was looking for her earring. I was just standing watching her. She said "Well what are you just standing there for, stupid? Help me find my earring." I bent down in the grass, not because she told me but because I had seen her earring

I said "Here is your ugly and stupid old earring." "Thanks Now hurry up and get your butt up and lets get out of here. You know that crazy old man (lives here) called shot gun said Monica. "Yeah its so quite. I almost forgot."
(quiet)

As we were walking away I heard some cursing. It was that man they called Shot gun. He was standing on his porch yelling and waving his hands that held a gun.

FIG. 13-19   *Excerpt from "Shot Gun"*

pleasure and her feeling of comfort with this apparently free-wheeling arrangement; she especially liked being in charge of her own learning. "I like deciding what I'm going to do and how I'm going to do it," she said one winter day. "When a person's grown, she better be independent. And that's what I'm learning [in here] to be!"

Kenetta, who was working quite independently by the end of first semester, created "Polkadot Party," a story that reflected her development as a writer; she demonstrated increasing skill at writing believable dialogue and including details,

A

Polkadot Party   5-90

"Dear, have you seen my gold earing?" asked Mrs. Thompson. "No honey, I'm sorry that I didn't see it. I hope you find it soon," replied Mr. Thompson. "Thanks any way," shouted Mrs Thompson ~~yelling~~ to her husband while digging through her jewlry box.

"Tony, come here. I would like to speak to you for a while." "Yes Mommy," replied Tony a short little inocent boy. "Honey, have you seen my gold earing? I really need it." "Sure I see it right now over on the floor next to your bed." He quickly ~~went~~ gave the shiny piece to his Nerves mother. "Thankyou. I don't know what I'd do without you," she said as she took the earing from Tony's small hand and kissed him on his cheek.

"Mommy where are you going?" asked Tony with a look on his face that said don't leave me.

"I'm going to a dinner party with ~~your~~ your dad." "Can I go Mommy?" "I'm sorry baby, but you can't go. It's for grownups only." "Please Mommy can I go? I love you very much so let me go with you please." "No I'm sorry." "You don't love me!" "Yes I do, you know how much I love you." "Where will I go and who will stay here with me?" "That is already ~~tooken~~ taken care of, Tony. Miss Nellie Noodlesoup is on her way over here now!"

FIG. 13-20   *Excerpt from "Polkadot Party"*

exaggeration, and humor. Figure 13-20 shows an excerpt from "Polkadot Party," which earned her an unequivocal A.

In her End-of-the-Year Survey, Kenetta concluded that she was indeed a reader but not a writer: "I like reading very much. If I'm bored I pick up a book and read it and ever since this class I like reading even more." To my surprise, Kenetta wrote: "I don't like to write that much, but people tell me that how can you like to read if you don't like to write." I believe that Kenetta made this important connection because we'd often talked about our practice of reading to write and writing to read.

I wondered how this avid reader and skillful writer, who regularly received grades of B or A in language arts, could translate her increased interest and growing skill in language learning to American history class, where her report card grade hovered between a D and an F. I hoped that with my help and that of other interested adults Kenetta would eventually learn the usual school ropes: reading texts and taking traditional tests. I hoped she would not lose her love for reading in the process, and that she would continue to find strength in her independence.

Tequila

Tequila, too, had come to SMS this year from a school in urban Cleveland. Quietly, she made what I considered to be wonderful progress in language arts: she read many books (most of them independently) and wrote stories, poetry, and responses to literature; she found her voice through fiction writing. As she learned to speak up during class discussions, she opened up and used language much more expansively and with much greater ease and power than she had earlier. Like Kenetta, Tequila benefited from the easy give-and-take in this particular class, the opportunity to make choices, and the camaraderie.

When Tequila decided to write "Imagination" (which is included in Chapter 4) and its sequel about the grandson of the young slave boy, she felt at ease in making choices and working independently yet within a community of serious learners. Because she felt increasingly responsible for her own learning, compiled fuller and more exotic writing portfolios, and initiated and participated more readily and fluently in intellectual conversations, Tequila received grades of B+ or A− from me and ended the year with an A. I believe she learned to value her language work as much as I did. If what I imagine is true, I feel certain that no matter how capricious school had been in the past or would be in the future, Tequila had a new awareness that she was an able language learner, especially a writer. At the end of eighth grade, she took home her bulging writing spiral, proof of her blossoming talent.

I want to share several pieces of Tequila's writing. Figure 13-21 shows a letter she wrote to me about Stella in *Home Before Dark*. I gave Tequila a B+/A− on this, her first draft, because I applauded her interesting questions and keen observations about this poor family of migrant workers. Tequila read her letter aloud to several of her classmates and me. We complimented her on the thoughtful questions she had raised and tried to answer them. Because she didn't elaborate, I wondered what Tequila meant when she said that Stella had "a very demanding life," although she did explain the demands of Stella's life—both physical and psychological. She and I conferred about the general organization of her piece, and I made a few suggestions she used in her revised version, which she turned into an essay.

In another response to *Home Before Dark* written three months later, she concentrated on subtle psychological dilemmas. She wrote, "Mae is drained from having so

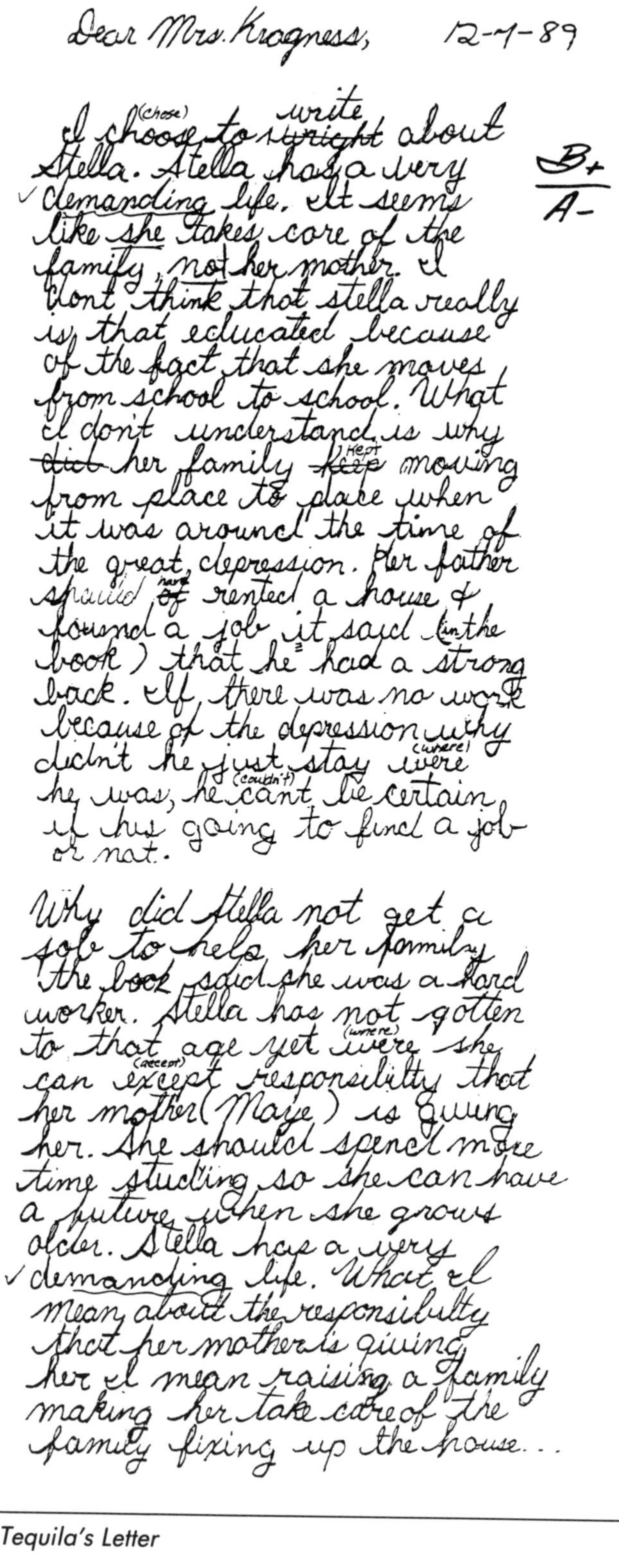

Dear Mrs. Kragness, 12-7-89

I ~~choose~~ (chose) to ~~wright~~ write about Stella. Stella has a very demanding life. It seems like she takes core of the family, not her mother. I dont think that stella really is that educated because of the fact that she moves from school to school. What I don't understand is why ~~did~~ her family ~~keep~~ kept moving from place to place when it was around the time of the great depression. Her father should ~~of~~ have rented a house & found a job it said (in the book) that he had a strong back. If there was no work because of the depression why didn't he just stay were (where) he was, he can't (couldn't) be certain if his going to find a job or not.

Why did Stella not get a job to help her family the book said she was a hard worker. Stella has not gotten to that age yet were (where) she can except (accept) responsilbilty that her mother (Maye) is giving her. She should spend more time studing so she can have a future when she grows older. Stella has a very demanding life. What I mean about the responsibilty that her mother is giving her I mean raising a family making her take care of the family fixing up the house...

B+ / A-

FIG. 13-21 *Tequila's Letter*

many children so close together. Mae doesn't want to be *helped* or *noticed*. She don't want Anne and Newton to take away the only value in her life, her children and then be ashamed. Mae's hair is hacked off in the back, her legs are unshaven, she do not take care of herself she has no life no education *no soul* or *spirit* in a way you can say she's the living Dead!! Mae doesn't seem to act like she's alive. She is in a depression so deep that it seems like the only real sign of life is her breathing."

Although Tequila didn't always put in periods at the ends of sentences, she *does* have a good sentence sense; even though she didn't always obey standard grammar rules, she *does* describe the character, Mae, "the living dead," powerfully. In comparison to her earlier piece on Stella, this one on Mae is more carefully organized and focused. In a note, I congratulated Tequila on her character analysis.

3/89

Dear Tequila,

I have given you a straight A on this analysis of Mae because you've focused on the woman's major problems; you understand that she is not merely a lazy mother, but a depressed woman suffering from "a depression so deep that it seems like the only real sign of life is her breathing." You have great empathy for humans, Tequila. You also seem to understand what is not obvious. I love the way you make words work!

This piece is also excellent because it has what writers call "voice." It has a good supply of soul and spirit—all that poor Mae doesn't have. I am thrilled with the progress you've made this year. Keep up the fine and sensitive work.

Mrs. Krogness

P.S. When you reread this piece *aloud,* you'll figure out where to place periods. You've omitted a few end marks. See me about a couple grammatical points.

MMK

Kenetta found courage and strength by knowing that she could be independent. Tequila found her voice through writing. Encouraging young people who might fall through the cracks to discover and then internalize their strengths can sometimes be enough to sustain their interest and pride in school.

Chi

Chi arrived in my seventh-grade class six or seven years after she had immigrated from Vietnam with her mother and sisters and brothers. A tiny, lively girl with an engaging smile and a sense of humor to match, she spoke only when called on and wrote only when required. It certainly wasn't that she was complacent or resistant to learning; she was simply overwhelmed trying to understand a new language and a new culture. An eager student, she was ready and willing to learn.

When students learning English as a second language demonstrate the willingness and ability to work, half the battle is won. I credit Chi for the wonderful progress she made during the school year, but she didn't do it alone. Her LD (Learning Disabilities) tutor, Josie Chapman, who was not specially trained in ESL (English as a Second Language) but was a warm, concerned, and capable woman, helped Chi work wonders. I relied on Josie because I have no ESL background myself, and Shaker Heights Middle School had no special ESL program. Even more important to Chi's development were Muriel and Jim Bristol, who lived next door to Chi and her older siblings and served as their surrogate parents. The Bristols helped Chi with her homework and came to

Chi is learning to take the lead by using English, her new language.

every school event and parent-teacher conference instead of her mother who, quite suddenly, had returned to Vietnam. The Bristols fed the younger members of this immigrant family breakfast each morning and packed lunches for them, showing the kind of daily devotion so critical to a student's growth.

During class, I helped Chi and Jung, who had come from Korea. I stopped by their desks often to confer, encourage, and explain to them what was going on and what to do. The other students became increasingly sensitive to the needs of Chi and Jung, likely because they themselves were gaining more confidence in school. Often they interrupted class and urged me to stop for a few minutes to explain to our two ESL students what we were talking about. The young students enjoyed and profited from helping Chi and Jung think through and then write down their ideas. Lisa S., in particular, derived great pleasure from helping Chi, a good friend, use her new language.

Chi's writing shows how her syntax improved as she practiced hearing and using the language. Her responses to literature, letters, stories, descriptions, and poetry are proof of her developing literacy. With each effort her repertoire expanded and her confidence in using words increased. Although Chi eventually learned how to start sentences with adverb clauses, develop key ideas in a well-focused manner, and communicate in rather sophisticated ways, as a new user of English she brought freshness to the language. In her written discussion of the book bag problem, for example, Chi wrote: "When the book bag is too heavy it is not good to your bones."

But I had to face the inevitable: assessing my two ESL students' work. How does a language arts/English teacher assess a student like Chi, who is struggling to learn a new language? I imagined that I would evaluate her first on the basis of her investment in language learning and her initiative in using English—just as I assessed my other students. But how does a teacher grade a non-English-speaking student? I considered simply writing Chi notes, thus giving her written feedback on daily papers without giving her a grade. Then I imagined using the I.E., the individual evaluation, to explain

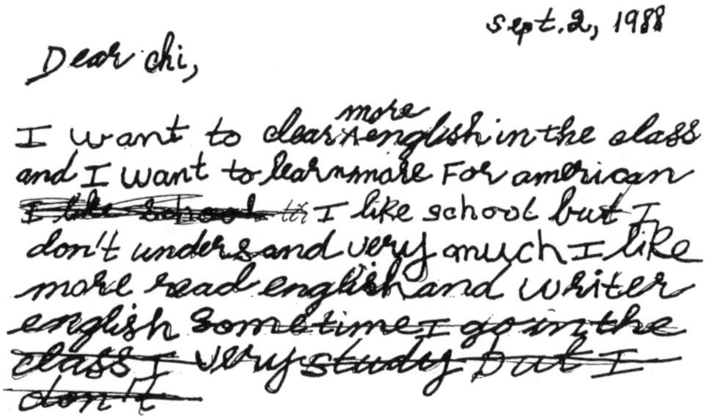

sept. 2, 1988

Dear chi,

I want to ~~clear~~ more english in the class and I want to learn more For american ~~I like school~~ I like school but I don't undersand very much I like more read english and writer english ~~Sometime I go in the class I very study but I don't~~

FIG. 13-22 *Chi's Letter of Intention*

her progress in using English instead of giving her a grade on her report card. But because members of her family were also learning English, sending home only written evaluations (notes on daily papers and an I.E. on her report card) would only confuse them. There was nothing to do but to write notes and give Chi grades on her daily work and give her a letter grade instead of an I.E. on her report card! As difficult as this is to admit, giving her grades was the right choice; after all, an immigrant already feels different and left out. I did, however, keep the Bristols informed of Chi's progress by telephone or note and told them how they could help her.

Generally, I gave Chi B's, since she worked diligently on every reading and writing project. Consequently, her language skill improved significantly. But she spoke only when called upon (in Vietnam, Chi hadn't been accustomed to talking during class). I knew, however, that one day she would feel comfortable enough to join our class discussion, and I was willing to wait. Access to the language was what she initially needed most, and I intended to immerse her in English.

Like all my students, Chi, who was in my back-to-back seventh-grade language arts/English class, began the year by writing a letter of intention (see Figure 13-22). I very simply asked her what she wanted to learn and how she wanted to learn. She struggled to explain her great desire "to clear more English," meaning she wanted to learn more English. She wanted to read and write English, too. For some reason, she crossed out the part about her willingness to be prepared because she had studied very hard.

Although I didn't grade Chi's first effort, I wrote her a brief, encouraging note in very simple English:

9-2-88

Dear Chi,

You will learn more English. You will learn how to read, write, and understand. We *will* help you, Chi.

You are a fine person. We all like you.

Mrs. Krogness

In the meantime, I talked with her and with Josie Chapman and the Bristols. We all agreed that I should start giving Chi writing assignments (to be done during class) in which she would write firsthand of coming to the United States and learning a new

B+

Sept, 6, 1988.

I am new person in nicistates, I like shaker HTS OHIO. ~~the start school I am scared~~ This year the ~~mit~~ New school I am so scared, because I am not undersand english very much, sometime I go ~~to school I don't undersand englishs sad~~ in the class I am crying because I don't undersand, and I am sad I need one person help me english, but not ~~e~~ everbody help me english because I am said, I want make Friend but I don't undersand, because not everybody like me. I hope I undersand english sooN this year.

FIG. 13-23   Chi's 9/6/88 Piece

10/4/88

One day Chi came to the United states of America. She moved from Viet Nam. Chi brought some clothes, some family pictures, I came here I saw everthing new to me. School is new. It does not look like my school in Viet Nam. The language is not the same my language I speak in VN. The food isnot looked my food in VN. Some times I cant eat. and in the United states in school use the pen not pencil. My country the weather not look like the U.S. summer here is very hot, the winter isit very cold.

FIG. 13-24   Chi's Vietnam/U.S. Piece

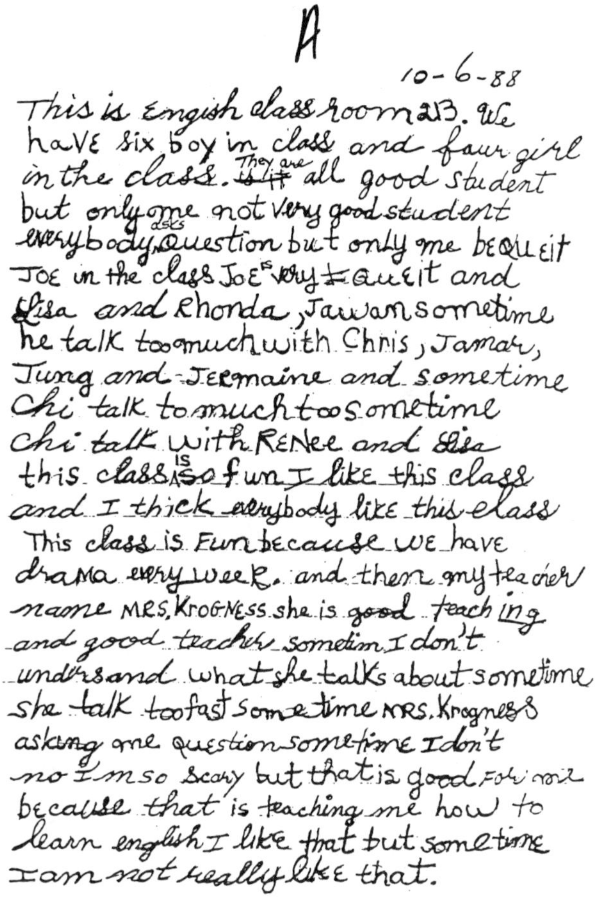

A

10-6-88

This is English class room 213. We have six boy in class and four girl in the class. They are all good student but only one not very good student everybody question but only me be quit Joe in the class Joe very quit and Lisa and Rhonda, Taiwan sometime he talk too much with Chris, Jamar, Jung and Jermaine and sometime Chi talk to much too sometime Chi talk with Renee and Lisa this class is so fun I like this class and I thick everybody like this class This class is Fun because we have drama every week. and then my teacher name Mrs. Krogness she is good teaching and good teacher sometime I don't understand what she talks about sometime she talk too fast sometime Mrs. Krogness asking me question sometime I don't no I'm so scary but that is good for me because that is teaching me how to learn english I like that but sometime I am not really like that.

FIG. 13-25   *Chi's English-Class Piece*

language; she would compare life in Vietnam with her new life here and her school life there and here. In this way she could capitalize on writing about what she knew best. Using her little Vietnamese/English dictionary and frequently asking for help, she wrote three pieces that reflect her desire to conquer the language, fit in with her peers, and become a part of her new culture. Each time Chi wrote, she gained greater mastery of the language, I think, because she ventured forth and tried to express ideas beyond the realm of her own needs and fears. Chi, Lisa S., and I took turns reading Chi's pieces of writing aloud. Lisa and I praised her for her excellent work.

On the piece dated 9/6/88 (see Figure 13-23), I gave Chi a B+ and wrote another encouraging note to reassure her that she *would* learn to read, write, and speak English and that she should not worry. I read my note aloud to her; then Chi read it aloud to me and beamed. About a month later she wrote a piece comparing and contrasting every-day things in Vietnam and the United States (see Figure 13-24). Again, I gave Chi a B and wrote her a note telling her that she was, indeed, learning her new language better each day. Two days later, on October 6, I encouraged Chi to write about our class. Specifically, I asked her to write about class members (whose names I printed on the board) and tell what we did in our class. Chi wrote a smashing full-page piece (see Figure 13-25) describing many of us to a T: "She [Mrs. Krogness] talk too fast," reminding me to do as Jawan had once advised, "Chill!" I noticed the length and increased complexity of her sentences. On this highly developed and expansive piece, I gave Chi an A. Everyone cheered and applauded Chi for her obvious success. Lisa S. asked Chi to read her class story aloud, but sudden shyness overtook her, and Lisa volunteered to read it while Chi read her words silently.

Here is the note I wrote (and read aloud very slowly and with clear diction) to Chi commending her on the story about our class:

10/8/88

Dear Chi,

This story about our class is wonderful! You describe many classmates. You describe your teacher very well. She does talk too fast. She will try to talk more slowly. I am glad you like drama. You are very good at drama. Drama helps you learn English. Writing helps you learn English. Reading helps you learn English. So does talking.

You are a hard worker. You are learning to speak, write, and read English because you practice it. Please keep on working hard each day.

Mrs. Krogness

In addition to writing personal stories and recording her observations, I expected Chi to read aloud with us, do written responses to literature, and answer open-ended questions—with our help, of course. The one-to-one help that Jeannine, Judith, and I gave her during class that first semester and the assistance she received from her tutor and the Bristols each evening supported Chi in her effort to achieve fluency in English

---

Shaker HTS.
Nov. 14, 1989

Dear Laura & John,
Thank you for visiting us . I am glad to see both of you . I enjoyed your drama. I much liked very, the game catch the pouch. that is so fun. I like that very much. I wish everyday I enjoyed your drama . Please come again,
Sincerely
Chi

FIG. 13-26   *Chi's Thank-you Letter*

Jan. 21, 1989

Dear Mrs. Bratt,
    I am sorry about your father being
dead. I know you feel so bad.
I know that because my father
he dead. I am feel so sad.
I hope to see you soon.

                        Sincerely,
                        Chi

FIG. 13-27   *Chi's Condolence Letter*

that year. I noticed that her written homework was smoother and syntactically more standard than her class work. At the end of the first grading period, I gave Chi a B, an E for her daily effort, and a 2 for her excellent citizenship (cooperation, respect, attention, preparedness).

By mid-November, Chi was able to write a cordial thank-you letter to Laura and John, our visiting actors, using standard conventions (see Figure 13-26). Her sentence structure, her spelling, and her punctuation had all improved, and I gave her a B. In January, we wrote condolence letters to our volunteer and advocate, Judith Bratt, whose father had died. Chi's letter, written during class, is empathic and quite literate, especially the first sentence (see Figure 13-27). Chi earned a B+ at the end of the second grading period, an E for her excellent and sustained effort, and a 2 for citizenship, indicating that she was a most remarkable student who came to class ready to learn and prepared to do her best work. The high citizenship grade also indicated her willingness to work with other students. I told Chi that if she were to try talking more during class discussions, she would earn higher letter and citizenship grades. When the rest of us stopped talking long enough to listen, Chi ventured forth more and more frequently, first with one-word comments, eventually with full sentences. Small literature discussion groups allowed her greater freedom and opportunity to express herself more fully.

By February, Chi had become quite accomplished at interpreting the literature we (and she) were reading aloud and responding to in class; she was able to give supporting evidence in the form of examples and details from the text. One homework assignment earned her an A: a description of her bedroom, written in standard English that is nicely focused and detailed (see Figure 13-28). By April, Chi had gained a high degree of fluency in her writing and used adverb clauses to start sentences in her list of solutions for the book bag problem, which earned her another A and a brief note of commendation. In May I asked the students to listen to their favorite radio station and pay special attention to the lyrics of songs they liked. Chi, who by this time had embraced certain aspects of Western culture, particularly the teen culture, enjoyed this assignment (see Figure 13-29). By now, she was doing much of her language arts homework independently. Just before school was out, Chi wrote two poems (Figure 13-30 shows one of them). Although at times she still forgot to make the plural form of nouns and verbs, she'd come a long way since September in using the English language to talk, read, write, think, and create.

A   2-89

Chi

My bedroom is the smallest room in our house but it is very neat. The rug and walls are tan, the curtains are white and my bed is white and blue. When I am in my bed I com look out my long window and see a big street. When I'm in my bed I turn toward my lelf hand, I can see my calender with chinese pictures on it. Next to my bed there is a small table with a lamp on the top. There is also a clock radio, and also another clock next to my nightstand is a special kind of dresser where I can hang my clothes. It has four doors and four drawers. /.

This is a fine piece of writing, Chi. I can picture your bedroom in my mind.

Mrs. K

FIG. 13-28   *Chi's Description of Her Bedroom*

Chi   5/89

Yesterday I was listening to my favorite song Sealed With A Kiss. I felt very strong and loving because the music is very slow and quiet. The words are so soft and sweet they touch my heart, and I like every song like that all the time.

FIG. 13-29   *Chi's Song-Lyric Piece*

Poem 6-2-89

Flowers and tears touch the window, stormy rain all night

Lonliness and dreams make you feel sad

Rain in the night makes you feel sadder

Searching for you dream in the night

FIG. 13-30   *Chi's Poem*

Not surprisingly Chi earned an A for the last grading period, an E for her steady progress and obvious accomplishments in language learning, and a 1 in citizenship for her increased leadership as a new member of our class and country. When Chi learned of her final grade, she playfully skipped around the room and then hopped up on a desk near Jawan: "See how tall I am," the petite girl laughed. "Yeah, I see, I see. You be growin', Chi. I see how far you have came this year, too," he laughed warmly.

FOURTEEN
A Journey with Boy Wonder

*"Life is a moment waiting to pass.
If you want to live it, grab it
fast." Dwight*

"I'm sitting in my room trying to figure out how I'm going to play football and be in a play as well. I can't do it. I'm too chicken, so I only dream about it. Walking through the hall [at school], I see a lot of people that know where there lives are going, but me, I don't know what I'm going all I know is whatever is going to happen better happen soon." This is the prologue to Dwight's original story, "The Avengers," which he began writing as a seventh grader and worked on during eighth grade.

We've met Dwight, the remarkable boy who polished his personal story about his cousin Thomas (see Chapter 9) to a glow and won the Reading Race hands down (see Chapter 5). He wound up his eighth-grade year having read more than sixty novels in and out of our language arts/reading class (see Figure 14-1). His progress kept me going.

For the teachers and administrators who judge students' (and teachers') progress by Standard Achievement Test scores, Dwight made impressive gains during eighth grade.

	September 1989	*June 1990*	*Growth*
Reading Comprehension			
Grade Equivalent	6.1	12.6	6.5
Vocabulary			
Grade Equivalent	10.9	12.7	1.8

Toward the end of the school year, I noticed that Dwight spoke a more standard English dialect and conformed more to the standard conventions of writing. P. K. Saha, a friend of mine and a professor of linguistics at Case Western Reserve University in Cleveland, gave me a possible explanation for Dwight's changing speech patterns. He thought the amount of reading Dwight had done—his immersion in standard English—had influenced his speech and written expression significantly.

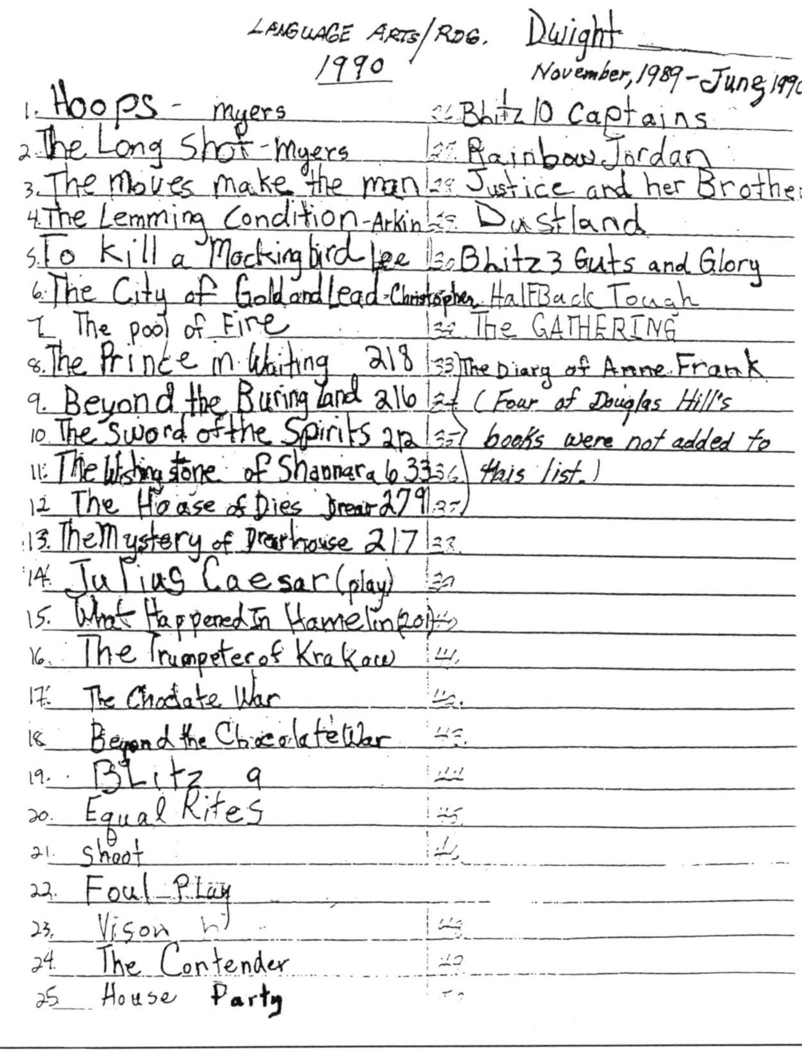
LANGUAGE ARTS/RDG. 1990 Dwight
November, 1989 – June 1990

1. Hoops - myers
2. The Long Shot - Myers
3. The Moves make the man
4. The Lemming Condition - Arkin
5. To kill a Mockingbird Lee
6. The City of Gold and Lead - Christopher
7. The pool of Fire
8. The Prince in Waiting 218
9. Beyond the Burning Land 216
10. The Sword of the Spirits 212
11. The Wishing stone of Shannara 633
12. The House of Dies Drear 279
13. The Mystery of Drear house 217
14. Julius Caesar (play)
15. What Happened In Hamelin 201
16. The Trumpeter of Krakow
17. The Chocolate War
18. Beyond the Chocolate War
19. Blitz 9
20. Equal Rites
21. Shoot
22. Foul Play
23. Vison
24. The Contender
25. House Party

26. Blitz 10 Captains
27. Rainbow Jordan
28. Justice and her Brother
29. Dustland
30. Blitz 3 Guts and Glory
31. HalfBack Tough
32. The GATHERING
33. The Diary of Anne Frank
(Four of Douglas Hill's books were not added to this list.)

FIG. 14-1 *Excerpt from Dwight's Reading Record*

A person, not a trophy

But make no mistake, Dwight was never *my* trophy. He was his own person, strong and single-minded and living life his way. I knew that this boy, who might have fallen through the cracks at school because of a serious reading problem during his early years, would probably benefit from guidance and support. But I kept a respectful distance and let him be in charge of his journey into language and literature. I simply responded to his oblique ways of showing interest.

Lending books to Dwight paid great dividends from the start. Untypically, one day he smiled and spoke expansively: "I *love* books!" I capitalized on his passion by talking with him about books and sending him to good authors. "Would you like to keep this book for your own collection?" I asked each time Dwight finished another and then another paperback.

During the first semester Dwight read at a fierce rate: between basketball season and track, he consumed five novels in six consecutive days—mostly nights, since he stayed up well past midnight to read. He read *What Happened in Hamelin* by Gloria Skurzynski, *The Trumpeter of Krakow* by Eric P. Kelly, *The Chocolate War* and *Beyond the Chocolate War* by Robert Cormier, and *Blitz 9* by Paul Nichols. All of these books I'd suggested except for *Blitz 9,* which he found in the drawer I'd filled to the brim with enticing paperbacks.

During the next couple of weeks, Dwight read *Equal Rites* by Terry Pratchett, a fantasy story I'd bought especially for him. He read *The Contender* by Robert Lypsite and several of Virginia Hamilton's books, *Justice and Her Brothers, Dustland,* and *The Gathering.* Dwight had enjoyed reading Hamilton's *The House of Dies Drear* for English class, which had prompted him to go to the library and find *The Mystery of Drear House,* its sequel.

How did I know Dwight had actually read all these books? For one thing, Dwight's scruples were beyond reproach; he wouldn't record the title of a book until he had finished reading it. But the real proof was the way he talked animatedly after school or on his way to or from my class. Though Dwight's enthusiasm for books was palpable, and his pursuit of literature intense (he'd look in the book drawer of my big yellow oak desk almost daily), I didn't press him to talk or write about characters, plots, and themes unless he initiated the conversation. I knew that he would have to feel in charge. Building trust and intellectual stamina takes time.

The act of reading

"If I didn't know how to read, my life would most likely feel empty," Dwight said one day. An only child whose parents had moved from his grandmother's house in Cleveland to Shaker Heights when he was in fifth grade, he escaped into literature, I suspect, for solace, finding safe companionship with heroic characters such as Taran in Lloyd Alexander's Prydain series. Fantasy stories satisfied his yearning for strength of body and spirit, wisdom, responsibility, adulation, independence, and above all, freedom. Dwight, who was searching for heroes, found them in the novels he read.

Books also offered Dwight an opportunity to reflect on his own dreams, to feel part of the universe. He understood in a subliminal way the book he identified as his favorite, Madeleine L'Engle's *A Wrinkle in Time.* Although he didn't talk about the terror a person who loses his individuality and personal freedom feels, I believe that he felt its meaning—as he also surely felt the power of love that dominates L'Engle's writing.

"Writing," Dwight wrote, "is something I wish I didn't know how to do because it is demanding. On the other hand, it lets me express myself to the max! I don't have to hide my feelings like I do when talking to someone."

The freedom to be

This restrained and often solitary boy was learning to let down his guard a little at a time. During rare moments, he could even be expansive about his new knowledge and

Motivator Les Brown helps Dwight build even more steam and esteem.

his dreams for the future. I watched him take hold of his life and give it new dimensions and new direction. Dwight was noticeably buoyed the Monday after Les Brown, the motivational expert, had spoken at our school. Very much an adolescent, Dwight sat *under* his writing table and wrote terse aphorisms:

"If you want to improve life, improve yourself."

"When life itself has become hard, understand that [that] is the best part of living."

"When you think of the perfect friend, think of yourself."

Thinking back on his adamant statement the first week of school, "I hate talking when there is no need to," I realized the progress that Dwight had made, and it was only the beginning of February! The Great Lakes Shakespeare actors would be with us soon to work on *Julius Caesar*. In partial preparation for their coming, I encouraged my eighth graders to memorize Brutus's speech and Mark Antony's powerful oration to the people after Julius Caesar's assassination.

Each day as we chanted the lines together, Dwight's voice rose above the rest of his classmates, and he relied on the script less and less frequently. He was preparing himself for his stage debut—the day that Christy and Erik, the actors from Great Lakes, would block the intense scene following Julius Caesar's bloody death, the scene in which Brutus attempts to explain to the restive crowd why slaying Caesar was necessary.

When Christy called for someone to play Mark Antony, Dwight's hand shot up. I watched expectantly as he pulled on a simple white cotton toga and then paced back and forth, quietly practicing his lines, as the two Shakespeare actors coached the members of the fickle crowd. When Dwight stood on a chair high above the throng to recite Mark Antony's "Friends, Romans, countrymen" speech, he was majestic; he was a presence. His classmates and I were spellbound. Dwight took Shakespeare's timeless words and made them his own.

"Friends, Romans, countrymen, lend me your ears; I come to bury Caesar, not to praise him. The evil that men do lives after them, the good is oft interred with their bones; so let it be with Caesar." Quietly I snapped pictures to record this occasion.

Here is the thank-you letter Dwight wrote to Christy and Erik:

February 14, 1990

Dear Christy and Erik,

I'm not going to bore you or insult you by saying "I liked it. It was fun." I believe if you are going to write a letter, do it as best you can. I'm from Shaker Heights Middle School, Miss Krogness's 5th period language arts class. If you don't remember, I was the stand-in for Christy during the scene when Mark Antony gave his fameous speech: Friends, Roman Countryman!!

You two have done something six teachers haven't been able to do! Because of your friendliness, I was able to get up and give a speech with confidence. I noticed that when you two would act, you would instantly transform into your character as if you were that person at that time. I don't think I could do that because I look at things from one perspective.

It's time to sign off. I hope I have a chance to see you two again in the theater.

Sincerely,
Dwight

Coming to know

On a cold Sunday when a blizzard blew into Cleveland, my husband, John, and I accompanied fifteen young people and five of their parents to the Cleveland Play House for a matinee performance of August Wilson's *Fences*. For most of my students, seeing live theater was a new experience, and going to the elegant Bolton Theatre of the Cleveland Play House was a first. The students sat quietly, captivated by the story, the set, and the characters. They laughed appreciatively, and in the right places.

On the way home, Dwight, Nona, and Roslind were sitting quietly in the backseat of our car when suddenly Roslind asked, "Why is the play called *Fences?*"

"Think about fences, Roslind. What do fences do?" I asked.

"They keep people out!" she replied.

"They also keep people in," Dwight countered. "Rose wanted to keep her husband, Troy, in and away from other women."

Roslind was satisfied with that explanation, but I asked again: "What else might the title *Fences* mean?"

Dwight said he'd been considering that question during intermission, when he'd walked around the grand lobby looking at the gallery of contemporary paintings.

"I think *Fences* refers to a limited life," Dwight mused. Indeed, Troy Maxson's dreams had been stopped at an invisible fence: the color barrier had precluded his becoming a major league baseball player.

Moments like these illuminated Dwight's soul. But life with this intense thirteen-year-old boy wasn't always smooth. While a milestone such as reciting Mark Antony's speech could send him flying, failing to meet his own excruciatingly high expectations in school or in sports often caused Dwight to plummet into dark despair. At these times, he avoided me in the hall and sulked class time away.

Beyond the classroom walls

Reading books and participating in football, basketball, and track were the ballast that kept Dwight together during the tumult of early adolescence. I wondered what would occupy this boy's sharp mind and fill all the empty hours during the summer just three months away. So early in March I began asking my students about their summer plans. What would they be doing with all that free time? Many shrugged and looked at me as though I'd taken leave of my senses.

"Summer? When's that?" Laurelia laughed ironically.

"I don't do nothin' in the summer except hang out with my friends," Jermaine responded.

Natachia, who rarely volunteered, spoke up: "I'm going to get a job bussing at a fast-food place this summer. I want to earn some money."

"I might be going down South with my grandmother to visit my great grandmother, aunts, uncles, and cousins," DeSean volunteered.

"Summer school is where I have to go," another student groaned.

Dwight looked alert but noncommittal. I knew he took pleasure in exciting settings where new challenges awaited him. In calling various institutions, I had learned about Volunteens, Mt. Sinai Hospital's volunteer program for teenagers. It sounded like an ideal place for Dwight. During our language arts class, Dwight telephoned the hospital to make an appointment with Bonnie Rudolph, volunteer director, for an interview. The day came. As we drove down to the big university hospital, I talked with him about questions she'd probably ask, the hypothetical questions we'd practiced answering during class while we were doing mock interviews for summer jobs.

Dwight listened intently but said little; this was his *first* real job interview. Just before he opened the door leading to Ms. Rudolph's office, I shook his hand firmly and wished him luck. Among the many matters of protocol my students and I had practiced in class, firmly gripping the hands of the adults who would interview them and looking them squarely in the eye were paramount. When Dwight came out of Ms. Rudolph's volunteer office, he looked confident.

"Did you get it?" I whispered. He nodded. Dwight had landed his first real job, a volunteer job that would not pay him a salary but would open his mind and broaden his vision that summer. The job, three days a week from 8:30 A.M. until 4:30 P.M., began several days after school let out.

I won't forget the summer day I visited the Mt. Sinai Hospital pediatrics ward to see two of my kids, Dwight and Radha, in their new setting. In the blue and white sweater with "Mt. Sinai Volunteens" embossed on it, Dwight looked self-assured. An irrepressible smile crept across his face when he said, "I can come and go as I please. All I have to do is check in with Tracy, the head nurse, who's my supervisor."

"Working here is one of the best recommendations you can get for the future," he told me proudly as he stood behind the ward information desk. Dwight and Radha played with and fed little children who were hospitalized; they paged nurses, ran errands all over the hospital, stocked and cleaned equipment, and gave a total of three-hundred volunteer hours that summer.

As they worked, Dwight and Radha used language to exchange information and pleasantries—even good-natured banter, they told me—with a new group of people in a new setting. They received instructions, asked questions, and carried messages. I'm not merely speculating when I say that this social/intellectual experience served to extend and expand Dwight's and Radha's capabilities as language makers and users quite beyond the four walls of a classroom. Clearly, both of them developed a new self-esteem and pride from becoming part of the work world where they were respected and valued for their contributions.

During the course of just one year, Dwight had become a more confident, more conversant, and more socialized young person not only on the football field, the basketball court, and the track, but also in the classroom. He regularly ate lunch with a group of boys, both African American and white; he talked and jived with other kids in the halls of our school. By the end of eighth grade, he exemplified youthful anticipation.

Like Taran, the assistant pig keeper in Lloyd Alexander's Prydain series, Dwight was impatient to grow up and get on with life, maybe even become the High King. Dwight, alias Boy Wonder, alias Quicksilver, was what seventh-grader Greg would call "a star catcher," a dreamer of dreams. For Dwight and all the other young people whose paths have crossed mine over the years I have one wish: may you remember all your lives how to catch a star.

References

Alexander, Lloyd. 1964. *The Book of Three*. Book 1 in the Prydain Series. New York: Dell.

Angelou, Maya. 1971. *Just Give Me a Cool Drink of Water 'Fore I Diiie*. New York: Random House.

Babbitt, Natalie. 1975. *Tuck Everlasting*. New York: Farrar, Straus & Giroux.

Baum, L. Frank. 1976. "Witches' Spells: Miss Trust's Incantation," in *Witch Poems,* ed. by Daisy Wallace. New York: Holiday House.

Bettelheim, Bruno. 1977. *The Uses of Enchantment: The Meaning and Importance of Fairy Tales*. New York: Vintage Books.

Bridgers, Sue Ellen. 1976. *Home Before Dark*. New York: Alfred A. Knopf.

Brown, Margaret Wise. 1947. *Goodnight, Moon*. New York: Harper & Row.

Clavell, James. 1963. *The Children's Story*. New York: Dell.

Clifton, Lucille. 1969. *Good Time Poems*. New York: Random House.

———. 1980. *Two-Headed Woman*. Amherst, MA: University of Massachusetts Press.

Cormier, Robert. 1985. *Beyond the Chocolate War*. New York: Dell.

———. 1974. *The Chocolate War*. New York: Dell.

Cummings, E. E. 1967. "in Just-" in *Reflections on a Gift of Watermelon Pickle,* ed. by Stephen Dunning, Edward Lueders, Hugh Smith. New York: Lothrop, Lee & Shepard.

Dunning, Stephen, Edward Lueders, and Hugh Smith. Eds. 1967. *Reflections on a Gift of Watermelon Pickle*. New York: Lothrop, Lee & Shepard.

Eliot, T.S. 1982. *Old Possum's Book of Practical Cats*. New York: Harcourt Brace Jovanovich.

Giovanni, Nikki. 1985. *Spin a Soft Black Song*. New York: Hill and Wang.

———. 1980. *Those Who Ride the Night Winds*. New York: William Morrow.

Granger's Index to Poetry. 1973. Ed. by William James Smith. New York/London: Columbia University Press.

Greenfield, Eloise. 1981. *Daydreamers*. New York: Dial.

———. 1972. *Honey, I Love and Other Love Poems*. New York: Harper & Row.

Hamilton, Virginia. 1980. *Dustland*. New York: Harcourt Brace Jovanovich.

———. 1989. *The Gathering*. New York: Harcourt Brace Jovanovich.

———. 1986. *The House of Dies Drear*. New York: Macmillan.

————. 1978. *Justice and Her Brothers*. New York: Harcourt Brace Jovanovich.

————. 1987. *The Mystery of Drear House*. New York: Collier/Macmillan.

————. 1982. *Sweet Whispers, Brother Rush*. New York: Avon.

Hayden, Torey L. 1980. *One Child*. New York: Avon.

Hinton, S. E. 1967. *The Outsiders*. New York: Dell.

————. 1988. *Taming the Star Runner*. New York: Dell.

————. 1979. *Tex*. New York: Dell.

Hopkins, Lee Bennett. 1972. *Pass the Poetry, Please!* New York: Citation.

Hughes, Langston. 1982. *Listen Children: An Anthology of Black Literature*, ed. by Dorothy S. Strickland. New York: Bantam Books.

Hurston Zora Neale. 1937. *Their Eyes Were Watching God*. New York: Harper & Row.

Janeczko, Paul. 1987. *This Delicious Day: 65 Poems*. New York: Orchard Books.

Katz, Bobbi. 1973. *Upside Down and Inside Out: Poems for All Your Pockets*. New York: Franklin Watts.

Kelly, Eric P. 1928. *The Trumpeter of Krakow*. New York: Collier/Macmillan.

Kennedy, X. J. 1982. *Knock at a Star*. Boston: Little, Brown.

————. 1976. "Wicked Witch's Kitchen" in *Witch Poems*, ed. by Daisy Wallace. New York: Holiday House.

Korman, Gordon. 1984. *No Coins, Please*. New York: Scholastic.

L'Engle, Madeleine. 1962. *A Wrinkle in Time*. New York: Scholastic.

Levoy, Myron. 1977. *Alan and Naomi*. New York: Harper Trophy/Harper & Row.

Livingston, Myra Cohn. 1988. *There Was a Place and Other Poems*. New York: Macmillan.

Lypsite, Robert. 1967. *The Contender*. New York: Harper & Row.

MacLachlan, Patricia. 1985. *Sarah, Plain and Tall*. New York: Harper & Row.

Madhubuti, Haki (Donald L. Lee). 1990. *Black Men: Obsolete, Single, Dangerous?* Chicago, IL: Third World.

Merriam, Eve. 1962. "I'm Sorry Says the Machine" in *CHORTLES New and Selected Wordplay Poems*. New York: Morrow.

Moore, Lilian. 1976. "Witch Goes Shopping," in *Witch Poems*, ed. by Daisy Wallace. New York: Holiday House.

Myers, Walter Dean. 1981. *Hoops*. New York: Dell.

————. 1979. *The Young Landlords*. New York: Viking.

Naidoo, Beverly. 1986. *Journey to Jo'Burg: A South African Story*. New York: Harper Trophy/ Harper & Row.

Nichols, Paul. 1989. *Blitz 9*. New York: Ballantine.

Nikolay, Sonja. 1976. "Witches' Menu" in *Witch Poems*, ed. by Daisy Wallace. New York: Holiday House.

Paterson, Katherine. 1977. *Bridge to Terabithia*. New York: Avon/Camelot.

Peck, Robert Newton. 1972. *A Day No Pigs Would Die*. New York: Dell.

Pratchett, Terry. 1987. *Equal Rites*. New York: ROC-Penguin.

Rochman, Hazel, sel. 1988. *Somehow Tenderness Survives: Stories of South Africa*. New York: Harper Keypoint/Harper Collins.

Rosenblatt, Louise. 1990. In *Transactions with Literature: A Fifty-Year Perspective*, ed. by Edmund J. Farrell and James R. Squire. Urbana, IL: The National Council of Teachers of English.

Rylant, Cynthia. 1982. *When I Was Young in the Mountains*. New York: Dutton.

Sanchez, Sonia. 1973. "To P.J. (2 yrs old who sed write a poem for me in Portland, Oregon)," in *Listen Children: An Anthology of Black Literature,* ed. Dorothy S. Strickland. Magnolia, MA: Peter Smith.

Sendak, Maurice. 1963. *Where the Wild Things Are*. New York: Harper & Row.

Serraillier, Ian. 1964. *The Enchanted Island: Stories from Shakespeare*. Cambridge: Oxford University Press.

Shreve, Susan. 1984. *The Flunking of Joshua T. Bates*. New York: Scholastic.

Silverstein, Shel. 1974. *Where the Sidewalk Ends*. New York: Harper & Row.

Skurzynski, Gloria. 1979. *What Happened in Hamelin*. New York: Four Winds.

Smith, Frank. 1988. *Joining the Literacy Club: Further Essays into Education*. Portsmouth, NH: Heinemann.

Spolin, Viola. 1963. *Improvisation for the Theater*. Evanston, IL: Northwestern University Press.

Steinbeck, John. 1939. *Grapes of Wrath*. New York: Viking/Penguin.

Taylor, Mildred. 1987. *The Friendship*. New York: Dial.

———. 1987. *The Gold Cadillac*. New York: Dial.

———. 1981. *Let the Circle Be Unbroken*. New York: Dial.

———. 1978. *Roll of Thunder, Hear My Cry*. New York: Bantam.

———. 1975. *Song of the Trees*. New York: Bantam.

Thurman, Judith. 1976. *Flashlight and Other Poems*. New York: Atheneum.

Twain, Mark. 1979. In *Empty Pages: A Search for Writing Competence in School and Society* by Clifton Fadimon & Jas Howard. Belmont, CA: Signature Books, Fearon Pitman.

Volavkova, Hana, ed. 1993. *I Never Saw Another Butterfly*. United States Holocaust Memorial Museum, expanded second edition. New York: Schocken.

Wallace, Ronald. 1981. "Hippopotamus," in *Plums, Stones, Kisses & Hooks*. Columbia: University of Missouri Press.

Worth, Valerie. 1987. *All the Small Poems*. New York: Farrar, Straus, & Giroux.

Index